Editor
Rabbi Mordechai Dinerman

Course Development
Rabbi Lazer Gurkow
Chava Shapiro
Rabbi Naftali Silberberg

Editorial Board
Rivkah Slonim
Rabbi Ari Sollish
Rabbi Avrohom Sternberg

Research
Rabbi Avraham Bergstein
Rabbi Yaakov Gerson
Rabbi Eli Raksin
Rabbi Shmuel Super

Design and Layout
Mendel Schtroks

Printed in the United States of America
© Published and Copyrighted 2016 by
The Rohr Jewish Learning Institute
822 Eastern Parkway, Brooklyn, NY 11213

(888) YOUR-JLI/718-221-6900
www.myJLI.com

THE JEWISH COURSE OF
WHY

JLI
JEWISH LEARNING INSTITUTE

The **Rohr Jewish Learning Institute**
gratefully acknowledges
the pioneering support of

George and Pamela Rohr

SINCE ITS INCEPTION,
the **Rohr JLI** has been
a beneficiary of the vision, generosity,
care, and concern
of the **Rohr family**

In the merit of
the tens of thousands of hours of Torah study
by **JLI** students worldwide,
may they be blessed with health,
Yiddishe nachas from all their loved ones,
and extraordinary success
in all their endeavors ❧

This course was enabled by
a generous grant from the estate of

Elliot James Belkin

אליהו בן משה ולאה הכהן

Vancouver, BC

*Out of loving concern for the spiritual
welfare of his fellow Jews, he made it possible
to share the inspiration he discovered at JLI
with the Jewish community worldwide.*

ENDORSEMENTS

This course will provide participants a deep understanding of numerous traditional Jewish practices and customs and their historical context. In addition, it will expose them to the rich literature that explains and clarifies these practices and their deep meaning. Participants will come to understand the complex processes that produced and encouraged so many of our beautiful customs. The deep understanding that they will acquire should greatly increase their appreciation for the unending intellectual quest that is a major part of Jewish life.

Lawrence H. Schiffman, PhD
Skirball Department of Hebrew and Judaic Studies
Director of the Global Network for
Advanced Research in Jewish Studies
New York University

The Jewish Course of Why is an excellent portal into the richness and relevance of Jewish ritual, belief, and practice that will leave students eager for more in-depth explorations of the topics—both timely and timeless—that are discussed.

Altie Karper
Editorial Director, Schocken Books

To meet the multitude of external and international challenges facing Jews and Judaism in the 21st century, it is essential that we are a knowledgeable, informed, and committed community. The key to achieving this is meaningful education made accessible to the largest numbers possible. There is a growing desire on the part of younger Jews to know, to understand, our great heritage introduced in the Torah and sacred texts.

Moses taught that the greatest perpetual dangers to the future of the Jewish people are not wars or natural disasters, but apathy, indifference, and ignorance. The response lies in *The Jewish Course of Why*. It will challenge the students of all ages, on intellectual, emotional, and personal levels. It addresses in a meaningful way the questions most perplexing to this generation that often become a barrier to the acceptance of Jewish practice and tenets. The course is a key to the treasure house of Jewish wisdom, scholarship, significance, and great relevance.

Popular culture and ignorance have often created mythological explanations or significance for our *mitzvot* and observances. Knowing the "why" will dispel these inaccuracies and provide a more meaningful and authentic basis for adherence to our glorious traditions.

Malcolm Hoenlein
Executive Vice Chairman, Conference of Presidents of Major American Jewish Organizations

We are at an inflection point in modern Jewish history. External challenges to core Jewish values and beliefs, including the concept of Jewish national identity and connection to the Land of Israel, are growing. The physical safety of Jews in parts of Europe and elsewhere is threatened. At the same time, levels of assimilation and ignorance within the Jewish community have never been higher. Many Jews, especially younger ones, don't have the same sense of connection to and responsibility for other Jews and the Jewish people. Initiatives to elevate Jewish literacy, like JLI's *The Jewish Course of Why,* are vital, not only for personal spiritual growth, but to ensure that Jews have the knowledge and motivation to address today's critical challenges.

Jonathan Greenblatt
National Director and CEO, Anti-Defamation League

The Jewish people have been called "the people of the book." Why? Different people will offer different explanations. But no one will question that the expression is ingrained in our culture. Some expressions are part of our vocabulary and our daily lives; we may know how and when to use them but not WHY they are part of who we are. The background and reasons behind 50 of these questions, distinguishing the attitudes and customs of the Jewish people, will come to life and be more meaningful through *The Jewish Course of Why.* It will enrich your appreciation and understanding of Jewish culture.

Carolyn Starman Hessel
Director of Sami Rohr Prize for Jewish Literature
Jewish Book Council, Executive Director Emeritus

There was a time when the most-asked question by Jews who wanted to strengthen their connection with G-d was "How?" How to fulfill the laws of Torah was the most important quest for generations past untouched by the Western mind-set of scientific inquiry and secular doubt. That age is gone. Today's generation needs to know why. And perhaps there is much to be gained by this modality—a faith strengthened by the profundity of Jewish thought and law which, when studied through the lens of rabbinic wisdom, makes us ever more convinced of the divine truth of the revelation at Sinai. How relevant then is a course such as this, which is unafraid to deal with the ultimate questions of why—and aids us to become more fervently attached to our faith by way of the illuminating answers.

Rabbi Benjamin Blech
Professor of Talmud, Yeshiva University
Author of thirteen books on Judaism, including
The Complete Idiot's Guide to Understanding Judaism

The new JLI initiative of *The Jewish Course of Why* presents the awesome intellectual, philosophical, and spiritual depth of Judaism in a remarkably accessible way. As the wisdom of Hashem, Torah Judaism has the answers to life's most difficult and profound questions. I would like to commend JLI for sharing the Torah's life-changing ideas with an audience that spans the full spectrum of Jewish life today.

Chief Rabbi Warren Goldstein, PhD
Chief Rabbi of South Africa
Author, *Defending the Human Spirit: Jewish Law's Vision for a Moral Society*

Endorsements

Too many American Jews know little about Judaism beyond what they learned from Woody Allen, Seinfeld, or their bar-and-bat-mitzvah preparations—in any case, hardly a sophisticated or challenging body of knowledge. This exciting and substantive class will provide a more fulfilling perspective, answering the troubling questions that many of us are reluctant to even ask.

Michael Medved
Nationally Syndicated Talk Radio Host
Author, Political Commentator, and Film Critic

Why? This is often the first question a child asks repeatedly. Perhaps the best way to answer that "Why?" is with a narrative—although it is the question that remains paramount. Questions serve as the catalyst for the narrative. Can the story of the Exodus from Egypt begin to be told at the Passover Seder unless someone (usually a child) asks the teller the Four Questions? As Jews, we are the "people of the story." As a storyteller-educator, I believe that two of the reasons why we tell stories and why stories still work powerfully in our contemporary electronic-oriented world are because stories provoke curiosity and inspire wonder. Curiosity and wonder are two major components of being human and Jewish. So what can be wiser than offering *The Jewish Course of Why,* that poses that seminal question in order to prompt Jewish cultural literacy?

Peninnah Schram
Professor Emerita, Yeshiva University
Storyteller, Award-winning author of eleven books including: *Jewish Stories One Generation Tells Another,* and *Jewish Stories of Love and Marriage.*
Recipient of Covenant Award for Outstanding Educator

The JLI course *The Jewish Course of Why* is a journey into the depth and beauty of Jewish thought and inquiry. This is a timely and important topic. So many people misunderstand Judaism on such a basic level—and these are precisely the issues and questions around which they focus. Through the exploration of misconceptions and perplexing questions in modern Judaism, one is introduced to the richness and elegance of the logic and ethic underlying Jewish belief and practice. The absolute gem of a course, it leaves one not only with answers to questions, but also with a level of cultural literacy that underscores the importance of the core Jewish values of curiosity and questioning.

Risa E. Dickson, PhD
Vice President for Academic Affairs,
University of Hawaii Educational System

A quality that differentiates human beings from animals is our ability to ask "why?" Judaism and *The Jewish Course of Why* encourage us to wonder and to wander among multiple perspectives on questions like: Why have Jews survived when many other groups of people have disappeared? Why do we pray? Why does Judaism have so many laws about food? It is the course everyone has been waiting for that will answer fifty of the most-asked questions—chosen from a survey of adult learners—and pave the way for even more inquiry and learning.

Betsy Dolgin Katz
Faculty Member, Spertus Institute for Jewish Learning and Leadership
Member, Board of Directors, The Covenant Foundation
Author, *Reinventing Adult Jewish Learning*

The Jews are an ever-questioning people, and the newest JLI course offers an excellent introduction to the art of the query. Jews are rarely satisfied with the facile answer "because," and we're proud of it. Enshrined in the Four Questions of the Passover Seder, we teach our children that one of the most valuable aspects of speaking is asking. "The embarrassed cannot learn," teach the sages, and JLI provides a safe intellectual space for Jews to dig deeper into the foundations of Jewish philosophy and practice.

Henry Abramson, PhD
Dean, Lander College of Arts and Sciences
Producer and Lecturer, *This Week in Jewish History* online series
Author of six books, including *Reading the Talmud*

I applaud The Rohr Jewish Learning Institute for providing *The Jewish Course of Why*. Its teachers present a wide range of Jewish topics with a depth that is both exciting and stimulating. I wish that such courses had existed when I started learning about Judaism. What a wonderful way for beginners as well as people with much background to expand their knowledge of Judaism.

Lisa Aiken, PhD
Psychologist, Lecturer
Author or co-author of thirteen books, including *To Be a Jewish Woman*

Today, when people are searching for answers that speak to them, a course that can provide intellectual depth and personal relevance is of the utmost importance. JLI's *The Jewish Course of Why* is a foundational course that can give students the means to find answers and meaning for both novice and scholar alike. If you have ever asked "Why?" this course is for you.

Ira Bedzow, PhD
Director, Biomedical Ethics and Humanities Program, New York Medical College

The intellectual depths of Judaism can only be explored through self-examination and listening to one's inner voice that questions, "why?" At the American Hebrew Academy we have the privilege of working with the leadership team of the Rohr Jewish Learning Institute, and our students' learning is enriched by the experience facilitated through the use of JLI course materials.

Glenn A. Drew
Executive Director and General Counsel, American Hebrew Academy

At a time when the legitimacy of the world's only Jewish state is under a sustained assault, and anti-Semitism rears its ugly head throughout the globe, the Rohr JLI's *The Jewish Course of Why* is indispensable for familiarizing us with Judaism's true essence and mammoth contribution to human civilization.

Efraim Karsh, PhD
Professor of Political Studies, Bar-Ilan University
Founding Director and Emeritus Professor of Middle East & Mediterranean Studies, King's College London

TABLE OF CONTENTS

ב"ה

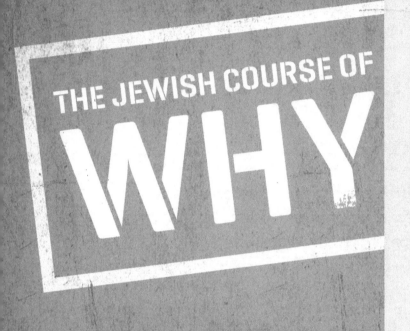

LESSON ONE

1. Why ask "Why?"? Isn't Judaism a *belief* system?

2. Why are there no miracles today of biblical proportion?

3. Why do we pray? Doesn't God know what He is doing? Can we really affect His will?

4. Why is there so much fragmentation in Jewish practice?

5. Why have the Jews survived millennia while so many other civilizations have vanished?

6. Why don't Jews accept the Christian messiah?

7. Why do we kindle *yartzeit* candles to commemorate the dead?

JEWISH LEARNING INSTITUTE

1. Why ask "why?" Isn't Judaism a *belief* system?

Why Question?

Text 1

Maimonides, *Mishneh Torah*, Laws of Substituting Sacrifices 4:14 📖

Rabbi Moshe ben Maimon
(Maimonides, Rambam)
1135–1204

Halachist, philosopher, author, and physician. Maimonides was born in Cordoba, Spain. After the conquest of Cordoba by the Almohads, he fled Spain and eventually settled in Cairo, Egypt. There, he became the leader of the Jewish community and served as court physician to the vizier of Egypt. He is most noted for authoring the *Mishneh Torah*, an encyclopedic arrangement of Jewish law, and for his philosophical work, *Guide for the Perplexed*. His rulings on Jewish law are integral to the formation of halachic consensus.

אַף עַל פִּי שֶׁכָּל חוּקֵי הַתּוֹרָה גְּזֵרוֹת הֵם, כְּמוֹ שֶׁבֵּיאַרְנוּ בְּסוֹף מְעִילָה, רָאוּי לְהִתְבּוֹנֵן בָּהֶן, וְכָל שֶׁאַתָּה יָכוֹל לִיתֵּן לוֹ טַעַם, תֵּן לוֹ טַעַם. הֲרֵי אָמְרוּ חֲכָמִים הָרִאשׁוֹנִים, שֶׁהַמֶּלֶךְ שְׁלֹמֹה הֵבִין רוֹב הַטְּעָמִים שֶׁל כָּל חוּקֵי הַתּוֹרָה.

Although all of the suprarational laws in the Torah are decrees, as I have explained elsewhere, it is appropriate to meditate upon them, and, wherever possible, provide a rationale. Indeed, the sages said that King Solomon understood many of the rationales for all the suprarational statutes of the Torah.

QUESTION FOR DISCUSSION

What is the benefit of contemplating rationales for God's laws?

Conditions (Optional)

Text 2

Rabbi Jonathan Sacks, *Rabbi Jonathan Sacks's Haggadah: Hebrew and English Text with New Essays and Commentary* [New York: Continuum, 2006], p. 108 ▮

There are three conditions, though, for asking a Jewish question. The first is that we seek genuinely to learn—not to doubt, ridicule, dismiss, reject. That is what the wicked son of the Haggadah does: he asks not out of a desire to understand but as a prelude to walking away.

Second is that we accept limits to our understanding. Not everything is intelligible at any given moment. There were scientists at the beginning of the twentieth century who believed that virtually every major discovery had already been made—not suspecting that the next hundred years would give rise to Einstein's relativity theory, Heisenberg's uncertainty principle, Godel's theorem, proof of the big bang origin of the universe, the discovery of DNA, and the decoding of the human genome. In relation to Torah, many German and American Jews in the nineteenth century could not understand Jewish prayers for a return to Zion, and deleted them from the prayer book. These facts should induce in us a certain humility. Not every scientific orthodoxy survives the test of time. Not everything in Judaism that we do not understand is unintelligible. The very features of Jewish life one generation finds difficult, the next generation may find the most meaningful of all. Faith is not opposed to questions, but it is opposed to the shallow certainty that what we understand is all there is.

Rabbi Jonathan Sacks, PhD
1948–

Former chief rabbi of the United Kingdom. Rabbi Sacks attended Cambridge University and received his doctorate from King's College, London. A prolific and influential author, his books include *Will We Have Jewish Grandchildren?* and *The Dignity of Difference*. He received the Jerusalem Prize in 1995 for his contributions to enhancing Jewish life in the Diaspora, was knighted and made a life peer in 2005, and became Baron Sacks of Aldridge in 2009.

Third is that when it comes to Torah, we learn by living and understand by doing. We learn to understand music by listening to music. We learn to appreciate literature by reading literature. There is no way of understanding Shabbat without keeping Shabbat, no way of appreciating how Jewish laws of family purity enhance a marriage without observing them. Judaism, like music, is something that can be understood only from the inside, by immersing yourself in it.

Given these caveats, Judaism is a faith that, more than any other, values the mind, encouraging questions and engaging us at the highest level of intellectual rigor. Every question asked in reverence is the start of a journey toward God, and it begins with the habit that, on Pesach, Jewish parents teach their children to ask, thereby to join the never-ending dialogue between human understanding and heaven.

KEY POINTS

- We ask "why?" because while the human mind cannot grasp the full breadth of our Creator's infinite will, God wants us to connect intellectually and emotionally with His Torah and *mitzvot*. This engages our full being in a relationship with God.

- When we ask a Jewish question, we ask not to dismiss but out of a genuine desire to learn; we accept that there are limits to our understanding; and we ask knowing that there are certain things we can only understand through immersion in Jewish life.

2. Why are there no miracles today of biblical proportions?

The Sub-Question (Optional)

QUESTION FOR DISCUSSION

Beyond curiosity, what might prompt someone to ask this question?

Pros vs. Cons

LEARNING EXERCISE 1

What are the advantages of miracles? Are there any disadvantages?

Advantages of Miracles	Disadvantages of Miracles

The Tumbling Walls of Jericho

Text 3

Rabbi Yechezkel Landau, cited in *Noda BiYehuda al HaTorah*, *Parashat Bereishit* 📖

אֲבָל יְהוֹשֻׁעַ שֶׁבָּא לִכְבּוֹשׁ אַרְצוֹת שִׁבְעָה גוֹיִם, וּבָא לְאַרְצָם, וְשָׁם לָקַח אֶרֶץ אֲחוּזָתָם מִיָּדָם, הָיָה לַחֲשׁוֹד כִּי לֹא עַל פִּי הַדִּבּוּר עָשָׂה. שֶׁהַקָּבַּ"ה אָמַר לוֹ "כָּל מָקוֹם אֲשֶׁר תִּדְרוֹךְ כַּף רַגְלְכֶם בּוֹ לָכֶם נְתַתִּיו"... (יְהוֹשֻׁעַ א, ג). וְהַגּוֹיִם יֹאמְרוּ כִּי שֶׁקֶר הוּא, שֶׁהוּא עַצְמוֹ בִּגְבוּרָתוֹ וּבִגְבוּרַת עַמּוֹ יִשְׂרָאֵל הוּא בָּא בִּזְרוֹעַ לָקַחַת אַרְצָם.

לָכֵן בִּתְחִלַּת הַכִּיבּוּשׁ, עִיר הָרִאשׁוֹנָה הָעוֹמֶדֶת בִּקְצֵה הַגְּבוּל הִיא עִיר יְרִיחוֹ, לֹא כָּבְשָׁהּ דֶּרֶךְ כִּיבּוּשׁ מִלְחָמָה דֶּרֶךְ טִבְעוֹ שֶׁל עוֹלָם, שֶׁאַנְשֵׁי הַחַיִל עוֹלִים מִבַּחוּץ עַל הַחוֹמָה, אוֹ שֶׁנּוֹגְשִׁים לִשְׁבּוֹר דַּלְתוֹת הַשְּׁעָרִים, אוֹ לְהָבִיא הָעִיר בְּמָצוֹר זְמַן רַב עַד שֶׁלֹּא יִהְיֶה לֶחֶם לִבְנֵי הָעִיר וְיִהְיוּ מוּכְרָחִים לִפְתּוֹחַ שַׁעֲרֵי הָעִיר. כָּל אֵלֶּה לֹא נַעֲשָׂה בְּכִיבּוּשׁ יְרִיחוֹ. אֲבָל סָבְבוּ הָעִיר שֶׁבַע פְּעָמִים, וְתָקְעוּ בַּשּׁוֹפָרוֹת, וְנָפְלָה חוֹמַת הָעִיר תַּחְתֶּיהָ. כַּכָּתוּב "וַיָּרַע הָעָם, וַיִּתְקְעוּ בַּשּׁוֹפָרוֹת, וַיְהִי כִשְׁמוֹעַ הָעָם אֶת קוֹל הַשּׁוֹפָר, וַיָּרִיעוּ הָעָם תְּרוּעָה גְדוֹלָה, וַתִּפּוֹל הַחוֹמָה תַּחְתֶּיהָ, וַיַּעַל הָעָם הָעִירָה אִישׁ נֶגְדּוֹ וַיִּלְכְּדוּ אֶת הָעִיר" (יְהוֹשֻׁעַ ו,כ). וְהִנֵּה בָּזֶה רָאוּ עַמִּים כֻּלָּם כִּי אִי אֶפְשָׁר דָּבָר זֶה בְּשׁוּם תַּחְבּוּלָה בְּטֶבַע וְלֹא בְּכֹחַ וּגְבוּרָה אֱנוֹשִׁית, רַק פֶּלֶא הוּא מִן הַבּוֹרֵא, וּבִרְצוֹנוֹ יְהוֹשֻׁעַ וְיִשְׂרָאֵל בָּאִים לִנְחוֹל אֶת הָאָרֶץ.

וְלָכֵן לֹא מָצִינוּ שׁוּב בִּשְׁאָר עָרִים בְּצוּרוֹת שֶׁכִּיבֵּשׁ יְהוֹשֻׁעַ שֶׁנָּפְלוּ הַחוֹמוֹת מֵעֲלֵיהֶם, אֲבָל כָּבַשׁ אוֹתָן בְּכִיבּוּשׁ מִלְחָמָה, כֵּיוָן שֶׁכְּבָר הוֹדִיעַ הַקָּבַּ"ה בִּתְחִלַּת הַכִּיבּוּשׁ שֶׁיְּהוֹשֻׁעַ הוּא שָׁלִיחַ מֵהַשֵּׁם יִתְבָּרֵךְ בְּמִלְחָמָה זוֹ, וְהוּא שַׂר צְבָא ה', שׁוּב לֹא הָיָה צוֹרֶךְ לְהוֹדִיעַ בְּכָל פַּעַם, כִּי פְקִיד ה' לֹא יִשָּׁנֶה וְלֹא יִכְבּוֹשׁ כִּי אִם מַה שֶּׁנִּצְטַוָּה.

When Joshua arrived to conquer Israel, the land of the seven nations, people could have suspected that God did not instruct him to do so. Although God told him, "Every place that the sole of your foot shall tread upon, I have given it to you . . ." (Joshua 1:3); nevertheless, the nations could have argued that this was false

Rabbi Yechezkel Landau
(*Noda BiYehuda*)
1713-1793

Halachist. Rabbi Landau was born in Poland. In 1755, he assumed the rabbinate of Prague and all of Bohemia. An influential authority on Halachah, he responded to queries from all over Europe, most of which have been collected and published in *Responsa Noda BiYehudah*. He also wrote explanatory commentaries on the *Shulchan Aruch* and a commentary on several Talmudic tractates.

and that Joshua was coming to misappropriate their land by his own might and the strength of his people.

This is why Jericho, the border city and the first city to be taken, was not conquered by natural means. Jews did not scale its walls, crash its gates, or lay a prolonged siege until the starving inhabitants would be forced to open the city gates. Rather, they walked around the city seven times, sounded their *shofars*, and the walls miraculously fell. As the verse says (Joshua 6:20), "The people shouted when they blew with the *shofars*: and it came to pass, when the people heard the sound of the *shofar*, and the people shouted with a great shout, that the wall fell down flat, so that the people went up into the city, every man straight before him, and they took the city." With this, all the nations saw that this was not a natural conquest and that human prowess was not responsible for it. They realized that it was a divine miracle, and that God willed that Joshua and the Jews take the Land.

We do not find Joshua conquering any other fortified city through such miraculous means. He conquered them with normative warfare. God already broadcasted at the outset of the conquest that Joshua was a divine messenger with respect to this war, and it was unnecessary to repeat this message each time. For a legitimate messenger of God would not contravene God's wishes and would not conquer that which God did not command him to conquer.

KEY POINTS

- We no longer witness miracles of biblical proportions because the purpose of these miracles was to transmit foundational statements about the Jewish faith. God relies on us to convey these messages to future generations.

- While our biblical ancestors witnessed God's power to suspend the rules of nature, we observe a deeper reality, that nature is God's tool and not separate from Him.

- God wants us to discover Him beneath the veil of the natural world. This will result in a more lasting and deeper relationship with God.

3. Why do we pray? Doesn't God know what He is doing? Can we really affect His will?

To Pray Means to Change (Optional)

Text 4a

Rabbi Tsvi Elimelech Shapiro, *Benei Yisaschar, Ma'amarei Shabbatot* 8 🎕

חָקְרוּ הַקַּדְמוֹנִים אֵיךְ אֶפְשָׁר לוֹמַר שֶׁתִּהְיֶה הַתְּפִלָּה פּוֹעֶלֶת, נִמְצָא שֶׁיֵּשׁ חַס וְשָׁלוֹם שִׁינוּי רָצוֹן, כַּאֲשֶׁר קוֹדֶם הַתְּפִלָּה הָיָה הָרָצוֹן בְּאוֹפֶן כָּזֶה, וְאַחַר כָּךְ עַל יְדֵי הַתְּפִלָּה נִשְׁתַּנָּה הָרָצוֹן.

וְהִנֵּה כָּתְבוּ עַל זֶה תַּלְמִידֵי הַבַּעַשׁ"ט לִהְיוֹת עַל יְדֵי הַתְּפִלָּה נִתְדַּבֵּק הָאָדָם בְּמָקוֹם אַחֵר יוֹתֵר גָּבוֹהַּ וְנֶהְפַּךְ לְאִישׁ אַחֵר. וְהַגַם שֶׁנִּגְזַר גְּזֵירָה עַל אוֹתוֹ הָאִישׁ, הִנֵּה בְּהִתְפַּלֵּל הָאָדָם אֶל הַשֵּׁם הוי"ה ב"ה הַמְהַוֶּוה כָּל הֲוָיוֹת, הִנֵּה נִתְדַּבֵּק בְּמָקוֹם יוֹתֵר גָּבוֹהַּ, וְנִתְהַוָּה לַהֲוָיָה אַחֶרֶת.

וְאֵין כָּאן שִׁינוּי רָצוֹן, כִּי עַל אוֹתָהּ הַהֲוָיָה שֶׁהוּא כָּעֵת לֹא נִגְזְרָה הַגְּזֵירָה.

Rabbi Tsvi Elimelech Shapiro
(*Benei Yisaschar*)
1783–1841

Rabbi Shapiro was the student of Rabbi Ya'akov Yitschak of Lublin and of his uncle, Rabbi Elimelech of Lizhensk. He was influential in bringing the Chasidic movement to Galician and Hungarian Jewry. He authored *Benei Yisaschar*. His descendants established the Chasidic dynasties of Dinov, Munkach, and Bluzhov.

Earlier scholars have questioned how prayer could be effective. An effective prayer implies that God changed His will—that before the prayer He wanted one thing and through prayer He wills something else.

In response, the students of the Ba'al Shem Tov taught that through prayer, you connect to a loftier place, and this renders you a new person. Although something particular may have been decreed upon you, your prayer to the Creator connects you with a higher place, and you experience a rebirth. Accordingly, there is no change in God's will; for God's original plan never pertained to the new person you have become through prayer.

LEARNING EXERCISE 2A

How might we approach prayer differently in light of the teaching that through prayer, we connect to a loftier place, and this changes us into a new person?

_____

_____

_____

_____

_____

_____

_____

_____

_____

Plan A, Plan B

Text 4b

Rabbi David Shlomo Eibeshitz, *Arvei Nachal, Parashat Balak* 1 📜

הַמְּחַקְרִים הִקְשׁוּ בְּמַה שֶׁאָנוּ רוֹאִין בְּכָל עֵת שֶׁיֵּשׁ אֵיזֶה צַעַר בָּעוֹלָם וּגְזֵירָה אֲזַי
מְבַטְּלִין עַל יְדֵי תְּפִלָּה . . . וְאֵיךְ יְצוּיַּיר אֶצְלוֹ שִׁינוּי רָצוֹן עַל יְדֵי הַתְּפִלָּה?

אָכֵן בְּשַׁ"ס יֵשׁ תֵּירוּץ עַל זֶה. וְהוּא אָמְרָם זַ"ל (חולין ס,ב): "מְלַמֵּד שֶׁיָּצְאוּ
דְשָׁאִים וְעָמְדוּ עַל פֶּתַח קַרְקַע, וְלֹא יָצְאוּ עַד שֶׁבָּא אָדָם הָרִאשׁוֹן וּבִיקֵּשׁ עֲלֵיהֶם
רַחֲמִים, וְיָרְדוּ גְשָׁמִים וְצָמְחוּ, מְלַמֵּד שֶׁהַקָּבָּ"ה מִתְאַוֶּה לִתְפִלָּתָן שֶׁל צַדִּיקִים".

אֲשֶׁר לְפִי זֶה אֵין כָּאן שִׁינוּי רָצוֹן, כִּי כָּךְ הָיָה הָרָצוֹן מִתְּחִלָּה
לְהַעֲצִיר הַגְּשָׁמִים כְּדֵי שֶׁיִּתְפַּלְלוּ וְאַחַר כָּךְ יֵרְדוּ גְשָׁמִים.

Rabbi David Shlomo Eibeshitz
1755–1814

Russian-born author and rabbi. After serving numerous rabbinical posts in Europe, Rabbi Eibeshitz moved to Safed, Israel. His most noted works are *Arvei Nachal*, a Chasidic and Kabbalistic commentary on the Torah, and *Levushei Serad*, a commentary to the *Code of Jewish Law*.

The philosophers ask about the fact that whenever we are in distress we attempt to change things through prayer. . . . Is it conceivable that prayer could change God's will?

The Talmud (Chulin 60b) provides an answer to this question. It states, "[On the third day of Creation], vegetation emerged from the earth but only slightly. It did not grow until Adam came into existence and prayed on its behalf, whereupon rain descended and the vegetation grew. This teaches us that God thirsts for the prayers of the righteous."

Accordingly, God does not change His plans through prayer. God's intention from the outset was to withhold rain so that man would pray and that only then rain would fall.

QUESTION FOR DISCUSSION

If God is willing to grant us certain things through prayer, why doesn't He grant them to us without prayer?

LEARNING EXERCISE 2B

How might we approach prayer differently in light of the statement that "God thirsts for our prayers" to enable a relationship with Him?

_____

_____

_____

_____

_____

_____

_____

_____

A New Will (Optional)

LEARNING EXERCISE 3

Describe the key difference between Text 4a and Text 4b.	
Describe a common denominator between these two texts.	

Text 4c

Rabbi Shmuel Schneersohn, *Torat Shmuel* 5627, p. 59 📖

הַתְּפִילָה הוּא "יְהִי רָצוֹן", פֵּירוּשׁ - לַעֲשׂוֹת רָצוֹן חָדָשׁ
לִהְיוֹת רוֹפֵא חוֹלִים וּמַתִּיר אֲסוּרִים.

Rabbi Shmuel Schneersohn of Lubavitch
(Rebbe Maharash)
1834–1882

Known by the acronym "Maharash"; fourth Chabad rebbe and leader of Russian Jewry. Born in Lubavitch, Russia, he was the youngest son of Rabbi Menachem Mendel Schneersohn (the Tsemach Tsedek). Much of his leadership was devoted to combating anti-Jewish policies. His discourses have been collected and published as *Likutei Torah, Torat Shmuel.*

The objective of prayer is summed up by the words, "May it be your will." This implies that our prayers initiate a new divine will to heal the sick and release the captured.

KEY POINTS

- Our prayers can be effective because through prayer we experience personal change. God's initial will does not apply to the new person we have become.

- Our prayers can be effective because there are certain things God decides to grant only upon request. God desires our prayers because asking for our needs enables us to have a tangible and consistent relationship with Him. Thus, it is not that we pray because we need; we need so that we will pray.

- Our prayers can be effective, according to the mystics, because we have the ability to initiate a new divine will. This is because prayer reveals our connection to God at a level that transcends the divine system through which the initial will was generated.

4. Why is there so much fragmentation in Jewish practice?

Different Strokes, Different Folks

Text 5

Rabbi Chaim Vital, *Peri Ets Chayim*, *Sha'ar Hatefilah*, Introduction 📖

בְּשָׁרְשֵׁי הַמִּנְהָגִים, שֶׁיֵּשׁ חִלּוּקִים בֵּין אַשְׁכְּנַזִים וּבֵין סְפָרַדִּיִּים, קַטָאלוֹנִיִּים
וְאִיטַלְיִּים וְכַיּוֹצֵא בָהֶם, שֶׁיֵּשׁ בָּהֶם מִנְהָגִים קַדְמוֹנִים שֶׁלָהֶם בְּסִידוּרֵי הַתְּפִלָּה,
וְלֹא בְּמַה שֶׁנּוֹגֵעַ לְפִיּוּטִים וּפִזְמוֹנִים הָאַחֲרוֹנִים רַק בְּשָׁרְשֵׁי הַתְּפִלּוֹת כְּפִי הַדִּין.

וְהָיָה אוֹמֵר מוֹרִי זלה"ה, שֶׁיֵּשׁ י"ב שְׁעָרִים בָּרָקִיעַ, נֶגֶד י"ב שְׁבָטִים,
וְכָל אֶחָד עוֹלָה תְּפִלָּתוֹ דֶּרֶךְ שַׁעַר אֶחָד, וְהֵם הַשְּׁעָרִים הַנִּזְכָּרִים
בְּשִׁלְהֵי סֵפֶר יְחֶזְקֵאל. וְאָמַר שֶׁוַּדַּאי לֹא הָיוּ הַשְּׁעָרִים וְדַרְכֵי הַשְּׁעָרִים
שָׁוִין, וְכָל אֶחָד מְשֻׁנֶּה מֵחֲבֵירוֹ, לָכֵן גַּם הַתְּפִלּוֹת מְשׁוּנּוֹת.

לָכֵן כָּל אֶחָד וְאֶחָד רָאוּי לְהַחֲזִיק כְּמִנְהָג תְּפִלָּתוֹ, כִּי מִי יוֹדֵעַ אִם הוּא
מִשֵּׁבֶט הַהוּא, וְאֵין תְּפִילָּתוֹ עוֹלָה אֶלָּא עַל יְדֵי שַׁעַר הַהוּא.

אַךְ מַה שֶׁהוּא דִּינִין מְפוֹרָשִׁין בַּתַּלְמוּד, זֶה שָׁוֶה לְכָל הַשְּׁבָטִים.

Rabbi Chaim Vital
ca. 1542–1620

Lurianic Kabbalist. Rabbi Vital was born in Israel, lived in Safed and Jerusalem, and later in Damascus. He was authorized by his teacher, Rabbi Yitschak Luria, the Arizal, to record his teachings. Acting on this mandate, Vital began arranging his master's teachings in written form, and his many works constitute the foundation of the Lurianic school of Jewish mysticism. His most famous work is *Ets Chaim*.

German, Spanish, Catalan, Italian, and other Jews have different customs pertaining to prayer, not only with regard to recently written liturgical poems and hymns, but also with regard to essential components of prayer that are mandated by Jewish law.

My teacher, the Arizal, would say that there are twelve supernal gates that correspond to the twelve tribes, and that these are alluded to at the end of the Book of Ezekiel. Each tribe's prayer ascends through its own gate. Each gate, and the spiritual paths that lead to them, is certainly not identical. Correspondingly, each tribe prays with variations.

People should therefore maintain their unique prayer customs. It is possible that the versions they were taught correspond to their particular tribe and are the means by which their prayers ascend.

However, laws that are clearly stated in the Talmud apply equally for all tribes.

Tribal Dwelling (Optional)

Text 6

Rabbi Ya'akov Aryeh Guterman, *Bikurei Aviv, Parashat Balak* 📖

בְּפָסוּק "וַיַּרְא אֶת יִשְׂרָאֵל שׁוֹכֵן לִשְׁבָטָיו" (בַּמִּדְבָּר כד,ב), פֵּירֵשׁ רַשִׁ"י, "רָאָה כָּל שֵׁבֶט וְשֵׁבֶט שׁוֹכֵן בִּפְנֵי עַצְמוֹ וְאֵינָם מְעוּרְבָּבִים".

קָשֶׁה: מַאי מַעֲלָה הוּא זֶה? . . .

אַבְרָהָם עָבַד הַשֵׁם יִתְבָּרֵךְ בְּאַהֲבָה יוֹתֵר מִיִּרְאָה, שֶׁהָיָה נִשְׁמָתוֹ מִסְפִירַת חֶסֶד, וְיִצְחָק אָבִינוּ עָבַד בְּיִרְאָה יוֹתֵר, שֶׁהָיָה נִשְׁמָתוֹ מִסְפִירַת גְּבוּרָה, יַעֲקֹב בְּתִפְאֶרֶת. וְכֵן כָּל אָדָם צָרִיךְ לֵידַע כֹּחַ נִשְׁמָתוֹ לַעֲבוֹד לְהַשֵׁם יִתְבָּרֵךְ לְפִי כֹּחַ נִשְׁמָתוֹ לְפִי סְפִירָה הַשׁוֹרֶשׁ נִשְׁמָתוֹ הוּא מִשָּׁם.

וְכֵן הָיוּ הַשְׁבָטִים: רְאוּבֵן הָיָה חֶסֶד סְפִירָה שֶׁלוֹ, אֲשֶׁר נִשְׁמָתוֹ נִלְקַח מִשָּׁם, וְהָיָה כֹּחַ אָב בַּבֵּן, וְהָיָה כָּל שִׁבְטוֹ נִשְׁמָתָם מִסְפִירַת חֶסֶד. עַל כֵּן הָיוּ יוֹדְעִים עֲבוֹדָה שֶׁלָהֶם לְתַקֵן נִשְׁמָתָם בְּאַהֲבָה גְדוֹלָה לְהַשֵׁם יִתְבָּרֵךְ. וְכֵן שִׁמְעוֹן הָיָה מִסְפִירַת גְּבוּרָה, וְהָיָה כֹּחַ אָב בַּבֵּן לְכָל שִׁבְטוֹ לִהְיוֹת בִּבְחִינַת יִרְאָה יוֹתֵר. וְהָיוּ יוֹדְעִים כָּל אֶחָד עֲבוֹדָה שֶׁלוֹ לַעֲבוֹד הַשֵׁם יִתְבָּרֵךְ. לֹא כְּמוֹ עַתָּה מְעוּרְבָּבִים הָעוֹלָם הַשְׁבָטִים, וּכְמוֹ שֶׁאַחֵר עוֹשֶׂה הוּא נַמִי עוֹשֶׂה . . .

וְזֶה רָאָה "שׁוֹכֵן לִשְׁבָטָיו", שֶׁהָיָה כָּל אֶחָד מַכִּיר שִׁבְטוֹ, וְהָיָה יֵדַע
כֹּחַ נִשְׁמָתוֹ לַעֲבוֹד הַשֵּׁם יִתְבָּרַךְ בְּזֶה שֶׁהוּא כֹּחַ נִשְׁמָתוֹ . . .

שֶׁאִם הָיָה מְעוֹרָבִים הָיָה אֶחָד עוֹשֶׂה מַה שֶׁחֲבֵירוֹ עוֹשֶׂה, אַף עַל פִּי
שֶׁאֵין הָעֲבוֹדָה הַשַּׁיָּיךְ לְשׁוֹרֵשׁ נִשְׁמָתוֹ. וְלֹא הָיָה לוֹ תִּיקוּן כְּלַל.

Rabbi Ya'akov Aryeh Guterman
1792–1874

Founder of the Radzyminer
Chasidic dynasty. Rabbi Guterman
was a pupil of Rabbi Simchah
Bunim of Peshischa and Rabbi
Yitschak Kalish, and he attracted
a large Chasidic following. His
teachings were published in
Divrei Aviv and *Bikurei Aviv*.

On the verse (Numbers 24:2), "And Balaam saw Israel dwelling by their tribes," Rashi comments: "He saw each tribe dwelling separately—not intermingled."

What is the virtue in this? . . . Abraham served God more through love than awe, as his soul emanated from the attribute of *chesed*, divine kindness. Isaac served more through awe than love, inasmuch as his soul was from the divine attribute of *gevurah*, strength and severity. Jacob served with *tiferet*, beauty and mercy. In the same way, people ought to know their respective souls' potentials so that they can serve God according to those potentials, according to the divine attribute in which their souls are rooted.

So it was with the tribes: Reuben's soul stemmed from the attribute of love and kindness, as did all souls of his tribe. They knew that their primary service was love of God. Simeon's soul was rooted in the attribute of severity, as were all souls of his tribe. Awe of God was the dominant aspect of their service. Each tribe knew its path in the service of God. Now, however, the tribes are intermingled, and people simply adopt the ways of their neighbors. . . .

This is the deeper meaning of, "And Balaam saw Israel dwelling by their tribes." Each tribe recognized its uniqueness and served God according to its potential. . . . Had they been intermingled, each would have imitated the other, even though such service would have had no relation to the root of their souls and would have offered their souls no rectification.

Nullify or Purify?

LEARNING EXERCISE 4

You possess a unique mix of personal characteristics, strengths, and talents. How might you use these to promote acts of goodness and kindness? How might you integrate your uniqueness into your relationship with the Creator?

_____

_____

_____

_____

_____

_____

_____

Avoiding the Pitfalls
of Difference (Optional)

QUESTION FOR DISCUSSION

Is it possible to embrace diversity while avoiding discord? How?

KEY POINTS

- There have always been variations in Jewish custom and practice, starting with the twelve tribes of Israel, rooted in a diversity of emotional approaches to divine service.

- Every individual has a distinctive soul with its own unique approach to divine service. Each of us should therefore use our God-given strengths, talents, and abilities to fulfill the purpose of our existence.

- We avoid fragmentation and discord, not by promoting uniformity, but by recognizing that we are like one body—each part has a crucial function and depends on the others. Moreover, despite our differences, we are part of a greater whole.

5. Why have the Jews survived millennia while so many other civilizations have vanished?

A Common Question

Text 7a

Blaise Pascal, *Thoughts*, trans. W. F. Trotter [New York: P. F. Collier & Son, 1910], pp. 209–210

The Jewish people at once attract my attention by the number of wonderful and singular facts which appear about them. . . . This family, or people, is the most ancient within human knowledge, a fact which seems to me to inspire a peculiar veneration for it. This people is not eminent solely by their antiquity, but is also singular by their duration, which has always continued from their origin till now. For whereas the nations of Greece and of Italy, of Lacedaemon, of Athens and of Rome, and others who came long after, have long since perished, these ever remain. And in spite of the endeavors of many powerful kings who have a hundred times tried to destroy them, as their historians testify, and as it is easy to conjecture from the natural order of things during so long a space of years, they have nevertheless been preserved (and this preservation has been foretold).

Blaise Pascal
1623–1662

French inventor, mathematician, physicist, and theological writer. In the 1640s, Pascal invented the Pascaline, an early calculator. In the 1650s, he laid the foundation of probability theory with Pierre de Fermat and published *Les Provinciales*, a groundbreaking work of religious theology. Pascal is also widely known for his body of notes, posthumously released as the *Pensées*.

Text 7b

Mark Twain, "Concerning the Jews," *Harper's New Monthly Magazine* 99:592 (September 1899), p. 535

Mark Twain
1835–1910

Pen name of Samuel Langhorne Clemens, popular American humorist, journalist, lecturer, and novelist. Best known for his novels *The Adventures of Tom Sawyer* and *The Adventures of Huckleberry Finn*, he is remembered as one of America's most beloved literary figures.

The Egyptian, the Babylonian, and the Persian rose, filled the planet with sound and splendor, then faded to dream-stuff and passed away; the Greek and the Roman followed, and made a vast noise, and they are gone; other peoples have sprung up and held their torch high for a time, but it burned out, and they sit in twilight now, or have vanished. The Jew saw them all, and is now what he always was, exhibiting no decadence, no infirmities of age, no weakening of his parts, no slowing of his energies, no dulling of his alert and aggressive mind. All things are mortal but the Jew; all other forces pass, but he remains. What is the secret of his immortality?

Text 7c

Arnold Toynbee and D. C. Somervell, *A Study of History*, *Abridgement of Volumes I–VI* [New York, Oxford University Press, 1947], p. 94

The Jews live on—the same peculiar people—today, long after the Phoenicians and the Philistines have lost their identity like all the nations. The ancient Syriac neighbors of Israel have fallen into the melting-pot and have been re-minted, in the fullness of time, with new images and superscriptions, while Israel has proved impervious to this alchemy—performed by History in the crucibles of universal states and universal churches and wanderings of the nations—to which we Gentiles all in turn succumb.

Arnold Toynbee
1889–1975

British historian, philosopher, and expert in international affairs. Toynbee is best known for his 12-volume *A Study of History*. With his prodigious scholarly output, Toynbee was one of the most widely read and discussed scholars of the 1940s and 1950s. A controversial figure, Toynbee's referring to contemporary Jews as "fossils" of a past civilization, compounded by his rhetoric concerning the State of Israel, were a source of much heated debate.

QUESTION FOR DISCUSSION

What might be some of the contributing factors to the survival of the Jewish people?

A Faithful Shepherd

Text 8

Midrash Tanchuma, Parashat Toldot 5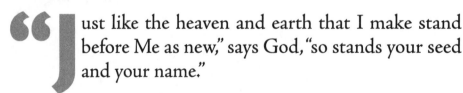

אַדְרִיָאנוּס אָמַר לְרַבִּי יְהוֹשֻׁעַ: גְּדוֹלָה הַכִּבְשָׂה הָעוֹמֶדֶת בֵּין שִׁבְעִים זְאֵבִים.

אָמַר לֵיהּ: גָּדוֹל הוּא הָרוֹעֶה שֶׁמַּצִּילָהּ וְשׁוֹמְרָהּ וְשׁוֹבְרָן לְפָנֶיהָ. הֲוֵי "כָּל כְּלִי יוּצַר עָלַיִךְ לֹא יִצְלָח" (יְשַׁעְיָהוּ נד,יז).

Hadrian said to Rabbi Yehoshua, "Is the lamb so great to survive the seventy wolves? [Certainly not! It must be that the wolves are kind to the lamb and do not seek to destroy her.]"

Said Rabbi Yehoshua, "Great is the Shepherd Who saves and guards her and drives her enemies away. As it is written, "No weapon formed against you shall prosper" (Isaiah 54:17).

Text 9

Isaiah 66:22

כִּי כַאֲשֶׁר הַשָּׁמַיִם הַחֲדָשִׁים וְהָאָרֶץ הַחֲדָשָׁה אֲשֶׁר אֲנִי עֹשֶׂה עֹמְדִים לְפָנַי נְאֻם ה', כֵּן יַעֲמֹד זַרְעֲכֶם וְשִׁמְכֶם.

"Just like the heaven and earth that I make stand before Me as new," says God, "so stands your seed and your name."

Text 10

Rabbi Ya'akov Emden, *Siddur*, Introduction 📖

אֲנַחְנוּ הָאוּמָה הַגּוֹלָה, שֶׂה פְזוּרָה, אַחַר כָּל מָה שֶׁעָבַר עָלֵינוּ מֵהַצָּרוֹת
וְהַתְּמוּרוֹת אֲלָפִים מֵהַשָּׁנִים. וְאֵין אוּמָה בָּעוֹלָם נִרְדָּפֶת כָּמוֹנוּ. מָה רַבִּים
הָיוּ צָרֵינוּ, מֶה עָצְמוּ נָשְׂאוּ רֹאשׁ הַקָּמִים עָלֵינוּ מִנְּעוּרֵינוּ, לְהַשְׁמִידֵנוּ
לְעָקְרֵנוּ לְשָׁרְשֵׁנוּ, מִפְּנֵי הַשִּׂנְאָה שֶׁסִּבָּתָהּ הַקִּנְאָה רַבַּת צְרָרוּנוּ. גַּם לֹא
יָכְלוּ לָנוּ לְאַבְּדֵנוּ וּלְכַלּוֹתֵינוּ. כָּל הָאוּמוֹת הַקַּדְמוֹת הָעֲצוּמוֹת, אָבַד זִכְרָם,
בָּטַל סִבְרָם, סָר צִלָּם, וְאָנוּ הַדְּבֵקִים בַּה' כֻּלָּנוּ חַיִּים הַיּוֹם . . .

מָה יַעֲנֶה בָּזֶה פִילוֹסוֹף חָרִיף? הַיָד הַמִּקְרֶה עָשְׂתָה כָּל אֵלֶּה? חֵי נַפְשִׁי, כִּי
בְּהִתְבּוֹנְנִי בְּנִפְלָאוֹת אֵלֶּה גָּדְלוּ אֶצְלִי יוֹתֵר מִכָּל נִסִּים וְנִפְלָאוֹת שֶׁעָשָׂה
הַשֵּׁם יִתְבָּרֵךְ לַאֲבוֹתֵינוּ בְּמִצְרַיִם וּבַמִּדְבָּר וּבְאֶרֶץ יִשְׂרָאֵל. וְכָל מַה שֶׁאָרַךְ
הַגָּלוּת יוֹתֵר, נִתְאַמֵּת הַנֵּס יוֹתֵר, וְנוֹדַע מַעֲשֵׂה תָקְפּוֹ וּגְבוּרָתוֹ.

We are the exiled nation, the lost sheep. With all the troubles that have passed over us through the millennia, there is no nation in the world that has been pursued as we have been. How numerous our enemies have been! From our earliest days, how mightily have they lifted their heads up, seeking to destroy us, to uproot us, because of the hatred caused by envy. But they have not succeeded in destroying us. All the mighty ancient nations, their memory is gone, their hope is naught, their protection has been removed. But we who cling to God, we are all alive today. . . .

How can a sharp skeptic rebut this? Could it have been the work of chance that caused all this? By my living soul! When I contemplate these wonders, they seem greater to me than all the wonders and miracles that God did for our ancestors in Egypt, in the wilderness, and in the Land of Israel. And the longer the exile continues, the more

Rabbi Ya'akov Emden (Ya'avetz)
1697–1776

Talmudist and Kabbalist. Rabbi Emden was the son of Rabbi Tsvi Ashkenazi, the Chacham Tsvi. He is famed for his vocal opposition to the Sabbateans, which led to several bitter controversies. In 1728, he became rabbi of Emden, Germany, but gave up that position soon thereafter. Emden wrote many works, including a *sidur* with halachic and Kabbalistic commentary, polemical writings, halachic responsa, and glosses on the Talmud.

this miracle is verified, and the more we know its power and might.

QUESTION FOR DISCUSSION

Why did Rabbi Ya'akov Emden believe that the survival of the Jews was a greater miracle than the miracles mentioned in the Bible?

A Stiff-Necked Nation

Text 11

Shemot Rabah

An early rabbinic commentary on the Book of Exodus. Midrash is the designation of a particular genre of rabbinic literature usually forming a running commentary on specific books of the Bible. *Shemot Rabah*, written mostly in Hebrew, provides textual exegeses, expounds upon the biblical narrative, and develops and illustrates moral principles. It was first published in Constantinople in 1512 together with four other midrashic works on the other four books of the Pentateuch.

Midrash, *Shemot Rabah* 42:9

"וְהִנֵּה עַם קְשֵׁה עוֹרֶף הוּא" (שְׁמוֹת לב,ט) . . . אַתָּה סָבוּר שֶׁהוּא לִגְנַאי וְאֵינוֹ אֶלָּא לִשְׁבָחָן. אוֹ יְהוּדִי אוֹ צָלוּב.

"He is a stiff-necked nation" (Exodus 32:9). . . . You might assume these words denigrate the Jews; in fact, they flatter us. [As the Jew is wont to say,] "Either Judaism or crucifixion."

Text 12

Maurice Samuel, *The Professor and the Fossil* [New York: Knopf, 1956], p. 163

As the Modern world opens, Jewry and Judaism are still very much on the scene. A fascinating historical drama is revealed. The auctioneer is Time, the buyer Oblivion. The peoples come up on the block, one after another, the hammer is lifted, the established formula is intoned: "Going! Going! Gone!" But there is one people that appears on the block regularly, and over it the words "Going! Going!" have been repeated again and again; again and again it has looked like a sale: but the third word has never been pronounced over it.

Maurice Samuel
1895–1972

Romanian-born novelist, translator, and lecturer. A Jewish and Zionist intellectual, Samuel is best known for *You Gentiles*, published in 1924. Most of his work concerns Judaism and the Jew's role in history and modern society. In 1944, he received the prestigious Anisfield-Wolf Book Award for his nonfiction work, *The World of Sholom Aleichem*.

KEY POINTS

- The Jewish people have survived because God promises to protect us both from annihilation and assimilation.

- We participate in the miracle of our survival. Our descendants will remain Jewish because of choices we make—even involving sacrifice—to live as Jews and pass Judaism on to our children.

6. Why don't Jews accept the Christian messiah?

The Barcelona Disputation

Text 13a

Rabbi Moshe ben Nachman, *Kitvei Ramban* 1:310–311; translation from Hyam Maccoby, *Judaism on Trial* [Rutherford, NJ: Fairleigh Dickinson University Press, 1982], pp. 119–120 📖

Rabbi Moshe ben Nachman
(Nachmanides, Ramban)
1194–1270

Scholar, philosopher, author, and physician. Nachmanides was born in Spain and served as leader of Iberian Jewry. In 1263, he was summoned by King James of Aragon to a public disputation with Pablo Cristiani, a Jewish apostate. Though Nachmanides was the clear victor of the debate, he had to flee Spain because of the resulting persecution. He moved to Israel and helped reestablish communal life in Jerusalem. He authored a classic commentary on the Pentateuch and a commentary on the Talmud.

עִיקַר הַדִּין וְהַמַּחֲלוֹקֶת שֶׁבֵּין הַיְּהוּדִים וּבֵין הַנּוֹצְרִים הוּא בְּמַה שֶׁאַתֶּם אוֹמְרִים בְּעִיקַר הָאֱ-לוֹהוּת דָּבָר מַר מְאוֹד. וְאַתָּה אֲדוֹנֵנוּ הַמֶּלֶךְ נוֹצְרִי בֶּן נוֹצְרִי [וּבֶן נוֹצְרִית], וְשָׁמַעְתָּ כָּל יָמֶיךָ גַּלָחִים [צְעִירִים וְדוֹרְשִׁים מְדַבְּרִים מִלֵּידַת יֵשׁוּ], וּמִלְאוּ מוֹחֲךָ וּמוֹחַ עַצְמוֹתֶיךָ מִדְּבַר הַזֶּה, וְשָׁב אֶצְלְךָ מִתּוֹךְ אוֹתוֹ הָרְגִילוּת.

אֲבָל הַדָּבָר אֲשֶׁר אַתֶּם מַאֲמִינִים, וְהוּא עִיקַר אֱמוּנַתְכֶם, לֹא יְקַבֵּל אוֹתוֹ הַשֵּׂכֶל, וְהַטֶּבַע אֵינוֹ נוֹתֵן, וְהַנְּבִיאִים מֵעוֹלָם לֹא אָמְרוּ כֵן, גַּם הַפֶּלֶא אֵינוֹ יָכוֹל לְהִתְפַּשֵּׁט בַּדָּבָר הַהוּא, כַּאֲשֶׁר אֲבָאֵר בִּרְאָיוֹת גְּמוּרוֹת בִּמְקוֹמוֹ וּבִשְׁעָתוֹ, שֶׁיִּהְיֶה בּוֹרֵא הַשָּׁמַיִם וְהָאָרֶץ [וְכָל אֲשֶׁר בָּם] חוֹזֵר [עוֹבֵר] בְּבֶטֶן יְהוּדִית אַחַת, וְיִגְדַּל בּוֹ ז' חֳדָשִׁים, וְיִוָּלֵד קָטָן, וְאַחַר כָּךְ יִגְדַּל, וְאַחַר כָּךְ יִימָסֵר בְּיַד שׂוֹנְאָיו, וְיִשְׁפְּטוּהוּ מִשְׁפַּט מָוֶת, וִימִיתוּהוּ, וְאַחַר כָּךְ תֹּאמְרוּ שֶׁחָיָה וְחָזַר לִמְקוֹמוֹ הָרִאשׁוֹן. לֹא יִסְבֹּל דַּעַת יְהוּדִי וְשׁוּם אָדָם.

וּלְחִינָם וְהֶבֶל תְּדַבְּרוּ דִּבְרֵיכֶם, כִּי זֶה הוּא עִיקַר מַחֲלוֹקְתֵנוּ.

The real point of difference between Jews and Christians lies in what you say about the fundamental matter of the deity; a doctrine which is distasteful indeed. You, our lord King, are a Christian and the son of a Christian, and you have listened all your life to priests who have filled your brain and the marrow of your bones with this doctrine, and it has settled with you, because of that accustomed habit. But the doctrine in which you believe, and which is the foundation of your faith, cannot be accepted by reason, and nature affords no ground for it, nor have the prophets ever expressed it. Nor can even the miraculous stretch as far as this, as I shall explain with full proofs in the right time and place, that the Creator of Heaven and earth resorted to the womb of a certain Jewess and grew there for nine months and was born as an infant, and afterwards grew up and was betrayed into the hands of his enemies who sentenced him to death and executed him, and that afterwards, as you say, he came to life and returned to his original place. The mind of a Jew, or any other person, cannot tolerate this; and you speak your words entirely in vain, for this is the root of our controversy.

QUESTION FOR DISCUSSION

Do you see any problems or inconsistencies with Rabbi Moshe ben Nachman's argument against Christianity?

The Messiah (Optional)

Text 13b

Rabbi Moshe ben Nachman, ibid., p. 311; translation
from Hyam Maccoby, ibid., pp. 120–121 📖

אֲבָל נְדַבֵּר גַּם מִן הַמָּשִׁיחַ כַּאֲשֶׁר הוּא רְצוֹנְכֶם.

אָמַר פְּרָאִי פּוֹל: וְתַאֲמִין שֶׁבָּא?

אָמַרְתִּי: לֹא. אֲבָל אֲנִי מַאֲמִין וְיוֹדֵעַ שֶׁלֹּא בָּא, וְלֹא הָיָה אָדָם מֵעוֹלָם שֶׁאָמַר
וְלֹא שֶׁיֹּאמְרוּ עָלָיו שֶׁהוּא מָשִׁיחַ זוּלָתִי יֵשׁוּ, וְאִי אֶפְשָׁר לִי (לְהַאֲמִין) בִּמְשִׁיחוּתוֹ.
שֶׁהַנָּבִיא אוֹמֵר בְּמָשִׁיחַ, "וּמִשָּׁלוֹ מִיָּם עַד יָם וּמִנָּהָר עַד אַפְסֵי אָרֶץ" (תְּהִלִּים עב,
ח), וְהוּא לֹא הָיָה לוֹ מֶמְשָׁלָה, אֲבָל בְּחַיָּיו הָיָה נִרְדָּף מֵאוֹיְבָיו וּמִתְחַבֵּא מִפְּנֵיהֶם,
וּלְבַסּוֹף נָפַל בְּיָדָם, וְלֹא הָיָה יָכוֹל לְהַצִּיל עַצְמוֹ, אֵיךְ יוֹשִׁיעַ כָּל יִשְׂרָאֵל? וְאַף (כִּי)
אַחֲרֵי מוֹתוֹ לֹא הָיָה לוֹ מֶמְשָׁלָה, כִּי מֶמְשֶׁלֶת רוֹמָה אֵינָה בַּעֲבוּרוֹ. אֲבָל קוֹדֶם
שֶׁהֶאֱמִינוּ בּוֹ הָיְתָה עִיר רוֹמָא מוֹשֶׁלֶת בְּרוֹב הָעוֹלָם, וּלְאַחַר שֶׁבָּאוּ בֶּאֱמוּנָתוֹ
הִפְסִידוּ מֶמְשָׁלוֹת רַבּוֹת. וְעַתָּה עוֹבְדֵי מוּחַמַּד יֵשׁ לָהֶם מֶמְשָׁלָה יוֹתֵר מֵהֶם.

וְכֵן הַנָּבִיא אוֹמֵר שֶׁבִּזְמַן הַמָּשִׁיחַ "לֹא יְלַמְּדוּ עוֹד אִישׁ אֶת רֵעֵהוּ וְאִישׁ אֶת
אָחִיו לֵאמֹר דְּעוּ אֶת ה' כִּי כוּלָּם יֵדְעוּ אוֹתִי וְכוּ'" (יִרְמְיָהוּ לב, לד). וְאוֹמֵר
(יְשַׁעְיָהוּ יא,ט) "כִּי מָלְאָה הָאָרֶץ דֵּעָה אֶת ה' כַּמַּיִם לַיָּם מְכַסִּים". וְאוֹמֵר
(יְשַׁעְיָהוּ ב,ד) "וְכִתְּתוּ חַרְבוֹתָם וְכוּ' וְלֹא יִשָּׂא גוֹי אֶל גּוֹי חֶרֶב וְלֹא יִלְמְדוּ
עוֹד מִלְחָמָה." וּמִימֵי יֵשׁוּ וְעַד הֵנָּה כָּל הָעוֹלָם מָלֵא חָמָס וְשׁוֹד וְהַנּוֹצְרִים,
שׁוֹפְכִים דָּמִים יוֹתֵר מִשְּׁאָר הָאוּמּוֹת, וְהֵם גַּם כֵּן מְגַלֵּי עֲרָיוֹת, וְכַמָּה יִהְיֶה
קָשֶׁה לְךָ אֲדוֹנִי הַמֶּלֶךְ, וּלְפָרָשֶׁיךָ אֵלֶּה [אִם] לֹא יִלְמְדוּ עוֹד מִלְחָמָה.

> **L**et us speak of the Messiah too, as this is
> your wish."
>
> Said Fray Paul, "Will you believe, then, that he
> has come?"
>
> Said I, "No. On the contrary, I believe and know that he has
> not come; and so far there has never been any other man

(leaving aside Jesus) who has claimed to be the Messiah (or has had that claim made for him) in whose Messiahship it is possible for me to believe. For the prophet says about the Messiah, 'His rule shall be from sea to sea, and from the river until the ends of the earth' (Psalms 72:8). Jesus, however, never had any power, but in his lifetime he was fleeing from his enemies and hiding from them, and in the end he fell into their hands and could not save himself, so how could he save all Israel? Even after his death he did not have any rule, for the power of Rome is not because of him. Even before they believed in Jesus, the city of Rome was ruling over most of the world, and after they adopted faith in him, they lost many provinces; and now the worshippers of Mohammed have greater power than they.

"The prophet says that in the time of the Messiah, 'They shall teach no more every man his neighbour, and every man his brother, saying, "Know the Lord": for they shall all know me' (Jeremiah 32:34); also, 'The earth shall be full of the knowledge of the Lord, as the waters cover the sea' (Isaiah 11:9); also, 'They shall beat their swords into ploughshares . . . nation shall not lift up sword against nation, neither shall they learn war any more' (Isaiah 2:4). Yet from the days of Jesus until now, the whole world has been full of violence and plundering, and the Christians are greater spillers of blood than all the rest of the peoples, and they are also practisers of adultery and incest. And how hard it would be for you, my lord King, and for your knights, if they were not to learn war anymore!"

Text 13c

Rabbi Moshe ben Nachman, ibid., p. 319; translation
from Hyam Maccoby, ibid., p. 142 📖

זֶה עִנְיַן הַוִּיכּוּחִים כּוּלָם. לֹא שָׁנִיתִי בָּהֶם דָּבָר לְדַעְתִּי.

אַחֲרֵי כֵן בּוֹ בַיוֹם, עָמַדְתִּי לִפְנֵי אֲדוֹנֵנוּ הַמֶּלֶךְ, וְאָמַר: יִשָּׁאֵר הַוִּיכּוּחַ. כִּי
לֹא רָאִיתִי אָדָם שֶׁאֵין הַדִּין עִמּוֹ שֶׁטָּעַן אוֹתוֹ יָפֶה כַּאֲשֶׁר עָשִׂיתִי.

This is the content of all of the discussions. I have not altered one thing in them, to my knowledge.

Afterwards, on the same day, I stood before our lord the King, and he said, "Let the disputation be discontinued; for I have never seen a man who was in the wrong argue as well as you did."

KEY POINTS

- We reject the notion of the Christian deity first and foremost because it has no basis in Jewish tradition, and furthermore, because it cannot be accepted by reason.

- We reject the Christian messiah because he did not fulfill the biblical messianic prophecies, including reigning over the world, spreading the knowledge of God throughout the earth, and ushering in world peace.

7. Why do we kindle *yahrtzeit* candles to commemorate the dead?

Lights of Honor

Text 14

Kol Bo 68 🕮

וְכָתַב הָרַב ר' אָשֵׁר (מִלּוּנִי״ל): וְנָהֲגוּ לִהְיוֹת כָּל אֶחָד מַדְלִיק בִּמְקוֹמוֹ
נֵר אוֹ פְּנַס בְּיוֹם הַכִּפּוּרִים לְכַפֵּר עַל אָבִיו וְעַל אִמּוֹ, כִּי כָּבוֹד הוּא
לַשֵּׁם יִתְבָּרֵךְ, וְכֵן אָמַר (יְשַׁעְיָה כד,טו) "בָּאֻרִים כַּבְּדוּ ה'", אָמַר הַקָּדוֹשׁ
בָּרוּךְ הוּא הַדְלִיקוּ לְפָנַי נֵר שֶׁאֶשְׁמוֹר נִשְׁמוֹתֵיכֶם שֶׁקְּרוּיָה נֵר.

Rabbi Asher of Luneil wrote: On the eve of Yom Kippur, it is customary for all those who lost a parent to kindle a candle or torch near where they will pray [in the synagogue] to atone for the deceased. This honors God, as it is written (Isaiah 24:15), "With lights you shall honor God," [and the Midrash comments:] "God says, light a candle before Me and I shall guard over your souls, which are called candles."

Kol Bo

Kol Bo (lit., "all is in it") is a collection of laws and customs dealing with a variety of subjects. Some assume it was composed by Rabbi Aharon ben Ya'akov HaKohen of Narbonne, who lived during the 13th and 14th centuries, author of *Orechot Chayim*. Rabbi David Conforte (17th century) cites a tradition claiming it was authored by an anonymous woman. It was first printed in Naples in 1490.

Continue your learning experience ONLINE

Visit www.myJLI.com/why1

for insightful and inspiring videos, articles, and readings on this topic.

KEY POINTS

- Because the soul is likened to a flame, we light a candle whenever we wish to honor and memorialize the soul of a deceased loved one.

- The children of the deceased can do a mitzvah on behalf of their parents and thereby help their souls acquire atonement.

Lesson Conclusion (Optional)

LEARNING EXERCISE 5

With a partner, identify a theme that has been present in most (or all) of the elements of this lesson.

1. Why ask "why?" Isn't Judaism a *belief* system?

2. Why are there no miracles today of biblical proportions?

3. Why do we pray? Doesn't God know what He is doing? Can we really affect His will?

4. Why is there so much fragmentation in Jewish practice?

5. Why have the Jews survived millennia while so many other civilizations have vanished?

6. Why don't Jews accept the Christian messiah?

7. Why do we kindle *yahrtzeit* candles to commemorate the dead?

ADDITIONAL READINGS

WHY AREN'T WE CHRISTIANS?

BY RABBI ARYEH KAPLAN

We hear quite a bit today about a movement called "Jews for Jesus." A small number of Jews seem to be finding the teachings of Christianity very attractive. The vast majority of Jews, however, still reject these teachings in the most emphatic terms.

For almost two thousand years, the Christians have been trying to win over the Jew. And for the same period of time, the Jew has resisted all such overtures. But why? Why don't we accept Jesus? In short: Why aren't we Christians?

In order to understand this, we must look at the origin of Christian beliefs. Christianity began with a Jew. Jesus lived as a Jew, around the same time as many of our greatest Talmudic sages. The great Hillel lived just a generation earlier, and Rabbi Akiba, a generation after. Our own sources, however, record very little about Jesus' life. Everything that we know about him is found in the Gospels of the New Testament, a book written by and for the early Christian church. This book, however, was written primarily to further the cause of Christianity, and it is therefore impossible to separate the historical person of Jesus from the "Christ" required by early Christian theology.

Soon after the death of Jesus, we find a marked change in the teachings of his followers. Christianity as we know it began during this period in the work of Paul of Tarsus. Paul, or as he was earlier known, Saul, was a disciple of the great Talmudist Rabbi Gamliel, and he began his career by actively opposing the ear-

Rabbi Aryeh Kaplan. (1934–1983) American rabbi, author, and physicist. Rabbi Kaplan authored more than 50 volumes on Torah, Talmud, Jewish mysticism, and philosophy, many of which have become modern-day classics. He is best known for his popular translation and elucidation of the Bible, *The Living Torah*, and his translation of the Ladino biblical commentary, *Me'am Lo'ez*.

ly Christians. In a dramatic incident on the road to Damascus, Paul converted to Christianity, and later became one of its foremost leaders. Although he had never seen Jesus alive, he claimed to have spoken to him in spirit. Under Paul's leadership, many of the distinctive doctrines of Christianity were first proclaimed, and, for the most part, they have never changed. His teachings are recorded in his Epistles, which form the second part of the New Testament.

Among Paul's major teachings, we find the following:

1) Jesus was the Messiah or Christ predicted by the Prophets of the Bible and awaited by the Jews. He is also the Son of G-d, and like any son, is essentially the same as his Father.

2) Man is evil and sinful. All mankind is damned because of Adam's sin. The Torah cannot save man, since its many commandments make it too difficult to keep. The only thing that can prevent man's utter damnation in hell is the belief in Christ.

3) The Jews were originally G-d's chosen people, but they were rejected when they refused to accept His son, Jesus. The name "Israel," G-d's chosen people, is no longer carried by the Jew, but by those who accept Jesus as the Messiah. Only these share G-d's love. Everyone else is damned in hell.

4) There is only one law now that Christ has come, and that is love. One must follow the example of Christ's sacrifice, and patiently hope that G-d will be gracious in return.

It is enough to state these articles of Christian faith to see why the Jews could not accept them. Taking them one by one, the Jewish viewpoint would be:

1) Jesus could not have been the Messiah. The Prophets predicted a world of peace and love after the Messiah's coming, and this certainly does not exist today. Furthermore, any talk of the Messiah as being the "son of G-d" is totally unacceptable. In no place do the Prophets say that he will be anything more than a remarkable leader and teacher.

2) Although the Torah does speak of Adam's sin, it teaches that man can rise above it. Man might not be able to perfect himself, but it was for this reason that G-d gave us the Torah. It is absurd to think that G-d would give a Torah that was impossible or too difficult to follow. In no place does Judaism teach that one can be saved from damnation by mere belief. Any true belief in G-d must lead a person to also follow His commandments.

3) It is impossible to imagine that G-d would ever reject the Jewish people. In many places, the Bible clearly states that His covenant with them will be forever.

4) In many places, the Bible says that the Torah was given forever. It is therefore impossible to say that it has been replaced by a new law or testament. Love alone is not enough, for one must know how to express it, and for this, we need the Torah as a guide. Love is only one of the Torah's commandments, and good deeds are its necessary expression.

Why do we believe these ideas rather than the ones expressed by Paul and Christianity?

For one thing, we see no evidence that Jesus was indeed the Messiah expected by Israel. The Messianic promise included such things as perfect peace and unity among men, love and truth, universal knowledge and undisturbed happiness, as well as the end of all evil, idolatry, falsehood and hatred. None of these things have been fulfilled by Christianity.

The Christian answer to this is the simple assertion that all things have indeed changed by the coming of Jesus. If the change is not visible, it is because man is evil and has not truly accepted Jesus and his teachings. Thus, the Messiah or Christ will have to return in order to prove his victory.

The Jew refuses to accept the excuse that the major prophecies concerning the Messiah will only be fulfilled in a "second coming." He expects the Messiah to complete his mission in his first attempt. The Jew therefore believes that the Messiah is yet to come.

But there is also another more important issue at stake than the mere identity of the Messiah. Christianity teaches that Jesus was also G-d in human form. The Jew sees this as a totally mistaken idea about G-d. It makes G-d too small, for in stating that He can assume human form, it diminishes both His unity and His divinity.

We disagree with Christianity not only with regard to belief, but also with regard to what man must do. Christianity tends to deny that man's actions are ultimately very useful. The only thing that can save man is his utter despair in his own sinfulness, and total dependence on G-d. The Jew, on the other hand, believes that man can come close to G-d by obeying Him and keeping His commandments.

Christianity thus starts with one idea about man, while Judaism starts with the exact opposite idea.

Judaism starts with the idea that man is created in the "likeness of G-d." He therefore does not have to go very far to discover the divine, both in himself and in others. There is always the opportunity to awaken the divine in oneself by obeying G-d's commandments. The Jew begins with this opportunity.

Christianity, on the other hand, begins with the basic assumption that man is depraved and sinful. Left to himself, man is utterly damned. He is naturally involved in evil, and must therefore do something to be saved from it.

The first question that the Christian asks is, "What have you done to be saved?" To the Jew, this question is almost meaningless. This is not the Jewish way of thinking at all. The Jew asks, "How can I serve G-d? How can I keep His commandments?" The central focus of Judaism is obeying the commandments of the Torah. We look at man and see his greatness, for he can obey these commandments and fulfill G-d's will.

Christianity teaches that man is so evil that he can never really serve G-d. The Torah is too difficult for man. The only thing that man can do is believe in Christ and wait for salvation.

The Jew replies that the very fact that G-d Himself gave us commandments and told us to obey them teaches us that we can indeed serve G-d and fulfill His will. It is unthinkable that G-d would give His people a Torah if it were impossible to keep it.

Although all of Jesus' disciples were Jews, they could not convince their fellow Jews of their teachings. The early dogmas of Christianity seemed closer to those of the pagan gentiles than to those of the Jews. More and more, Christianity was rejected by the Jews and accepted by the gentiles. It thus gradually developed into a gentile church, and its attitude toward the Jews became more and more unfriendly. It may have constantly appealed to the Jews to convert, sometimes even resorting to cruelty and force, but the Jew stood firm. Christianity may have changed human history,

but it could never win over the Jews. The Jew stood by his Torah and walked his own way.

In essence, there were two Christian teachings that the Jew could never accept. Christianity taught that G-d had assumed human form in Jesus, and that the Torah no longer mattered. The Jew rejected these two dogmas, even under pain of death.

In rejecting Christianity, Judaism therefore did not reject anything that it needed spiritually. There was nothing in all the teachings of Jesus that would have added even one iota to the strength of the Torah. If Christianity made any contribution at all, it was to the non-Jewish world.

The Jew knew that his Torah provided him with a unique relationship with G-d. Everything that he saw in Christianity seemed to contradict this relationship. It is for this reason that throughout the centuries, the Jew has found it impossible to accept the teachings of Christianity. He believed with perfect faith that G-d had shown him the way, and he had no intention of ever leaving it.

The Real Messiah?: A Jewish Response to Missionaries [NCSY and OU Press, New York, 2005], pp. 3–6
Reprinted with permission of OU Press

THE ART OF ASKING QUESTIONS

BY RABBI JONATHAN SACKS

Socrates (469-399 B.C.E.), the great Greek philosopher and mentor of Plato, was in the habit of asking disconcerting questions. To this day, persistent questioning in search of clarity is known as the Socratic method. For this habit, among other things, he was put on trial by the Athenians, accused of 'corrupting the young,' and sentenced to death. Nothing could be less like Judaism, in which teaching the young to ask questions is an essential feature of Pesach, so much so that the Haggadah—the narration—must be in response to a question asked by a child. If there is no child present, adults must ask one another, and if one is eating alone, one must ask oneself. In Judaism, to be without questions is not a sign of faith, but of lack of depth. 'As for the child who does not know how to ask, you must begin to teach him how.' Many of the customs of seder night (dipping the parsley and removing the seder plate are two examples) were introduced solely to provoke a child to ask 'Why?' Judaism is a religion of questions.

Abraham Twerski, the American psychiatrist, remembers how, when he was young, his teacher would welcome questions, the more demanding the better. When faced with a particularly tough challenge, he would say, in his broken English: 'You right! You hundred prozent right! Now I show you where you wrong.' The Nobel prize-winning Jewish physicist Isidore Rabi once explained that his mother taught him how to be a scientist. 'Every other child would come back from school and be asked, "What did you learn today?" But my mother used to ask, instead, "Izzy, did you ask a good question today?"' In the yeshiva, the home of traditional Talmudic learning, the highest compliment a teacher can give a student is *Du fregst a gutte kasha*, 'You raise a good objection.'

Rabbi Jonathan Sacks, PhD. (1948–) Former chief rabbi of the United Kingdom. Rabbi Sacks attended Cambridge University and received his doctorate from King's College, London. A prolific and influential author, his books include *Will We Have Jewish Grandchildren?* and *The Dignity of Difference*. He received the Jerusalem Prize in 1995 for his contributions to enhancing Jewish life in the Diaspora, was knighted and made a life peer in 2005, and became Baron Sacks of Aldridge in 2009.

Where did it come from, this Jewish passion for questions? Clearly it owes much to the fact that three times in the Torah, Moses speaks of children asking for an explanation of religious practice, and in another place it says, 'On that day you shall tell your son . . .' Together, these four verses serve as the basis for the 'four sons' of the Haggadah. Education is not indoctrination. It is teaching a child to be curious, to wonder, reflect, enquire. The child who asks becomes a partner in the learning process. He or she is no longer a passive recipient but an active participant. To ask is to grow.

But questioning goes deeper than this in Judaism—so deep as to represent a *sui generis* religious phenomenon. The heroes of faith asked questions of God, and the greater the prophet, the harder the question. Abraham asked, 'Shall the judge of all the earth not do justice?' Moses asked, 'O Lord, why have You brought trouble upon this people?' Jeremiah said, 'You are always righteous, O Lord, when I bring a case before You, yet I would speak with You about Your justice: Why does the way of the wicked prosper? Why do all the faithless live at ease?' The Book of Job, the most searching of all explorations of human suffering, is a book of questions asked by man, to which God replies with four chapters of questions of His own. The earliest sermons (known as the *Yelamdenu* type) began with a question asked of the rabbi by a member of the congregation. One of the classic genres of rabbinical literature is called *She'elot uteshuvot*, 'questions and replies.' Questioning is at the heart of Jewish spirituality.

Religious faith has often been seen as naïve, blind, accepting. That is not the Jewish way. Judaism is not the suspension of critical intelligence. It contains no equivalent to the famous declaration of the Christian thinker Tertullian, *Certum est quia impossibile est*, 'I believe it because it is impossible.' To the contrary: asking a question is itself a profound expression of faith in the intelligibility of the universe and the meaningfulness of human life. To ask is to believe that somewhere there is an answer. The fact that throughout history people have devoted their lives to extending the frontiers of knowledge is a compelling testimony to the restlessness of the human spirit and its constant desire to go further, higher, deeper. Far from faith excluding questions, questions testify to faith—that history is not random, that the universe is not impervious to our understanding, that what happens to us is not blind chance. We ask, not because we doubt, but because we believe.

There are three kinds of question, each corresponding to a different aspect of God, humanity and the intellectual quest. The first belongs to the sphere of *chokhmah*, 'wisdom,' and includes scientific, historical, and sociological inquiry. Rashi interprets the phrase on the creation of man 'in Our image, according to Our likeness' to mean 'with the power to understand and discern.' *Homo sapiens* is the only being known to us capable of framing the question, 'Why?' Maimonides includes scientific and philosophical understanding as part of the commands to love and fear God, because the more we understand of the universe, the more awe-inspiring it and its Architect reveal themselves to be. The sages coined a special blessing for seeing a sage distinguished for his or her worldly knowledge ('Blessed are You . . . who has given of His wisdom to flesh and blood'). The first request we make in the daily *Amidah* prayer is 'favour us with knowledge, understanding and insight.' Human dignity is intimately related to our ability to fathom the workings of the universe, natural and social. *Chokhmah* is an encounter with God through creation. Making man in His image, the creative God endowed mankind with creativity.

Second are the questions we ask about Torah, like the four that open the seder: 'Why is this night different? Why do we do this, not that? What is the reason for the law?' It is one of the most striking features of biblical Hebrew that though the Torah is full of commands—613 of them—there is no biblical word that means 'obey.' Instead the Torah uses the word *shema*, meaning, 'to hear, listen, reflect on, internalize and respond.' God wants not blind obedience, but understanding response. Moses tells the Israelites that the commands are 'their wisdom and understanding in the eyes of the nations,' implying that they are amenable to human reason. In one of the historic moments of adult education, Ezra, returning from Babylon, assembles the people in Jerusalem and reads publicly from the Torah with the assistance of Levites whose task was 'to make it clear and explain the meaning so that the people could understand what was being read.' The saintly Hillel, known for his gentleness to all, none the less said, 'An ignorant person cannot be pious.' The more we ask, search and understand the Torah, the better able we are to internalize its values and apply them to new situations. Torah is a meeting with God in *revelation*.

Undoubtedly, though, the most unique of Judaism's questions and the one most associated with the prophetic tradition is about justice: why bad things happen to good people, why evil seems so often to triumph, why there is so much undeserved suffering in the world. Karl Marx once called religion 'the opium of the people.' He believed that it reconciled them to their condition—their poverty, disease and death, their 'station in life,' their subjection to tyrannical rulers, the sheer bleakness of existence for most people most of the time. Faith anaesthetized. It made the otherwise unbearable, bearable. It taught people to accept things as they are because that is the will of God. Religion, he argued, was the most powerful means ever devised for keeping people in their place. It spread the aura of inevitability over arbitrary fate. So, argued Marx, if the world is to be changed, religion must be abandoned.

Nothing could be less true of Judaism—the faith born when God liberated a people from the chains of slavery. The question that echoes through the history of Judaism—from Abraham to Jeremiah to Job to rabbinic *midrash* to medieval lament to Hassidic prayer—is not acceptance of, but a protest against, injustice. There are some questions to which the response is an answer. But there are other questions to which the response is an act. To ask, 'Why do the righteous suffer?' is not to seek an explanation that will reconcile us to the slings and arrows of outrageous fortune. It is to turn to God with a request for action, and to discover, in the very process of making the request, that God is asking the same of us.

There are three scenes in Moses' early life. He sees an Egyptian attacking an Israelite, and he intervenes. He sees two Israelites fighting, and he intervenes. He sees non-Israelite shepherds mistreating the non-Israelite daughters of Jethro, and he intervenes. To be a Jew is to be prepared to act in the face of wrongdoing. When Rabbi Chaim of Brisk was asked, What is the role of a rabbi?, he replied, 'To redress the grievances of those who are abandoned and alone, to protect the dignity of the poor, and to save the oppressed from the hands of their oppressor.' Judaism is God's question-mark against the random cruelties of the world. It is His call to us to 'mend the world' until it becomes a place worthy of the Divine presence, to accept no illness that can be cured, no poverty that can be alleviated, no injustice that can be rectified. To ask the prophetic question is not to seek an answer but to be energized to action. That is what it is to meet God in *redemption*.

The three types of question are therefore inter-related. When we use our understanding of creation in conjunction with the commands of revelation, we help to bring redemption—an act at a time, a day at a time, knowing that it is not given to us to complete the task but neither may we stand aside from it.

There are three conditions, though, for asking a Jewish question. The first is that we seek genuinely to learn – not to doubt, ridicule, dismiss, reject. That is what the 'wicked son' of the Haggadah does: ask not out of a desire to understand but as a prelude to walking away.

Second is that we accept limits to our understanding. Not everything is intelligible at any given moment. There were scientists at the beginning of the twentieth century who believed that virtually every major discovery had already been made—not suspecting that the next hundred years would give rise to Einstein's relativity theory, Heisenberg's uncertainty principle, Gödel's theorem, proof of the 'Big Bang' origin of the universe, the discovery of DNA and the decoding of the human genome. In relation to Torah, there were many German and American Jews in the nineteenth century who could not understand Jewish prayers for a return to Zion, and deleted them from the prayer book. These facts should induce in us a certain humility. Not every scientific orthodoxy survives the test of time. Not everything in Judaism that we do not understand is unintelligible. The very features of Jewish life one generation finds difficult, the next generation may find the most meaningful of all. Faith is not opposed to questions, but it is opposed to the shallow certainty that what we understand is all there is.

Third is that when it comes to Torah, we learn by living and understand by doing. We learn to understand music by listening to music. We learn to appreciate literature by reading literature. There is no way of understanding Shabbat without keeping Shabbat, no way of appreciating how Jewish laws of family purity enhance a marriage without observing them. Judaism, like music, is something that can only be understood from the inside, by immersing yourself in it.

Given these caveats, Judaism is a faith that, more than any other, values the mind, encouraging questions and engaging us at the highest level of intellectual rigour. Every question asked in reverence is the start of a journey towards God, and it begins with the habit which, on Pesach, Jewish parents teach their children: to ask, thereby to join the never-ending dialogue between human understanding and heaven.

Rabbi Jonathan Sacks's Haggadah: Hebrew and English Text with New Essays and Commentary [Jerusalem: Maggid Books, 2015], pp. 106-108
Reprinted with permission of the publisher.

WHO AM I? WHO ARE WE?

BY RABBI JONATHAN SACKS

Years after I left Cambridge I found myself watching a television documentary about the great Egyptian temples. They had been built some three thousand three hundred years ago by the pharaoh assumed by most scholars to be the ruler at the time of the Exodus: Rameses II. Lovingly, the camera took us on a tour of those magnificent buildings at Luxor, Karnack and Abu Simbel. The commentator spoke about their magnificence, their scale, their beauty, their sheer endurance across the millennia. They still stand in little less than their former glory, defying time.

For twenty minutes or so I was carried along by his enthusiasm. Then I found myself asking what survives today of the Egypt of the pharaohs-the greatest, most powerful and by far the most long-lived of the empires of the ancient world? The buildings, the temples and the monuments remain, but not the people, the faith, or the civilization. Already in the reign of Rameses II, the Egypt of the pharaohs had reached its peak. After his death it would begin its decline. By the time of the Alexandrian empire ancient Egyptian culture had run its course. It had lasted many centuries but like most other civilizations it had proved all too mortal. The stones remained; the world they celebrated was no more.

It occurred to me that among the builders of those temples must have been some of my ancestors. They were slaves in Egypt at the time. The Bible tells us that they were employed to build the cities of Pithom (Per-Atum) and Rameses, two of Rameses II's greatest projects. The contrast between the people and the king could not have been greater. The slaves were known as Hebrews, perhaps from the ancient word *Habiru*. They were, as the name implies, nomads, immigrants. They were *Ivrim,* meaning those who journey from place to place. In Egypt they had become slaves. They had no power, no wealth, no rights, no freedom. They were, of all people, the lowest of the low.

Egypt, at the time, was an indomitable power. Not only was it a country of immense technical prowess, but it ruled the entire region of the Middle East. Rameses was not so much served as a king; he was worshipped as a god. Colossal statues of him were to be found throughout the country. The prefix *Ra* tells us that he was seen as the sun god. This explains an otherwise puzzling feature of the biblical story of the Exodus. The ten plagues that struck Egypt mounted in a rising scale of devastation, a sequence broken by the ninth, darkness, which seems less like an affliction than an inconvenience. The ninth plague, we now understand, was a judgement, not against the people but its most significant deity, the Pharaoh who saw himself as the god of the sun.

Suppose that we could travel back in time and tell the inhabitants of those days that it would not be the Egypt of the pharaohs, its empire and dynasty that would survive. It would instead be that nation of slaves, known to others as Hebrews, to themselves as the children of Israel, and to later history as the Jews. Nothing would have struck them as more absurd. Indeed, the earliest known reference to the Israelites outside the Bible is an inscription on the Merneptah stele, a giant slab of black granite dating from the thirteenth century B.C.E. It reads, "Israel is laid waste. His seed is no more." Not only would the Egyptians not have believed that the people of Israel would survive, they believed that they were already on the verge of extinction. Ancient Egypt and ancient Israel, therefore, seem to stand at opposite extremes of the great gamble we take with time. What endures and what wanes? What survives and what is eclipsed? It is a question we can never answer in advance, only in retrospect. But retrospect is what we have.

Egypt and Israel three millennia ago were nations that asked themselves the most fundamental human question of all: How do we defeat death and conquer mortality? How, in the brief span of a human life, do we participate in something that will endure long after we are no longer here? The Egyptians gave one answer—an answer that through the ages has tempted emperors and tyrants, rulers and kings. We defeat mortality by building monuments that will stand for thousands of years. Their stones will outlive the winds and sands of time. The Jews gave an entirely different answer.

The Israelites, slaves in Egypt for more than two hundred years, were about to go free. Ten plagues had struck the country. Whatever their cause, they seemed to convey a message: The God of Israel is on the side of freedom and human dignity. On the brink of their release, Moses, the leader of the Jews, gathered them together and prepared to address them. He might have spoken about freedom. He could have given a stirring address about the promised land to which they were travelling, the "land flowing with milk and honey." Or he might have prepared them for the journey that Jay ahead, the long march across the wilderness.

Instead, Moses delivered a series of addresses that seemed to make no sense in the context of that particular moment. He presented a new idea, revolutionary in character whose implications remain challenging even now. He spoke about children, and the distant future, and the duty to pass on memory to generations yet unborn. Three times he turned to the theme:

> And when your children ask you, 'What do you mean by this rite?' you shall say . . .

> And you shall explain to your child on that day, 'It is because of what the Lord did for me when I went free from Egypt.'

> And when, in time to come, your child asks you, saying, 'What does this mean?' you shall say to him . . .

About to gain their freedom, the Israelites were told that they had to become a nation of educators.

Freedom, Moses suggested, is won, not on the battlefield, nor in the political arena, but in the human imagination and will. To defend a land, you need an army. But to defend freedom, you need education. You need families and schools to ensure that your ideals are passed on to the next generation and never lost, or despaired of, or obscured. The citadels of liberty are houses of study. Its heroes are teachers, its passion is education and the life of the mind. Moses realized that a people achieves immortality not by building temples or mausoleums, but by engraving their values on the hearts of their children, and they on theirs, and so on until the end of time.

The Israelites built living monuments-monuments to life-and became a people dedicated to bringing new generations into being and handing on to them the heritage of the past. Their great institutions were the family and education via the conversation between the generations. In place of temples they built houses of prayer and study. In place of stones they had words and teachings. They saw God not as the power that enslaves but as the power that sets free. Instead of worshipping mighty rulers they affirmed the dignity of the widow, the orphan, the stranger, the vulnerable, the weak and the neglected. In that counterintuitive reversal they discovered the secret of eternity. Whether through accident or design or something greater than either, the Hebrew slaves who built Rameses' temples had lived through one of the great revelations of history. These were our ancestors, and we are their heirs.

* * *

Was I right or wrong to see in this story something out of the ordinary? Only later did I discover that three other people, none of them Jews, had shared my own sense of amazement and had been persuaded by it that somewhere in the tale of Jewish survival was a mystery of great significance. Each of them, for different reasons, had been led to reflect on the nature of history. Each had been startled into a discovery that there was one people whose history broke all the rules. The first was Blaise Pascal, a mathematician and physicist in the seventeenth century who invented the first digital calculator and the syringe, and discovered Pascal's law of pressure and the principle of the hydraulic press. More significantly, he was the founder of the modern theory of probability. At the age of thirty he abruptly ended his scientific work and devoted the rest of his life to thinking about religious faith. His theological reflections led him to formulate what has come to be known as "Pascal's wager," the idea that under conditions of uncertainty we have more to lose by disbelieving than by believing in God. However, Pascal also applied the idea of probability to history and came to a striking conclusion: that among all the myriad peoples that have lived on earth, only one defies probability:

> It is certain that in certain parts of the world we can see a peculiar people, separated from the other peoples of the world, and this is called the Jewish people. . . . This people is not only of remarkable antiquity but has also lasted for a singularly long time. . . . For whereas the peoples of Greece and Italy, of Sparta, Athens and Rome, and others who came so much later have perished so long ago, these still exist, despite the efforts of so many powerful kings who have tried a hundred times to wipe them out, as their historians testify, and as can easily be judged by the natural order of things over such a long spell of years. They have always been preserved, however, and their preservation was foretold. . . . My encounter with this people amazes me. . . .

In *War and Peace* Leo Tolstoy also wrestled with the question of the meaning of history. Is the course of events determined by the decisions of great leaders and military commanders? Or is there some deeper underlying thread of meaning, a destiny whose outline can be discerned beneath the surface of apparently random happenings? Critics have often been irritated by Tolstoy's philosophizing, which cuts across the vivid drama of the novel, the fate of five aristocratic families set against the panoramic background of Napoleon's invasion of Russia. Yet Tolstoy was driven by a conviction that there is a moral and spiritual dimension to history, and this idea left him no peace. At the height of his career, having completed *Anna Karenina,* he abandoned his life as an aristocrat and started living the life of a peasant, devoted to faith, love and the virtues of simplicity. One of the things that, for him, proved the existence of a mysterious and providential pattern in history was the story of the Jews:

> He whom neither slaughter nor torture of thousands of years could destroy, he whom neither fire nor sword nor inquisition was able to wipe off the face of the earth, he who was the first to produce the oracles of God, he who has been for so long the guardian of prophecy, and who has transmitted it to the rest of the world-such a nation cannot be destroyed. The Jew is as everlasting as eternity itself.

The third figure, Nicolay·Berdyayev, was one of the great thinkers of the Russian Revolution. The destiny of civilizations, he believed, was ruled by material forces, economies, wars, the physical indices of power. Something happened, though, to make him change his mind. In his study of history he came across one people whose fate could not be accounted for in these terms-the Jewish people. Their existence and survival was a refutation of Marxist theory. This discovery changed Berdyayev's life. He became religious. He no longer believed in materialism but instead in the "light which breaks through from the transcendent world of the spirit." Eventually, he was expelled from Russia and spent the rest of his life in Berlin and Paris, teaching religion. In *The Meaning of History,* he tells how he made his discovery:

> I remember how the materialist interpretation of history, when I attempted in my youth to verify it by applying it to the destinies of peoples, broke down in the case of the Jews, where destiny seemed absolutely inexplicable from the materialistic standpoint. . . Its survival is a mysterious and wonderful phenomenon demonstrating that the life of this people is governed by a special predetermination, transcending the processes of adaptation expounded by the materialistic interpretation of history. The survival of the Jews, their resistance to destruction, their endurance under absolutely peculiar conditions and the fateful role played by them in history: all these point to the particular and mysterious foundations of their destiny.

Here were three people whose lives were changed by their encounter with the Jewish story. Judaism confirmed their own religious faith and suggested to them the important idea that God might be found not only in nature but in history. And if we search for revelation in history, we will find it, more compellingly than anywhere else, in the history of that unusual people, our ancestors. For almost two thousand years Jews remained a distinctive nation without any of the usual prerequisites of nationhood. They had no land, no sovereignty, no power, no overarching political structures, not even a shared culture. They were scattered over the face of the earth, and almost everywhere they were a minority. For the most part, they refused active efforts to convert them and resisted the passive pull of assimilation. No other people kept its identity intact for so long in such circumstances.

Rabbi Jonathan Sacks, *Radical Then, Radical Now: On Being Jewish* [London: Continuum Books, 2003], pp. 29-36

WHY DON'T MIRACLES HAPPEN ANYMORE?

BY RABBI ZALMAN POSNER

Miracles—the word itself is hazy. Just what is a miracle? A world-shocking event such as the parting of the Red Sea at the time of the Exodus? Or the constant human act of breathing? Neither of these two phenomena can truly be explained, but one of them is a familiar, ongoing occurrence while the other is an exotic, one-time happening. Let's talk about these two types of miracles and see whether miracles have really ceased.

The greatest miracle of all is described in the opening words of the Book of Genesis: "In the beginning, Gd created . . ." Suddenly "nothing" was transformed into "something." We are all familiar with the transformation of matter into energy or of energy into matter, but each of these changes involved a previously existing "something." Where "nothing" exists, there can be no change. Creating ex nihilo—literally "out of nothing""—is beyond man's capabilities. This is a hurdle of acceptance that must be confronted at the outset. G-d, and G-d alone can create. The miracle of creation is the miracle of the first order, beyond duplication by man.

The more familiar miracles described elsewhere in the Torah—the parting of the Red Sea, the manna in the wilderness, the Menorah that burned in the Sanctuary for eight days (the miracle of Chanukah), and so forth—these are all miracles of the second order. They did not entail creation ex nihilo, but merely change. Water, which is liquid, suddenly behaved like a solid; this, in brief is what happened when the Red Sea was parted to enable Israel to pass through it on dry land. A quantity of oil which normally can burn for only one day burned for eight full days because its rate of combustion had been slowed to one-eighth the ordinary rate. This, in brief, is the story of Chanukah. As the Talmud puts it, "He Who ordered oil to burn, and it burns, will order vinegar to burn and it, too, will burn."

But there is yet a third order of miracles—the miracles that are with us every day of our lives. The Sages teach us to "praise Him for every breath we draw." We are to give thanks to G-d for our every heartbeat, for the smooth performance of all our vital functions, and indeed for all the day-by-day workings of nature. "But," I hear someone protest, "that's only nature!" Correct. But the ordinary, the "natural," the everyday and commonplace happenings in nature and in our bodies are no less the work of G-d's hand than the parting of the Red Sea and, for that matter, the act of Creation itself. Thus we see that miracles are in-

Rabbi Zalman I. Posner. (1926–2014) Chabad *shliach*. Rabbi Posner and his wife were sent in 1949 to serve as emissaries of the 6th Lubavitcher Rebbe, Rabbi Yosef Yitschak Schneersohn, to Nashville, Tennessee. There, Rabbi Posner served as the spiritual leader of Congregation Sherith Israel for many years. A well-known Chasidic authority, he edited and translated many works, including sections of the *Tanya* and the *Nusach Ha'Ari Sidur*. He is the author of *Think Jewish* and *Reflections on the Sedra*, a collection of sermons.

deed still taking place and, in fact, are happening all the time.

This, by the way, is the explanation of the miracle of Purim, the deliverance of the Jewish people from Haman's wicked scheming: a succession of events which are not in themselves "supernatural," a series of what appears to be mere "coincidences," but [rather] which come about at a time when they can do, and do, the most good.

The Lubavitcher Rebbe once compared the Torah perspective and the non-Torah (we might call it "scientific") perspective succinctly: the Torah view seeks the supernatural in the natural; science seeks the natural in the supernatural.

The function of the scientist is to find reasons for all the phenomena of nature, and then to apply his findings to all the natural events he subsequently encounters. He sets out from the premise that there is a reason for everything; he has faith in cause and effect. If an apparently healthy man suddenly falls sick and dies, the scientist cannot simply attribute it to the inscrutable will of Gd. His job is to find the cause of that illness, perhaps to cure others stricken with a similar disease, or perhaps to prevent the disease from striking others. Let it be emphasized that all this, in itself, is perfectly consonant with Torah doctrine.

What are the physical causes of thunder and lightning, of rainbows, floods, earthquakes, eclipses, and famines—indeed, of anything in the universe? An occurrence that seems to defy explanation simply presents that much more of a challenge. "At the present stage in our knowledge we cannot adequately explain this phenomenon," the scientist will note. But the fact remains that, as a scientist, he must find a "natural" explanation for whatever happens in the world in which we live.

Torah imparts a different perspective. From the vantage point of Torah, everything is "supernatural"—including nature. Nature itself is a miracle, created by the hand of G-d; without His charge, "Let there be . . . ," it would have remained nothingness. Do your lungs

work properly? If so, give thanks to G-d for that. The natural functions of your body have concealed within them the hand of G-d; without Him they would not continue. That tree and that sunset are not just a beautiful tree and a glorious sunset; they are the manifestation of G-d Himself through His creations.

These two perspectives, science and Torah are, of course, not mutually exclusive. The physician who is a Torah Jew will use all his professional skill to treat his patient, and remain sufficiently humble to recite some Tehillim (Psalms) as well. Or, we might express the same thought in reverse; the Torah Jew who is a physician will offer prayers for his patient, but at the same time employ all his medical skills to treat him. Two different perspectives may both be valid. A physicist might see a sunset as a refraction of light rays, while a painter might view the same scene as a cascade of colors. Rabbi Chaim Brisker (a nineteenth-century great Torah luminary), observed a sunset on Yom Kippur and described it as the atoning power of the Day of Forgiveness slowly sinking below the horizon—an unusual perspective but a perfectly valid one.

Miracles, certainly the miracles of nature, are with us, all the time. But, repeating the original question, why don't "supernatural" miracles, the miracles of the second order, happen anymore today?

Let us try to answer that question without entering into the various views on the purpose of the Biblical miracles. Take as our case in point the parting of the Red Sea. We are told (Exodus 14:31) that Israel "beheld the hand of G-d" at the Red Sea. The Children of Israel recognized the miracle for what it was. Those generations of the Biblical era, to which it was given to witness miracles, had the capability of accepting them as such, and of being impressed.

Then, these ancients implemented their recognition of the "hand of G-d" by living in accordance with the "word of G-d," because they had experienced Him directly and personally. The generations of antiquity lived in a pre-scientific age. G-d wanted to show them that there was a Power greater than wealth and the chariots of Pharaoh, greater than the waves of the sea, and they were prepared to learn the lesson which the miracle had been intended to teach.

But people have changed since then.

If we were to gather at the banks of the Mississippi River today and I were to promise that at dawn the next morning, I would strike the river with a staff and the waters would part and then, the next morning, I would indeed strike that river a mighty blow and the waters would really part, what would you say?

That G-d sent me? That it was a miracle? Or would you suggest that it was a trick which I performed with the aid of a ton of Jell-O under the levee or some other sleight of hand? Or, if we were to meet tomorrow at that mountain in the Sinai desert and to hear a voice thundering forth from a cloud, would we declare that this must be the voice of G-d, or would we suspect the presence of a hidden loudspeaker or some other gadget?

The question we should ask is not whether miracles do or do not happen today, and why, but what effect miracles have upon us. Miracles show man that G-d is master over nature, over all the world. Miracles are a form of communication, but communication needs two partners. To be sure, G-d can perform miracles, but how would we react to them? Perhaps, when we are ready for miracles, when we are able to recognize a miracle when we see one, it will be given us to witness miracles.

But then, is it really true that the kind of miracles that are described in the Bible never occur today? I am not a military strategist, but how about the Six-Day War of 1967, Israel's crossing of the Suez Canal during the Yom Kippur war and the Entebbe rescue? And, more recently, the Gulf War scuds, the fall of Communism, and the massive Jewish emigration form the former Soviet Union? I have read many explanations of these events, but frankly, I find it easier to perceive them as miracles which reveal the hand of G-d in the history of man rather than to accept the "rational" explanations.

Excerpted from *Think Jewish: A Contemporary View of Judaism, A Jewish View of Today's World* [Kesher Press: Nashville, TN, 1978] Reprinted with permission of the publisher.

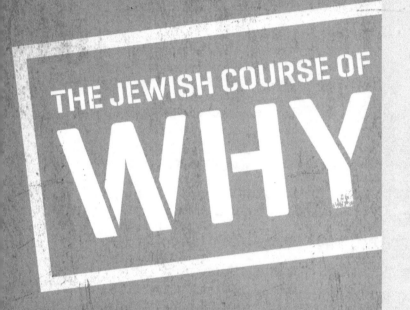

THE JEWISH COURSE OF
WHY

LESSON TWO

1. Why is the Star of David a Jewish symbol?

2. Why does a *mikveh* "purify"?

3. Why do people require such "purification"?

4. Why are there so many dos and don'ts in Judaism?

5. Why do many Jews sway when they pray?

6. Why do traditional synagogues have separate seating for men and women?

7. Why is Israel important to the Jews?

8. Why does the Bible call for animal sacrifices?

JLI

JEWISH LEARNING INSTITUTE

1. Why is the Star of David a Jewish symbol?

Trust in God's Omnipresence

Text 1

Rabbi Moshe Feinstein, *Responsa Igrot Moshe, Orach Chayim* 3:15 📖

הִנֵּה כְּפִי שֶׁיָּדוּעַ, זֶה מֵאוֹת בְּשָׁנִים שֶׁעָשׂוּ צִיּוּר מָגֵן דָּוִד עַל פָּרֹכוֹת וְעַל מְעִילִים וּמִטְפָּחוֹת, וְלֹא הָיָה מִי שֶׁיְּעַרְעֵר עַל זֶה. וְאַף שֶׁאֵין לָנוּ מָקוֹר צוּרַת הַמָּגֵן דָּוִד, אֵין בָּזֶה שׁוּם קְפֵּידָא.

וְגַם יֵשׁ בָּזֶה עִנְיָן לְהַזְכִּיר שֶׁהַשֵּׁם יִתְבָּרֵךְ מֶלֶךְ לְמַעֲלָה וּלְמַטָּה וּלְכָל ד' רוּחוֹת הַשָּׁמַיִם. וְשַׁיָּכוּת שֵׁם דָּוִד לֹא יָדוּעַ. וְאוּלַי הוּא סִימָן לְדָוִד שֶׁבָּטַח בְּמִלְחֲמוֹתָיו עַל הַשֵּׁם יִתְבָּרֵךְ, שֶׁהוּא מֶלֶךְ לְמַעֲלָה, וּלְמַטָּה, וּבְכָל רוּחוֹת הַשָּׁמַיִם, שֶׁלָּכֵן לֹא הָיָה יָרֵא מִמַּלְכֵי בָּשָׂר וָדָם וּמֵחַיָּילוֹתֵיהֶם כְּצִיּוּי הַתּוֹרָה.

Rabbi Moshe Feinstein
1895–1986

Leading halachic authority of the 20th century. Rabbi Feinstein was appointed rabbi of Luban, Belarus, in 1921. He immigrated to the U.S. in 1937 and became the dean of Mesivta Tiferet Yerushalayim in New York. Rabbi Feinstein's halachic decisions have been published in a multivolume collection entitled *Igrot Moshe*.

It is well known that the Star of David has been used on ark curtains and Torah covers for centuries without any controversy. Although we do not know the origins of the Star of David, this alone does not constitute an objection to its use.

In fact, [one can find important symbolism in the Star of David] in that it serves to remind us that God reigns over what is above and below and over the four directions. Perhaps the connection with David is that when he went to war, he placed his trust in God's all-encompassing reign, and therefore, in accordance with the Torah's instruction to not be afraid while in battle, he was not intimidated by human armies and kings.

Two United Sets of Three (Optional)

Text 2

Rabbi Shlomo Zalman Ehrenreich, *Avnei Hamakom, Even Habe'er* 3 📖

יֵשׁ לוֹמַר עַל פִּי מַה שֶּׁדָּרַשׁ הַאי גְּלִילָאָה (בְּשַׁבָּת פח,א) "בְּרִיךְ רַחֲמָנָא דְיָהִיב לָן אוֹרְיָין תְּלִיתָאִי לְעַם תְּלִיתָאִי" - הִיא הַתּוֹרָה הַקְּדוֹשָׁה שֶׁהִיא מִג' חֲלָקִים, תּוֹרָה נְבִיאִים וּכְתוּבִים. [אִי נַמִי כְּמוֹ שֶׁכָּתַב הָעִיּוּן יַעֲקֹב, תּוֹרָה שֶׁבִּכְתָב, וְתוֹרָה שֶׁבְּעַל פֶּה, וְסִתְרֵי תוֹרָה.] וְעַם יִשְׂרָאֵל הוּא מִג' חֲלָקִים, כֹּהֲנִים לְוִיִּם וְיִשְׂרָאֵלִים.

וְהִנֵּה הֵם ב' מְשׁוּלָשִׁים, כָּזֶה, וְהַמָּגֵן דָּוִד הוּא ב' מְשׁוּלָשִׁים, אֶחָד מְשׁוּלָב בְּתוֹךְ חֲבֵירוֹ . . .

וְהִנֵּה הָיוּ מְלָכִים בְּיִשְׂרָאֵל שֶׁלָּחֲמוּ בִּמְסִירוּת נֶפֶשׁ עֲבוּר יִשְׂרָאֵל, אֲבָל רַק בִּשְׁבִיל עַם יִשְׂרָאֵל, וְלֹא בִּשְׁבִיל הַתּוֹרָה הַקְּדוֹשָׁה, וְלֹא אִיכְפַּת לְהוּ הַתּוֹרָה הַקְּדוֹשָׁה מִידִי, אַדְרַבָּה לֹא שָׁמְרוּ הַתּוֹרָה כְּלָל, וְהָיוּ רְשָׁעִים גְּמוּרִים. אֲבָל בֶּאֱמֶת, עַם יִשְׂרָאֵל בְּלֹא הַתּוֹרָה הֵם כְּגוּף בְּלֹא נְשָׁמָה. וּבְלֹא תוֹרָה אֵין יִשְׂרָאֵל נֶחְשָׁב לִמְאוּמָה, וּכְלֹא הֵם. וְהַתּוֹרָה הַקְּדוֹשָׁה וְיִשְׂרָאֵל צְרִיכִין שֶׁיִּהְיוּ מְחוּבָּרִים יַחַד בְּקֶשֶׁר אַמִּיץ וְחָזָק, שֶׁלֹּא יִפָּרְדוּ זֶה מִזֶּה לְעוֹלָם. וּבָזֶה יְכַוֵּן הֲרָמַת קֶרֶן יִשְׂרָאֵל אִם הֵם מְשׁוּלָבִים וּמְחוּבָּרִים עִם הַתּוֹרָה הַקְּדוֹשָׁה.

אָמְנָם דָּוִד הַמֶּלֶךְ עָלָיו הַשָּׁלוֹם, הַמֶּלֶךְ הַחָסִיד, הוּא לָחַם מִלְחֲמוֹת ה' בְּעַד הַתּוֹרָה הַקְּדוֹשָׁה וַעֲבוּר יִשְׂרָאֵל, שְׁנֵיהֶם מְקוּשָּׁרִים וּמְשׁוּלָבִים יַחַד. עַל כֵּן נִקְרָא מָגֵן דָּוִד, שֶׁאֵלּוּ הַב' הַמְּשׁוּלָשִׁים יַחְדָּיו יֻדְבָּקוּ. וְעַל זֶה מוֹרֶה צוּרַת הַמָּגֵן דָּוִד.

The Talmud recounts (Shabbat 88a) how a certain Galilean lectured, "Blessed is God Who gave the three-dimensioned Torah to a three-dimensioned people."

"Three-dimensioned Torah" refers to the Bible, which consists of the Pentateuch, Prophets, and Writings (or, that the Torah comprises the Written Torah, Oral Torah, and Kabbalah).

"Three-dimensioned people" refers to the fact that the Jews consist of Priests, Levites, and Israelites.

The Star of David, which consists of two interlaced triangles, each with three points, alludes to these tripartite entities. . . .

There were kings of Israel who fought valiantly on behalf of the Jewish people—but only for the people and not the Torah. In fact, many of them were wayward and neglected the Torah. But the Jews without the Torah are like a body without a soul; without the Torah, we cannot be a people. The bond between the Jewish people and the Torah ought never to be severed. This bond will establish a vigorous Jewish continuity.

Indeed, David, the pious and righteous king, fought his wars to protect both the Jewish people and the Torah. He thus linked the Torah of three with the people of three. This is the message conveyed by the Star of David.

Recipient of Six (Optional)

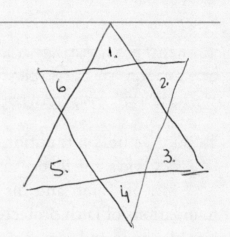
Text 3

Rabbi Avraham Chaim Hakohen Katz, *Erets Hachayim*, Psalms 18:3

הָיָה חִילוּק בֵּין מָגִינֵי מַלְכֵי יִשְׂרָאֵל לְמַלְכֵי בֵּית דָוִד. כִּי לְמַלְכֵי יִשְׂרָאֵל הָיָה מָגֵן
שֶׁל שָׁלֹשׁ קְצָווֹת כָּזֶה, וּמַלְכוּת בֵּית דָוִד הָיָה שֶׁל שִׁשָּׁה קְצָווֹת, לְהוֹרוֹת שֶׁיֵּשׁ
לוֹ אֲחִיזָה בְּמִדַּת מַלְכוּת, וּמְקַבֵּל שֶׁפַע מִן שִׁשָּׁה קְצָווֹת, וְדָוִד הוּא הַשְּׁבִיעִי.

The kings of Israel and the kings [of Judah] who descended from David carried differently shaped shields. The kings of Israel had triangular shields. The kings of Judah carried six-pointed shields to show that they were rooted in the seventh divine attribute of *malchut* (sovereignty) and were nourished by the six preceding attributes.

Rabbi Avraham Chaim Hakohen Katz
18th century

Kabbalist and author. Rabbi Katz was the grandson of the famed *Sema,* author of a noted commentary on *Shulchan Aruch.* He served as the Rabbi of Nikolsburg (currently part of the Czech Republic) until he moved to Israel with his son in 1748. He authored *Eretz Hachaim,* a Kabbalistic commentary to Psalms.

A Shield with a Different Symbol (Optional)

Text 4

Rabbi Moshe Isserles, *Torat Ha'olah* 1:20 📖

Rabbi Moshe Isserles
(Rema)
1525–1572

Halachist. Rema served as rabbi in Krakow, Poland, and is considered the definitive authority on Jewish law among Ashkenazic Jewry. Rema authored glosses on the *Shulchan Aruch* (known as the *Mapah*) and *Darchei Moshe*, a commentary on the halachic compendium *Arba'ah Turim*.

וְלָכֵן מְקוּבָּל גַּם כֵּן שֶׁהַמְּנוֹרָה הָיְתָה מְצוּיֶּרֶת בְּמָגֵן דָּוִד, לִהְיוֹת כִּי זְכוּת הַתּוֹרָה וְהָאֱמוּנוֹת הָאֲמִיתִּיּוֹת עִם עִקְרֵי הַדָּת הָיוּ עוֹמְדִים לְדָוִד בְּמִלְחֲמוֹתָיו. וְלָכֵן הָיְתָה הַמְּנוֹרָה לְמָגֵן וּלְמַחֲסֶה אֵלָיו.

We hold a tradition that a menorah adorned David's shield because the merit of David's study of Torah and his adherence to our beliefs and foundations of faith protected him in battle. The menorah was his shield and armor.

KEY POINTS

- The six-pointed Star of David, representing the six directions, reminds us of God's all-encompassing sovereignty and enables us to trust Him in the face of life's challenges.

- The Star of David, which consists of two interlaced triangles, alludes to two tripartite entities: the Torah and the Jewish people. This indicates that the Jewish people and the Torah are inextricably linked.

- The six points on King David's shield represented the six divine attributes that precede *malchut* (sovereignty). As the embodiment of *malchut*, David received these six channels of divine energy and conveyed them to the world.

---

2. Why does a *mikveh* purify?

Divine Decree

Text 5

Maimonides, *Mishneh Torah*, Laws of *Mikva'ot* 11:12 📖

הַטְּבִילָה מִן הַטּוּמְאוֹת מִכְּלַל הַחֻקִּים הוּא. שֶׁאֵין הַטּוּמְאָה
טִיט אוֹ צוֹאָה שֶׁתַּעֲבוֹר בַּמַּיִם. אֶלָּא גְּזֵרַת הַכָּתוּב הִיא.

I mmersing in a *mikveh* to emerge from a state of impurity is an ordinance whose rationale exceeds human
understanding. It has nothing to do with filth that can
be washed away by water. It is a divine decree.

Rabbi Moshe ben Maimon
(Maimonides, Rambam)
1135–1204

Halachist, philosopher, author, and
physician. Maimonides was born in
Cordoba, Spain. After the conquest
of Cordoba by the Almohads, he
fled Spain and eventually settled
in Cairo, Egypt. There, he became
the leader of the Jewish community
and served as court physician to the
vizier of Egypt. He is most noted
for authoring the *Mishneh Torah*, an
encyclopedic arrangement of Jewish
law, and for his philosophical work,
Guide for the Perplexed. His rulings
on Jewish law are integral to the
formation of halachic consensus.

In the Beginning . . .

Text 6a

Rabbi Eliyahu de Vidas, *Reishit Chochmah*, *Sha'ar Ha'ahavah* 11 📖

הָאָדָם בְּהִכָּנְסוֹ אֶל הַמִּקְוֶה הוּא כְּדֵי לְהִכָּלֵל וְלַחֲזוֹר הַנְּשָׁמָה הַפְּגוּמָה וְהָאֵיבָרִים
הַפְּגוּמִים מִמָּקוֹם שֶׁיָּצְאוּ, וְשָׁם מִתְעַלְּמִים כְּעוּבָּר הַמִּתְעַלֵּם בְּבֶטֶן אִמּוֹ . . . וּבִיצִיאַת
הָאָדָם מֵהַמִּקְוֶה הֲרֵי נִתְקְנוּ אֵיבָרָיו וְנִשְׁמָתוֹ, וַהֲרֵי הוּא חָדָשׁ, וְאֵין לַחִיצוֹנִים
חֵלֶק בּוֹ, וְיַרְגִּישׁ הָאָדָם בְּעַצְמוֹ רוּחַ חֲדָשָׁה מִנִּיצוֹץ הַנְּשָׁמָה שֶׁחָזְרָה אֵלָיו.

וְרָאוּי הוּא שֶׁקּוֹדֶם שֶׁיִּכָּנֵס בַּמִּקְוֶה שֶׁיְּהַרְהֵר תְּשׁוּבָה מֵעֲוֹנוֹתָיו.

Rabbi Eliyahu de Vidas
1518–1592

Born in Safed; he is considered one of the prominent kabbalists of the 16th century. A student of Rabbi Moshe Cordovero and Rabbi Yitschak Luria, he is best known as the author of *Reishit Chochmah*, a compendium of moral teachings culled from various sources in the Talmud, Midrash, and Zohar. He is buried in Hebron.

We enter the *mikveh* to return our spiritually blemished bodies and souls to their origins. In the *mikveh*, we are enveloped like a fetus in the womb of its mother. . . . When we emerge from the *mikveh*, our bodies and souls are restored. We become like new, and negative forces have no part in us. We should sense a new spirit from the spark of the soul that has been returned to us.

Before entering the *mikveh*, it is appropriate to repent for our wrongdoings.

Text 6b

Sefer Hachinuch, Mitzvah 173 📖

שֶׁיִּרְאֶה הָאָדָם אֶת עַצְמוֹ אַחַר הַטְּבִילָה כְּאִילּוּ נִבְרָא בְּאוֹתָהּ שָׁעָה,
כְּמוֹ שֶׁהָיָה הָעוֹלָם כּוּלּוֹ מַיִם טֶרֶם הֱיוֹת בּוֹ אָדָם, וּכְמוֹ שֶׁכָּתוּב
(בְּרֵאשִׁית א,ב) "וְרוּחַ אֱלֹקִים מְרַחֶפֶת עַל פְּנֵי הַמָּיִם".

וְיִתֵּן אֶל לִבּוֹ בְּדִמְיוֹן כִּי כְּמוֹ שֶׁנִּתְחַדֵּשׁ בְּגוּפוֹ יְחַדֵּשׁ גַּם כֵּן פְּעוּלּוֹתָיו לְטוֹב.

Sefer Hachinuch

A work on the biblical commandments. Four aspects of every mitzvah are discussed in this work: the definition of the mitzvah; ethical lessons that can be deduced from the mitzvah; basic laws pertaining to the observance of the mitzvah; and who is obligated to perform the mitzvah and when. The work was composed in the 13th century by an anonymous author who refers to himself as "the Levite of Barcelona." It has been widely thought that this referred to Rabbi Aharon Halevi of Barcelona (Re'ah); however, this view has been contested.

We should regard ourselves after immersion as if we were created anew at that moment. For with immersion, we return to the primordial state, when existence was enveloped by water, as it says (Genesis 1:2), "And the spirit of God was hovering over the face of the water."

We ought to contemplate that just as our bodies have undergone renewal, so too, our behavior should be renewed for the better.

— During the women Menses there's void in her.

The concept is to be envelopes in pure water like a

Fetus in water. Everything is Submerged in holiness.

Sea-Like Consciousness (Optional)

Text 7a

Rabbi Shne'ur Zalman of Liadi, *Siddur im Dach*, p. 318

בִּתְחִלַּת הַבְּרִיאָה הָיוּ הַמַּיִם מְסַבְּבִים כָּל הָאָרֶץ, וְהָאָרֶץ הָיְתָה מוּבְלַעַת בְּתוֹךְ הַיָּם, עַד שֶׁאָמַר "יִקָּווּ הַמַּיִם כו' וְתֵרָאֶה הַיַּבָּשָׁה כו'" (בְּרֵאשִׁית א,ט).

וְכָךְ לְמַעֲלָה, עַלְמָא דְאִתְגַּלְיָא הָיָה מוּבְלָע וְכָלוּל תְּחִלָּה בְּעַלְמָא דְאִתְכַּסְיָא שֶׁנִּקְרָאת בְּחִינַת יָם.

In the beginning, water encompassed all of existence. What is now dry land was subsumed in the sea, until God spoke, "Let the waters gather, etc., and let the dry land appear" (Genesis 1:9).

Similarly, in a spiritual sense, what was to become an independent existence was initially part of a submerged existence.

Rabbi Shne'ur Zalman of Liadi (Alter Rebbe)
1745–1812

Chasidic rebbe, halachic authority, and founder of the Chabad movement. The Alter Rebbe was born in Liozna, Belarus, and was among the principal students of the Magid of Mezeritch. His numerous works include the *Tanya*, an early classic containing the fundamentals of Chabad Chasidism, and *Shulchan Aruch HaRav*, an expanded and reworked code of Jewish law.

Text 7b

Rabbi Shne'ur Zalman of Liadi, ibid. 📖

כַּאֲשֶׁר הָאָדָם, שֶׁהוּא מֵעַלְמָא דְּאִתְגַּלְיָא, מִן הָאֲדָמָה כוּ', יִטְבּוֹל בְּמֵי
הַמִּקְוֶה, שֶׁהֵן עַלְמָא דְּאִתְכַּסְיָא, יִהְיֶה בָּזֶה גַּם כֵּן הִתְכַּלְלוּת עַלְמָא דְּאִתְגַּלְיָא
בְּעָלְמָא דְּאִתְכַּסְיָא, שֶׁיּוּכְלַל וְיָבֹא בִּמְקוֹר חוֹצְבוֹ, וּמִשָּׁם יוּכַל לְהִשְׁתַּנּוֹת.

When human beings, dwellers of a world that senses independence from God, immerse in a *mikveh*, which represents a subsumed state of existence, they return to their original source, from which change can flow.

KEY POINTS

- To immerse in a *mikveh* is to symbolically return to a pristine and unblemished primordial state from which we can emerge as a new person.

- Immersion in a *mikveh* represents a consciousness in which we acutely sense God's all-encompassing presence and our dependence on Him.

---

3. Why do people require purification?

Text 8

Rabbi Menachem Mendel Morgenstern, *Ohel Torah*, Leviticus 12:2 📖

הַטַּעַם מֵעִנְיָן טוּמְאַת יוֹלֶדֶת נִרְאֶה שֶׁהוּא עַל פִּי מַאֲמָרָם זִכְרוֹנָם לִבְרָכָה
(תַּעֲנִית ב,א), ג׳ מַפְתְּחוֹת בְּיָדוֹ שֶׁל הַקָּבָּ״ה שֶׁלֹּא נִמְסְרוּ לְשָׁלִיחַ, וְחַד מִנַּיְיהוּ
מַפְתֵּחַ שֶׁל חַיָּה, מִדִּכְתִיב (בְּרֵאשִׁית ל,כב) ״וַיִּזְכֹּר אֱלֹקִים אֶת רָחֵל וַיִּשְׁמַע
אֵלֶיהָ אֱלֹקִים וַיִּפְתַּח אֶת רַחְמָהּ״ – שֶׁהַקָּבָּ״ה עַצְמוֹ פּוֹתֵחַ הָרֶחֶם . . .

וְאִם כֵּן, בְּיוֹלֶדֶת בְּעֵת שֶׁכּוֹרַעַת לֵילֵד, שׁוֹרֶה שָׁם קְדוּשָׁה עֶלְיוֹנָה. וְאַחַר
כָּךְ בְּצֵאת לַאֲוִיר הָעוֹלָם, מִמֵּילָא מִסְתַּלֶּקֶת הַשְּׁכִינָה וְהַקְּדוּשָׁה, וַאֲזַי
נוֹלַד בַּמָּקוֹם הַזֶּה הַטּוּמְאָה, כִּי בְּכָל מָקוֹם שֶׁיֵּשׁ הִסְתַּלְּקוּת קְדוּשָׁה נוֹלַד
בִּמְקוֹמָהּ טוּמְאָה, כְּמוֹ טוּמְאַת מֵת שֶׁהוּא גַּם כֵּן מֵהַאי טַעְמָא.

The reason that a woman who gives birth becomes *tamei* (ritually impure) can be explained per the Talmudic statement (Ta'anit 2a) that there are three keys that remain in God's hand and are not delegated to messengers, one of them being the key to childbirth. As it says (Genesis 30:22), "And God remembered Rachel, He hearkened to her, and opened her womb," teaching us that God Himself is intimately present in the birthing process. . . .

Rabbi Menachem Mendel Morgenstern
1787–1859

Chasidic rabbi and leader. Born near Lublin, Poland, Rabbi Menachem Mendel went on to succeed the Chozeh (Seer) of Lublin and Rabbi Simchah Bunem of Peshischa as a Chasidic rebbe in Kotsk. His teachings, some of which are gathered in *Ohel Torah* and *Emet Ve'emunah*, are well-known in the Chasidic world for their sharpness.

[Handwritten notes:] After birth there's a holiness that is missing. Mikveh will reconnect her. * When there's a void of sanctity the Mikveh fills the void

It follows, therefore, that a lofty level of holiness is present at the time of birth. Once a baby is born, this holiness departs from the mother, and *tumah* ensues. When there is a void of holiness, there can be *tumah*. Indeed, this is why a corpse is *tamei*.

KEY POINTS

- Ritual impurity has nothing to do with uncleanliness. Rather, when holiness departs, ritual impurity can result.

4. Why are there so many dos and don'ts in Judaism?

Three Understandings

LEARNING EXERCISE 1

With your *chavruta* partner, study Texts 9a, 9b, and 9c, which elucidate three perspectives on the purpose of *mitzvot*. After you read them, write in the chart below how the author of each text might have answered our question.

	Why the Torah's "dos and don'ts" span virtually every area of our lives
Text 9a	
Text 9b	
Text 9c	

Text 9a

Rabbi Moshe ben Nachman, Deuteronomy 22:6 📖

"לֹא נִתְּנוּ הַמִּצְוֹת אֶלָּא לְצָרֵף בָּהֶם אֶת הַבְּרִיּוֹת" (בְּרֵאשִׁית רַבָּה מד,א):
. . . שֶׁאֵין הַתּוֹעֶלֶת בְּמִצְוֹת לְהַקָּבָּ"ה בְּעַצְמוֹ יִתְעַלֶּה, אֲבָל הַתּוֹעֶלֶת
בָּאָדָם עַצְמוֹ לִמְנוֹעַ מִמֶּנּוּ נֶזֶק, אוֹ אֱמוּנָה רָעָה, אוֹ מִדָּה מְגוּנָה, אוֹ
לִזְכּוֹר הַנִּסִּים וְנִפְלָאוֹת הַבּוֹרֵא יִתְבָּרֵךְ וְלָדַעַת אֶת הַשֵּׁם.

וְזֶהוּ "לְצָרֵף בָּהֶן", שֶׁיִּהְיוּ כְּכֶסֶף צָרוּף, כִּי הַצּוֹרֵף הַכֶּסֶף אֵין מַעֲשֵׂהוּ
בְּלֹא טַעַם, אֲבָל לְהוֹצִיא מִמֶּנּוּ כָּל סִיג, וְכֵן הַמִּצְוֹת לְהוֹצִיא
מִלִּבֵּנוּ כָּל אֱמוּנָה רָעָה, וּלְהוֹדִיעֵנוּ הָאֱמֶת, וּלְזוֹכְרוֹ תָּמִיד.

Rabbi Moshe ben Nachman
(Nachmanides, Ramban)
1194–1270

Scholar, philosopher, author, and physician. Nachmanides was born in Spain and served as leader of Iberian Jewry. In 1263, he was summoned by King James of Aragon to a public disputation with Pablo Cristiani, a Jewish apostate. Though Nachmanides was the clear victor of the debate, he had to flee Spain because of the resulting persecution. He moved to Israel and helped reestablish communal life in Jerusalem. He authored a classic commentary on the Pentateuch and a commentary on the Talmud.

"The *mitzvot* were solely given to refine human beings" (Midrash, *Bereishit Rabah* 44:1).... The *mitzvot* are not to benefit God. Their purpose is to benefit humankind—to keep them safe from harm; shield them from negative beliefs and base character traits; remind them of the miracles and wonders of the Creator; and help them know God.

The Midrash says that *mitzvot* are intended to "refine" human beings, as we would refer to refining silver. The act of refining silver is not senseless; it removes all impurities. So too, the *mitzvot* remove from our hearts every harmful belief, inform us of the truth, and enable us to keep it continuously in our minds.

Text 9b

Rabbi Shne'ur Zalman of Liadi, *Tanya*, ch. 46 📖

זֶהוּ שֶׁאוֹמְרִים: "אֲשֶׁר קִדְּשָׁנוּ בְּמִצְוֹתָיו".

כְּאָדָם הַמְקַדֵּשׁ אִשָּׁה לִהְיוֹת מְיֻחֶדֶת עִמּוֹ בְּיִחוּד גָּמוּר, כְּמוֹ שֶׁכָּתוּב (בְּרֵאשִׁית ב,כד) "וְדָבַק בְּאִשְׁתּוֹ וְהָיוּ לְבָשָׂר אֶחָד". כָּכָה מַמָּשׁ וְיָתֵר עַל כֵּן לְאֵין קֵץ הוּא יִחוּד נֶפֶשׁ הָאֱלֹקִית הָעוֹסֶקֶת בְּתוֹרָה וּמִצְוֹת וְנֶפֶשׁ הַחִיּוּנִית וּלְבוּשֵׁיהֶן הַנַּ"ל בְּאוֹר אֵין סוֹף בָּרוּךְ הוּא.

וְלָכֵן הִמְשִׁיל שְׁלֹמֹה עָלָיו הַשָּׁלוֹם בְּשִׁיר הַשִּׁירִים יִחוּד זֶה לְיִחוּד חָתָן וְכַלָּה, בִּדְבֵיקָה חֲשִׁיקָה וַחֲפִיצָה בְּחִיבּוּק וְנִישׁוּק.

This is the meaning of [the blessing we recite before we fulfill a mitzvah: "Blessed are You . . .] Who has sanctified us with His commandments."

[The Hebrew word *kideshanu*—generally rendered as "sanctified us"—can also translate as "betrothed us." Thus, the blessing implies that God betrothed us through giving us His *mitzvot*.] Just as a man betroths a woman in order to unite with her in a perfect bond—as it is written (Genesis 2:24), "He shall cleave to his wife, and they shall be one flesh"—similarly, and infinitely more so, is our union with the infinite light of God when we engage in Torah and *mitzvot*.

This is why King Solomon, in Song of Songs, depicts our union with God by means of a metaphor of a groom and bride whose relationship is characterized by attachment, longing, desire, embraces, and kisses.

Text 9c

Rabbi Shne'ur Zalman of Liadi, *Tanya*, ch. 36–37 📖

וְהִנֵּה מוּדַעַת זֹאת מַאֲמַר רַזַ"ל שֶׁתַּכְלִית בְּרִיאַת עוֹלָם הַזֶּה
הוּא שֶׁנִּתְאַוָּה הַקָּבָּ"ה לִהְיוֹת לוֹ דִּירָה בְּתַחְתּוֹנִים . . .

וְהִנֵּה תַּכְלִית הַשְּׁלֵימוּת הַזֶּה . . . תָּלוּי בְּמַעֲשֵׂינוּ וַעֲבוֹדָתֵנוּ כָּל זְמַן מֶשֶׁךְ הַגָּלוּת.
כִּי הַגּוֹרֵם שְׂכַר הַמִּצְוָה הִיא הַמִּצְוָה בְּעַצְמָהּ. כִּי בַּעֲשִׂיָּתָהּ מַמְשִׁיךְ הָאָדָם גִּילּוּי
אוֹר אֵין סוֹף בָּרוּךְ הוּא מִלְמַעְלָה לְמַטָּה לְהִתְלַבֵּשׁ בְּגַשְׁמִיּוּת עוֹלָם הַזֶּה.

It is a well-known rabbinic statement that the purpose
of the Creation of this world is that God desired that
the lowest world become a worthy home for His presence. . . .

The culminating fulfillment of this . . . depends on our actions and service throughout the duration of our exile. For
the reward of a commandment is the commandment itself,
meaning, by virtue of performing a mitzvah, a person suffuses infinite divine energy from above downward, to be
clothed in the corporeality of the world.

We are always connecting with G-D everyday.

KEY POINTS

- The intention of *mitzvot* is to purify and refine our character, to
  enable us to have a relationship with God, and to reveal Godliness in a world seemingly devoid of any sanctity.

- *Mitzvot* encompass all realms of life because this enables us to
  refine all areas of our existence, foster a relationship with God
  in all aspects of our identities, and reveal Godliness in even the
  most mundane spheres of our lives.

G-D gave us Mitzvot for him to have a home in this world

5. Why do many Jews sway when they pray?

Dearth of Books (Optional)

Text 10

Rabbi Yehudah Halevi, *Kuzari* 2:80

כִּי מִפְּנֵי שֶׁיְּכוֹלִים לִקְרוֹא רַבִּים מֵהֶם פֶּה אֶחָד, הָיָה אֶפְשָׁר שֶׁיִּתְקַבְּצוּ עֲשָׂרָה מֵהֶם אוֹ יוֹתֵר עַל סֵפֶר אֶחָד. וּבַעֲבוּר זֶה הָיוּ סְפָרֵינוּ גְדוֹלִים. וְיִצְטָרֵךְ כָּל אֶחָד מֵהָעֲשָׂרָה שֶׁיַּטֶּה עִם הָעִתִּים לְעַיֵּין הַתֵּיבָה, וְיָשׁוּב. וְהוּא נוֹטֶה וְשָׁב תָּמִיד מִפְּנֵי שֶׁהַסֵּפֶר בָּאָרֶץ.

וְהָיָה זֶה הַסִּבָּה הָרִאשׁוֹנָה. וְאַחַר כֵּן שָׁב מִנְהָג מִפְּנֵי הַהִסְתַּכְּלוּת וְהָרְאִיָּה וּלְהִדַּמוֹת כַּאֲשֶׁר הוּא טֶבַע בְּנֵי אָדָם.

I t often happened that many persons read from the same book at the same time; it was possible that ten or more read from one volume, which is why our books were so large. Each of these readers was thus obliged to bend down in his turn in order to read a passage and to turn back again. This resulted in a continual bending and sitting up while the book was lying on the ground.

This was the original cause. Then, as is human nature, people adopted this as a habit upon observing and imitating others.

Rabbi Yehudah Halevi
ca. 1075–1141

Noted author, physician, and poet. Rabbi Yehudah Halevi is best known as the author of the *Kuzari*, a philosophical work, written in the form of a discussion between a Jew, a Christian, and a Muslim before the King of the Khazars. In addition to the *Kuzari*, he wrote thousands of poems, of which only a few hundred survive today.

All Limbs Proclaim

Text 11

Rabbi David Abudraham, *Siddur, Birkot Hashachar*

Rabbi David ben Yoseph Abudraham
14th century

Resided in Seville, Spain, and is famous for his work on Jewish prayers and blessings. The work—completed around the year 1340—is a commentary on the daily, Shabbat, and festival prayers and collects many customs and laws relating to them. He is believed to have been a disciple of Rabbi Ya'akov ben Asher, author of *Arba'ah Turim*.

וְנָהֲגוּ יִשְׂרָאֵל לְהִתְנוֹעֵעַ בְּשָׁעָה שֶׁקּוֹרִין . . . וּכְתִיב (תְּהִלִּים לה,י) "כָּל עַצְמוֹתַי תֹּאמַרְנָה ה' מִי כָמוֹךָ". לְהוֹדִיעַ כִּי הוּא וְכָל עַצְמוֹתָיו עֲסוּקִים יַחַד לְהַלֵּל וּלְשַׁבֵּחַ לַשֵּׁם.

It is customary to sway while reading the Torah. . . . As it says (Psalms 35:10), "All of my limbs shall say, 'God! Who is like you!'" We thereby testify that we, with all of our limbs, are harmoniously praising the Creator.

Inner Flame

Text 12

Zohar 3:218b–219a 📖

מַאי הַאי . . . יִשְׂרָאֵל . . . דְּכָד לָעָאן בְּאוֹרַיְיתָא מִתְנַעְנְעָן הָכָא וְהָכָא
בְּלֹא לְמוֹדַע דְּבַר נַשׁ בְּעָלְמָא, וְלֹא יָכְלִין לְמֵיקַם בְּקִיּוּמַיְיהוּ? . . .

דִּכְתִיב (מִשְׁלֵי כ,כז) "נֵר ה' נִשְׁמַת אָדָם" . . . כֵּיָון דְּאָמַר מִלָּה
חֲדָא דְּאוֹרַיְיתָא, הָא נְהוֹרָא דָּלִיק, וְלֹא יָכְלוּן אִינוּן לְאִשְׁתַּכְּכָא,
וּמִתְנַעְנְעָן לְכָאן וּלְכָאן וּלְכָל סִטְרִין כִּנְהוֹרָא דְּשַׁרְגָּא.

Why is it that . . . we . . . sway to and fro when we study Torah—a habit that comes naturally to us—and we are unable to keep still? . . .

It is written, "The soul of man is God's candle" (Proverbs 20:27). . . . When we utter even one word of Torah, the flame of the soul is kindled. We cannot keep still, but sway to and fro like the flame of a wick.

Zohar

The seminal work of Kabbalah, Jewish mysticism. The Zohar is a mystical commentary on the Torah, written in Aramaic and Hebrew. According to Arizal, the Zohar contains the teachings of Rabbi Shimon bar Yocha'i who lived in the Land of Israel during the 2nd century. The Zohar has become one of the indispensable texts of traditional Judaism, alongside and nearly equal in stature to the Mishnah and Talmud.

KEY POINTS

- Some sway during prayer and study so that their entire bodies will be involved in this important endeavor. Furthermore, like a flickering flame, swaying represents the soul's yearning to cleave to God.

- This custom teaches us that when we study and pray, our souls experience an intimate bond with God. And yet, our spiritual pursuits of prayer and study ought not to be merely a soul endeavor, but experiences that relate to our bodies as well.

6. Why do traditional synagogues have separate seating for men and women?

The History (Optional)

Text 13

Jonathan D. Sarna, "The Debate over Mixed Seating in the American Synagogue," in *The American Synagogue: A Sanctuary Transformed* [New York: Cambridge University Press, 1987], p. 366

Jonathan D. Sarna, PhD
1955–

Historian. Dr. Sarna is the Joseph H. & Belle R. Braun Professor of American Jewish History and chair of the Hornstein Jewish Professional Leadership Program at Brandeis University, the chief historian of the National Museum of American Jewish History in Philadelphia, as well as a member of JLI's Academic Advisory Board. Sarna has written, edited, or coedited more than 30 books. He is best known for his book *American Judaism: A History*, winner of the Jewish Book Council's "Jewish Book of the Year Award" in 2004. Dr. Sarna served as the chief course consultant for JLI's *To Be a Jew in the Free World*.

Beginning in the mid-eighteenth century, church seating patterns began to change. Families at first won permission to sit together in church on a voluntary basis, and subsequently family seating became the norm.... The family pew won rapid and widespread acceptance in church circles, and Americans, forgetting that there were other possibilities, came to believe that "the family that prays together stays together."

The overwhelming move to adopt family seating stems from great changes in the history of the family that have been amply detailed elsewhere. The growing differentiation between home and work saw families take on a new symbolic role, termed by [historian John Putnam] Demos "the family as refuge," the image being that of family members clustering together for protection against the evils of anomic industrial society. Fear of family breakdown naturally led to a host of new rituals and forms (including the cult of domesticity) designed to "strengthen the family" against the menacing forces threatening to rend it asunder.

The family pew was one of these new forms. By raising the family's status over that of the single individual, and by symbolically linking family values to religious values, the family pew demonstrated, as separate seating did not, that the church stood behind the family structure one hundred percent.

QUESTION FOR DISCUSSION

The need to link family values to religious values is understandable and necessary. How could Jewish law be disposed to ignore this rationale?

The Center of Jewish Life is At home
The Center of our Relationship with G-D is in Temple. & nothing should get in the way.
Everything has its time & should not Distract From it.

The Jewish Sanctuary

Text 14

Rabbi Samson Raphael Hirsch, Genesis 28:22

Rabbi Samson Raphael Hirsch
1808–1888

Born in Hamburg, Germany; rabbi and educator; intellectual founder of the *Torah Im Derech Eretz* school of Orthodox Judaism, which advocates combining Torah with secular education. Beginning in 1830, Hirsch served as chief rabbi in several prominent German cities. During this period he wrote his *Nineteen Letters on Judaism*, under the pseudonym of Ben Uziel. His work helped preserve traditional Judaism during the era of the German Enlightenment. He is buried in Frankfurt am Main.

This is the mistake so often made by civilizations that pride themselves in building beautiful cathedrals and "houses of God." They build, as the prophet (Ezekiel 43:8) puts it, "their doorsteps next to My doorstep." They visit God in His house, but forbid His entry into theirs—where His presence with His thoughts might certainly be inconvenient.

That was not the thought with which the first foundation stone was laid for the first "House of God." The sanctity of the home is the necessary condition for the sanctity of the House of God. The House of God is sanctified not because it is the place to which holiness is relegated, but because from there, holiness is to flow out and penetrate the entire human sphere.

Know Before Whom You Stand

Text 15

Talmud, Berachot 28b

Babylonian Talmud

A literary work of monumental proportions that draws upon the legal, spiritual, intellectual, ethical, and historical traditions of Judaism. The 37 tractates of the Babylonian Talmud contain the teachings of the Jewish sages from the period after the destruction of the 2nd Temple through the 5th century CE. It has served as the primary vehicle for the transmission of the Oral Law and the education of Jews over the centuries; it is the entry point for all subsequent legal, ethical, and theological Jewish scholarship.

וּכְשֶׁאַתֶּם מִתְפַּלְלִים - דְּעוּ לִפְנֵי מִי אַתֶּם עוֹמְדִים.

When you pray, know before Whom you stand.

FIGURE 2.2

Prayer Laws

Any designs and artwork on synagogue walls need to be placed above eye level so as not to distract the congregants during prayer.
(Shulchan Aruch, Orach Chayim 90:23, and Magen Avraham 37)

Windows should be placed above eye level.
(Responsa Chatam Sofer, Orach Chayim 27)

During prayer, one's eyes should be directed downward.
(Talmud, Yevamot 105b)

One may not pray facing a mirror.
(Responsa Machshevet Hakodesh 2:29)

Though normally one may not eat before morning prayers, one may eat prior to prayer if one's hunger will detract from concentration.
(Shulchan Aruch, Orach Chayim 89:4)

KEY POINTS

- The Jewish home—not the synagogue—has always been the nerve center of Jewish life, where family values, linked to Jewish values, are fortified.

- Prayer is an intimate act of bonding with God, and thus to pray properly requires a high degree of mental focus. Among other restrictions intended to minimize distractions and aid in concentration, men sit separately from women.

7. Why is Israel important to the Jews?

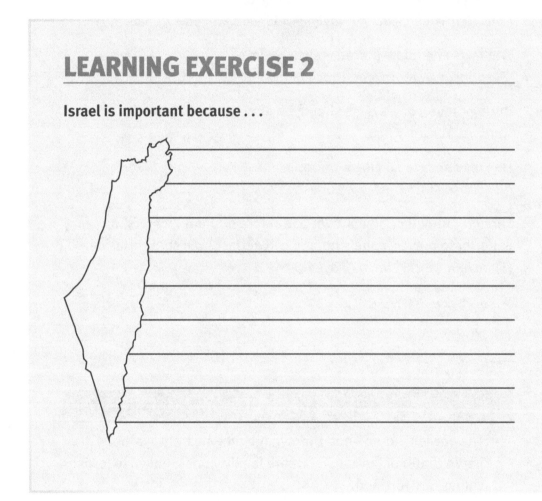

LEARNING EXERCISE 2

Israel is important because . . .

_____

_____

_____

_____

_____

_____

_____

_____

_____

To Conquer Earthliness

Text 16

Rashi, Genesis 1:1 🔖

לֹא הָיָה צָרִיךְ לְהַתְחִיל הַתּוֹרָה אֶלָּא מֵ"הַחֹדֶשׁ הַזֶּה לָכֶם" (שְׁמוֹת יב,ב),
שֶׁהִיא מִצְוָה רִאשׁוֹנָה שֶׁנִּצְטַוּוּ יִשְׂרָאֵל. וּמַה טַּעַם פָּתַח בְּ"בְּרֵאשִׁית"?

מִשּׁוּם . . . שֶׁאִם יֹאמְרוּ אוּמּוֹת הָעוֹלָם לְיִשְׂרָאֵל, "לִסְטִים אַתֶּם, שֶׁכְּבַשְׁתֶּם אַרְצוֹת
שִׁבְעָה גּוֹיִם", הֵם אוֹמְרִים לָהֶם: "כָּל הָאָרֶץ שֶׁל הַקָּדוֹשׁ בָּרוּךְ הוּא הִיא, הוּא בְּרָאָהּ
וּנְתָנָהּ לַאֲשֶׁר יָשָׁר בְּעֵינָיו, בִּרְצוֹנוֹ נָתְנָהּ לָהֶם וּבִרְצוֹנוֹ נָטְלָהּ מֵהֶם וּנְתָנָהּ לָנוּ".

It would have been more appropriate to begin the Torah with the words "This month is to be for you [the first month]" (Exodus 12:2), which is the first commandment given to the Jews, [namely, to establish the Jewish calendar]. Why does the Torah start with "In the beginning [God created heaven and earth]"?

So that . . . if the nations of the world should say to Israel, "You are robbers, for you conquered by force the lands of the seven nations [of Canaan]," Israel will reply, "The entire earth belongs to God; He created it [as we learn from the story of Creation] and gave it to whomever He deemed proper. He gave it to them, and when He wished, He took it away from them and gave it to us.

Rabbi Shlomo Yitschaki (Rashi)
1040–1105

Most noted biblical and Talmudic commentator. Born in Troyes, France, Rashi studied in the famed *yeshivot* of Mainz and Worms. His commentaries on the Pentateuch and the Talmud, which focus on the straightforward meaning of the text, appear in virtually every edition of the Talmud and Bible.

Text 17

The Rebbe, Rabbi Menachem Mendel Schneerson, *Likutei Sichot* 30:250–251 📖

תַּכְלִית עֲבוֹדָתָם שֶׁל בְּנֵי יִשְׂרָאֵל הִיא לַעֲשׂוֹת לוֹ יִתְבָּרֵךְ דִּירָה **בַּתַחְתּוֹנִים**

דַּוְקָא, שֶׁקְּדוּשָׁתוֹ יִתְבָּרֵךְ תְּשְׁרֶה בְּ"אַרְצִיּוּת" שֶׁל עוֹלָם הַזֶּה הַגַּשְׁמִי

דַּוְקָא (שֶׁלָּכֵן רוֹב מִצְוֹת הַתּוֹרָה הֵן מִצְוֹת **מַעֲשִׂיּוֹת**, כְּדֵי שֶׁעַל יְדֵי קִיּוּם

הַתּוֹרָה וּמִצְווֹת תּוּמְשַׁךְ קְדוּשָׁה (גַּם) בְּעִנְיָנִים הַגַּשְׁמִיִּים) . . .

דַּוְקָא מִשּׁוּם זֶה נִיתְּנָה לוֹ אֶרֶץ יִשְׂרָאֵל, אֶרֶץ גַּשְׁמִית, שֶׁבָּהּ תְּלוּיוֹת

כַּמָּה וְכַמָּה מִצְוֹת הַתּוֹרָה . . . מֵאַחַר שֶׁזֶּהוּ עִנְיָן בְּנֵי יִשְׂרָאֵל וְהַתּוֹרָה –

"לִכְבּוֹשׁ" אֶת הָ"אַרְצִיּוּת" שֶׁל עוֹלָם הַזֶּה וְלַעֲשׂוֹתוֹ דִּירָה לוֹ יִתְבָּרֵךְ.

Rabbi Menachem Mendel Schneerson
1902–1994

The towering Jewish leader of the 20th century, known as "the Lubavitcher Rebbe," or simply as "the Rebbe." Born in southern Ukraine, the Rebbe escaped Nazi-occupied Europe, arriving in the U.S. in June 1941. The Rebbe inspired and guided the revival of traditional Judaism after the European devastation, impacting virtually every Jewish community the world over. The Rebbe often emphasized that the performance of just one additional good deed could usher in the era of Mashiach. The Rebbe's scholarly talks and writings have been printed in more than 200 volumes.

The mission and purpose of the Jewish people is to turn the lowest reality into a home for God, meaning, that God should be expressed through the materiality of this physical world. (This is why most *mitzvot* are action-based—so that sanctity will be expressed in the physical realm as well.) . . .

For this reason, the Land of Israel was given to the Jewish people, a physical land where many of the *mitzvot* find their only expression . . . because the purpose of the Jewish people and the Torah is to conquer the materiality of this world and turn it into a home for God.

Divine Choice (Optional)

Text 18

Rabbi Aryeh Kaplan, *Jerusalem: The Eye of the Universe*
[Brooklyn, NY: Mesorah Publications, 1997], pp. 81–83

The last question we need to discuss is why God chose the Land of Israel as the chosen land? . . .

If you look at a map, you will see that the geographical location of the Land of Israel virtually guaranteed that it would play a key role in the tides of civilization. The Old World consisted of two great land masses, Eurasia (Europe and Asia) and Africa. It was impossible to travel from Eurasia to Africa without passing through the Holy Land. Therefore, every conqueror, every civilization that passed from one continent to the other, had to pass through the Holy Land and come in contact with the Jew. The Land of Israel thus interacted with virtually every great civilization, and all of them were, to some degree, influenced by the teachings of the Torah.

Besides being a gateway between North and South, the Holy Land is part of the keystone link between East and West. . . . Today, [the Atlantic and Pacific] Oceans are linked by the Suez Canal, but in the past, most caravan routes linking the Atlantic and Pacific passed directly through the Holy Land.

The Land of Israel was therefore literally the crossroads of civilization. Its capital and spiritual center, Jerusalem, was the focus of a process where the Jew would interact with all peoples, absorbing all the wisdom of the ancient

Rabbi Aryeh Kaplan
1934–1983

American rabbi, author, and physicist. Rabbi Kaplan authored more than 50 volumes on Torah, Talmud, Jewish mysticism, and philosophy, many of which have become modern-day classics. He is best known for his popular translation and elucidation of the Bible, *The Living Torah*, and his translation of the Ladino biblical commentary, *Me'am Lo'ez*.

world, while at the same time touching every great civilization with the wisdom of the Torah. It was thus taught that "Jerusalem is the center of the world" (*Midrash Tanchuma, Kedoshim* 10). God also told His prophet, "This is Jerusalem, I have set her in the midst of nations, and countries are around her" (Ezekiel 5:5). Considering both the centrality of its location and its spiritual influence, it is not at all surprising that Jerusalem today is a sacred city to the majority of the world's population.

Text 19

Midrash Tanchuma

A midrashic work bearing the name of Rabbi Tanchuma, a 4th-century Talmudic sage quoted often in this work. Midrash is the designation of a particular genre of rabbinic literature usually forming a running commentary on specific books of the Bible. *Midrash Tanchuma* provides textual exegeses, expounds upon the biblical narrative, and develops and illustrates moral principles. *Tanchuma* is unique in that many of its sections commence with a halachic discussion, which subsequently leads into non-halachic teachings.

Midrash Tanchuma, Parashat Re'eh 8

חֲבִיבָה אֶרֶץ יִשְׂרָאֵל שֶׁבָּחַר בָּה הַקָּדוֹשׁ בָּרוּךְ הוּא.

The Land of Israel is cherished for God chose it.

KEY POINTS

- Our sovereignty over a physical land is integral to the Jewish mission: to conquer the materiality of this world and turn it into a home for God.

- Israel's location ensured that it interacted with, and thus had the opportunity to influence, virtually every great civilization, spreading the wisdom of Torah throughout the world.

8. Why does the Bible call for animal sacrifices?

Subdue It

Text 20

Genesis 1:28

וַיְבָרֶךְ אֹתָם אֱלֹקִים, וַיֹּאמֶר לָהֶם אֱלֹקִים, פְּרוּ וּרְבוּ, וּמִלְאוּ אֶת הָאָרֶץ וְכִבְשֻׁהָ, וּרְדוּ בִּדְגַת הַיָּם וּבְעוֹף הַשָּׁמַיִם וּבְכָל חַיָּה הָרֹמֶשֶׂת עַל הָאָרֶץ.

God blessed [Adam and Chavah], and God said to them, "Be fruitful and multiply and fill the earth and subdue it, and rule over the fish of the sea and over the fowl of the sky and over all the beasts that tread upon the earth."

Text 21

Rabbi Yosef Yitschak Schneersohn
(Rayats, Frierdiker Rebbe, Previous Rebbe)
1880–1950

Chasidic rebbe, prolific writer, and Jewish activist. Rabbi Yosef Yitschak, the 6th leader of the Chabad movement, actively promoted Jewish religious practice in Soviet Russia and was arrested for these activities. After his release from prison and exile, he settled in Warsaw, Poland, from where he fled Nazi occupation, and arrived in New York in 1940. Settling in Brooklyn, Rabbi Schneersohn worked to revitalize American Jewish life. His son-in law, Rabbi Menachem Mendel Schneerson, succeeded him as the leader of the Chabad movement.

Rabbi Yosef Yitschak Schneersohn, cited in *Hayom Yom*, 7 Adar II

אַז מֶען גֶעהט אִין גאַס, דאַרְף מֶען טְראַכְטֶען דְבְרֵי תּוֹרָה . . . אָבֶּער אַז עֶר גֶעהְט
אוּן אִיז נִיט פאַרְנוּמֶען אִין דְבְרֵי תּוֹרָה, זאָגְט אִים דֶער שְׁטֵיין אוֹיף וֶועמֶען עֶר
טְרֶעט: בּוּלאַךְ (גּוֹלֶם) וואָס טְרֶעטְסְטוּ אוֹיף מִיר? מִיט וואָס בִּיסְטוּ הֶעכֶער פוּן מִיר?

While walking in the street, one must think words of Torah. . . . But when someone goes about not occupied with Torah, the stone he treads upon exclaims, "*Bulach!* (Clod), How dare you trample me! How are you any higher than I am?"

A Concession (Optional)

Text 22a

Maimonides, *Guide for the Perplexed* 3:32 📖

שֶׁאִי אֶפְשָׁר לָצֵאת מִן הַהֵפֶךְ אֶל הַהֵפֶךְ פִּתְאוֹם, וְלָזֶה אִי אֶפְשָׁר
לְפִי טֶבַע הָאָדָם שֶׁיַּנִּיחַ כָּל מָה שֶׁהֻרְגַּל בּוֹ פִּתְאוֹם.

וְכַאֲשֶׁר שָׁלַח הַשֵּׁם מֹשֶׁה רַבֵּנוּ עָלָיו הַשָּׁלוֹם לְתִתֵּנוּ "מַמְלֶכֶת כֹּהֲנִים וְגוֹי
קָדוֹשׁ" (שְׁמוֹת יט,ו) בִּידִיעָתוֹ יִתְבָּרֵךְ . . . וּלְהִנָּתֵן לַעֲבוֹדָתוֹ . . . וְהָיָה הַמִּנְהָג
הַמְפֻרְסָם בָּעוֹלָם כֻּלוֹ שֶׁהָיוּ אָז שֶׁהָיוּ רְגִילִין בּוֹ, וְהָעֲבוֹדָה הַכּוֹלֶלֶת אֲשֶׁר גֻּדְּלוּ עָלֶיהָ,
לְהַקְרִיב מִינֵי בַּעֲלֵי חַיִּים בְּהֵיכָלוֹת הָהֵם אֲשֶׁר הָיוּ מַעֲמִידִים בָּהֶם הַצְּלָמִים,
וּלְהִשְׁתַּחֲוֹת לָהֶם, וּלְקַטֵּר לִפְנֵיהֶם . . . לֹא גָּזְרָה חָכְמָתוֹ וְתַחְבּוּלָתוֹ הַמְּבוֹאֶרֶת
בְּכָל בְּרִיאוֹתָיו שֶׁיְּצַוֵּנוּ לְהָנִיחַ מִינֵי הָעֲבוֹדוֹת הָהֵם כֻּלָּם וּלְבַטְּלָם, כִּי אָז הָיָה
מַה שֶּׁלֹּא יַעֲלֶה בְּלֵב לְקַבְּלוֹ, כְּפִי טֶבַע הָאָדָם שֶׁהוּא נוֹטֶה תָּמִיד לַמּוּרְגָּל.

וְהָיָה דּוֹמֶה אָז כְּאִלּוּ יָבֹא נָבִיא בִּזְמַנֵּנוּ זֶה שֶׁיִּקְרָא לַעֲבוֹדַת הַשֵּׁם,
וְיֹאמַר, הַשֵּׁם צִוָּה אֶתְכֶם שֶׁלֹּא תִּתְפַּלְלוּ אֵלָיו, וְלֹא תָצוּמוּ, וְלֹא תְּבַקְשׁוּ
תְּשׁוּעָתוֹ בְּעֵת צָרָה, אֲבָל תִּהְיֶה עֲבוֹדַתְכֶם מַחְשָׁבָה מִבִּלְתִּי מַעֲשֶׂה.

וּמִפְּנֵי זֶה הִשְׁאִיר הַשֵּׁם מִינֵי הָעֲבוֹדוֹת הָהֵם וְהֶעֱתִיקָם מֵהְיוֹתָם לִנְבְרָאִים
וּלְעִנְיָינִים דִּמְיוֹנִיִּים שֶׁאֵין אֲמִתּוּת לָהֶם, לִשְׁמוֹ יִתְבָּרֵךְ . . . וְהִגִּיעַ הַתַּחְבּוּלָה
בְּזֹאת הָעָרְמָה הָאֱלֹקִית שֶׁנִּמְחָה זֵכֶר עֲבוֹדָה זָרָה, וְהִתְקַיְּימָה הַפִּנָּה הַגְּדוֹלָה
הָאֲמִתִּית בְּאוּמָתֵנוּ, וְהוּא מְצִיאוּת הַשֵּׁם וְאַחְדוּתוֹ, וְלֹא יִבְרְחוּ הַנְּפָשׁוֹת
וְיִשְׁתּוֹמְמוּ בְּבִטּוּל הָעֲבוֹדוֹת אֲשֶׁר הֻרְגְּלוּ וְלֹא נוֹדְעוּ עֲבוֹדוֹת זוּלָתָם.

It is impossible to go suddenly from one extreme to the other. By nature, people cannot abruptly discontinue something to which they are accustomed.

God sent Moses to make [the Israelites] "a kingdom of priests and a holy nation" (Exodus 19:6) by means of the knowledge of God . . . and the devotion to His service. . . . But the custom which was in those days common among all people, and the general mode of worship in which the

Israelites were brought up, consisted of sacrificing animals in those temples that contained certain images, to bow down to those images, and to burn incense before them.... It was in accordance with the wisdom and plan of God, as displayed in the whole Creation, that He did not command us to give up and to discontinue all these manners of service; for to obey such a commandment would have been contrary to the nature of human beings, who generally cleave to what they are accustomed.

Had God banned this service in those days, it would have made the same impression as a prophet would make at present if he called us to the service of God and told us in His name that we should not pray to Him, not fast, not seek His help in time of trouble; that we should serve Him in thought, but not by any action.

For this reason, God allowed this kind of service to continue. He transferred to His service that which had formerly served as a worship of created beings, of things imaginary and unreal....

By this divine plan it was effected that the traces of idolatry were blotted out, and the great principle of our faith, the existence and unity of God, was firmly established. This result was thus obtained without deterring or confusing the minds of the people by the abolition of the service to which they were accustomed and which alone was familiar to them.

Text 22b

Maimonides, *Mishneh Torah*, Laws of Misappropriating Temple Property 8:8 📖

וְהַמִּשְׁפָּטִים הֵן הַמִּצְוֹת שֶׁטַּעֲמָן גָּלוּי, וְטוֹבַת עֲשִׂיָּתָן בָּעוֹלָם הַזֶּה
יְדוּעָה, כְּגוֹן אִיסוּר גֵּזֶל, וּשְׁפִיכוּת דָּמִים, וְכִיבּוּד אָב וָאֵם.

וְהַחוּקִים הֵן הַמִּצְוֹת שֶׁאֵין טַעֲמָן יָדוּעַ . . . וְיִצְרוֹ שֶׁל אָדָם נוֹקְפוֹ
בָּהֶן, וְאוּמּוֹת הָעוֹלָם מְשִׁיבִין, כְּגוֹן אִיסוּר בְּשַׂר חֲזִיר, וּבָשָׂר
בְּחָלָב . . . וְכָל הַקָּרְבָּנוֹת כּוּלָן מִכְּלַל הַחוּקִים הֵן.

Mishpatim are those *mitzvot* whose rationales are openly revealed and whose benefits are known—for example, the prohibitions against robbery and bloodshed, and the obligation to honor one's parents.

Chukim are the *mitzvot* whose rationales are not known.... Our selfish inclinations pester us about these laws, and the nations of the world challenge them. Examples include the prohibition to eat pig or milk mixed with meat . . . All of the sacrifices are in this category of *chukim*.

QUESTION FOR DISCUSSION

Can Maimonides' explanation for sacrifices in Text 22a be reconciled with his statement in Text 22b that sacrifices are *chukim*?

Self-Sacrifice

Text 23

Sefer Hachinuch, Mitzvah 95 📖

עִיקְרֵי הַלְּבָבוֹת תְּלוּיִין אַחַר הַפְּעוּלוֹת. וְעַל כֵּן, כִּי יֶחֱטָא אִישׁ, לֹא יִטּוֹהַר לִבּוֹ יָפֶה בְּדָבָר שְׂפָתַיִם לְבָד, שֶׁיֹּאמַר בֵּינוֹ וּלְכוֹתֶל "חָטָאתִי לֹא אוֹסִיף עוֹד". אֲבָל בַּעֲשׂוֹתוֹ מַעֲשֶׂה גָּדוֹל עַל דְּבַר חֶטְאוֹ, לָקַחַת מִמִּכְלְאוֹתָיו עַתּוּדִים, וְלִטְרוֹחַ לַהֲבִיאָם אֶל הַבַּיִת הַנָּכוֹן אֶל הַכֹּהֵן, וְכָל הַמַּעֲשֶׂה הַכָּתוּב בְּקָרְבְּנֵי הַחוֹטְאִים, מִתּוֹךְ כָּל הַמַּעֲשֶׂה הַגָּדוֹל הַהוּא יִקְבַּע בְּנַפְשׁוֹ רוֹעַ הַחֵטְא, וְיִמָּנַע מִמֶּנּוּ פַּעַם אַחֶרֶת . . . מִזֶּה הַשּׁוֹרֶשׁ צִיוָּנוּ הָאֵ-ל לְהַקְרִיב לְעוֹלָם מֵהַדְּבָרִים שֶׁלֵּב אָדָם הוֹמֶה בָּהֶן, כְּמוֹ הַבָּשָׂר וְהַיַּיִן וְהַפַּת, כְּדֵי שֶׁיִּתְעוֹרֵר הַלֵּב יוֹתֵר עִם הָעֵסֶק בָּהֶם . . .

וְעוֹד יֵשׁ הִתְעוֹרְרוּת אַחֵר לַלֵּב בְּקָרְבַּן הַבְּהֵמוֹת מִצַּד הַדִּמְיוֹן, שֶׁגּוּף הָאָדָם וְהַבְּהֵמָה יִדְמוּ בְּכָל עִנְיְנֵיהֶם, לֹא יִתְחַלְּקוּ רַק שֶׁבָּזֶה נָתַן הַשֵּׂכֶל וְלֹא בָזֶה. וּבִהְיוֹת גּוּף הָאָדָם יוֹצֵא מִגֶּדֶר הַשֵּׂכֶל בְּעֵת הַחֵטְא, יֵשׁ לוֹ לָדַעַת שֶׁנִּכְנַס בְּעֵת הַהִיא בְּגֶדֶר הַבְּהֵמוֹת אַחֵר שֶׁלֹּא יְחַלְּקֵם רַק הוּא לְבַדּוֹ, וְעַל כֵּן נִצְטַוֶּה לָקַחַת גּוּף בָּשָׂר כְּגוּפוֹ, וּלְהַבִיאוֹ אֶל הַמָּקוֹם הַנִּבְחָר לְעִלּוּי הַשֵּׂכֶל וּלְשָׂרְפוֹ שָׁם, וּלְהַשְׁכִּיחַ זִכְרוֹ, כָּלִיל יִהְיֶה, לֹא יִזָּכֵר וְלֹא יִפָּקֵד, תַּחַת גּוּפוֹ, כְּדֵי לְצַיֵּיר בְּלִבָבוֹ צִיּוּר חָזָק שֶׁכָּל עִנְיָנוֹ שֶׁל גּוּף בְּלִי שֵׂכֶל אָבַד וּבָטֵל לְגַמְרֵי, וְיִשְׂמַח בְּחֶלְקוֹ בְּנֶפֶשׁ הַמַּשְׂכֶּלֶת שֶׁחֲנָנוֹ הָאֵ-ל שֶׁהִיא קַיֶּימֶת לְעוֹלָם . . . וּבְקָבְעוֹ צִיּוּר זֶה בְּנַפְשׁוֹ יִזָּהֵר מִן הַחֵטְא הַרְבֵּה.

Our feelings are dependent on our actions. Hence, when a person sins, his character is not cleansed merely by uttering to the wall, "I have sinned; I shall not repeat." He must engage in a grand act. He must seize goats from his pens and labor to bring them to the priest at the House of God, and he must follow all of the laws that are spelled out regarding sin offerings. This intense drama will impress upon his soul the corruption of sin and the resolve to refrain from its harms in the future. . . .

We experience another sort of emotional impact by offering the sacrifice. There is a commonality between human and animal bodies. The primary difference between them is the mind and soul. When we sin, our bodies essentially disengage from our minds and souls. During these moments, our bodies are akin to the animal. We are therefore commanded to take an animal, a being with a body like ours, and to bring it to the place that promotes pursuits of the mind and the spirit, and to burn there the animal's remains, which brings a total end to the animal's existence. The act of bringing the sacrifice will impress upon us in a forceful manner that the body without the mind vanishes, and that we ought to be grateful that God graced us with a mind and soul that endure forever. . . . When we absorb this imagery, we will be cautious from sin.

Elevating All Animal Life (Optional)

Text 24

Rabbi Shne'ur Zalman of Liadi, *Tanya*, ch. 34 📖

וְאַף שֶׁאֵינוֹ נוֹתֵן אֶלָּא חוֹמֶשׁ, הֲרֵי הַחוֹמֶשׁ מַעֲלֶה עִמּוֹ כָּל הָאַרְבַּע יָדוֹת לַה׳, לִהְיוֹת מָכוֹן לְשִׁבְתּוֹ יִתְבָּרֵךְ.

כַּנּוֹדַע מַאֲמַר רַזַ״ל שֶׁמִּצְוַת צְדָקָה שְׁקוּלָה כְּנֶגֶד כָּל הַקָּרְבָּנוֹת, וּבְקָרְבָּנוֹת הָיָה כָּל הַחַי עוֹלֶה לַה׳ עַל יְדֵי בְּהֵמָה אַחַת. וְכָל הַצּוֹמֵחַ עַל יְדֵי עִשָּׂרוֹן סֹלֶת אֶחָד בָּלוּל בְּשֶׁמֶן.

Even though you distribute no more than a fifth of your income, this fifth carries the other four parts with it up to God. All of your income will now become a dwelling for the Creator.

Everything has a purpose

Lesson **2**   Animal Sacrifice

81

This idea can be derived from the Talmudic statement that the commandment of charity is akin to the sacrifices. With respect to the sacrifices, all living creatures were elevated unto God through the offering of one beast, and all plants through one-tenth of a measure of fine meal mixed with oil.

Continue your learning experience ONLINE

Visit www.myJLI.com/why2

for insightful and inspiring videos, articles, and readings on this topic.

KEY POINTS

- The right to utilize God's creations, including animal life, is contingent on our doing so while fulfilling the divine mission to sublimate the material world to its Godly purpose.

- Action fuels emotion. The intense act of animal sacrifice was intended to stimulate an emotional realization of the harmfulness of transgression and the futility of excessive bodily pursuits and awaken our drive for meaning and goodness.

- By using an animal for a holy purpose, all animal life is elevated.

Lesson Conclusion (Optional)

LEARNING EXERCISE 3

With a partner, identify a theme that has been present in most (or all) of the elements of this lesson.

1. Why is the Star of David a Jewish symbol?

2. Why does a *mikveh* purify?

3. Why do people require purification?

4. Why are there so many dos and don'ts in Judaism?

5. Why do many Jews sway when they pray?

6. Why do traditional synagogues have separate seating for men and women?

7. Why is Israel important to the Jews?

8. Why does the Bible call for animal sacrifices?

ADDITIONAL READINGS

EYE OF THE UNIVERSE

BY RABBI ARYEH KAPLAN

The last question we must discuss is why God chose the Land of Israel as the chosen land; and in particular, why He chose Jerusalem as its spiritual focus. Of course, we have seen how the Altar in Jerusalem played an important role from the time of Adam, but still, why was it this spot in particular that was chosen, and none other? If you look at a map, you will see that the geographical location of the Land of Israel virtually guaranteed that it would plan a key role in the tides of civilization. The Old World consisted of two great land masses, Eurasia (Europe and Asia) and Africa. It was impossible to travel from Eurasia to Africa without passing through the Holy Land. Therefore, every conqueror, every civilization that passed from one continent to the other, had to pass through the Holy Land and come in contact with the Jew. The Land of Israel thus interacted with virtually every great civilization, and all of them were, to some degree, influenced by the teachings of the Torah.

Besides being a gateway between north and south, the Holy Land is part of the keystone link between east and west. There are mountains in Israel where a cup of water spilled on the western slope will eventually flow in to the Atlantic Ocean, while one spilled on the eastern slope will flow into the Pacific. Today, these oceans are linked by the Suez Canal, but in the past, most caravan routes linking the Atlantic and Pacific passed directly through the Holy Land.

The Land of Israel was therefore literally the crossroads of civilization. Its capital and spiritual center, Jerusalem, was the focus of a process where the Jew would interact with all peoples, absorbing all the wisdom of the ancient world, while at the same time touching every great civilization with the wisdom of the Torah. It was thus taught that "Jerusalem is the center of the world."[1] God also told His prophet, "This is Jerusalem, I have set her in the midst of nations, and countries are around her" (Ezekiel 5:5). Considering both the centrality of its location and its spiritual influence, it is not at all surprising that Jerusalem today is a sacred city to the majority of the world's population.

Even today, when land routes are no longer as important as they were in the past, Jerusalem is still a center of human concern. One need only to think of how Providence placed the major portion of the world's supply of oil—the main source of transportation energy—within a stone's throw of Jerusalem. The world would otherwise not give the Holy City a second thought, except perhaps as an ancient sacred shrine. As it is, decisions made in Jerusalem today can influence even the greatest world powers. Jerusalem thus still occupies an important role in the councils of nations. All this is certainly more than mere coincidence.

On a much deeper level, however, we see Jerusalem not only as a center of civilization, but also as the very center of creation.

As discussed earlier, the most important single object in Jerusalem was the Ark, containing the Tablets and the Original Torah. This stood in the Holy of Holies

---

Rabbi Aryeh Kaplan. (1934–1983) American rabbi, author, and physicist. Rabbi Kaplan authored more than 50 volumes on Torah, Talmud, Jewish mysticism, and philosophy, many of which have become modern-day classics. He is best known for his popular translation and elucidation of the Bible, *The Living Torah*, and his translation of the Ladino biblical commentary, *Me'am Lo'ez*.

[1] *Tanchuma, Kedoshim* 10, *Pesikta Rabatai* 10:2, *Zohar* 2: 157a, 2:222b, Ramban on Genesis 14:18, *Shalshelet HaKaballah* p. 31, *Likutey Torah* (R. Shneur Zalman of Liadi) *Masai* 91b.

on an outcrop of bedrock known as the *Evven She-tiyah,* literally, the Foundation Stone.[2] The Talmud states that it is called the "Foundation Stone" because it was the foundation of the universe. As the Talmud explains, this is because it was the very first point at which God began the act of creation.[3]

This is based on the teaching that creation began at a single point, and from this point, the universe unfolded until God decreed that it should stop. This is the significance of Shadai, which is one of God's names. It comes from the word *Dai,* meaning "enough," and it indicates the Attribute through which God stopped the expansion of creation at a certain stage.[4]

Here we must seek to understand why creation had to begin at a single point, and what is the significance of this point. Why could creation not have been brought into existence all at once? Why did it all have emanate from a single point in space?

The answer to these questions involves an understanding of the entire concept of the spiritual and physical, as well as the difference between the two. There are numerous discussions regarding the difference between the physical and the spiritual, but this difference is often not spelled out precisely. Very closely related is the question why God created a physical world in the first place. God Himself is certainly spiritual, as is the ultimate purpose of creation. It is therefore somewhat difficult to understand the need for a physical world at all.

With a little insight, the difference between the spiritual and the physical is readily apparent. In the physical realm, there is a concept of physical space; while in the spiritual, this concept is totally absent. All that exists in the spiritual realm is conceptual space. Two things that are similar are said to be close, while

things that are different are said to be far from one another. While in the physical world it is possible to push two different things together, this is impossible in the spiritual realm.[5]

We see a good example of this in the case of the teachings involving angels. It is taught that one angel cannot have two missions while two angels cannot share the same mission.[6] There is no spatial concept unifying an angel. Therefore, if an angel had two missions, by definition it would become two angels. On the other hand, if two angels had the same mission, there could be no physical space separating them, and by definition they would be a single angel.[7]

We now begin to see why a physical world is needed. If only a spiritual world existed, there would be no way in which two different things could be brought together. Because they are different, by definition they are separated, and there would be no physical space in which they could be "pushed" together.

Spiritual entities, however, can be bound to physical objects, very much as the soul is bound to the body. The only way, then, in which two different spiritual entities or forces can be brought together is when they are bound to the same physical thing, or to two physical things which themselves are brought together.

A good example of this involves the impulses for good and evil in man, respectively known as the *Yetzer Tov* and the *Yetzer HaRa.* In a purely spiritual sense, good and evil are opposites, which can never be brought together. Without man's physical body, they could not be brought together in a single entity, indeed, in angels, which are purely spiritual, good and evil cannot coexist.[8] It is only in a physical body that good and evil can be brought together, and man therefore had to be created with such a body before

[2] *Yoma* 5:2 (53b), *VaYikra Rabbah* 20:4, *Pesikta* 26 (171a), *Zohar* 1:71b (end), 1:231a, *Zohar Chadash* 28a; *Yad, Bet HaBechirah* 4: I, Rashi on Job 39:28. See *Likutey Moharan* 61:6, from Job 31:35.

[3] *Tosefta, Yoma* 2:12; *Yoma* 54b, *Pirkey Rabbi Eliezer* 35 (82b), *Midrash Tehillim* 91, *Zohar* 1:131a, 1:86b, 87a, Ramban, Bachya, on Genesis 28:19. Also see *Zohar* 1:231a, 222a, *Tikuney Zohar* 67 (98a). God's Name is inscribed on this stone, see *Targum J.* on Exodus 28:39, Ecclesiastes 3:11.

[4] *Bereshit Rabbah* 5:8. Creation began at a single point, *Bereshit Rabbah* 4:2.

[5] *Moreh Nebukhim,* introduction to part 2, #16; *Or HaShem* 1:1:16, *Shefa Tal* 1:3 (Hanau 5372) p. 13c in note, *Pardes Rimonim* 2:7, *Amud HaAvodah, Vikuach Shoel U'Meshiv* 99. See note 7. Also see my book, "God, Man and Tefillin" (NCSY, New York, 1973) p. 42. *Cf. Toledot Yaakov Yosef* 197c, *Tzafnat Paneach* 26d, 68d, *Sefer Baal Shem Tov, Ekev* 72, *Bereshit* 41.

[6] *Bereshit Rabbah* 50:2, *Targum,* Rashi, on Genesis 18:2, *Zohar* 1:127a.

[7] For a similar argument, see *Yad, Yesodey HaTorah* 1:7, 2:5, see Commentary *ad loc.*

[8] *Shabbat* 89a, *Bereshit Rabbah* 48:11.

he could have within himself the combination of good and evil that would allow him to have free will and free choice.[9]

God created many different spiritual concepts, forces and entities with which to create and direct the universe. Spiritual concepts can consist of such opposites as good and evil, or justice and mercy; as well as the basic concepts of giving and receiving, which are the spiritual roots of masculinity and femininity. There are also countless angels and spiritual potentials, all interacting to bring about the processes through which the universe is directed and guided.

All these are different, and in some cases opposite, and there would be no way for them to come together so that they could act in concert. The only way in which all spiritual forces can be brought together is for all of them to be associated with a single physical point. This point is the *Evven Shetiyah—the* Foundation Stone of all creation.

Jerusalem's original name was Shalem (Salem), coming from the same root as *Shalom,* meaning peace. One of the main concepts of Jerusalem is peace, as it is written, "Seek Jerusalem's peace" (Psalms 122:6). But, as the *Zohar* explains, this peace is not only in the physical world; it also implies peace in the spiritual world.[10] The meaning of this is that all spiritual forces are brought together so that they can act in concert and in harmony.[11]

The act of creation involved all these spiritual forces acting in concert. Before they could do so, however, a physical point had to be created, which would serve as a focus for all these forces. This was the Foundation Stone, the first point of creation. Since it was the focus of all spiritual forces, it brought them all into play in the creation of the physical universe. It is therefore not surprising to find that the very first word in the *Torah—Bereshyt—*contains an allusion to this spot that was the focus of creation.[12]

It was in this same place that God created man. When God was about to create man, the Torah relates that He said, "Let us make man in our image" (Genesis 1:26). The meaning of this is that God was speaking to all the spiritual forces that He had created, bringing them all into the creation of man, the final goal of His creation. In order to bring all these forces to bear upon the creation of man, God created him in the very place where all these forces are focused.[13]

In a dynamic sense, all these forces are actually concentrated in man himself, and this is the meaning of the teaching that man is a microcosm.[14] But man would multiply and become many, while these forces would have to be focused on a single stationary place. Jerusalem, and particularly the Foundation Stone, is therefore a place of gathering, first only for the Jewish people, but ultimately for all mankind. As all men return to their spiritual source, they tend to strengthen the spiritual concentration in this place.[15]

The sages teach that God created man from the place of the Great Altar, the place of his atonement.[16] The meaning of this is that the sacrifices, brought on the Altar, would ultimately atone for man's sins. This, however, can also be understood in light of the above. The entire concept of sin is one of spiritual separation, where spiritual forces are separated from each other, and where man is thus separated from God.[17] The concept of sacrifice, on the other hand, is to reunite these forces, thus bringing man back to God. Indeed for this reason, the Hebrew word for

---

[9] *Pitchey Chakhmah VaDaat* #4, *Shefa Tal* 3:1.

[10] *Zohar* 3:90b.

[11] It is thus written, "He makes peace in His high places" (Job 25:2), see Rashi *ad loc., Bereshit Rabbah* 12:8, *BaMidbar Rabbah* 12:8, *Bahir* 11, 59, 153. Also see *Chagigah* 12a, *Bereshit Rabbah* 4:7, Rashi on Genesis 1:8.

[12] The word *Bereshyt* can thus be read as *Bara Shyt—"He* created the *Shyt "—the Shyt* being the foundation and drainage pit of the Altar, see *Succah* 49a. Note that *Shyt* is masculine, while *Shetiyah* is feminine, both words sharing the same root. The *Shetiyah* was the foundation of both the physical and spiritual worlds, see *Yoma* 54b. It was a place of constriction *(tzimtzum)* of spiritual forces, *cf. Likutey Moharan* 61:6.

[13] *Bereshit Rabbah* 8:3. Note that the Jew was also created on the spot, since key events in the lives of the Patriarchs occurred here, see Chapter 6, notes 28, 45, 49.

[14] *Avot Rabbi Natan* 31:3, Saadya Gaon on *Sefer Yetzirah* 4:1, *Tikkuney Zohar* 17a.

[15] *Cf. Metzudot David* (Radbaz) 266.

[16] See Chapter 6, note 4.

[17] Isaiah 59:2, Rambam, *Shemonah Perakim* #8, *Reshit Chakhmah* 1:7 (22d), *Nefesh HaChaim* 1:18.

sacrifice, *Korban,* comes from the root *Karav,* meaning to "be close."[18] But sacrifice and atonement would be accomplished primarily in close proximity to this Foundation Stone, which is the one point that unifies and brings together all spiritual forces. Indeed, the primary purpose of the entire Temple Service was to rectify and strengthen the bond between these forces.

Upon this Foundation Stone stood the Ark, containing the Two Tablets upon which God had written the Ten Commandments, as well as the Original Torah written by Moses. This was to underscore the fact that all creation is sustained by the Covenant of the Torah, as God said, "If not for My covenant day and night, I would not have appointed the decrees of heaven and earth" (Jeremiah 33:25).[19] All creation was contingent upon this covenant, which was made when Israel accepted the Torah from God.[20] The fact that the Ark stood on the Foundation Stone of creation means that all creation is infused with the power of the Torah.

Since this spot is where all spiritual forces come together to influence the physical world, this is indeed the "Gate of Heaven." It is from this spot—between the two Cherubim on the Ark—that prophecy emanates, and through there all prayers are channeled. This spot is the focus of all spiritual forces, and all communication that we have with these forces is through this location. It is thus taught that spiritual channels emanate from the Foundation Stone, bringing spiritual sustenance to all the world.[21]

This also explains the meaning of Jacob's dream, where he saw "A ladder standing on the earth, with its head reaching the heaven" (Genesis 28:12). The concept of a ladder is that of a single entity in which many steps are united. There are many steps on a ladder, but they are all connected by the body of the ladder itself. The same is true of the Foundation Stone,

the place where Jacob slept. This too was a single entity to which all spiritual levels are attached.[22]

Since the Foundation Stone unites all spiritual forces, there must be a realm in the spiritual domain where all these forces come together. In the words of our sages, this realm is called "Jerusalem on High," and is said to parallel the physical Jerusalem.[23] This supernal Jerusalem is the realm where all the spiritual forces are brought together to interact. In the words of some of our sages, this "Jerusalem on High" is called Shalem, from the root *Shalom,* since this is where even opposing spiritual forces exist together in harmony.[24]

As Creator of all spiritual forces, God Himself is infinitely higher than even the highest of them. The difference between God and any created entity, even the highest is infinitely greater than the difference between even the very highest and very lowest things in creation. God is the Creator while everything else is created, and there can be no greater fundamental difference than this.

This, however, presents some very serious difficulties. If God is utterly different from all spiritual forces, how can they have any association with Him? We know that God constantly acts upon these forces, this being the entire mechanism of Divine Providence.[25] Furthermore, like everything else, these constantly depend on God for existence itself—if God did not constantly infuse them with His creative force, they would instantly cease to exist.[26] But if both God and these forces are spiritual and different, then they are separated to the ultimate degree. It would only be through a physical entity that the two could be united.

In many places, when speaking of the Chosen City, the Torah calls it, "The place that God will choose

---

[18] See Chapter 5, note 15.

[19] See *Shabbat* 33a, 137b, *Pesachim* 68b, *Taanit* 27b, *Megillah* 31b, *Nedarim* 31b, *Avodah Zarah* 3a, *Tosefta, Berakhot* 6:18, *Yebamot* 2:6, Commentaries on *Avot* 1:2.

[20] *Shabbat* 88a, Rashi on Genesis 1:31.

[21] *Kohelet Rabbah* 2:7, *Tanehuma, Kedoshim* 10, Rashi on Ecclesiastes 2:5, *Sichot HaRan* 60.

[22] *Tsioni ad loc., Sodey Razia* (Bilgorei 5696) p. 35a, *Megalah Amukot* 121, 128, 131, 134, 178.

[23] *Taanit Sa,* Rashba (in *Eyin Yaakov*) *ad loc., Chagigah* 12b, *Tanchuma, Pekudey* 1, *Zohar* 1:80, 1: 183a, 2:59a,Ramban on Genesis 14: 18; *Yerushalmi, Berakhot* 4:5 (35b), Ibn Ezra on Psalm 76:3, Rashi on Genesis 28:17, *Targum,* Rashi, on Psalm 122:3.

[24] *Zohar* 1:87a, 3:90b.

[25] *Derekh HaShem* 2:5:4, 3:2:5.

[26] *Yad, Yesodey Ha Torah* 2:9, *Moreh Nebukhim* 1:69, *Likutey Amarim* (Tanya), *Shaar Ha Yichud VeHaEmunah* 1.

to make His Name dwell there."[27] To the extent that we can understand it, this means that God associates Himself with this place. This is very difficult for the human mind to comprehend, and indeed, Solomon, the wisest of all men, found it impossible to understand. He thus said to God, "Behold the heavens and the heavens of heaven cannot contain You, how much less this house that I have built" (1 Kings 8:27). Yet, he knew that God had somehow associated Himself with this place, as God himself had proclaimed in His Torah. [28]

But if both God and the entire array of spiritual forces are associated with this spot—the Foundation Stone—then they can indeed interact. Thus, it is by associating with the Temple and the Stone that God also associates with all the spiritual forces that He created, sustaining and directing them. As mentioned above, however, the array of spiritual forces is called "Jerusalem on High."[29]

We thus see that God does not associate with "Jerusalem on High" until He does so with the physical Jerusalem. This is the meaning of the Talmudic teaching, "God swore that He would not enter Jerusalem on High until He enters Jerusalem down below."[30]

This is also the meaning of the fact that God Himself appeared at the top of the ladder in Jacob's dream. This is the concept of unification, not only affecting all spiritual levels, but also attaching them to God Himself.

The entire purpose of the Temple service was to strengthen this bond between God and the spiritual forces, thus enhancing them and giving them greater power to elevate the physical world. For example, on the festival of Succot, seventy sacrifices were brought, one for each of the seventy archetypal nations of the world.[31] Through this, the directing angels overseeing these nations would be elevated, and, as a result, the nations themselves would be brought to a higher spiritual level.

In a similar manner, other aspects of the Temple service served to enhance other spiritual aspects of humanity. Since the time that the Temple was destroyed, these spiritual aspects have also diminished.

This also explains why all our prayers are directed toward the Foundation Stone, the place of the Ark. We do not pray to any spiritual force or entity, even the highest, but only to God alone. The content of our prayer, however, is to rectify the various spiritual forces, bringing God's light to shine upon them.[32] Since the main connection between God and the spiritual forces is the place of the Ark, we focus our prayers toward this spot.

Through this, we can understand another very difficult Talmudic teaching:[33]

Rabbi Yochanan said in the name of Rabbi Yosi (ben Zimra): How do we know that God prays? It is written, "I will bring them to My holy mountain, and make them rejoice in the house of My prayer, [for My house is a house of prayer for all nations]" (Isaiah 56:7). The scripture does not say "their prayer," but "My prayer." We thus see that God prays.

And what is His prayer?

Rav Zutra bar Tovia said in the name of Rav: It is "May it be My will that My mercy should overcome My anger, and that My mercy dominate My

---

27 Deuteronomy 12:11, 14:23, 16:2, 16:6, 16:11, 26:2. See 1 Kings 8:29. Also see Chapter 6, note 1.

28 See *Sichot HaRan* 40.

29 Jerusalem is thus identified with *Yesod*-Foundation, the Attribute that unites Male and Female, see *Etz Chaim*, *Shaar HaArat HaMochin* 5 (p. 126), *Shaar Kitzur ABYA* 1 (p. 393). *Cf. Zohar* 2: 184b, *Mavo Shaarim* 4:2:7 (p. 165), *Shaarey Gan Eden* 89a, *Siddur Rabbi Shneur Zalman of Liadi* p. 53d, 59b, 62c, *Torah Or* 37d, *Likutey Torah, Ekev* (16c,d).

30 *Taanit* 5a. See *Pardes Rimonim* 8:26, *Shnei Luchot HaBrit, Torah SheBeKtav*, beginning of *VaYechi* (3:66b), *Likutey Torah* (R. Shneur Zalman), *Pekudey* (4a).

31 *Succah* 55b. Regarding these seventy directing angels, see *Targum J.* on Deuteronomy 32:8, Genesis 11:7,8, *Pirkey Rabbi Eliezer* 24, Ibn Ezra on Zechariah 1:8, *Derekh HaShem* 2:4:8.

32 See Bachya on Deuteronomy 4:7, *Tshuvot Rivash* 157, *Elemah Rabatai, Eyin Kall* 1:2, *Pardes Rimonim* 32:2, *Metzudot David* (Radbaz) 2, *Shomer Emunim* (HaKadmon) 2:64,65, *Kisey Melekh* (on *Tikuney Zohar* 22) 94b #50.

33 *Berakhot* 7a, *Otzar HaKavod ad loc.*, *Siddur Rabbi Shneur Zalman of Liadi* p. 136c.

Attributes. May I act toward My children with the Attribute of Mercy, and go beyond the requirements of the law."

At first thought this appears beyond all comprehension. How can we say that God prays? And if He does, to whom does He pray? And what is the precise meaning of His prayer?

But if we look carefully at the basic concept of prayer, this becomes somewhat easier to understand. When we pray, the object of our prayer is to bring God's spiritual Light to bear on the spiritual forces, so that they in turn should enhance the world in which we live. Prayer is therefore the enhancement and elevation of the spiritual forces. Of course, the One who enhances these forces is none other than God Himself, infusing them with His Light and creative force. When God acts upon these forces in this manner, He is said to be "praying."

This also explains the content of God's prayer. The concept of God's anger and His Attribute of Justice is essentially when He withdraws His Light from the spiritual forces, allowing them to function on their own. These forces then function almost automatically, dispensing justice according to a strict rule, in an almost mechanical fashion. This is the idea of God's "hiding His face."[34]

The concept of God's Mercy, on the other hand, is when God makes His Light shine on these forces, taking complete control of them, as it were. Thus, when God prays that His Mercy should dominate His Attributes, it means that He is infusing these Attributes with His Light and creative force. This is the concept of God praying. . . .

It is important to note that God's prayer is associated with the Temple in Jerusalem—"For My house is the house of My prayer." According to what we have said earlier, however, the reason for this is obvious. God's prayer refers to His infusing all Attributes and spiritual forces with His Light, which takes place through the Foundation Stone, the focus of all prayer.

It is also very significant to note the ending of this verse, "For My house is a house of prayer to all nations." Here again, at first thought, it is difficult to see what connection this has to God's prayer. Why is the verse that teaches the concept of God's prayer associated with that of the Temple being a place of prayer for all peoples?

We must realize that the main reason there is distinction between Jew and Gentile is because of the withholding of God's light. As a result of the sins of Adam, of the generation of the Flood, and of the builders of the Tower of Babel, God gradually withdrew His Light from the world, restricting it to one people, the Jews, who would inhabit Jerusalem and serve God there.[35] Therefore, there are directing angels over the gentile nations, but they are on a lower level than the spiritual forces associated with Israel.[36]

The concept of God's prayer, however, is that His Light should shine through all spiritual forces with its full intensity, and thus, to all mankind as well. Therefore, when God's house is the "house of His prayer," it is then also "a house of prayer for all nations."[37]

This again brings us to the location of the Foundation Stone, the focus of all spiritual forces. It was set on the crossroads of civilization, so that all peoples should interact with these forces and throughout history, be influenced by them. In this manner, all mankind is gradually elevated by these forces, paving the way for the ultimate rectification of the world. This will be realized in the Messianic Age, when Jerusalem becomes a center for God's teaching for all mankind: "Out of Zion shall come forth the Torah, and God's word from Jerusalem" (Micah 4:2).

Jerusalem: The Eye of the Universe [NCSY/OU Press: New York, 1976], pp. 77–86
Reprinted with permission of OU Press

---

[34] *Likutey Moharan* 2:6.

[35] For details, see "The Jew," Collegiate Hashkafa Series, Young Israel, New York, 1973.

[36] See note 31.

[37] This was thus the place of the creation of Adam, the father of the entire human race.

ON THE ESSENCE OF RITUAL IMPURITY

BY SUSAN HANDELMAN, PhD

One of the most widely misunderstood concepts in the Torah is contained in the words *tum'ah* and *taharah*. Translated as "unclean" and "clean," or "impure" and "pure," *tum'ah* and *taharah*—and, by extension, the laws of *niddah* and Family Purity—often evoke a negative response. Why, it is asked, must a woman be stigmatized as *tamei*, "impure"? Why should she be made to feel inferior about the natural processes of her body?

It might be said that, at the bottom, these objections arise from a fundamental misunderstanding. *Tum'ah* and *taharah* are, above all, spiritual and not physical concepts.

The laws of *tum'ah*, *niddah* and *mikvah* belong to the category of commandments in the Torah known as *chukkim*—Divine "decrees" for which no reason is given. They are not logically comprehensible, like the laws against robbery or murder, or those commandments that serve as memorials to events in our national past such as Passover and Sukkot. The laws of *tum'ah* and *taharah* are supra-rational, "above" reason. And it is precisely because they are of such high spiritual level, beyond what intellect can comprehend, that they affect an elevated part of the soul, a part of the soul that transcends reason entirely.

But even if the human mind can't understand these Divine decrees logically, we can nevertheless try to understand them spiritually and search for their inner meaning and significance. In this endeavor, the teachings of chassidic philosophy are of invaluable aid, for the study of Chassidut reveals the inner aspect of Torah, its "soul," and can guide us through realms where unaided human intellect cannot reach. Chassidism strives for the direct perception of G-dliness underlying everything, and illuminates the spiritual sources of all physical phenomena.

Tum'ah as the Absence of Holiness

Chassidic teaching explains that in essence, *tum'ah*, "spiritual impurity," is definable as the "absence of holiness." Holiness is called "life," "vitality"; it is that which is united with and emanates from the source of all life, the Creator. Chassidic philosophy further elucidates that true union with G-d, true holiness, means that one's own independent existence is in a state of *bittul*, "nullification" to G-d.[2] On the other hand, that which is distant or separated from its source is called "death" and "impurity." According to Torah law, death is the principal cause of all *tum'ah*; the highest magnitude of *tum'ah* comes from contact with a dead body.

The forces of evil are, in kabbalistic and chassidic terminology, the *sitra achara*, the "other side." They are what is "outside," what is far from G-d's presence and holiness. They flourish in the realm where He is most concealed and least felt, where there is least holiness. In a place where G-d is least felt, there is naturally more room for "opposition" to Him. Spiritually speaking, what is most evil and most impure in a person is, above all, the assertion of self: one pushes G-d's presence away and creates a void, a vacuum where His presence should be.

That is the deeper meaning, according to chassidic teaching, of the phrase "to cause a *chilul Hashem*," to desecrate G-d's name: it means to make a *chalal* (void), a place empty of His presence. Holiness is synonymous with *bittul*: it has no sense of any true existence independent of G-d. That is why, our sages tell us, arrogance is equivalent to idolatry—for idolatry, in essence, means that something is regarded as independent of the Creator and asserts itself in place of Him.

Susan Handelman, PhD. Dr. Handelman is a Chicago native and professor of English at Bar Ilan University. She is the author of *Fragments of Redemption*, *Slayers of Moses*, and *Make Yourself a Teacher*.
[1] *Likkutei Sichot* of the Lubavitcher Rebbe, vol. 8, pp. 72, 85.

[2] *Tanya*, part 1, chapter 6: "So, too, are all the utterances and thoughts which are not directed towards G-d and His will and service. For this is the meaning of *sitra achara*, 'the other side,' i.e., not the side of holiness. For the holy side is nothing but the indwelling and extension of the holiness of the Holy One, blessed be He, and He dwells only on such a thing that abnegates itself *(batel)* completely to Him . . ."

Hence, if we strip the words "pure" and "impure" of their physical connotations, and perceive their true spiritual meaning, we see that what they really signify is the presence or absence of holiness.

An Important Distinction Between Two Types of *Tum'ah*

At this point we must ask: why must *tum'ah* exist at all? What purpose can it have in G-d's creation?

"The Almighty has created one thing opposite the other," the Book of Ecclesiastes tells us, and as chassidic teaching interprets this verse, everything in the realm of holiness has its counterpart in the realm of unholiness.

On the one hand, these opposing realms are created so that we may have "free choice" in our behavior. On a deeper level, as Chassidism explains, when we reject the evil and choose the good and, moreover, when we further transform the evil itself into good, we effect an elevation not only in ourselves but in the entire world, bringing it closer to its ultimate perfection.

Hence, the ultimate purpose of *tum'ah*, the "other side," is for us to achieve higher levels. As the well-known chassidic saying has it, "Every descent is for the purpose of a greater ascent," and all concealments of G-d make way for a greater revelation. When the soul comes down to this world, for example, to be vested in a material body, it undergoes an incomparable descent from its previous purely spiritual existence. The purpose of this descent, though, is that the soul may rise even higher in its apprehension of G-d and attain a more elevated rank than it had before it descended to this world. It can attain this elevation only through the vehicle of the body, through serving G-d in this lower physical world.

On the one hand, there is concealment and impurity in this lowly material world; on the other hand, only through its struggles here can the soul rise higher.

We must distinguish, then, between two types of *tum'ah*, two types of "descent." There is the *tum'ah* that we ourselves create when we intentionally push

G-d's presence away and create a void; and there is the *tum'ah* that G-d creates as part of nature.

This distinction is crucial to our understanding of *niddah* (laws pertaining to menstruation). The *tum'ah*, the impurity that attaches to a sin, is a void we create and by which we degrade ourselves. The *tum'ah* of *niddah*, however, is a built-in part of a woman's natural monthly cycle. Her "descent" from a peak level of potential holiness (i.e., where the creation of a new life is possible) does not mean that she is, G-d forbid, "sinful" or "degraded," "inferior" or "stigmatized." On the contrary, precisely because there is such holiness involved in a woman's possession of the G-dly power to create, as if *ex nihilo*, a new life within her body, there is the possibility for greater *tum'ah*—but also a great elevation.

Let us try to understand further the idea that the more holiness, the more opportunity there is for the forces of impurity to enter. This is no contradiction to what was stated earlier—that the forces of the "other side" can flourish in the absence of holiness. The forces of evil are also called *kelipot*, "husks" or "shells," not only because they cover over and conceal the inner sparks of holiness that gives life to all things, but also because—like the husks or peels of a fruit—they can derive whatever life they have only from this inner spark, the truly living part. When separated from the inner part, they have no more sustenance and "die."

An excess of holiness can provide "room" for the extraneous forces to derive sustenance, just as, for example, if a barrel is filled to the top, some water will spill over and water weeds as well.

In this light we can further understand the explanation of the Kotzker Rebbe[3] that *tum'ah* can set in only where holiness has been and gone. We can connect this with our understanding of the kind of *tum'ah* that is part of *niddah*.

The Torah says that when a woman gives birth, she is in a state of *niddah* for a variable amount of time: if

---

[3] *Sefer HaLikkutim—Dach* "Tzemach Tzedek," vol. 6, s.v. Niddah.

the child is male, she will be *tamei* for seven days, and if female, fourteen days.

Why should there be *tum'ah* at childbirth? The Kotzker Rebbe explains that *tum'ah* can set in only when holiness departs. As the Talmud tells us, G-d is directly involved with every childbirth and does not delegate any powers to His "messengers." Thus, there is a very great level of holiness at birth: the birth of a child involves one of the most sublime powers of G-d, the ability to create *ex nihilo*—something from nothing. After birth, this intense holiness, this powerful force of G-d, "departs" and there is greater potential for *tum'ah*.

One might conjecture further that the reason the birth of a female involves a longer period of *niddah* is that a female contains within her the G-dly power to create yet another new life from "nothing." Because of this higher potential for holiness, there can be more *tum'ah*.

The same is true of a woman's monthly cycle. Every month, this great potential for holiness, a woman's potential to engage in the sublime power of creation, reaches a peak in her body (an "ascent"). When the potential is not fulfilled and the holiness departs, the now-lifeless remnants leave the body. And this "descent" is susceptible to *tum'ah*. It is precisely because of the high level of G-dliness involved in the procreative process that *tum'ah* can occur at all.

But here again, this "descent" into *niddah* is for the purpose of a higher ascent, through purification in the *mikvah* and a new cycle of building up to a higher level of holiness the next month. The *mikvah*—as will be presently explained—enables one to ascend even higher than the previous month.

In this sense the *mikvah* and the monthly cycle of a woman may be compared to Shabbat and the weekly cycle of every Jew. The alternation of the holy day of Shabbat with the mundane days of the week is the same cycle of ascent and descent, reenacted every seven days. The six mundane days lead up to Shabbat, during which the world becomes elevated, purified, ascends to its source. Every Jew then receives

an "extra soul," which he loses as the Shabbat departs and he must "go down" again into the struggles of the coming week. It is the very struggle to purify ourselves and the world we confront during the six days that becomes elevated on the Shabbat, and enables us to ascend higher and higher every week, in constant progression.

Or, let us take another cycle: the daily alternation of sleeping and waking. According to Torah law, every person upon awakening must wash his hands, to remove the "impure spirit" that adheres to them during sleep. In sleep, there is a "departure of holiness" from the body—the soul, it is said, "ascends to its source" above. Again, this "natural law" allows for impurity to set in. Our hands are *tamei* upon awakening, to be sure, but they are not "evil." The same is true of *tum'ah* during a woman's monthly "natural low." It is the result of a departure of holiness, but not a state of degradation, inferiority or shame.

Rabbi Menachem Mendel Schneerson, the Lubavitcher Rebbe, offers an even more profound understanding of the inner nature of these "lows," these descents. Since, he says, the descent is in fact a necessary preparation for the ascent, and its ultimate purpose is the ascent, the descent is nothing other than a part of the ascent itself. The Rebbe explains[4] why the Torah, in speaking of all the journeys of the Jews in the desert, also describes the places where they rested as "journeys." Since the resting was a preparation for the journey that followed, the resting places are in fact part of the journey onward. Or as in our previous example: sleep gives strength to elevate oneself even more the following day, and is thus part of that ascent itself—though it appears to be a lower state for the body.

And on a broader level, the same is true, the Rebbe explains,[5] of the exile of the Jewish people among the nations. If the exile were only for the purpose of punishing us for our sins, it should have lessened with time. Instead, it grows worse from day to day. (The concealment and darkness, however, are a prepara-

---

[4] *Likkutei Sichot*, vol. 6, Pekudei.
[5] *Likkutei Sichot*, vol. 2, pp. 358, 360–363.

tion for—and their ultimate purpose is—a great revelation, the great light that will come in the era of Moshiach; and so the closer we approach that great light, the thicker the darkness becomes.) The inner purpose of the exile is that, through refining ourselves and the world, we will ultimately attain a higher level of holiness and unity with G-d than existed even during the times of the First Temple.

A Comparison with the Moon

In essence, these "natural lows"—absences of holiness that G-d has created within the monthly cycle of a woman, the weekly cycle of Shabbat, the nightly cycle of sleep, or the entire lifecycle of the Jewish people as a whole—are, in their innermost sense, all parts of the process of spiritual ascent.

Nor is the connection between these different cycles artificial. The Talmud compares the Jewish people to the moon, for just as the moon waxes and wanes every month, so too do the Jews undergo phases of concealment and renewal in exile and redemption. The appearance of the new moon, Rosh Chodesh, is a minor holiday, marking the beginning of a new month. And this day is also a special holiday for women, given to them as a reward for not participating in the making and worship of the Golden Calf. A woman's body, of course, also follows a monthly cycle, and chassidic teaching illumines a deeper correspondence between the cycle of *niddah* and the new moon.

The third Lubavitcher Rebbe (the "Tzemach Tzedek") explains[6] that on Rosh Chodesh the moon is renewed, "purified," and again "unites" with the sun; it again receives its reflection. This union of the sun and the moon on Rosh Chodesh corresponds to the union of man and woman after the days of *niddah* are over. And in the same way that a woman is renewed monthly, so will the Jewish people be renewed at the time of their redemption, which will culminate in their higher union with G-d.

As the Talmud states, when the Jews were exiled, the *Shechinah*, the "indwelling presence" of G-d, went into exile with them. And as the Tzemach Tzedek points out, the Hebrew letters of the word *niddah* also mean *nod Hei*, "G-d wanders." He is in exile with the people of Israel.

Hence the reunion of the sun and the moon on Rosh Chodesh reflects the union of man and woman, and of G-d and the Jewish people whose relationship is compared to that of husband and wife.

Understanding *Mikvah*

We have seen that these natural descents are aspects of ascent. Why, however, must this process be accompanied by immersion in a *mikvah*, and what has water to do with changing one's status from *tamei*, "impure," to *tahor*, "pure"?

The chassidic masters explain[7] that in progressing from one level to another, there has to be a period of "nothingness in between." For example, when a seed is planted in the ground, it must first disintegrate, lose its first existence, in order to be able to flower. To reach a higher state, one must first lose or nullify his previous state.

This is the inner purpose of the *mikvah*: to enable one to attain this state of *bittul*, "nullification," the "nothingness in between" the two progressive levels. As chassidic teaching points out,[8] the letters of the Hebrew word for *bittul*, when rearranged, spell *tevilah*—"immersion"—a further indication of their spiritual interconnection.

To fulfill the mitzvah of *mikvah*, one must immerse completely, be entirely enveloped by the waters. This total immersion of self means losing one's independent existence, going out from oneself, elevating oneself by becoming a vessel for holiness. Maimonides writes in his code of Jewish Law, the *Mishneh Torah*, that this immersion requires the intent of the heart, the intent to purify oneself spiritually from all

---

6 *Sefer HaLikkutim—Dach* "Tzemach Tzedek," vol. 6, s.v. Niddah, pp. 38–40.

7 *Yom Tov Shel Rosh HaShanah* 5666, Discourse 2 (beginning *Zeh HaYom*).

8 *Likkutei Sichot*, vol. 1, pp. 4–5; Siddur, *Kavanot HaMikvah*, end.

wrongful thoughts and bad traits, to bring one's soul into "the waters of pure understanding."

Chassidut makes a further illuminating connection between this concept of *mikvah* and the nature of the great flood that occurred in the days of Noah.[9] Why, the question is asked, was water the chosen instrument for removing the wicked from the world, and why did the flood have to last for such a long time, forty days and forty nights? Surely if G-d simply wanted to punish the sinners, He could have done so immediately.

The answer, chassidic teaching explains, is that the flood was not just a punishment, but also a purification for the world. It completely enveloped the earth, and its forty days and forty nights correspond to the measure of forty *se'ah* of water required to make a ritually fit *mikvah*. The waters of the flood cleansed the world by immersion in the same way one is purified by immersion in the waters of the *mikvah*. The separation and removal of all extraneous and undesirable elements has the ultimate purpose of bringing the world (and a person) to a higher level.

And this brings us back to the beginning: the ultimate cause of *tum'ah* is separation from G-d; and to be united means to be "nullified" to Him, to lose the sense of one's independent existence and be attached to one's source.

According to Torah law, however,[10] one is purified only upon leaving the *mikvah*, not while inside it. As the Lubavitcher Rebbe explains,[11] this means that the ultimate purpose of our elevated spiritual states, our "ascents," is not to be removed from the world; the purpose of creation is "to make a dwelling-place for G-d in the lower worlds." That is, we must affect the "outside"—bring holiness into the very lowest levels. Despite one's high spiritual state, one is not purified until "going out"—until affecting the "outside."

In practical terms, this means that "the essential thing is the deed"—action in the world, in the refinement of one's inner self, and also one's particular share of the world, to make a "dwelling-place for G-d." Just as the elevated state of Shabbat is called the "source of blessing" for the entire week, and Rosh Chodesh is the same for the entire month, so too the purification of oneself in the *mikvah* should permeate all one's thoughts, words and actions when one leaves the *mikvah*.

Chassidut further explains[12] that the performance of mitzvot provides "garments" for the soul. The moment of conception is particularly crucial, for the frame of mind and purity of the parents determines, to a great extent, what manner of "garments" that soul will have. In sum, not only do the laws of Family Purity have a deep spiritual meaning, but as the Lubavitcher Rebbe explains,[13] the fulfillment of this mitzvah has a profound, direct influence on both the spiritual and the physical health of one's children—and by extension, on all Jewish generations to eternity.

Total Immersion: A Mikvah Anthology [Jason Aronson Publishers, Northvale NJ, 1996], pp. 61–68
Reprinted with permission of the author

---

9 *Likkutei Sichot*, loc. cit.; *Torah Ohr*, Noach, discourse beginning *Mayim Rabim*.

10 Maimonides, *Mishneh Torah, Hil. Avot HaTum'ah* 6:16.

11 *Likkutei Sichot*, vol. 1, pp. 14–15.

12 *Tanya*, part 1, end of ch. 2; part 4, sec. 3.

13 *Likkutei Sichot*, vol. 13, pp. 258–262; see also references there.

MY BELOVED *MECHITZAH*

BY JOELLE KEENE

I didn't know these lovebirds, but there they were, unmistakably just that, standing at Sabbath morning services amid a sea of men and women with his arm around her waist, she leaning into his shoulder and the two of them swaying gently back and forth to the sound of the prayers. How nice, I thought, that they're learning Torah together. Where it will take them no one can say, but they're together on a great and splendid journey.

Since then my own journey, begun in part in that same room, has led me to a place where I could not possibly stand in prayer with my husband's arm around my waist. Praying might just be the most important thing we humans do, setting the stage for all of the rest of our behavior, but it is not the easiest. For most of us it takes tremendous concentration, a great erasing of everything outside and at the same time a bringing of everything we are into one small moment framed by a particular piece of ancient text. The problem is that love is so powerful—especially love for a spouse, but even premonitions of love like crush and curiosity—that in any given moment, prayer cannot compete.

Perhaps that's why Jewish tradition invented something called the *mechitzah*, surely the most widely maligned—I would say misunderstood—of any institution in Judaism today. A *mechitzah*, literally "separation," is a screen or other barrier in a traditional synagogue that separates women from men during worship; in this separation, some say, the women are demeaned. The religious idea is that men should not be able to see women while they're praying, for if they do, their prayer will not be heard. To me, that's not demeaning; it's a statement of obvious fact. It's hard enough to pray when you're alone.

Try this exercise: Imagine that you need to speak with G-d. Imagine that you need something very, very badly, and that G-d really is all-powerful and the only One Who can grant it to you. Or imagine that you've done something terribly wrong and need some great forgiveness, or that your first child has just been born and you want to offer thanks. Close your eyes. Find the words. Now try, really try, to send them up to heaven.

Could you do this while cuddling with your spouse? Could you do it while ogling the latest beauty to join the synagogue, or that guy you see each Saturday who's so cute it makes you laugh? Maybe you could—everyone's different—but I strive mightily just to sense G-d's listening when I pray.

Sometimes I picture great tree limbs, an overarching Father seeing every word and deed, or see myself as human clay addressing Him who formed it. Or I conjure up an awesome, holy Throne bathed in rays of light, considering with mercy my so tiny, distant plea. Yet with all these tools and more, still it's hard. We need all the help we can get.

And so we have a curtain—to center us perhaps, to make a place that forms a space where we can pray. There are as many kinds of *mechitzahs* as there are synagogues—I've seen sleek wood carved in modern shapes, and balconies where height is the *mechitzah*, and gathered lace on curtain rods that roll.

But all *mechitzahs* hold us back from one another and group our prayers by gender rising heavenward. Perhaps this helps G-d hear us, too; perhaps we sound clearer, are more ourselves, unmediated by our opposites. Judaism loves categories and celebrates them every way—night and day, milk and meat, Sabbath versus holidays and ordinary days—and gender's no exception.

The men's section is front and center because men have more ritual commandments in the synagogue, while women are responsible for bringing Torah into the home. Synagogue becomes one place where we can be with our own gender, something not without a pleasure all its own.

So you can say the *mechitzah* exists to keep women out, that the genders are identical and all else is cultural conceit. For many of us, though, the *mechitzah* opens a door in, perhaps into a more concentrated experience of who we are and certainly into the presence of G-d where holiness and much direction lie. In prayer, we reach outside our earthly yearnings and search for something different, something that ennobles us, sets our sights high and improves us from the inside out. In love, we find an outlet for those improvements, for our goodness, kindness, generosity. Love is arguably our most G-d-like activity, and also our greatest earthly reward; in its physical expression, it is said to bring G-d's presence to rest on us directly. Each paves the way for the other; I'm a better wife for praying, and drawn closer to G-d through the love my marriage brings. Each creates a chasm we can cross.

And so I wonder again about those Sabbath lovebirds, trying to make their yearnings heard above the din of daily life, studying Torah and singing psalms, arms linked, perhaps journeying down paths deep into wisdom.

There's no one way to pray, and none of us can say for sure whose prayers are heard. But perhaps their love has grown so much that they can't sit together in services anymore, or their love for G-d has grown in such a way that they don't want to. Maybe it would take more than a curtain to keep them apart—and perhaps just a curtain to link them

Reprinted with permission from *OLAM Magazine*.

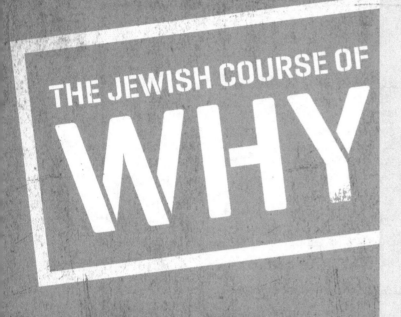

THE JEWISH COURSE OF WHY

LESSON THREE

JLI

JEWISH LEARNING INSTITUTE

1. Why are there so many Jews in Hollywood?

Economics of Discrimination

Text 1

Neal Gabler, *An Empire of Their Own: How the Jews Invented Hollywood* [New York: Crown Publishers, 1988], pp. 5–6

Neal Gabler
1950–

American journalist, historian and film critic. Gabler holds advanced degrees in both film and American culture from the University of Michigan. He has authored four books, including *An Empire of Their Own: How the Jews Invented Hollywood* (1988), and *Life the Movie: How Entertainment Conquered Reality* (1998).

The movie industry held out a number of blandishments to these Jews, not the least of which that it admitted them. There were no social barriers in a business as new and faintly disreputable as the movies were in the early days. There were none of the impediments imposed by the loftier professions and the family entrenched businesses to keep Jews and other undesirables out. Financial barriers were lower too and that attracted Jews and other entrepreneurs. In fact, one could conceivably open a theater for less than four hundred dollars.

The Jews also had a special compatibility with the industry, one that gave them certain advantages over their competitors. For one thing, having come primarily from fashion and retail, they understood public taste and were masters at gauging market swings, at merchandising, at pirating away customers and beating the competition. For another, as immigrants themselves, they had a peculiar sensitivity to the dreams and aspirations of other immigrants and working-class families, two overlapping groups that made up a significant portion of the early moviegoing audience. . . .

If the Jews were proscribed from entering the real corridors of gentility and status in America, the movies offered an ingenious option. Within the studios and on the screen, the Jews could simply create a new country—an empire of their own, so to speak—where they would not only be admitted, but would govern as well. They would create its values and myths, its traditions and archetypes. It would be an America where fathers were strong, families stable, people attractive, resilient, resourceful and decent. This was *their* America and its invention may be their most enduring legacy.

Laughing Matter (Optional)

Text 2

Steve Lipman, "Jews Serious When It Comes to Humor,"
The Jewish Week, September 8, 2013

Buried in the Pew Research Center's serious findings about Jewish belief and Jewish practice in the United States is one not-so-serious fact—about Jewish humor.

According to the "Portrait of Jewish Americans" study, which was released last week, 42 percent of American Jews consider "having a good sense of humor" to be "an essential part of what being Jewish means."

That places humor a single percentage point behind "caring about Israel." And it's far ahead of such other indications of Jewish identity as "being part of a Jewish community" or "observing Jewish law."

Text 3

"Jews and Humor," *Religion & Ethics Newsweekly*, January 10, 2014, www.pbs.org

Tim Kazurinsky
1950–

American actor and screenwriter. Kazurinsky is known for his tenure as both a writer and featured player on *Saturday Night Live* (1981–1984) as well as for his role as Officer Sweetchuck in the *Police Academy* film series. He is a mainstay of the Chicago theatre scene.

Ruth Wisse
1936–

Professor of Yiddish literature and professor of comparative literature at Harvard University. Wisse was born in Czernowitz, Ukraine, and grew up in Montreal, Canada. Her books include *Jews and Power*, *The Modern Jewish Canon*, and *No Joke: Making Jewish Humor* (2013).

Tim J. Kazurinsky: As somebody once said, "Tragedy plus time equals comedy," and given that equation it fits right in. In terms of tragedy, the Jews have kind of got a headlock on that.

[Bob] Faw: And that gulf between being God's anointed and all that misery, says [Professor] Ruth Wisse—that incongruity is at the core of Jewish humor.

Professor Wisse: Some people call it laughter through tears. I would suggest you could call it laughter through fears. Humor, being able to laugh at this, is a way of being able to maintain this delicate balance without going mad, you know. Humor is the one form that gives you the last word.

Text 4

Talmud, Ta'anit 22a

אַדְהָכִי וְהָכִי אָתוּ הַנָּךְ תְּרֵי אָחִי. אָמַר לֵיהּ: הַנָּךְ נַמִי בְּנֵי עַלְמָא דְאָתֵי נִינְהוּ.

אֲזַל לְגַבַּיְיהוּ. אָמַר לְהוּ: מַאי עוּבְדַיְיכוּ?

אָמְרוּ לֵיהּ: אִינְשֵׁי בְּדוּחֵי אֲנָן, מַבְדְחִינָן עֲצִיבֵי.

W hile [Rabbi Beroka and Elijah the Prophet were conversing in the marketplace,] two brothers passed by. Elijah remarked, "These two also have a share in the World to Come."

Rabbi Beroka approached them and asked, "What is your occupation?"

They replied, "We are comedians; we cheer up those who are sad."

Babylonian Talmud

A literary work of monumental proportions that draws upon the legal, spiritual, intellectual, ethical, and historical traditions of Judaism. The 37 tractates of the Babylonian Talmud contain the teachings of the Jewish sages from the period after the destruction of the 2nd Temple through the 5th century CE. It has served as the primary vehicle for the transmission of the Oral Law and the education of Jews over the centuries; it is the entry point for all subsequent legal, ethical, and theological Jewish scholarship.

For What?

Text 5

Rabbi Levi Yitschak of Berditchev, cited in *Pitgamin Kadishin*, p. 16

יֵדַע הָאָדָם בִּידִיעָה בְּרוּרָה וּצְלוּלָה, שֶׁכָּל נְסִיעוֹת וַהֲלִיכוֹת הָאָדָם לְאֵיזֶה מְקוֹמוֹת, הַכֹּל לֹא בְּמִקְרֶה הוּא חָלִילָה, רַק מֵאֵת ה' הָיְתָה זֹּאת, וּבְהַשְׁגָּחָה פְּרָטִית . . . וּכְמוֹ שֶׁאָמַר הַבַּעַל שֵׁם טוֹב זְכוּתוֹ יָגֵן עָלֵינוּ: "מֵה' מִצְעֲדֵי גֶבֶר כּוֹנָנוּ" (תְּהִלִּים לז,כג), דְּהַיְינוּ שֶׁהַשֵּׁם יִתְבָּרֵךְ עוֹשֶׂה לְהָאָדָם חֵשֶׁק לֵילֵךְ וְלִנְסוֹעַ לְאֵיזֶה מָקוֹם, וְכַוָּונָתוֹ יִתְבָּרֵךְ הוּא . . . שֶׁיַּעֲשֶׂה שָׁם הָאָדָם הַלָּזֶה אֵיזֶה עוּבְדָּא מֵעֲבוֹדָתוֹ יִתְבָּרֵךְ כְּדֵי שֶׁיְּתַקֵּן שָׁם הָאָדָם אֵיזֶה תִּיקוּן הַצָּרִיךְ לוֹ, כְּנִזְכָּר לְעֵיל.

וְעַל כֵּן חַיָּיב הָאָדָם לִרְאוֹת אֶת עַצְמוֹ בִּהְיוֹתוֹ בָּא אֶל אֵיזֶה מָקוֹם לִיתֵּן אֶל לִבּוֹ מַה זֶּה וְעַל מַה זֶּה הֵבִיא אוֹתוֹ הַשֵּׁם יִתְבָּרֵךְ לְכָאן, וַדַּאי לֹא לְחִנָּם הוּא.

Rabbi Levi Yitschak of Berditchev
1740–1809

Chasidic rebbe. Rabbi Levi Yitschak was one of the foremost disciples of the Magid of Mezeritch and later went on to serve as rabbi in Berditchev, Ukraine. His Chasidic commentary on the Torah, *Kedushat Levi*, is a classic that is popular to this day. He is known in Jewish history and folklore for his all-encompassing love, compassion, and advocacy on behalf of the Jewish people.

We should clearly recognize that our travels to different places are not random, God forbid, but specifically directed by God. . . . The Ba'al Shem Tov, of righteous memory, explained the verse (Psalms 37:23), "God establishes the steps of man," to mean that God imparts the desire to a person to travel to a specific place, His intention being that the person should engage in a particular divine service . . . thereby rectifying what this person must rectify.

Therefore, when we come to a particular place, we must take this to heart and ask ourselves, "Why am I here? For what purpose did God bring me here?" It is certainly not for naught.

LEARNING EXERCISE 1

How can you leverage your position of influence (through employment or otherwise) to reinforce faith, goodness, and moral values?

_____

_____

_____

_____

_____

_____

KEY POINTS

- Jewish immigrants to America in the early twentieth century, denied admission into many industries, turned to the movie business, where social and financial barriers were low. They subsequently brought in more of their own and eventually became known for their disproportionate presence in Hollywood.

- God directs our steps for a purpose. Jews in any industry need to leverage their position of influence to promote good values.

2. Why do we believe that Jews cannot convert out of Judaism?

A Jew Is a Jew

Text 6

Rabbi Shlomo Duran, *Responsa 89* 📖

Rabbi Shlomo Duran
(Rashbash)
ca. 1400–1470

Halachic authority. Born in Algiers, Rashbash was the son and successor of Rabbi Shimon ben Tsemach Duran, and like his father, he authored many responsa. In 1437, he composed a defense of the Talmud, which was published under the title *Milchemet Chovah*. Additionally, Duran also defended Judaism against Christian theological polemics in his treatise, *Setirat Emunat Hanotsrim*.

בְּנֵי אֵלּוּ הַמְשׁוּמָדִים, הַנִּקְרָאִים אָנוּסִים, הָעֲרֵלִים, כְּשֶׁבָּאִים לַחֲזוֹר בִּתְשׁוּבָה, צָרִיךְ לְבָרֵר דִּינָם בְּעִנְיַן תְּשׁוּבָתָם וּמִילָתָם וּטְבִילָתָם.

וְאוֹמֵר שֶׁדִּינָם הוּא כְּיִשְׂרָאֵל לְכָל דִּבְרֵיהֶם, דְּהֲלָכָה רוֹוַחַת הִיא בְּיִשְׂרָאֵל, דְּיִשְׂרָאֵל מְשׁוּמָּד אַף עַל פִּי שֶׁחָטָא יִשְׂרָאֵל [הוּא] כִּדְאִיתָא בִּבְכוֹרוֹת בְּפֶרֶק עַד כַּמָּה (ל,ב), וּבְסַנְהֶדְרִין בְּפֶרֶק נִגְמַר הַדִּין (מד,א) . . . וּבָנָיו כְּמוֹהוּ אִם נוֹלַד מִמְשׁוּמֶדֶת, כִּדְאִיתָא בְּפֶרֶק הָאוֹמֵר בְּקִדּוּשִׁין (סח,ב), וּבִיבָמוֹת בְּפֶרֶק קַמָּא (יז,א), וּבְפֶרֶק ב' (כג,א), וּבְפֶרֶק הַחוֹלֵץ (מז,ב). . .

וַאֲפִילוּ עַד כַּמָּה דוֹרוֹת עַד סוֹף הָעוֹלָם, יִשְׂרָאֵל חֲשַׁבִינַן לֵיהּ . . .

וְאַחַר שֶׁנִּתְבָּרֵר שֶׁאֵין לָהֶם דִּין גֵּרִים, אִם כֵּן אֵין לְהוֹדִיעָם קְצָת מִצְווֹת קַלּוֹת וַחֲמוּרוֹת וְעוֹנְשָׁן. וְהַדָּבָר הַזֶּה מוּכְרָע מֵעַצְמוֹ הוּא. שֶׁאִם תֹּאמַר שֶׁהוּא אֵינוֹ רוֹצֶה לְקַבְּלָם, אִם כֵּן נִפְטוֹר אוֹתוֹ מֵהֶם כְּגוֹי? חָלִילָה וְחָס שֶׁלֹּא עָלְתָה עַל דַּעַת, לְפִי שֶׁהוּא מְחוּיָּיב בָּהֶם כָּמוֹנוּ. וְאֵין לְיִרְאוּ וּלְבַהֲלוּ אֲבָל לְמָשְׁכוֹ חֶסֶד, וּמוּשְׁבָּע וְעוֹמֵד מִסִּינַי הוּא.

We need to clarify the law regarding the uncircumcised progeny of the *conversos*, known as *anusim*, who wish to return to Judaism.

These people are Jews in every respect. It is a widely known law that apostate Jews, "although they have sinned, are still

Jews," as clearly stated in the Talmud (Bechorot 30b; Sanhedrin 44a). . . . The same applies to their children, if they are born from a Jewess, even an apostate, as clearly stated in the Talmud (Kidushin 68b; Yevamot 17a; 23a; 47b). . . . Even if this were to continue for innumerable generations, the children would still be Jews. . . .

Having established that these people are not converts, we should not initiate them as we do converts—that is, by informing them about commandments that require less effort, those that involve more hardship, and the consequences of not observing them. We engage converts in this process to help them decide if they truly desire to embrace the Jewish path. But there is no reason to do so with the *conversos* because they have no option to turn away. They are foresworn from Sinai to observe the commandments like the rest of us. We should not make them anxious about embracing Judaism; we ought to draw them closer with loving-kindness.

A Divine Calling

Text 7

Joshua Malina, in Judea and Ruth Pearl, eds., *I Am Jewish: Personal Reflections Inspired by the Last Words of Daniel Pearl* [Woodstock, Vt: Jewish Lights Pub., 2004], p. 10

For me the statement, "I am Jewish" is no different from the statement "I am."

Joshua Malina
1966–

Actor and producer. Malina was born in New York City. His parents, Fran and Robert Malina, were founding members of Young Israel of Scarsdale. The name Malina originates from the Polish word for raspberry. He is known for his performances in *The West Wing*, *Scandal*, and *A Few Good Men*.

Subtle Expression (Optional)

Text 8a

Abigail Pogrebin, *Stars of David: Prominent Jews Talk about Being Jewish* [New York: Broadway, 2005], pp. 266–268

Abigail Pogrebin
1965–

Jewish-American author. Pogrebin began her career in broadcast journalism as a producer on PBS, and then on CBS News' *60 Minutes.* She has written columns in numerous newspapers and magazines, and has authored two books: *Stars of David: Prominent Jews Talk about Being Jewish,* and *One and the Same: My Life as an Identical Twin and What I've Learned About Everyone's Struggle to be Singular.*

Ruth Reichl
1948–

American chef and food writer. Reichl is the coproducer of *Gourmet's Diary of a Foodie,* the host of PBS's *Gourmet's Adventures With Ruth,* and the final editor-in-chief of the now shuttered *Gourmet* magazine. In 2009, she published *Gourmet Today,* a cookbook teeming with more than 1,000 recipes.

Despite Ruth Reichl's varied culinary exploits as restaurant critic for *The New York Times* (1993–1999) and as editor in chief of *Gourmet* magazine since then, she has never had a great Jewish meal. "It's the only food I don't much like. . . ."

"My parents didn't belong to a temple," she says. "But when I was in eighth grade, my mother announced that she thought I should get some Jewish background. So she went and joined Temple Emanu-El. And she came home and announced that I was going to go to Sunday school and be confirmed. And my father said, 'How did you join the temple?' And my mother said she put down their names on the membership, 'Mr. and Mrs. Ernst Reichl.' And my father said, 'You will go and take my name off; I will not belong to a temple.' It's the only time in my life I ever saw him really put his foot down. . . .

"The next year, they sent me to a French Catholic boarding school in Canada, so I finished my confirmation by mail: I wrote my confirmation thesis on why I didn't believe in God." ...

Reichl says her mother was pleased that Ruth's first husband, Doug, wasn't Jewish. (Her second husband, Michael Singer, is.) "Michael would tell you that my parents were self-loathing Jews," Reichl says. "I don't think that's true. But my mother would probably have been happier if she herself wasn't Jewish." ...

Text 8b

Abigail Pogrebin, ibid., pp. 269–270

I ask if it would give her pause were [her son] Nicholas to end up with a non-Jewish spouse. Reichl shakes her head: "No. I expect he will. What will give me pause—what would make me unhappy—is if he were ever not to identify himself as a Jew. But that's not going to happen."

And if he decides to raise his children as Christians? Reichl responds by relating a personal story that clearly shook her up: Her father's only sister, Lili, had "experienced part of the Holocaust," but escaped to America and decided to convert to Protestantism. Lili's son, Robert—Reichl's first cousin—married a Protestant. Robert's son, Mark, married a Catholic. Mark was speaking to Reichl [about property in Europe]. . . . And I said, 'Wait a minute: Are you telling me that your father doesn't want your in-laws to know that he's Jewish? And he said, 'My father's not Jewish.'"

Reichl gets wide-eyed with anger—"I mean, I was *stunned*: I said, 'I beg your pardon, but he was *one hundred percent* Jewish; he was *certainly* Jewish enough for Hitler; as would *you* have been.' And I hung up the phone and I haven't spoken to him since. I was stunned at how furious I became when he said to me, 'My father's not Jewish.' It just came over me; 'How dare you!? I mean, this is my only living relative of my father and you're telling me he's not a Jew? How *dare* you?'"

I'm curious why she thinks it disturbed her so much. "I think it speaks to everything that is important to me: not denying this kernel of who you are. I loved my Aunt Lili very much; she was this lovely Jewish woman, whether she changed her religion or not."

KEY POINTS

- To be a Jew is not a matter of having certain beliefs, practicing certain rituals, or identifying as a Jew; rather, our Jewishness stems from the fact that we were chosen by God to fulfill a particular mission, and this forms the core of who we are.

3. Why did our ancestors continue to identify as Jews despite being victims of so much suffering through the ages?

Text 9a

Bernard Lewis, in Judea and Ruth Pearl, eds., *I Am Jewish: Personal Reflections Inspired by the Last Words of Daniel Pearl*, [Woodstock, Vt: Jewish Lights Pub., 2004], pp. 102–103

It was more than sixty years ago, but I still vividly remember the occasion and the conversation. It was in the middle of the night, and apart of the routine rumble of shells and bombs, things were relatively quiet. I was on night watch. In the branch of His Majesty's service in which I served, we took turns staying awake, two at a time, all night long, to deal with any emergency that might arise. It so happened that this was a quiet night, and we whiled away the time chatting about nothing in particular. . . .

Suddenly, my colleague George started a new and very different conversation. "Forgive me," he said, "I don't want to intrude, but am I right in thinking that you are Jewish?"

"You are right," I replied, "I am Jewish, and there is nothing to forgive."

Bernard Lewis
1916–

British-American historian. Lewis was born to middle-class Jewish parents in Stoke Newington, London. An expert in the history of Islam and its interaction with the West, he is most noted for his works on the history of the Ottoman Empire. During the Second World War, Lewis served in the Royal Armoured Corps and Intelligence Corps.

"Forgive me," he said again, "but I have the impression that you are not a devout and observant Jew."

"You are right again," I said.

"Then I don't understand," he said. "Why do you bother?"

"Now I don't understand," I said. "What do you mean by that?"

"Let me try to explain," said George. "You must agree that being Jewish is often difficult and sometimes dangerous."

"Yes indeed," I said. One could hardly deny this statement in a branch of the intelligence service in 1942.

"Then I don't understand," said George yet again. "I can see that you may be ready to face persecution or death for your religious beliefs. But if you don't hold or live by those beliefs, then why bother?"

This time I began to understand George's question....

Text 9b

Bernard Lewis, ibid., pp. 103–104

There have always been some who indeed did "not bother," finding the retention dangerous, difficult, or merely burdensome. . . . But for most, even for those whose religious faith is at best tenuous and whose Jewish identity is overshadowed by other, larger identities, denying that Jewish identity would be an act of falsehood, if not to others, then to oneself.

KEY POINTS

- Jews have retained their identity despite much suffering on account of their Jewishness. This phenomenon can be attributed to the feeling that one's Jewish identity is deeply embedded in one's psyche and soul, which results in an unwillingness to betray one's authentic self.

4. Why does a mourner recite *Kaddish*?

For the Deceased

Text 10

Rabbi Adin Even-Israel (Steinsaltz), *HaSiddur Vehatefilah* 1:295 📖

כָּל אָדָם בְּיִשְׂרָאֵל הוּא בְּמוּבָן מְסֻיָּם אֶחָד מֵאֵלֶּה הַנּוֹשְׂאִים וּמְקַיְּמִים אֶת מַלְכוּת ה' בָּעוֹלָם, וּכְדִבְרֵי הַכָּתוּב "אַתֶּם עֵדַי נְאוּם ה'" (יְשַׁעְיָ' מג,י). מִשּׁוּם כָּךְ, חֶסְרוֹנוֹ שֶׁל כָּל אֶחָד מִיִּשְׂרָאֵל יוֹצֵר כִּבְיָכוֹל חָלָל וְחָסֵר בְּמַלְכוּת ה' בָּעוֹלָם. וּכְדֵי לְהַשְׁלִים הַחֶסְרוֹן, אֶת פְּגַם הַמְּצִיאוּת, צְרִיכִים הָאֲחֵרִים לְהִתְגַּבֵּר בְּיֶתֶר שְׂאֵת, וּלְהַכְרִיז שׁוּב בְּשֵׁם עַצְמָם וּבְשֵׁם הַנִּפְטָרִים, "יִתְגַּדַּל וְיִתְקַדַּשׁ".

וְכַאן הוּא גַם מָקוֹר הַהַכָּרָה כִּי אֲמִירַת הַקַּדִּישׁ הִיא עִלּוּי לְנִשְׁמַת הַמֵּת. חֶשְׁבּוֹן מַעֲשָׂיו וּפְעֻלּוֹתָו שֶׁל אָדָם הֵם בְּעִיקָּר הַתַּמְצִית שֶׁל חַיָּיו שֶׁל מַה שֶׁהִצְלִיחַ לַעֲשׂוֹת בִּזְמַן הֱיוֹתוֹ עַל הָאֲדָמָה. אוּלָם, חֶשְׁבּוֹן זֶה אֵינוֹ נִגְמָר תָּמִיד עִם הַמָּוֶות. הַהַעֲרָכָה הַשְּׁלֵמָה שֶׁל אָדָם קְשׁוּרָה לֹא רַק בְּמַה שֶׁהוּא עַצְמוֹ עָשָׂה, אֶלָּא גַם בִּדְבָרִים שֶׁנּוֹצְרוּ וְצָמְחוּ מִכּוֹחוֹ וְעַל יָדוֹ. וּמִשּׁוּם כָּךְ, כַּאֲשֶׁר הַמַּמְשִׁיכִים הַחַיִּים (וּבְיֶתֶר שְׂאֵת – הַבָּנִים וְהַצֶּאֱצָאִים, שֶׁעֶצֶם קִיּוּמָם הָיָה תָּלוּי בְּהוֹרֵיהֶם) עוֹשִׂים מַעֲשִׂים טוֹבִים – הֲרֵי הֵם מַשְׁלִימִים אֶת הַהַעֲרָכָה עַל הָאָדָם, שֶׁאַף שֶׁאֵינוֹ פּוֹעֵל יוֹתֵר בְּעַצְמוֹ בָּעוֹלָם, מַמְשִׁיכִים דְּבָרִים וְנַעֲשִׂים מִכּוֹחוֹ.

וּמִשּׁוּם כָּךְ, אֲמִירַת הַקַּדִּישׁ הִיא עִלּוּי לְנִשְׁמַת הַנִּפְטָר, שֶׁהֲרֵי בִּגְלָלוֹ וְלִשְׁמוֹ מַמְשִׁיכִים וּמוֹסִיפִים לִפְעוֹל בְּתוֹךְ הַמְּצִיאוּת.

Every member of the community of Israel is responsible for establishing and proclaiming God's sovereignty in this world. As the verse states, "You [Israel] are My witnesses, God proclaims" (Isaiah 43:10). Therefore, the absence of a Jewish person creates a void in the expression of God's sovereignty in the world. In order to fill this void, others need to intensify their work and proclaim—on behalf of themselves as well as the deceased—"May His name be exalted and hallowed!"

This is why reciting *Kaddish* elevates the soul of the deceased. While a person's overall accomplishments are defined by what the person achieved while alive, the complete tally of a person's achievements do not conclude at the moment of death. A complete evaluation of a person's accomplishments must also include all that is accomplished as a result of the person's inspiration and actions. Therefore, when those who remain alive (and especially the person's children and descendants, whose very existence is a credit to their forebears) do good deeds, they contribute to the deceased's accomplishments. For although the deceased is no longer active in this world, his or her actions continue to inspire positive deeds and actions.

The recitation of *Kaddish* elevates the soul because God is being exalted in this world due to and in the name of the deceased.

Rabbi Adin Even-Israel (Steinsaltz)
1937–

Talmudist, author, and philosopher. Rabbi Even-Israel is considered one of the foremost Jewish thinkers of the 20th century. Praised by *Time* magazine as a "once-in-a-millennium scholar," he has been awarded the Israel Prize for his contributions to Jewish study. He lives in Jerusalem and is the founder of the Israel Institute for Talmudic Publications, a society dedicated to the translation and elucidation of the Talmud.

For the Mourner

Text 11

The *Kaddish*

יִתְגַּדַּל וְיִתְקַדַּשׁ שְׁמֵהּ רַבָּא, בְּעָלְמָא דִּי בְרָא כִרְעוּתֵהּ . . .

May the Great Name [of God] be exalted and sanctified in the world that He created according to His will. . . .

KEY POINTS

- We all have a responsibility to promote divine awareness, and the death of a loved one creates a void in this respect. Proclaiming God's sovereignty (*Kaddish*), on behalf of and in the name of the deceased, fills this void.

- Through the recitation of *Kaddish*, the mourner affirms that God orchestrates every detail of our existence according to His will. In this way, *Kaddish* helps the mourner move from non-acceptance toward healing.

5. Why do Jews place pebbles on headstones?

6. Why is it not customary to leave flowers at the grave?

Text 12

Rabbi Shalom of Neustadt, *Hilchot Uminhagei Maharash* 490 📖

וּמַה שֶּׁתּוֹלְשִׁין עֵשֶׂב מִן הַקֶּבֶר אוֹ נוֹטְלִין צְרוֹר וּמְשִׂימִין עַל הַמַּצֵּבָה,
אֵינָהּ אֶלָּא מִשּׁוּם כָּבוֹד הַמֵּת לְהַרְאוֹת שֶׁפֹּה הָיוּ עַל קִבְרוֹ.

Our custom to tear grass from the area of a grave or to place a pebble on the headstone is only to bring honor to the deceased by indicating that people were at the grave.

Rabbi Shalom of Neustadt
Ca. 1350–1413

Austrian rabbi and scholar. Rabbi Shalom was born in Wiener Neustadt, a city located south of Vienna, where he went on to serve as rabbi, teaching and mentoring the famed Rabbi Ya'akov Moelin (Maharil). While most of his writings have been lost, his work on Jewish law and custom survives, and in 1977, it was finally published.

KEY POINTS

- By leaving a pebble on a headstone, we indicate that we were present at the gravesite and thereby bring honor to the deceased.

- One suggestion as to why the Jewish custom is not to leave flowers at the grave is that flowers are a form of beautification, and the only way to truly beautify the deceased is to do a mitzvah in his or her merit.

7. Why does Jewish law exempt women from certain ritual obligations that are obligatory for men?

A Matter of Time

Text 13

Mishnah, Kidushin 1:7 📖

Mishnah

The first authoritative work of Jewish law that was codified in writing. The Mishnah contains the oral traditions that were passed down from teacher to student; it supplements, clarifies, and systematizes the commandments of the Torah. Due to the continual persecution of the Jewish people, it became increasingly difficult to guarantee that these traditions would not be forgotten. Rabbi Yehudah Hanasi therefore redacted the Mishnah at the end of the 2nd century. It serves as the foundation for the Talmud.

כָּל מִצְוַת עֲשֵׂה שֶׁהַזְּמַן גְּרָמָה, הָאֲנָשִׁים חַיָּיבִין וְהַנָּשִׁים פְּטוּרוֹת.

וְכָל מִצְוֹת עֲשֵׂה שֶׁלֹּא הַזְּמַן גְּרָמָה, אֶחָד אֲנָשִׁים וְאֶחָד נָשִׁים חַיָּיבִין.

Positive *mitzvot* that are time contingent—men are obligated whereas women are exempt.

Positive *mitzvot* that are not time contingent—both men and women are obligated.

Exposing the Lie

Text 14

Ellen Jane Willis, *Beginning to See the Light* [Minneapolis: University of Minnesota Press, 2012], p. 314

The big lie of male supremacy is that women are less than fully human; the basic task of feminism is to expose that lie and fight it on every level. Yet for all my feminist militance, I was, it seemed, secretly afraid that the lie was true—that my humanity was hopelessly at odds with my ineluctable female sexuality—while the *rebbetsen*, staunch apostle of traditional femininity, did not appear to doubt for a moment that she could be both a woman and a serious person. Which was only superficially paradoxical, for if you were absolutely convinced that the Jewish woman's role was ordained by God, and that it was every bit as important spiritually as the man's, how could you believe the lie?

Ellen Jane Willis
1941–2006

American feminist and journalist. Willis was the founder of Redstockings, a short-lived radical feminist group, and her writings were often featured in *New York Magazine*. Her essays were collected into a number of books such as *Beginning to See the Light* (1981), *No More Nice Girls* (1992), and *Don't Think, Smile! Notes on a Decade of Denial* (1999).

KEY POINTS

- Western thinking revolves around *rights* whereas Jewish law and philosophy revolve around *obligations*. In addition, while Judaism has always championed equality, it emphasizes and thrives upon differentiation of roles and responsibilities. God set up this system of diversity to meet His goals and vision for the world.

- Judaism believes that the unique role of the Jewish woman was ordained by God and is every bit as important as the man's.

8. Why are ten men required for a *minyan*?

Chanah's Prayer (Optional)

Text 15

Talmud, Berachot 31a 📖

כַּמָּה הִלְכְתָא גַּבְרָוָותָא אִיכָּא לְמַשְׁמַע מֵהָנֵי קְרָאֵי דְּחַנָּה (שְׁמוּאֵל א, א,יג).

"וְחַנָּה הִיא מְדַבֶּרֶת עַל לִבָּה" - מִכָּאן לְמִתְפַּלֵּל צָרִיךְ שֶׁיְּכַוֵּין לִבּוֹ.

"רַק שְׂפָתֶיהָ נָעוֹת" - מִכָּאן לַמִּתְפַּלֵּל שֶׁיַּחְתּוֹךְ בִּשְׂפָתָיו.

"וְקוֹלָהּ לֹא יִשָּׁמֵעַ" - מִכָּאן, שֶׁאָסוּר לְהַגְבִּיהַּ קוֹלוֹ בִּתְפִלָּתוֹ.

"וַיַּחְשְׁבֶהָ עֵלִי לְשִׁכֹּרָה" - מִכָּאן, שֶׁשִּׁכּוֹר אָסוּר לְהִתְפַּלֵּל.

How many most important laws can be learned from these verses (I Samuel 1:13) relating to Chanah!

"Chanah was praying in her heart." From this we derive that when we pray we must have heartfelt intention.

"Her lips were moving." From this we derive that when we pray we must recite the words distinctly with our lips.

"But her voice was not heard." From this we derive that it is forbidden to raise our voices in prayer.

"Eli mistakenly thought she was drunk." From this we derive that a drunk person is forbidden to pray.

Obligation=Participation

Text 16

Rabbi Ya'akov Reischer, *Responsa Shevut Ya'akov* 2:25 📖

Rabbi Ya'akov Reischer
ca. 1670–1733

Renowned rabbi, halachic authority, and author. He served on rabbinical courts in Prague, Ansbach, Worms, and Metz. He was accepted by contemporary rabbis as the ultimate authority on halachic issues, and problems were addressed to him from all over the Diaspora and Israel. His most famous works are *Chok Ya'akov*, an exposition on the section of the *Shulchan Aruch* pertaining to the laws of Passover, and his *Responsa Shevut Ya'akov*.

דְּכוּלֵי עַלְמָא מוֹדוּ, דְּקוֹדֶם שֶׁנִּקְבַּר הַמֵּת, דְּכֵיוָן שֶׁפָּטוּר מִן הַתְּפִילָה, דְּאֵינוֹ מִצְטָרֵף כְּלַל לְמִנְיָן עֲשָׂרָה.

The halachic consensus is that a mourner whose next of kin has yet to be buried is not counted in a *minyan* because he is exempt from prayer.

KEY POINTS

- There are two separate obligations pertaining to prayer: to recite prayers each day, and to gather as a community to pray. While both men and women have the first obligation, the sages only placed the second obligation on men.

---

9. Why doesn't God respond to my requests?

Text 17

Rabbi Moshe of Trani
(Mabit)
1505–1580

Rabbi and scholar. Rabbi Moshe was born in Ottoman-ruled Salonika, Greece. At the age of sixteen, he left for Safed, Israel to study under the tutelage of Rabbi Yaakov Beirav. Later, he served as the rabbi of Safed for 55 years, during which time he penned many books on philosophy, halachic responsa, Talmud, and Bible. These include *Bet Elokim* and *Kiryat Sefer*. He is buried in the ancient cemetery in Safed, near the Arizal.

Rabbi Moshe of Trani, *Beit Elokim, Sha'ar Hatefilah* 15

גַּם כִּי תְּפִלָּתוֹ עַל עִנְיַן שְׁאֵלָתוֹ לֹא תִּהְיֶה מְקוּבֶּלֶת, לְסִבָּה שֶׁכְּבָר נִגְזְרָה גְּזֵרָה עָלָיו, אוֹ לְסִבָּה יְדוּעָה לְפָנָיו יִתְבָּרֵךְ, עִם כָּל זֶה, תְּפִלָּתוֹ תֵּחָשֵׁב לוֹ לִצְדָקָה בָּעוֹלָם הַבָּא. וְגַם בָּעוֹלָם הַזֶּה יֹאכַל פֵּירוֹת הַתְּפִלָּה דְּמִיוֹן מַה שֶּׁשָּׁאַל מֵהָאֵ-ל יִתְבָּרֵךְ.

כְּמוֹ שֶׁמָּצִינוּ בְּמֹשֶׁה רַבֵּינוּ ע"ה, כִּי גַּם שֶׁלֹּא נִתְקַבְּלָה תְּפִלָּתוֹ לִיכָּנֵס לָאָרֶץ, הִשִּׂיג דְּמִיוֹן הַכְּנִיסָה, שֶׁהֶרְאָהוּ הָאֵ-ל יִתְבָּרֵךְ אֶת כָּל הָאָרֶץ, וְכָל מַה שֶּׁיֶּאֱרַע לְיִשְׂרָאֵל מִיוֹם שֶׁיִּכָּנְסוּ וְעַד יוֹם שֶׁיֵּצְאוּ מִמֶּנָּה. וְכֵן מַה שֶּׁיֶּאֱרַע לְיִשְׂרָאֵל עַד סוֹף הָעוֹלָם. כְּמוֹ שֶׁאָמַר הַכָּתוּב (דְּבָרִים לד,ב) "עַד הַיָּם הָאַחֲרוֹן" וְדָרְשׁוּ חַז"ל (סִפְרֵי, דְּבָרִים שנז): "עַד הַיוֹם הָאַחֲרוֹן". וְזֶה הָיָה בְּסִבַּת תְּפִלָּתוֹ שֶׁהִתְפַּלֵּל בְּכַוָּונָה גְּדוֹלָה.

Even when, for whatever reason known to God, your prayer is not granted, you will be rewarded for it in the World to Come. You will also benefit in this world by reaping fruit that is similar to what you prayed for.

Indeed, we find with Moses, that although his prayer to enter the Land was not accepted, still, he received a taste of his request. God showed him the whole Land and all that would transpire with the Jewish people from the day they enter the Land until the day they would leave it, and even after that—forever. As the verse says (Deuteronomy 34:1–2), "God showed Moses the whole Land—from Gilead to Dan . . . unto the utmost sea (the Mediterranean)." And the sages derived (*Sifrei*, Deuteronomy 357) that God showed Moses all that would occur "until the final day." All of this was the result of his heartfelt prayers.

KEY POINTS

- All prayers are effective in some way.
- The fact that our prayers are not always effective in the way we expected or wanted reminds us that we are servants of God; while God hands us the reins to a certain extent, ultimately, He implements His vision.

10. Why does God give us negative, even harmful, inclinations?

A Quest for Imperfection

Text 18

Talmud, Shabbat 88b–89a 📖

בְּשָׁעָה שֶׁעָלָה מֹשֶׁה לַמָּרוֹם, אָמְרוּ מַלְאֲכֵי הַשָּׁרֵת לִפְנֵי הַקָּדוֹשׁ בָּרוּךְ הוּא: רִבּוֹנוֹ שֶׁל עוֹלָם, מַה לִּילוּד אִשָּׁה בֵּינֵינוּ?

אָמַר לָהֶן: לְקַבֵּל תּוֹרָה בָּא.

אָמְרוּ לְפָנָיו: חֲמוּדָה גְּנוּזָה שֶׁגְּנוּזָה לְךָ . . . אַתָּה מְבַקֵּשׁ לִיתְּנָהּ לְבָשָׂר וָדָם? "מָה אֱנוֹשׁ כִּי תִזְכְּרֶנּוּ וּבֶן אָדָם כִּי תִפְקְדֶנּוּ" (תְּהִלִּים ח,ה). "ה' אֲדֹנֵינוּ מָה אַדִּיר שִׁמְךָ בְּכָל הָאָרֶץ אֲשֶׁר תְּנָה הוֹדְךָ עַל הַשָּׁמָיִם" (שָׁם, ב).

אָמַר לוֹ הַקָּדוֹשׁ בָּרוּךְ הוּא לְמֹשֶׁה: הַחֲזֵיר לָהֶן תְּשׁוּבָה.

. . . אָמַר לְפָנָיו: רִבּוֹנוֹ שֶׁל עוֹלָם, תּוֹרָה שֶׁאַתָּה נוֹתֵן לִי מַה כְּתִיב בָּהּ – "אָנֹכִי ה' אֱלֹקֶיךָ אֲשֶׁר הוֹצֵאתִיךָ מֵאֶרֶץ מִצְרַיִם" (שְׁמוֹת כ,ב). אָמַר לָהֶן: לְמִצְרַיִם יְרַדְתֶּם? לְפַרְעֹה הִשְׁתַּעְבַּדְתֶּם? תּוֹרָה לָמָּה תְּהֵא לָכֶם?

שׁוּב מַה כְּתִיב בָּהּ – "לֹא יִהְיֶה לְךָ אֱלֹקִים אֲחֵרִים" (שָׁם, ג). בֵּין הַגּוֹיִים אַתֶּם שְׁרוּיִין שֶׁעוֹבְדִין עֲבוֹדָה זָרָה? שׁוּב מַה כְּתִיב בָּהּ – "זָכוֹר אֶת יוֹם הַשַּׁבָּת לְקַדְּשׁוֹ" (שָׁם, ח). כְּלוּם אַתֶּם עוֹשִׂים מְלָאכָה שֶׁאַתֶּם צְרִיכִין שְׁבוּת? שׁוּב מַה כְּתִיב בָּהּ – "לֹא תִשָּׂא" (שָׁם, ז). מַשָּׂא וּמַתָּן יֵשׁ בֵּינֵיכֶם? שׁוּב מַה כְּתִיב בָּהּ – "כַּבֵּד אֶת אָבִיךָ וְאֶת אִמֶּךָ" (שָׁם, יב). אָב וָאֵם יֵשׁ לָכֶם? שׁוּב מַה כְּתִיב בָּהּ - "לֹא תִרְצַח, לֹא תִנְאָף, לֹא תִגְנֹב" (שָׁם, יג). קִנְאָה יֵשׁ בֵּינֵיכֶם, יֵצֶר הָרַע יֵשׁ בֵּינֵיכֶם?

מִיָּד הוֹדוּ לוֹ לְהַקָּדוֹשׁ בָּרוּךְ הוּא.

When Moses ascended on high [to receive the Torah], the ministering angels spoke before the Creator, "Master of the Universe! What business does a mortal being have among us?"

"He has come to receive the Torah," God answered them.

The angels said to God, "That secret treasure, which has been hidden by You . . . You want to give to flesh and blood? 'What is man that You should consider him?' (Psalms 8:5). 'O God, how exalted is Your name throughout the Earth! Your glory [the Torah], should remain upon the Heavens!' (ibid., 8:2).

"Answer them," God said to Moses. . . .

Moses said, "Master of the Universe! The Torah that You have given me, what is written therein? 'I am the Lord your God, Who brought you out from the Land of Egypt'" (Exodus 20:2). [Turning to the angels,] Moses said, "Did you go down to Egypt? Were you enslaved to Pharaoh? Why then should the Torah be yours?

"It is also written therein, 'You shall have no other gods' (ibid., 20:3). Do you live among people who engage in idolatry?

"It is also written therein, 'Remember the Shabbat day, to keep it holy' (ibid., 20:8). Do you perform work from which you need to rest?

"It is also written therein: 'You shall not take God's name in vain' (ibid., 20:7). Do you engage in business [that would require oath taking]?

"It is also written therein: 'Honor your father and mother' (ibid., 20:12). Do you have fathers and mothers?

"It is also written therein: 'You shall not murder. You shall not commit adultery. You shall not steal' (ibid., 20:13). Is there jealousy among you? Is the evil inclination among you?"

Upon hearing this, the angels conceded.

QUESTION FOR DISCUSSION

Why did the angels protest against giving the Torah to human beings?

Text 19

Midrash, *Kohelet Rabah* 3:15 📖

"וְהִנֵּה טוֹב" (בְּרֵאשִׁית א,לא) - זֶה יֵצֶר טוֹב. "מְאֹד" (שָׁם) - זֶה יֵצֶר הָרָע.

> t is good" (Genesis 1:31) refers to the human inclination to do good. "It is *very* good" (ibid.) refers to the human's evil inclination.

Kohelet Rabah

A Midrashic text on the Book of Ecclesiastes. Midrash is the designation of a particular genre of rabbinic literature. The term "Midrash" is derived from the root d-r-sh, which means "to search," "to examine," and "to investigate." This particular Midrash provides textual exegeses and develops and illustrates moral principles. It was first published in Pesaro, Italy, in 1519, together with four other Midrashic works on the other four biblical *megilot*.

Healthy Self-Concept

Text 20

Rabbi Shne'ur Zalman of Liadi, *Tanya*, ch. 27 📖

וְאִם הָעַצְבוּת אֵינָהּ מִדַּאֲגַת עֲוֹנוֹת אֶלָּא מֵהִרְהוּרִים רָעִים וְתַאֲווֹת רָעוֹת שֶׁנּוֹפְלוֹת בְּמַחְשַׁבְתּוֹ . . . אַדְרַבָּה יֵשׁ לוֹ לִשְׂמֹחַ בְּחֶלְקוֹ, שֶׁאַף שֶׁנּוֹפְלוֹת לוֹ בְּמַחְשַׁבְתּוֹ, הוּא מֵסִיחַ דַּעְתּוֹ מֵהֶן, לְקַיֵּם מַה שֶׁנֶּאֱמַר (בַּמִּדְבָּר טו,לט) "וְלֹא תָתוּרוּ אַחֲרֵי לְבַבְכֶם וְאַחֲרֵי עֵינֵיכֶם". . .

וְאַדְרַבָּה הָעַצְבוּת הִיא מִגַּסּוּת הָרוּחַ, שֶׁאֵינוֹ מַכִּיר מְקוֹמוֹ. וְעַל כֵּן יֵרַע לְבָבוֹ עַל שֶׁאֵינוֹ בְּמַדְרֵגַת צַדִּיק. שֶׁלַּצַּדִּיקִים בְּוַדַּאי אֵין נוֹפְלִים לָהֶם הִרְהוּרֵי שְׁטוּת כָּאֵלּוּ. כִּי אִילּוּ הָיָה מַכִּיר מְקוֹמוֹ שֶׁהוּא רָחוֹק מְאֹד מִמַּדְרֵגַת צַדִּיק, וְהַלְוַאי הָיָה בֵּינוֹנִי . . . הֲרֵי זֹאת הִיא מִדַּת הַבֵּינוֹנִים וַעֲבוֹדָתָם, לִכְבּוֹשׁ הַיֵּצֶר וְהַהִרְהוּר הָעוֹלֶה מֵהַלֵּב לַמֹּחַ.

> f your despondency is not from concern over actual transgressions but from negative thoughts and negative desires that befall your mind . . . then, on the contrary, you should rejoice in your lot. For although these [negative thoughts and desires] befall your consciousness, you avert your mind from them, thereby fulfilling [the divine

Rabbi Shne'ur Zalman of Liadi (Alter Rebbe)
1745–1812

Chasidic rebbe, halachic authority, and founder of the Chabad movement. The Alter Rebbe was born in Liozna, Belarus, and was among the principal students of the Magid of Mezeritch. His numerous works include the *Tanya*, an early classic containing the fundamentals of Chabad Chasidism, and *Shulchan Aruch HaRav*, an expanded and reworked code of Jewish law.

commandment], "You shall not go astray after your heart and after your eyes . . ." (Numbers 15:39).

In fact, despondency [over such thoughts] actually stems from conceit. [It comes from the fact] that you do not know your place, and therefore you feel bad that you are not on the level of a *tsadik*, who is not plagued by such thoughts of folly. But if you knew your place, that you are very far from the level of a *tsadik*, and that you should aspire to be a *beinoni* . . . then indeed, this is the character of the *beinonim* and their task in life: to subjugate the [negative] impulse and thought rising from the heart to the mind.

Continue your learning experience ONLINE

Visit www.myJLI.com/why3

for insightful and inspiring videos, articles, and readings on this topic.

KEY POINTS

- God created us with negative inclinations because He desires that we overcome negativity and subdue it. This is the purpose of all of Creation and why God gave the Torah to human beings and not to the angels.

- Our negative inclinations and unholy desires should make us joyful for the opportunity to overcome them and fulfill our divine mission of turning negativity into goodness.

Lesson Conclusion (Optional)

LEARNING EXERCISE 2

With a partner, identify a theme that has been present in most (or all) of the elements of this lesson.

1. Why are there so many Jews in Hollywood?

2. Why do we believe that Jews cannot convert out of Judaism?

3. Why did our ancestors continue to identify as Jews despite being victims of so much suffering through the ages?

4. Why does a mourner recite *Kaddish*?

5. Why do Jews place pebbles on headstones?

6. Why not leave flowers at the grave?

7. Why does Jewish law exempt women from certain ritual obligations that are obligatory for men?

8. Why are ten men required for a *minyan*?

9. Why doesn't God respond to my requests?

10. Why does God give us negative, even harmful, inclinations?

ADDITIONAL READINGS

KADDISH

BY LEON WIESELTIER

Is death itself a sin? Twenty years ago, in an English writer of the seventeenth century, I came across this sentence: "I am not so much afraid of death, as ashamed thereof." I found it shocking then, and I do now. Here was a man for whom human mortality was a contradiction to human dignity.

It is a mistake to be embarrassed by finitude, but it is a gorgeous mistake.

The bay across from my mother's house was not troubled and it was not untroubled. The waters were in a condition of mild, infinite motion. They preached the permanence of impermanence. I heard them clearly. Small boats passed back and forth, to and from the sea.

The car came to a stop on the unpaved lane at the back of the cemetery. Car doors opened and closed. Arms were taken in arms. There were whispers. An indescribable sobriety. And there stood facing us the strangest thing I have ever seen: a stone that said WIESELTIER.

More cars pulled up. Cousins mainly, and a few of my father's friends. All of a sudden a winter wind arrived, out of season, for this moment. It blew bitterly. The rabbi summoned us to begin. I read a psalm: "And he shall be like a tree planted by the rivers of water, that bringeth forth his fruit in his season; his leaf also shall not wither." My sister read a psalm: "As

Leon Wieseltier. American writer, critic, and magazine editor. A child of Holocaust survivors, Wieseltier was born in Brooklyn, New York, and attended the Yeshiva of Flatbush, Columbia University, Oxford University, and Harvard University. From 1983 to 2014, Wieseltier was the literary editor of *The New Republic*. He is currently a senior fellow at the Brookings Institution and a contributing editor and critic at *The Atlantic*.

for man, his days are as grass; as a flower of the field, so he flourisheth. For the wind passeth over it, and it is gone." The rabbi said a few words about my father, all of them true. People were shivering in the cold. I asked a younger cousin to recite the memorial prayer that beseeches a merciful God to "devise a right rest" for the departed, and he recited it in a breaking voice. The rabbi commanded my mother to remove the cheesecloth that covered the foot-stone that bears my father's name, and the names of his brother and his sister. She did, and the names were revealed. Finally my mother had buried somebody she loved.

My father, my father, buried and unveiled.

It was not the sight of my father's grave that caused me to lose control of my sadness. It was the sight of the old men huddled against the wind, the old men in their caps and coats, who had come to bury one more of their own, to harken to one more prayer for one more dead, the firm, selfless old men with the accents and the histories. My exhausted and inexhaustible elders, unmoved again by the gusts. They are getting to their end, I thought; and I loved them; and I wept.

I was bursting with descent.

The living and the dead, I miss them all.

Then the rabbi instructed me to read another psalm. "The Lord is my shepherd; I shall not want." I chose to sing it, in the sweet, sepulchral manner in which it as sung on Sabbath afternoons. I stepped closer to the grave and sang, and as I sang I broke away from my dread. I sang to the death of wailing. My song grew as if to make room within it for all the true and punished people who gathered around it, to shield them with its splendor and to seal them with its peace. Lean on my time, lean on my heart, lean on my fire. I will not bend beneath your load, I will not bend. "Surely goodness and mercy shall follow me all the days of my life; and I will dwell in the house of the lord forever."

The living and the dead, I miss them all.

I will dance with them at the mourner's ball

Then I said the *kaddish*. I stood in the ashes of fury and spoke the sentences of praise. Was that voice my voice? It was no longer the effusion of woe. Magnified, I said.

Sanctified. I said. I looked above me, 1 looked below me. I looked around me. With my own eyes, I saw magnificence.

Kaddish [Vintage, New York, 1998], pp. 583-584

JEWISH IDENTITY

BY RUTH R. WISSE

Words depend on the context within which they are uttered. During the course of my normal life, whether "I am a Jew" or not is usually either obvious or irrelevant or both at once: obvious at the kosher butcher shop, irrelevant at the bank; obvious in the synagogue, irrelevant in the subway. When I teach Yiddish literature at the university, I use the first person pronoun to refer to us students, not us Jews. While my own interest in Yiddish may have been inspired by my Jewishness, some of my non-Jewish students were drawn to the subject by the desire to master an unfamiliar culture. Being Jewish may be the point or beside the point of the passion for literary studies. The American way of life affords us the freedom to live as we please, within the bounds of the law. We may choose to live as Jews, visibly and vitally, or else slip anonymously into the gentile mainstream.

Since I have always enjoyed being a Jew it never occurred to me to live otherwise. I appreciate the tough-mindedness of the Jewish religious tradition that knows how hard it is to achieve a mature civilization; I admire my ancestors who brought Jewish civilization to such a high level of maturity. Although I don't follow all the requirements of Halakhah, my

observance is higher than that of my parents whose observance was lower than that of their parents. I love the cycle the Jewish year, particularly the contrasted experiences of Rosh Hashanah and Passover. The culture and history of the Jewish people engages much of my intellectual energy. And the pleasure of being a member of the Jewish community usually outweighs its frustrations.

Most of all I cherish those of my fellow Jews who settled and who maintain the State of Israel, which I consider the highest manifestation of the human spirit in modern times. Jews always tried to take full responsibility for their actions in every human sphere, but not until we reclaimed responsibility for our political life could we provide a haven for Jews in danger. The more Hebrew I learn to speak and read, the longer and more often I am in Israel the more friends and relatives I acquire in the country, the greater my debt to its defenders. The achievements of Israel depend entirely on the patience of its defenders, for it is the only democracy in the world that has had to fight for its life from inception to the present. Not since the Romans crushed the second Jewish commonwealth have Jewish soldiers been able to protect the Jewish polity from its enemies. It goes unappreciated that these defenders of Israel are also the front line of defense for the democratic world.

Ruth Wisse. (1936–) Professor of Yiddish literature and professor of comparative literature at Harvard University. Wisse was born in Czernowitz, Ukraine, and grew up in Montreal, Canada. Her books include *Jews and Power*, *The Modern Jewish Canon*, and *No Joke: Making Jewish Humor* (2013).

The presence of enemies introduces a different context for the affirmation of Jewish identity. Jean Paul Sartre believed that the presence of anti-Semites required that Jews embrace their identity for they would otherwise become inauthentic foils of their adversaries and escapists from their existential condition. In 1942, at the height of the Nazi slaughter of the Jews of Europe, the Soviet Yiddish poet ltsik Feffer wrote a poem titled, "I Am a Jew." Feffer was a colonel in the Red Army, a member of the Communist Party, and an agent for the Soviet secret police. In the preceding years, he had obeyed Stalinist dictates to avoid all Jewish national expression. But the rules changed once Germany invaded Russia, and Feffer's poem came out as subtle as a drum:

> Pharoah and Titus, Haman made their aim
> To slay me in their times and lands
> Eternity still bears my name
> Upon its lands.
> And I survived in Spain the rack,
> The Inquisition Fires, too.
> My horn sounded this message back:
> "I am a Jew!"

–Itsik Feffer, translated by Joseph Leftwich

Every stanza ended with the same refrain of defiant Jewish self-affirmation. Not surprisingly, six years later, when Stalin ordered the arrest of Feffer, among other prominent Jews, on capital charges of anti-Soviet treachery, the poem was brought as evidence of Feffer's Jewish nationalist propaganda. At the trial a fellow defendant protested: "There cannot be anything criminal in the phrase 'I am a Jew.' If I approach someone and say, 'I am a Jew,' what could be bad about that?"[1] His comment was just, but, under the circumstances, naive. When the goal of aggressors is the ruin of the Jewish people, an otherwise unexceptional statement of fact acquires powers of resistance. This resistance became manifest when Soviet Jewry took up where Feffer left off in proclaiming, "We are Jews." Many claimed the right to live as Jews by immigrating to the Jewish homeland.

No Jew should have to affirm his identity in response to a knife at his throat. No regime or leader should seek aggrandizement at the expense of the Jewish people or deny us the same rights that they claim for themselves to land, to peace, to national existence. But as long as our enemies threaten, it is unutterably shameful to ignore their presence. Those of us who live outside Israel should be confronting its defamers no less vigorously than the Israel Defense Forces resist invaders and terrorists. I consider it my highest duty and priority as a Jew to oppose the propaganda war against the Jewish state, which has been waged with increasing sophistication and resources by Arab leaders who should have been improving their own societies. Precisely because America allows me the choice to be or not to be a Jew, I am free to expose our attackers for as long as it takes them to stop their attacks.

I Am Jewish

Excerpted from *I Am Jewish: Personal Reflections Inspired by the Last Words of Daniel Pearl,* ed. by Judea and Ruth Pearl, c 2005, Published by Jewish Lights Publishing, PO Box 237, Woodstock, Vermont 05091, www.jewishlights.com.
Permission granted by Jewish Lights Publishing, a division of LongHill Partners, Inc.

---

[1] *Stalin's Secret Pogrom: The Postwar Inquisition of the Jewish Anti-Fascist Committee,* ed. Joshua Rubenstein and Vladimir P. Naumov, trans. Laura Esther Wolf on (New Haven: Yale University Press, 2001), p. 158.

I AM JEWISH

BY NATAN SHARANSKY

There were more than a few Jews among the leaders of the Bolshevik Revolution, just as there have been more than a few Jews among the leaders of many other movements that have sought to save mankind. They believed with all their souls that the way to redeem humanity and create a better world was to achieve absolute equality. All human beings are equal, and equality means no differences. All human beings should therefore be identical. Ethnicity, class, religion, and national characteristics belonged to an old and decaying world. The time or such distinctions had passed. The Jewish revolutionaries wanted to release the iron reins that held each person to his tribe, that tied each Jewish man and woman to unique heritage and culture, and to create a new man–Homo sovieticus.

While these were assimilated Jews, a very Jewish aspiration was the basis for their actions. They wanted to be a light to the gentiles. To have influence, to lead, to mend the world. The way to do that, as they understood it, was to leave their villages, the *shtetls,* to erase their particularist Jewish identity, to meld utterly into their surroundings in order to create the new man who would live in the better world they so longed for.

I was one of the millions of new human beings in the Bolshevik experiment, which was successful far beyond its makers' expectations. Section five in my identity papers informed me that I was a Jew, but I hadn't a clue as to what that meant. I knew nothing of Jewish history, language, or customs, nor had I even heard of their existence. My father, who loved to tell stories, would sometimes tell us tales from the Bible. We heard about Joseph and his brothers, about Samson and Delilah, but they were stories just like all his other stories. No one told us that these were the history of our nation, no one thought to mention that these stories were connected to us in any way. Like all Soviet Jews of my generation, I grew up rootless, unconnected, without identity.

With our Jewish identity lacking positive content, only anti-Semitism gave it any meaning at all. To be a Jew was to be hated and discriminated against, to have fewer options. To be a Jew was to have a perpetual problem. We were weak, and we sought ways to escape our fate. Excelling at science, art, or chess were all ways to run away from that mysterious, inexplicable Jewishness. It not only failed to give us strength, identity, and meaning, but was actually a burden and interfered with our lives.

The strength arrived, unexpectedly, from a far-off land and war. The stellar Israeli victory in the Six Day War enabled us to stand tall. People suddenly treated Jews differently. Even the anti-Semitic joke changed. They were no longer about the cowardly, mendacious Jew. They were about the upstart, brave, and victorious Jew.

It was through the war that I became aware of the Jewish state, and of the language and culture it embodied. I was suddenly exposed to the existence of the Jewish people, to the existence of tradition and culture. I was no longer a disconnected individual in an alienating world ho tile world. I was a person with an identity and roots. 1 felt that I had a history, a nation, and a country behind me. That I had, at the end of the earth, a homeland. That I belonged. That feeling was my companion through years of struggle for human rights, in the framework of the Zionist movement, and through long years in prison. Even in solitary confinement I believed that the Jewish people and the State of Israel would fight for me. I was not alone. I was arrested a few month after the Entebbe operation. The operation signified that Israel was prepared to go any distance to save its citizens, and it made a huge impression on me. During my years in prison, every aircraft in Siberia's skies sounded to me like the rescue force coming to liberate me. True, I was not rescued by an airplane or a bold military mission, but I was certainly released

---

Natan Sharansky. (1948–) Former Soviet dissident and Israeli politician. Sharansky is the chairman of The Jewish Agency. He spent years in Soviet prison as a political prisoner for his human rights activism. He was released after his wife led an international campaign for his freedom. He has served in various ministerial positions, and as deputy prime minister in the Israeli government.

from my prison by the Jewish people and the State of Israel. I truly was not alone.

Identity and a sense of belonging give life strength and meaning. A person who has his Jewish identity is not enslaved. He is free even if they throw him in prison, even if they torture him. For me and for my colleagues in the Zionist movement, Jewish identity was a source of pride, and pride gave us the strength to fight. At first for our own self-respect, and afterward for our national honor, and in the end for the destruction of the evil Communist empire and for freedom throughout the world.

The Jews who led the Bolshevik Revolution believed that rubbing out their Jewish identity was the way to redeem the world. In practice, they lent a hand to one of the cruelest regimes mankind has known. Instead of being a light to the gentiles, they brought a great darkness on the world. Slashing off their roots did not create a new, strong, and free man. Instead, it trampled on human dignity and turned the individual into a slave and chattel. We have learned that liberation in fact depend on strengthening identity, on returning to one's roots. Only a person who is connected to his past, to his people, and to his roots can be free, and only a free person has the strength to act for the benefit of the rest of humanity.

Daniel Pearl's last words testify that he was a man who knew where he came from. He was not alienated from his identity. Only such a man could have been free and brave enough to take upon himself the important and dangerous mission during which he was murdered. The freedom that beat within him, the freedom that came from within his identity, is what gave him the strength to leave his land and his family and to do what he thought was right and important, for the sake of the rest of the world.

Excerpted from *I Am Jewish: Personal Reflections Inspired by the Last Words of Daniel Pearl*, ed. by Judea and Ruth Pearl, c 2005, Published by Jewish Lights Publishing, PO Box 237, Woodstock, Vermont 05091, www.jewishlights.com.
Permission granted by Jewish Lights Publishing, a division of LongHill Partners, Inc.

PARENTHOOD: NATURAL AND REDEEMED

BY RABBI JOSEPH B. SOLOVEITCHIK, PhD

Natural Parenthood

The Bible tells us that "The man called his wife's name Eve *(Havah)* because she was the mother of all living things *(hai)*" (Gen. 3:20). But man's name is not identified with fatherhood; he is called *adam* or *ish,* but not *av.* His role as a father was not portrayed symbolically by his name, while Eve's role as a mother was; nothing reflects Adam's task as a father. In contradistinction to Adam's, Abraham's fatherhood did find an expression in his name. God added the letter *hei* to his name in order to make Abraham's fatherhood universal, to make him "a father of many nations" (Gen. 17:5). Why did a change take place when Abraham, the father of our nation, appeared on the scene? Apparently a new idea of fatherhood that was unknown to Adam was revealed to the world with the arrival of Abraham.

Adam was the father of the natural, unredeemed community; Abraham was the father of a redeemed, spiritual community. Adam sinned and acted contrary to God's will; Abraham proclaimed God's word as the highest law for man to abide by. Adam lost the paradise; Abraham wanted to restore the paradise to man. Apparently, the role of the father within the confines of the natural, sinful-egotistic, pleasure-minded and power-oriented community differs from that within the redeemed, covenantal, ethical,

Rabbi Joseph B. Soloveitchik. (1903–1993) Talmudist and philosopher. A scion of a famous Lithuanian rabbinical family, Rabbi Soloveitchik was one of the most influential Jewish personalities, leaders, and thinkers of the 20th century. In 1941, he became professor of Talmud at RIETS—Yeshiva University; in this capacity, he ordained more rabbis than anyone else in Jewish history. Among his published works are *Halakhic Man* and *Lonely Man of Faith.*

love-oriented and humble community. Within the first community, founded by Adam, the father's role is of such minimal significance that it is not worth being demonstrated by the name, while in the covenantal community the role is redeemed and elevated, infused with new meaning deserving of emphasis and mention.

In the natural community, the woman is more concerned with motherhood than the man with fatherhood. Motherhood, in contrast to fatherhood, bespeaks a long-enduring peculiar state of body and mind. The nine months of pregnancy, with all its attendant biological and psychological changes, the birth of the child with pain and suffering, the nursing of the baby and, later, the caretaking of and attending to the youngster–all form part of the motherhood experience. In a word, the woman is bound up with the child and she experiences her motherhood role in all her thought and feeling. The father, if he wants, can deny his fatherhood and forego responsibility. The mother is bound up with the child; the father can roam around forgetting everything. Motherhood is an experience—unredeemed and hence brutish, yet an experience. Physically, fatherhood implies nothing tangible and memorable. The male, bodily and mentally, does not experience his fatherhood.

In short, within the natural community the mother occupies a central position while the father is relegated to a role that is intangible and vague, since it does not imply any restrictive bonds. Motherhood is a fact that is foisted upon a woman. That is why the name of the woman was derived from her role as a mother, while Adam's name has nothing in common with his fatherhood. "Can a woman forget her baby or disown the child of her womb?" (Isaiah 49:15).

Redeemed Parenthood

With the emergence of Abraham and the founding of a new kind of community, the covenantal one, the vague role of fatherhood and the all-absorbing experience of motherhood were redeemed. New commitments were accepted; man began to live not only for himself, but for others as well. He became concerned with the destiny of others, and discovered in himself responsiveness not only to biological pressure but to

the call of conscience, through which God addresses Himself to him. The fatherhood idea was redeemed, purged of its orgiastic-hedonic element, infused with life, and turned into a central reality on par with that of motherhood.

What is fatherhood in the covenantal society? It is the great educational commitment to the *masorah*, the tradition, the freely assumed obligation to hand down, to pass on to the child the covenant, a message, a code, a unique way of life, a tradition of *mishpat u-tzedakah*, of justice and charity. In the covenantal community, the father is promoted to teacher, and his role *ipso facto* is shifted from the periphery to the center on par with that of the mother. That is why Adam—as the representative of the natural community—was not aware of his fatherhood. Only with the emergence of the covenantal community and with the formulation of the doctrine of father-teacher was the fatherhood commitment suddenly revealed to us.

Motherhood expresses, as I explained before, a natural, unalterable reality, a factum. The woman becomes involved with her child within the natural community, while the man freely accepts fatherhood only in the covenantal community. However, not only did the role of the male undergo a change in the covenantal community, but that of the female did as well. Abraham personified fatherhood as a great commitment. Sarah became the first mother in the sense that her motherhood stemmed not only from instinctual involvement due to biological pressure but from free commitment as well. What was Sarah's commitment? The same as Abraham's: an educational *masorah* commitment to hand down and teach the covenant, God's word, the way of a covenantal life of *hesed u-tzedakah*, of kindness and charity.

Mother's job changed into a great mission; her preoccupation with the child was endowed with ethical meaning. She not only nurses the child physically, she brings him up; she assumes the role of educator. Motherhood is not only an experience but a commitment as well. At this juncture motherhood is hallowed on account of another idea which is linked up with the spontaneous free choice of motherhood on the part of the woman in the covenantal community.

As "mother-teacher," the woman is no more connected with only the fruit of her womb, with the child she bore. As long as motherhood, like fatherhood, was rooted in biological facticity, its confine was very narrow and extended only to a clan. One can experience biological motherhood only in respect to one's own child. However, when motherhood was transformed into a commitment and being a mother was equated with being a teacher, an apostle of God, the carrier of God's covenant, His prophet, then motherhood, like fatherhood, was elevated to a universal spiritual level. Instead of being just the father and mother of their offspring in a clannish sense, Abraham and Sarah accepted responsibility for the multitudes, for the world community of the committed. The father and mother of the clan were promoted to father- and mother-teachers of the entire covenantal community with all its universal aspirations. The letter *hei* was added to both of their names, signifying a transformation to universality. God promised Abraham that he would be "a father of many nations" (Gen. 17:4) and that Sarah "shall give rise to nations; rulers of peoples shall be of her" (17:16).

Sarah replaced Eve. The freely committed universal mother supplanted the instinctually involved natural mother. Eve was "the mother of all living"; Sarah, the mother of nations and kings. Eve's motherhood consisted in giving life in a natural sense to her child. It lacked, however, the element of leadership. Her motherhood was a result of a biological pressure, the consummation of a natural process. Sarah's was due to great vision, to a new mission she took on. She and "all the persons they had acquired in Haran" (Gen. 12:5)—her children/pupils—formed a covenantal community, one founded on education, a living tradition and commitment. Sarah redeemed the motherhood experience by taking a factum, a natural reality, and changing it into a commitment. Passive involvement became an active commitment; natural entanglement was elevated to a normative choice. The woman herself rose from a receptive to an active role. And the most important dimension which was added is that of universality, the capacity to assume motherhood vis-a-vis all children.

No more should a childless couple feel desolate and forsaken because the Almighty has not blessed them with an heir. The barren woman may lack the natural motherhood experience, but she can attain covenantal if not natural motherhood by choice, by commitment, by helping others, by contributing toward the strengthening of the covenantal community, by exposing children of other parents to the word of God. The Romans—to whom the idea of covenant was alien, who, in spite of their advanced technological achievements, never freed themselves from the bonds of the natural community—tried to compensate the childless man and woman by establishing the institution of adoption. Judaism did not need to create such an institution. The letter *hei* added to Abraham's and Sarah's names symbolized the exalted idea of covenantal fatherhood and motherhood, one which is realized not through natural but through spiritual-educational media which transcend the boundaries of a clan and extend into the open spaces of universality.

The Need for Sacrificial Action

However, any act of redemption is bound up with sacrificial action. A physiological reaction changes into meaningful hallowed action at any time the individual displays courage and the ability to answer the violent, orgiastic, hypnotic call of nature in the negative, thus incurring pain and suffering because of his refusal to cooperate with biological pressures that have not found their total release. Judaism identified sanctity with sacrifice, this identification being reflected in the status of utter and immutable sanctity, *kedushat ha-guf*, assigned halakhically to a *korban*. One cannot hallow anything unless one is ready to surrender, give up, and be defeated.

Let us analyze from this viewpoint the redeeming passional action of the covenantal mother.

Motherhood *per se*, even at the level of naturalness, is described by the Bible as a passional experience. On the one hand, the woman pays a much higher price than the father for engaging in sex. While the father is permitted by nature to walk off free, the mother becomes burdened with responsibilities for many long years. She loses her freedom and ability to order her life in accordance with her desires. In fact, she must give the whole of herself to the child. To be a mother—even at a natural level—means to shift all other responsibilities and concerns to the periphery. Even the most primitive motherhood experience is fraught with pain and suffering.

On the other hand, the woman, discriminated against by nature and charged to carry the heavy load of motherhood alone, is not ready to give up her role as mother and cast off the burden. This compulsive will in the woman to be a mother at all costs emphasizes the pathos in her role. The tragedy of the woman becomes the more pronounced the less she can avoid it. The woman in the Bible yearns for a child with her heart and soul and is not able to suppress the urge for motherhood. The experience would not be so sorrowful if it could be dispensed with, if the woman felt happy without it.

However, the Bible denies that such a possibility exists. The woman wants to be a mother; she cannot get along without involvement in this kind of a passional experience. The longing for children, for a home, for the parent-child community, is by far more intense in the woman than in man.

The lot of the unmarried woman is by far more miserable than that of the unmarried man. The impact of sexual loneliness upon a woman is more devastating, both physically and mentally, than it is upon a man. The woman finds herself in a paradoxical predicament. On the one hand, she craves a husband and child; on the other hand, this longing, which penetrates into the very depth of her personality, can be fulfilled only by means of pain and suffering.

The story of creation describes this role in a short verse. "To the woman He said, 'I will greatly multiply your sorrow and your conception. In sorrow you shall bring forth children; and your desire shall be to your husband, and he shall rule over you'" (Gen. 3:16). In other words, the desire of the woman is tragic, masochistic. On the one hand she yearns for children, a husband and a home; on the other hand, she pays the high price (in terms of her freedom, safety and leisure) for the attainment of this desire.

With the emergence of the covenantal community and the change of the mother role from an inevitable experience to a free commitment, the passional component of this experience and the tragic dichotomy were redeemed. I say "redeemed" and not liquidated or eliminated, since there is no power in the world which can nullify God's will. The pain and suffering involved in being a mother can never be eliminated. However, it is subject to redemption, to infusion with meaning and purposiveness. While Eve suffers, her passional experience is absurd, purposeless, a waste of energy and human feelings. While Sarah suffers, her experience is hallowed as a sacrifice for a great, exalted idea: the perpetuation of the covenantal community.

The Yearning for Children
Let us analyze the covenantal mother and her redeemed passional experience.

She wants a child. Her yearning for children is perhaps more powerful than that of the mother in the unredeemed natural community. Rachel exclaimed in utter despair, "Give me children; if not I shall die" (Gen. 30:1). Hannah's story (I Samuel, chapter 1) is replete with tenderness, human tragedy, suffering and faith. She is a woman in distress, a woman who thought that she had lost everything in life, that she had boon completely forsaken by God and men, a woman who felt a great poverty, the absurdity in living. She sought relief in prayer, for from a human viewpoint, the situation she found herself in was hopeless. No doubt her yearning for a child was by no means less intense than that of Eve. Yet there was a basic difference. Eve's yearning for a child was not related to a great goal. It was purely egotistic, instinctual, primitive desire. Eve wanted to be a mother because she felt a need not only to be loved but to love, to shower someone with affection.

As long as this desire is not redeemed and purged of its instinctual elements, a mother wants a child only to satisfy her desire for loving and caring for someone. She wanted a child because she was in need of giving vent to emotional pressure, to gratify a *per se* good instinctual drive, that is, to shower someone with love. What this leads to was irrelevant for Eve.

The purpose is fulfilled in dandling, hugging, or kissing anything.

However, in the covenantal community the urge to love is purged of its egotistic instinctual elements and turns into a need to serve, to sacrifice, to participate in the great adventure of being a people of God and a messianic community. The woman is no more a dandling, playing mother. She is a mother who teaches, educates, trains, and consecrates the child to God.

The covenantal mother's desire and craving for a child flow from the deep recesses of her personality where God's image is engraved. She tries to imitate the Creator. Jewish mystics asked: Why did God create the world? Does God, the Almighty, infinite, eternal, omniscient and transcendent, need a frail, finite, transient, and conditioned world? Yes, they said, He needs the world in order to have somebody on whom to practice kindness and mercy, in order to let somebody share in the great I-awareness of being, in order to give love and bestow *hesed*. God did not need the world for Himself; He wanted it in order to give man the possibility of attaining greatness.

So, too, the covenantal mother needs a child to make happy, to have the latter join the great community of the covenant, to serve the great cause, to consecrate the child to God. She is required to surrender her child. Jewish covenantal training is basically identical with an act of consecrating the child to God. A mother can be affectionate—Judaism has never condemned the manifestation of love by a mother. But covenantal mother has to withdraw from her child; her total possessive claims are curtailed in the covenantal community. For dedication to the covenantal cause and unlimited affection are mutually exclusive.

Hannah is the woman who proclaimed that motherhood asserts itself in consecration of the child, in giving him away, in surrendering him to God. "O Lord of hosts, if Thou wilt indeed look on the affliction of Your handmaid and remember me and not forget Thy handmaid but wilt give to Thy handmaid a man-child, I will give him to the Lord all the days of his life ..." (I Samuel 1:11). And what did Jewish mothers do throughout the millennia if not exactly the same thing that Hannah pledged? What does a Jewish mother do now when she brings her child to a yeshivah?

Jews introduced a system of public compulsory education 2100 years ago, while the so-called Western world was roaming the forests in Northern and Central Europe. "It was enacted to establish teachers of young children at every city and town, and to bring the children to them at the age of six or seven" (Bava Batra 21a). The child used to be taken away from the embrace of his mother at a very tender age and brought into a new world of Torah, teaching and training. Even now a Jewish child leaves home early in the morning and comes home late in the evening. When Hannah said, "For as long as he lives he is lent to the Lord" (I Samuel 1:28), she did not mean that he would retreat into some cloister; she did not think of physical solitude or a monastic life. Judaism has always opposed an unnatural life. What she had in mind was a life of service to God by serving the covenantal community. We are all still practicing this.

Let us recapitulate. In the natural community, the woman is involved in her motherhood-destiny; father is a distant figure who stands on the periphery. In the covenantal community, father moves to the center where mother has been all along, and both together take on a new commitment, universal in substance: to teach, to train the child to hear the faint echoes which keep on tapping at our gates and which disturb the complacent, comfortable, gracious society.

Two Complementary Missions

There is a distinction between mother's and father's mission within the covenantal community, since they represent two different personalistic approaches. Father's teaching is basically of an intellectual nature. Judaism is to a great extent an intellectual discipline, a method, a system of thought, a hierarchy of values. In order to be acquainted with all these aspects, one must study, comprehend, acquire knowledge and be familiar at least with its basic principles. Let me confide: it is not too easy a task. The teaching must be strict, exact and conscientious. If the father cannot accomplish it all by himself, he must see to it that his child obtains the necessary instruction.

However, Judaism is not only an intellectual tradition but an experiential one as well. The Jew not only observed but *experienced* the Shabbat, the Jew *experienced* Rosh Hashana and Yom Kippur. He did not only recite prayers on those days. The *seder* was not just a ceremonial, but a great *experiential* event. There is beauty, grandeur, warmth, and tenderness to Judaism. All these qualities cannot be described in cognitive terms. One may behold them, feel them, sense them. It is impossible to provide one with a formal training in the experiential realm. Experiences are communicated not through the word but through steady contact, through association, through osmosis, through a tear or a smile, through dreamy eyes and soft melody, through the silence at twilight and the recital of *Shema*. All this is to be found in the maternal domain. The mother creates the mood; she is the artist who is responsible for the magnificence, solemnity and beauty. She tells the child of the great romance of Judaism. She somehow communicates to him the tremor, the heartbeat of Judaism, while playing, singing, laughing and crying.

Leadership in Times of Crisis

While intellectual involvement is important, in times of crisis and distress the experiential commitment is indispensable. Were it not for the mother, the Jews would not have been able to defy and to survive so many crises which threatened to annihilate our people. Again the contrast between the natural and covenantal mother is striking.

The natural woman, Eve, becomes involved involuntarily, not only in natural motherhood, but also in many human situations. She is vulnerable to the smooth but evil tongue of the serpent, sinks easily into her receptive role, into her quest for pleasure, and loses her independence of mind and will. She cannot resist the satanic persuasive arguments and false promises. "And the woman saw that the tree was good for food and that it was pleasant to the eyes... she took of its fruit and did eat..." (Gen. 3:6). The natural mother, Eve, abandoned her freedom of choice based on critical scrutiny; she let herself be easily hypnotized by the serpent, seduced by him. She could not rise to the heights of a courageous personality; she yielded. In crisis, she displayed weakness, confusion and fear.

By redeeming the motherhood experience, Sarah restored the dignity of the woman. A new task was given to her, namely, to rise *heroically* in moments of dismay and spiritual chaos, when man, notwithstanding his great intellectual prowess, finds himself entranced and is about to fail in the implementation of his fatherhood commitment.

The mother in times of crisis assumes the role of her husband's keeper, his guardian and teacher. In the covenantal community, motherhood is a more powerful spiritual force than fatherhood. The shy, modest, reserved mother turns into an active personality whenever critical action is called for.

Man's mind roams about in a world of abstractions and twisted ideas. He is at times too critical, too skeptical to realize the simple truth which brooks no interference from the oversophisticated intellect. That is why the Bible has always portrayed the woman as the determining influence, saving the male from committing grave errors. She quite often changed the course of destiny.

The woman is a crisis personality. In normal times, when routine decisions are reached, the man makes up his mind and the Biblical woman follows him. However, in times of upheaval and transition, when the covenantal community finds itself at crossroads and the choice of alternative courses of action is about to be made, a choice that will shape destiny—it is then that the mother steps to the fore and takes command. The greatness of the man expresses itself in everyday action, when situations lend themselves to logical analysis and discursive thinking. The greatness of the woman manifests itself at the hour of crisis, when the situation does not lend itself to piecemeal understanding but requires instead instantaneous action that flows from the very depths of a sensitive personality. "God gave woman *binah yeterah*, an additional measure of understanding over men" (Niddah 45b).

Motherhood and the Covenantal Community

Sarah is responsible for the survival of the covenantal community. Abraham had two sons, Ishmael and Isaac. The covenant was confined to Isaac and not given to Ishmael. Why? Because the mother of Ishmael was Hagar, and the mother of Isaac was Sarah.

Let us just read the Biblical text pertaining to the event of the covenant and the birth of Isaac.

> *And when Abram was ninety-nine years old, the Lord appeared to Abram and said to him: "I am the Almighty God; walk before me and be perfect, and I will make My covenant between Me and you and will multiply you exceedingly... As for Me, behold my covenant is with you, and you shall be a father of many nations. Neither shall your name be called Abram, but your name shall be Abraham, for a father of many nations have I made you... And I will establish my covenant between Me and you and your seed after you in their generations for an everlasting covenant, to be a God unto you, and to your seed after you" (Gen. 17:1–7).*

We do not yet know whether God refers to Isaac or to Ishmael. However, God qualifies his statement by saying: "As for Sarah, your wife, you shall not call her name Sarai, but Sarah shall be her name, and I will bless her and give you a son through her, yea, I will bless her that she shall give rise to nations..." (Gen. 17:5–16). The covenant is restricted to Sarah and her offspring, and does not include Ishmael. Abraham feels embarrassed and he begs God that Ishmael may also be admitted to the covenant. "O that Ishmael might live before Thee" (Gen. 17:18). God, however, rejects Abraham's plea and He says: "Sarah, your wife, shall bear you a son indeed, and you shall call his name Isaac, and I will establish My covenant with him for an everlasting covenant, and with his seed after him. As for Ishmael I have heard you. Behold I have blessed him... But My covenant will I establish with Isaac whom Sarah shall bear unto you..." (Gen. 17:18–21).

God lays emphasis upon Sarah's role in the realization of the covenantal society. Abraham's offspring are not taken into this esoteric community if their mother happens to be Hagar and not Sarah. Later, when Sarah demands the expulsion of Ishmael, and Abraham is not eager to comply with her request, God tells him in terse terms, "Let it not be grievous in your sight because of the lad, and because of your bondwoman; in all that Sarah has said unto you, hearken unto her voice, for in Isaac shall your seed be called" (Gen. 21:12).

Rebecca is responsible for the covenant being transmitted to Jacob instead of Esau (Gen. 27). Isaac had contemplated entrusting the spiritual heritage to his oldest son. At the hour of crisis Rebecca intervened and thereby determined the historical destiny of the covenantal community. She sent Jacob to Haran to marry her nieces. Miriam is responsible for the emergence of Moses as a leader and redeemer of his people. If not for her, he would have never been imbued with great passionate love for his poor brethren. She suggested to the princess that a Hebrew wet-nurse be employed for the infant, preventing Moses from disappearing in anonymity and ignorance: "And his sister stood afar off, to know what would be done to him... Then said the sister to Pharaoh's daughter, 'Shall I go and call for you a nurse of the Hebrew women...'; and the maid went and called the child's mother" (Ex. 2:4, 7, 8). Similarly, Deborah saved the people from oppression and slavery when she organized the rebellion under the military command of Barak (Judges 4–5). And the Aggadah relates that the women refused to contribute to the Golden Calf (*Pirkei de-Rabbi Eliezer* 45) while they gave generously to the Tabernacle (Ex. 35).

The woman is both a demonic and Divine crisis personality. Eve and Delilah represent the woman-demon; our matriarchs, the Divine individuality. The destiny of mankind and of the covenantal people was shaped by the woman.

The Book of Proverbs dedicated its last section (31:11–31) to the woman of valor in whom the heart of her husband trusts. Valor as a trait of the feminine personality was born in the covenantal community where motherhood, instead of being a factum, became a challenge and an ideal.

The Tragedy in Motherhood

And yet the story of the Biblical woman, the covenantal mother, ends with a tragic note. The very moment she brings her job to a close, the instant she completes her task, when the crisis is over, she returns quickly to her tent, draws down the curtain of anonymity and disappears. She is outside of the hustle and bustle of the male society. Abraham sits "in front of the tent" (Gen. 18:1). His name appears in the press and many know him; he is the leader, the father, the teacher; his lips drip honey; he enlightens the minds; he fascinates the passersby. Hardly anyone knows that there is a Sarah, humble, modest, publicly shy. Somewhere in the tent is the person who is perhaps responsible for all the accomplishments credited to Abraham, for all the glory that is bestowed upon Abraham, who is superior to him, who leads the leader and teaches the teacher and guides the master, who inspires the visionary and interprets his dreams.

Sarah, the Biblical woman, is modest, humble, self-effacing. She enters the stage when she is called upon, acts her part with love and devotion in a dim corner of the stage, and then leaves softly by a side door without applause and without the enthusiastic response of the audience which is hardly aware of her. She returns to her tent, to anonymity and retreat. Only sensitive people know the truth. Only three travelers inquired about her. These travelers were not ordinary people whose eyes see only the surface. They were the angels of God. Their glimpse penetrated and apprehended the image of the true leader, teacher, prophetess, to whom everything should be credited. Nonchalantly they remarked, "Where is Sarah, your wife?" (Gen. 18:9). In other words, we know that without her you could not play the part that God assigned to you. Where is she? Why do not people know the truth? Why has she been just trailing behind you? Why did she not march in front of you? After all, the covenant cannot and will not be realized without her. Abraham answered tersely, "She is in the tent" (Gen. 18:9). Indeed she is enveloped in mystery.

It is quite interesting that although Abraham survived Sarah by thirty-eight years, his historical role came to an end with Sarah's passing. Isaac leaves the stage together with Rebecca. Jacob relinquishes his role to Joseph with the untimely death of Rachel. Without Sarah there would be no Abraham; no Isaac were it not for Rebecca; no Jacob without Rachel.

And yet, and here the tragedy manifests itself with all its impact, we say, "God of Abraham, God of Isaac, God of Jacob," but not "God of Sarah, God of Rebecca, God of Rachel and Leah," even though they had an equal share in *Borei Olam*, the Creator of the World.

The Halakhah was cognizant of the greatness of the covenantal mother when it formulated the rule that *Kedushat Yisrael*, one's status as a Jew, can be transmitted only through the woman. The Halakhah was also conscious of the loneliness and the tragic note in the feminine commitment when it accepted a contradictory rule that the child takes his father's name and family status.

The Duality of Fatherhood

A question arises in the Mishnah and Tosefta Bikkurim whether a proselyte may, when praying, address himself to God as "our God and the God of our fathers." The Halakhah has accepted the viewpoint of Rabbi Judah in the Jerusalem Talmud (Bikkurim 1:4) that the proselyte may recite the fixed text of the Bikkurim portion, including "which Thou didst swear unto our ancestors" (Deut. 26:15). Maimonides writes, relative to this problem: "The proselyte brings [*bikkurim,* his first fruits] and reads [the portion in Deuteronomy 26] for it was said by God to Abraham, 'and you shall be a father of many nations' (Gen. 17:4). Thus he [Abraham] is the father of the entire world that enters under the wings of the Divine Providence" (Maimonides, *Hilkhot Bikkurim* [Laws of the First Fruit Offering] 4:3).

Maimonides did not interpret the phrase "a father of many nations" in the sense of natural fatherhood, that Abraham will be naturally fruitful and fertile, the progenitor of many peoples. He saw it rather as denoting another kind of fatherhood, the spiritual. Abraham is the father of all those who gather under the wings of the *Shekhinah,* the Divine Presence, of those who cleave to the God of Israel and commit themselves to His teachings. The change from Abram to Abraham is symbolic of the transition from the relationship of biological progeny and offspring to that of metaphysical father/teacher and child/disciple.

When a man begets a child who is biologically his, a natural being becomes an Abram. This role is not a distinct privilege bestowed upon man exclusively. Procreation is a natural function of man and beast alike. But fatherhood that is rooted in the great idea-experience surpasses by far fatherhood due to a natural process of fertilization of the ovum. This message was conveyed to us through the covenant with Abraham. The covenant freed our ancestor from the natural restrictions of nature and widened his fatherhood experience to universal proportions. Whoever in the hour of enlightenment decides to return to God is embraced by Abraham as a beloved child.

In a word, fatherhood is a double experience, a natural and a personal-metaphysical one. At the first level, man is procreative and sues for a status of fatherhood which is doomed to failure because he will never develop the proper relationship with his offspring. He will have to resign himself to unmitigated contempt on the part of the son or daughter, as the young will always resent and despise the old; or he may have to establish a veritable tyranny in his home, a result of a meaningless and absurdly resentful relationship. At the second level, father and child form a relationship which adds a new quality to their existential experience. They form an ontic community, a community of being, within which man is relieved of the loneliness which lashes him with untold ruthlessness and existential insensateness. Only within this fellowship is real fatherhood found.

However, when I speak of the Abrahamic fatherhood which is attained through education, I understand the latter not only in terms of technical training of the child, of the development of his aptitudes and talents, of actualizing the child's full natural potential, of exercising his or her innate physical and intellectual capabilities. However important and essential this type of education is to the full realization of the child, the idea of Abrahamic fatherhood implies a new dimension, one which is to be found beside the realm of education as it is understood by philosophers and pedagogues. The service Abraham rendered to Isaac did not consist in educating him in skills and aptitudes in the Platonic sense, in bringing out what already was endowed in him, but in introducing him to a new existence, a covenantal, redeemed one. Abraham ushered Isaac into the covenantal community consisting of four *personae,* I, thou, he (lower case) and He (upper case). Abraham revealed to Isaac the regenerating Law of God, or His ways. Abraham became a part of the scheme of revelation of God's Law. While education aims only at being human, Abraham is within finitude involved with Isaac as to the latter's *trans-humanitas.* He gave him something which lies beyond and above the finite reality. He discovered for him the idea of self-transcendence and self-redemption, of catharsis.

"For I have known him that he shall command his children and his household after him that they shall keep the way of the Lord, to do righteousness and justice, so that the Lord may bring upon Abraham that which He had spoken of him" (Gen. 18:19). Fatherhood expresses itself in a testamental act, in transmitting the great experience and law of *revelatio Dei.* Not only does the father prepare his children for life, not only does he adapt them to an existing reality, as the naturalistic theory interprets the educational activity, but he also commits them to a higher transcendental reality. The fatherhood of Abraham is covenantal and was firmly established at the Mount Moriah with the *Akedah* drama, his willingness to sacrifice Isaac (Gen. 22). Many a modern father who tries to give his children an excellent technical education fails to become Abraham, to re-experience his fatherhood in letting his children discover a new reality of a committed, redeemed existence.

Clan and Nation

When God changed Abraham's name from Abram, He changed his task as well as that of his children. Abraham's role was changed from that of a private person, an individual, into that of a father of a nation. The land was granted not to a father of a *clan* but to a father of a *nation.* The promise was related to a nation: "I have made you the father of many nations... I will make nations come out of you" (Gen. 17:4,6).

He will no more be just the head of a clan, of a tribe or many tribes. He will be the father of a nation, of an aboriginal covenantal entity. The father personifies the nation; he is a nation disguised as an individual. Abram denotes the natural link, the father of a family; Abraham signifies the existential link between a father and his offspring when he experiences ontological unity, oneness of being, and comity, as if he lived in them in a future generation, as if he will continue to exist through them. A nation is not a clan. It is an entity *per se,* a personality, an individuality. It is not a collective thing integrated of the many, but an aboriginal unity. *Keneset Yisrael,* corporate Israel, is a being. It exists in the same manner as I, you and he exist. For instance, we believe that the promised land belongs to us. To whom? To me, to you, to him? To all of us? No! It belongs not to one of us, nor to all of us in partnership! It belongs to *Keneset Yisrael* as an individuality, an original being. *Keneset Yisrael* may encompass all of mankind, since everybody can join through *gerut,* conversion. No racial legitimation is required.

Once the children of Abraham will form a nation, once Abraham will be elevated to the father of a people, a nation, another question arises: who will be the mother of the nation? A clan can be formed by having a common ancestor, either a father or a mother. It is a purely biological blood link. A nation, however, is not dependent upon a blood relation. A nation has a common father-teacher. The father of a nation passes on to future generations not just genetic characteristics but a spiritual heritage, a way of life, a morality, an accumulation of values—in a word, a great world, a specific existential experience; he wills his own self to the generations, creating a sense of ontological unity, "...that he shall command his children and his household after him that they shall keep the way of the Lord, to do righteousness and justice" (Gen. 18:19).

The Torah has emphasized that both father and mother were created in the image of God and that both of them express themselves by using their re-spective image-consciousness in a unique way. Together they reflect the total glory and majesty which God invested in them. Hence, the nation cannot come into existence and become God's own nation unless the nation receives the moral code from the mother as well as the father. God speaks to his people either as a father or as a mother. He entrusted teaching to both. Hence, a nation must have a mother.

That is why the Torah tells us that Sarah could not bear a child (Gen. 11:30, 16:1). Without her, there will be no birth of a nation. The whole covenant would have been null and void if Sarah had not been involved. Abraham turned into a spiritual father, a universal teacher, or into an idea; so did Sarah. She became a mother of people, not a mother of a clan. She was transformed into an idea. Of course, she will teach her children the same moral code that Abraham formulated. However, she will interpret the same code in the unique style which only a mother knows. Abraham interprets events in his individual fashion. Sarah interprets events and things under the aspect of involvement and sharing.

How beautifully the Torah tells us the story of a father whom God charged with the mission of forming a nation and who could not implement his assignment because Sarah, the choicest of all women, could not join him since she was barren. God had to resort to a miracle in order that a charismatic nation be formed. Sarah *will* be the mother of the nation. "I will bless her and give you a son through her. I will bless her that she shall give rise to nations; rulers of people shall issue from her" (Gen. 17:16). The Almighty reemphasized that without Sarah there will be no covenant with a nation. The great historic task was entrusted to two people. They reflect the greatness of man *in toto.* Through them the great nation will achieve completeness.

Family Redeemed: Essays on Family Relationships [New Jersey: Toras Horav Foundation, 2000], pp. 105–125.
Reprinted with permission of the publisher

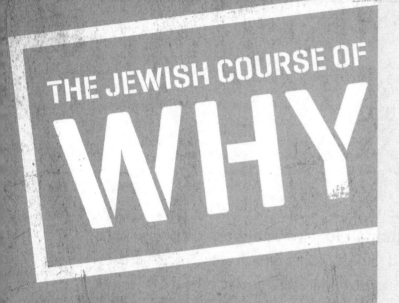

THE JEWISH COURSE OF

WHY

LESSON FOUR

1. Why doesn't Judaism seek converts?

2. Why does the Torah say that the Jews are the "chosen people"? Isn't that racist?

3. Why do we believe that we have free choice if God always knew how we would choose?

4. Why does the Torah permit slavery?

5. Why does Jewish law obsess over details?

6. Why is it permitted to have sexual relations on Shabbat?

7. Why does the Bible refer to sexual relations as "knowing"?

8. Why aren't vegan foods and restaurants Kosher by default?

9. Why do we say *lechayim* as a drinking salutation?

JLI

JEWISH LEARNING INSTITUTE

1. Why doesn't Judaism seek converts?

Tribalism, Universalism, Judaism

Text 1

Rabbi Jonathan Sacks, The Dignity of Difference: How to Avoid the Clash of Civilizations [London: Continuum, 2003], pp. 52–53 ▌

Rabbi Jonathan Sacks, PhD
1948–

Former chief rabbi of the United Kingdom. Rabbi Sacks attended Cambridge University and received his doctorate from King's College, London. A prolific and influential author, his books include *Will We Have Jewish Grandchildren?* and *The Dignity of Difference*. He received the Jerusalem Prize in 1995 for his contributions to enhancing Jewish life in the Diaspora, was knighted and made a life peer in 2005, and became Baron Sacks of Aldridge in 2009.

Judaism has a structural peculiarity so perplexing and profound that though its two daughter monotheisms, Christianity and Islam, took much else from it, they did not adopt this: it is a particularist monotheism. It believes in one God but not in one exclusive path to salvation. *The God of the Israelites is the God of all mankind, but the demands made of the Israelites are not asked of all mankind.*

There is no equivalent in Judaism to the doctrine *extra ecclesiam non est salus,* "outside the Church there is no salvation." On the contrary, Judaism's ancient sages maintained that "the pious of the nations have a share in the world to come."

Indeed, the Bible takes it for granted that the God of Israel is not only the God of Israel. He is also the God of Abraham's contemporary, Melchizedek, king of Salem, not a member of the covenantal family but still a "priest of the Most High God." He is acknowledged by Jethro, Moses'

[handwritten notes in margin:]
Tribalism = Many gods
Universalism = One god, one way to serve him
Judaism One God, multiple ways to serve him

father-in-law and a Midianite priest, who gives Israel its first lesson in government—the appointment of heads of thousands, hundreds, fifties, and tens.

Jewish Laws – 360
Noah's laws – 7 to continue Morality in the world
until the Nations Are created anew after

Text 2
The Flood.

The Lubavitcher Rebbe, Rabbi Menachem Mendel Schneerson, English correspondence, 12 Shevat, 5744 (January 16, 1984)

When it comes to contemplating the existence of G-d, one must first of all realize that a finite human being, even the wisest of men, cannot grasp the "mind" and "thought" of the Creator, Whose attributes are essentially incomprehensible as Himself—except to the extent that He willed to reveal in the Torah. . . .

Now insofar as the human race is concerned, the Torah tells us that it has evolved, by the design of the Creator, into a variety of components, rather than one massive uniform block, just as the physical human body consists of a variety of organs and parts, each with its purpose and function; nothing in it is useless or superfluous. For, as our Sages tell us (Talmud, Shabbat 77b), "The Creator has not created anything useless in His world."

Of course one may wonder why did G-d choose one nation out of all mankind to give it His Torah and *mitzvos* and designate it as "A kingdom of *kohanim* (G-d's servants) and a holy nation" (Exodus 19:6)? . . . But this would be like asking, why must the human body consist of such a variety of different parts, from the brain and heart to the foot and sole? Why not make it all heart or all brain?

Everything in Creation has its purpose. Each nation
has valid

Rabbi Menachem Mendel Schneerson
1902–1994

The towering Jewish leader of the 20th century, known as "the Lubavitcher Rebbe," or simply as "the Rebbe." Born in southern Ukraine, the Rebbe escaped Nazi-occupied Europe, arriving in the U.S. in June 1941. The Rebbe inspired and guided the revival of traditional Judaism after the European devastation, impacting virtually every Jewish community the world over. The Rebbe often emphasized that the performance of just one additional good deed could usher in the era of Mashiach. The Rebbe's scholarly talks and writings have been printed in more than 200 volumes.

The Proselyte (Optional)

Text 3

Babylonian Talmud

A literary work of monumental proportions that draws upon the legal, spiritual, intellectual, ethical, and historical traditions of Judaism. The 37 tractates of the Babylonian Talmud contain the teachings of the Jewish sages from the period after the destruction of the 2nd Temple through the 5th century CE. It has served as the primary vehicle for the transmission of the Oral Law and the education of Jews over the centuries; it is the entry point for all subsequent legal, ethical, and theological Jewish scholarship.

Talmud, Yevamot 22a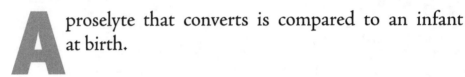

גֵּר שֶׁנִּתְגַּיֵּיר כְּקָטָן שֶׁנּוֹלַד דָּמֵי.

A proselyte that converts is compared to an infant at birth.

KEY POINTS

- Judaism does not seek converts because of the fundamental belief that non-Jews serve God in a way that is unique from Jews and necessary to the purpose of Creation.

- Judaism accepts sincere converts, for the genuine desire to be Jewish is an expression of the convert's real destiny and mission in life.

---

2. Why does the Torah say that the Jews are the "chosen people"? Isn't that racist?

Chosen For . . .

Text 4a

Exodus 19:4–6 📖

אַתֶּם רְאִיתֶם אֲשֶׁר עָשִׂיתִי לְמִצְרָיִם, וָאֶשָּׂא אֶתְכֶם
עַל כַּנְפֵי נְשָׁרִים, וָאָבִא אֶתְכֶם אֵלָי.

וְעַתָּה אִם שָׁמוֹעַ תִּשְׁמְעוּ בְּקֹלִי וּשְׁמַרְתֶּם אֶת בְּרִיתִי,
וִהְיִיתֶם לִי סְגֻלָּה מִכָּל הָעַמִּים כִּי לִי כָּל הָאָרֶץ.

וְאַתֶּם תִּהְיוּ לִי מַמְלֶכֶת כֹּהֲנִים וְגוֹי קָדוֹשׁ.

You have seen what I did to the Egyptians, and [how] I bore you on eagles' wings, and I brought you to Me.

And now, if you obey Me and keep My covenant, you shall be to Me a treasure out of all peoples, for Mine is the entire earth.

And you shall be to Me a kingdom of princes and a holy nation.

Text 4b

Rabbi Ovadiah Seforno, ad loc.

→ **Rabbi Ovadiah Seforno**
1475–1550

Biblical exegete, philosopher, and physician. Seforno was born in Cesena, Italy. After gaining a thorough knowledge of Talmud and the sciences, he moved to Rome where he studied medicine and taught Hebrew to the German scholar Johannes Reuchlin. Seforno eventually settled in Bologna where he founded and directed a yeshivah until his death. His magnum opus is a biblical commentary focused on the simple interpretation of text, with an emphasis on philology and philosophy.

"וִהְיִיתֶם לִי סְגֻלָּה מִכָּל הָעַמִּים": אַף עַל פִּי שֶׁכָּל הַמִּין הָאֱנוֹשִׁי יָקָר אֶצְלִי מִכָּל יֶתֶר הַנִּמְצָאִים הַשְּׁפָלִים, כִּי הוּא לְבַדּוֹ הַמְכֻוָּן בָּהֶם, כְּאָמְרָם ז"ל, "חָבִיב אָדָם שֶׁנִּבְרָא בְּצֶלֶם" (אָבוֹת ג,יד), מִכָּל מָקוֹם אַתֶּם תִּהְיוּ לִי סְגוּלָה מִכֻּלָּם.

"You shall be to Me a treasure out of all peoples": The entire human race is more precious to Me than all lower creatures, because the purpose of Creation is [fulfilled through] them. Indeed, our sages of blessed memory taught (Mishnah, Avot 3:14), "Beloved are human beings for they were created in the image of God." Nevertheless, from among all, you shall be my treasure.

In the world nothing will be developed without the people's being. Why are all people special? They're here to contribute to the better of society. Together All nations complete a whole body.

Text 4c

Rabbi Ovadiah Seforno, ad loc.

"וְאַתֶּם תִּהְיוּ לִי מַמְלֶכֶת כֹּהֲנִים": וּבָזֶה תִּהְיוּ סְגוּלָה מִכֻּלָּם, כִּי תִּהְיוּ מַמְלֶכֶת כֹּהֲנִים לְהָבִין וּלְהוֹרוֹת לְכָל הַמִּין הָאֱנוֹשִׁי לִקְרוֹא כֻלָּם בְּשֵׁם ה', וּלְעָבְדוֹ שְׁכֶם אֶחָד.

"And you shall be to Me a kingdom of princes": You will be a treasure to me in the sense that you will be a kingdom of priests, to guide and teach the entire human race to invoke God's name and to worship Him shoulder to shoulder.

Jews are the Chosen = work harder to make this world better, be a light to others

Text 5a

John Adams, letter to F. A. Vanderkemp, 16 February 1809, in *The Works of John Adams* [Boston: Little, Brown and Company, 1854], 9:608–609

In spite of Bolingbroke and Voltaire, I will insist that the Hebrews have done more to civilize man than any other nation. If I were an atheist, and believed in blind eternal fate, I should still believe that chance had ordered the Jews to be the most essential instrument for civilizing the nations. If I were an atheist to the other sect, who believed or pretended to believe that all is ordered by chance, I should believe that chance has ordered the Jews to preserve and propagate to all mankind the doctrine of a supreme, intelligent, wise, almighty sovereign of the universe, which I believe to be the great essential principle of all morality, and consequently of all civilization. I cannot say that I love the Jews very much neither, nor the French, nor the English, nor the Romans, nor the Greeks. We must love all nations as well as we can, but it is very hard to love most of them.

John Adams
1735–1826

Second president of the United States and political theorist. Adams, a Boston lawyer and public figure, was an active and influential leader in the American Revolution and helped Thomas Jefferson draft the Declaration of Independence. Adams served two terms as George Washington's vice president before being elected president.

Text 5b

Paul Johnson, *History of the Jews* [New York: Harper & Row, 1987], p. 585

Paul Johnson

English journalist, historian, speechwriter, and author. First came to prominence in the 1950s as a journalist writing for, and later editing, the *New Statesman* magazine. He has written over 40 books and contributed to numerous magazines and newspapers. In 2006, Johnson was honored with the Presidential Medal of Freedom by U.S. President George W. Bush.

One way of summing up 4000 years of Jewish history is to ask ourselves what would have happened to the human race if Abraham had not been a man of great sagacity, if he had stayed in Ur and kept his higher notions to himself, and no specific Jewish people had come into being. Certainly, the world without the Jews would have been a radically different place. . . .

All the great conceptual discoveries of the intellect seem obvious and inescapable once they have been revealed, but it requires a special genius to formulate them for the first time. The Jew has this gift. To them we owe the idea of equality before the law, both divine and human; of the sanctity of life and the dignity of the human person; of the individual conscience and so of personal redemption; of the collective conscience and so of social responsibility; of peace as an abstract ideal and love as the foundation of justice, and many other items which constitute the basic moral furniture of the human mind. Without the Jews, it might have been a much emptier place.

Divine Treasure (Optional)

Text 6

Rashi, Exodus 19:5

"סְגֻלָּה:" אוֹצָר חָבִיב, כְּמוֹ "וּסְגֻלַּת מְלָכִים" (קֹהֶלֶת ב,ח), כְּלֵי יָקָר וַאֲבָנִים טוֹבוֹת שֶׁהַמְּלָכִים גּוֹנְזִים אוֹתָם. כָּךְ אַתֶּם תִּהְיוּ לִי סְגוּלָה מִשְּׁאָר אומות.

Segulah: A beloved treasure, as it says, "The treasure of kings" (Ecclesiastes 2:8), which refers to the costly vessels and precious stones that kings store away. So will you be My treasure from among the nations.

Rabbi Shlomo Yitschaki (Rashi)
1040–1105

Most noted biblical and Talmudic commentator. Born in Troyes, France, Rashi studied in the famed *yeshivot* of Mainz and Worms. His commentaries on the Pentateuch and the Talmud, which focus on the straightforward meaning of the text, appear in virtually every edition of the Talmud and Bible.

Text 7

Rabbi Shne'ur Zalman of Liadi, *Igeret Hakodesh* 2 📖

שֶׁבְּכָל חֶסֶד וָחֶסֶד שֶׁהַקָּדוֹשׁ בָּרוּךְ הוּא עוֹשֶׂה לָאָדָם, צָרִיךְ לִהְיוֹת שְׁפַל רוּחַ בִּמְאֹד.

כִּי חֶסֶד דְּרוֹעָא יְמִינָא. וִימִינוֹ תְּחַבְּקֵנִי. שֶׁהִיא בְּחִינַת קִרְבַת אֱלֹקִים מַמָּשׁ בְּיֶתֶר שְׂאֵת מִלְּפָנִים. וְכָל הַקָּרוֹב אֶל ה' בְּיֶתֶר שְׂאֵת וְהַגְבָּהָ לְמַעֲלָה מַעְלָה, צָרִיךְ לִהְיוֹת יוֹתֵר שְׁפַל רוּחַ לְמַטָּה מַטָּה, כְּמוֹ שֶׁכָּתוּב (יִרְמְיָהוּ לא,ב), "מֵרָחוֹק ה' נִרְאָה לִי".

וּכְנוֹדַע דְּכֹלָּא קַמֵּיה דַּוְוקָא כְּלָא חָשִׁיב, וְאִם כֵּן כָּל שֶׁהוּא קַמֵּיה יוֹתֵר, הוּא יוֹתֵר כְּלָא וְאַיִן וְאָפֶס.

Rabbi Shne'ur Zalman of Liadi (Alter Rebbe)
1745–1812

Chasidic rebbe, halachic authority, and founder of the Chabad movement. The Alter Rebbe was born in Liozna, Belarus, and was among the principal students of the Magid of Mezeritch. His numerous works include the *Tanya*, an early classic containing the fundamentals of Chabad Chasidism, and *Shulchan Aruch HaRav*, an expanded and reworked code of Jewish law.

Every act of kindness that God bestows upon us has to render us more humble.

God's kindness is "an embrace of God's right arm," a metaphor for God bringing us closer to Himself, far more intensely than before. The closer we are to God, the more humble we need to be, as it is written (Jeremiah 31:2), "From afar the Lord has appeared to me."

It is known that all that is before Him is esteemed as nothing, which implies that the more one is "before Him," the more one is like naught and nonexistent.

KEY POINTS

- Chosenness is a call to responsibility—to guide and teach the world about ethical monotheism. Denying our chosenness would be a disservice to humanity.

3. Why do we believe that we have free choice if God always knew how we would choose?

Our Choice First

Text 8

Rabbi Shmuel de Uceda, *Midrash Shmuel*, Avot 3:21

לְפִי שֶׁהַשֵּׁם יִתְבָּרֵךְ הוּא מַבִּיט לְסוֹף דָּבָר בְּקַדְמוּתוֹ, וְכָל מַה שֶׁיַּעֲבוֹר עַל הָאָדָם עַד עֵת מוֹתוֹ הַכֹּל הוּא לְפָנָיו. וּמֵעֵת תְּחִלַּת יְדִיעָתוֹ מִנִּי אָז, רָאָה זֶה הָאָדָם מֵת מוּטָל לְפָנָיו, וְרָאָה בַּמֶּה בָּחַר כְּבָר. כִּי הוּא יִתְבָּרֵךְ אֵינוֹ תַּחַת הַזְּמַן, וְלֹא שַׁיָּךְ בֵּיהּ קְדִימָה וְאִיחוּר.

אִם כֵּן מַה שֶׁאֵירַע אֵינָה גְזֵרָה מֵאִתּוֹ יִתְבָּרֵךְ חַס וְשָׁלוֹם. רַק הִבִּיט וְרָאָה וְצָפָה מַה שֶׁהָאָדָם יִבְחַר הַפְּשׁוּטָה בִּבְחִירָתוֹ עַד סוֹף יָמָיו . . .

וְהִמְשִׁיל הָרַב ר' מֹשֶׁה אַלְמוֹשְׁנִינוּ ז"ל מָשָׁל בָּזֶה, וְאָמַר אִם אֲנִי רוֹאֶה אֶת רְאוּבֵן בַּהֹוֶה שֶׁהוּא רָץ, הִנֵּה יְחוּיָּב שֶׁיִּהְיֶה כֵּן, וְלֹא יִתָּכֵן בְּשׁוּם צַד שֶׁיִּהְיֶה בִּלְתִּי רָץ בִּהְיוֹתוֹ רָץ בַּהֹוֶה, שֶׁאִם כֵּן יִהְיוּ שְׁנֵי הֲפָכִים בְּנוֹשֵׂא אֶחָד בִּזְמַן אֶחָד. וְעִם כָּל זֶה, לֹא יֵאָמַר שֶׁהוּא מוּכְרָח בִּמְרוּצָתוֹ מִצַּד רְאִיָּיתִי וִידִיעָתִי שֶׁאֲנִי רוֹאֶה אוֹתוֹ רָץ, כִּי אִם שֶׁרְאִיָּיתִי וִידִיעָתִי אֲמִיתִית, הִנֵּה פְּעוּלָּתוֹ הִיא אֶפְשָׁרִית.

כֵּן יְדִיעָתוֹ יִתְבָּרֵךְ אֵינָה מַכְרַחַת פְּעוּלַּת הָאָדָם, אַף שֶׁיְּדָעָה, יַעַן הוּא יוֹדֵעַ אוֹתָם תָּמִיד בַּהֹוֶה, כִּי אֵין עָתִיד לְפָנָיו יִתְבָּרֵךְ שֶׁהוּא לְמַעֲלָה מִן הַזְּמַן, וְכָל הַזְּמַנִּים הָעֲתִידִים בְּעֶרְכֵּנוּ לְאֵין תַּכְלִית הֵם הֹוִים לְפָנָיו. וּכְמוֹ שֶׁבְּעֶרְכֵּנוּ יְדִיעָתֵנוּ אֵינָה מַכְרַחַת, כֵּן יְדִיעָתוֹ, לִהְיוֹתָהּ תְּמִידִי בְּעֶרְכּוֹ בַּהֹוֶה, אֵינָה מַכְרַחַת.

וְנִתְחַיֵּיב הַטָּעוּת בַּסָּפֵק הַזֶּה, לְמַה שֶׁאֵין אָנוּ יְכוֹלִים לְצַיֵּיר אֵיךְ תִּהְיֶה יְדִיעָתוֹ תָּמִיד בַּהֹוֶה, אַף בְּמַה שֶׁהוּא עָתִיד אֶצְלֵנוּ, וּבִהְיוֹתֵנוּ מַקִּישִׁים יְדִיעָתוֹ יִתְבָּרֵךְ אֶל יְדִיעָתֵנוּ נִתְחַיֵּיב אֶצְלֵנוּ הַסָּפֵק.

Rabbi Shmuel de Uceda
ca. 1545–1604

Author and Kabbalist. His name, Uceda, originates from the town of that name in the archbishopric of Toledo. Rabbi Shmuel was born in Safed, where he was a pupil of the Arizal and Rabbi Chaim Vital, with whom he studied Kabbalah. He grew to become a rabbi and teacher in Safed and later in Constantinople. He wrote commentaries to some biblical books, but is most noted for his *Mirash Shmuel* commentary on *Ethics of the Fathers*.

Rabbi Moshe Almosnino
1510–1580

Distinguished Jewish scholar. Rabbi Moshe Almosnino was eminent for knowledge of rabbinical matters and for scholarship in the sciences of his day, particularly natural physics and astronomy, furnishing commentaries upon many treatises translated from the Arabic and Latin. In 1565, he successfully represented his brethren at an audience with the Sultan Selim II, petitioning for the confirmation of their civil rights. He wrote a commentary on the Biblical *Megilot* under the title *Yedei Moshe* and an exposition on *Ethics of the Fathers*.

God sees in the present what the future will be. He foreknows everything that will befall us until the day we die. From the beginning of time, He observes our inevitable demise and all of our choices during our lifetime. For He is not subject to the limitations of time. The lines between past and future are not drawn.

Accordingly, our choices were not decreed by Him, God forbid. Rather, He looks and sees what we will choose until our last day. . . .

Rabbi Moshe Almosnino suggested the following parable:

If I see Reuben running, although my knowledge of this fact is flawless, one cannot say that Reuben is forced to run due to my seeing and knowing that he is running. Despite my knowledge, he is running by choice.

Similarly, God's knowledge does not compel our choices. God's knowledge is knowledge of the present. There is no future for Him, because He transcends the confines of time. Our future is God's present. And just like our knowledge of the present does not affect people's choices, so too, His knowledge—always about the present—does not affect our choices.

The confusion that we have in this regard is rooted in the fact that we cannot fathom the notion of God knowing the future in the present, which, in turn, is due to our thinking of God's knowledge through the prism of our own limited knowledge.

A Pointed Paradox (Optional)

Text 9

Maimonides, *Mishneh Torah*, Laws of *Teshuvah* 5:5 📖

דַּע שֶׁתְּשׁוּבַת שְׁאֵלָה זוֹ אֲרוּכָה מֵאֶרֶץ מִדָּה וּרְחָבָה מִנִּי יָם . . . וּכְשֵׁם שֶׁאֵין כֹּחַ בָּאָדָם לְהַשִּׂיג וְלִמְצוֹא אֲמִתַּת הַבּוֹרֵא, שֶׁנֶּאֱמַר, "כִּי לֹא יִרְאַנִי הָאָדָם וָחָי" (שְׁמוֹת לג,כ), אֵין כֹּחַ בָּאָדָם לְהַשִּׂיג וְלִמְצוֹא דַּעְתּוֹ שֶׁל בּוֹרֵא. הוּא שֶׁהַנָּבִיא אָמַר "כִּי לֹא מַחְשְׁבוֹתַי מַחְשְׁבוֹתֵיכֶם וְלֹא דַרְכֵיכֶם דְּרָכָי" (יְשַׁעְיָהוּ נה,ח). וְכֵיוָן שֶׁכֵּן הוּא, אֵין בָּנוּ כֹּחַ לֵידַע הֵיאַךְ יֵדַע הַקָּדוֹשׁ בָּרוּךְ הוּא כָּל הַבְּרוּאִים וְהַמַּעֲשִׂים. אֲבָל נֵדַע בְּלֹא סָפֵק שֶׁמַּעֲשֵׂה הָאָדָם בְּיַד הָאָדָם, וְאֵין הַקָּדוֹשׁ בָּרוּךְ הוּא מוֹשְׁכוֹ, וְלֹא גּוֹזֵר עָלָיו לַעֲשׂוֹת כָּךְ, וְלֹא מִפְּנֵי קַבָּלַת הַדָּת בִּלְבַד נוֹדַע דָּבָר זֶה, אֶלָּא בִּרְאָיוֹת בְּרוּרוֹת מִדִּבְרֵי הַחָכְמָה.

Know that the resolution to this question is longer than the earth and broader than the sea. . . . Just as human knowledge cannot comprehend and conceive the Creator, as it states, "No person will perceive Me and live" (Exodus 33:20), we similarly cannot comprehend the nature of His knowledge. This was the intent of the prophet's statement, "For My thoughts are not your thoughts, nor your ways My ways" (Isaiah 55:8). Accordingly, we do not have the potential to conceive how God knows all the creations and their deeds. However, we know without any doubt that our actions are in our own hands and that God does not lead us in a particular direction nor decree that we do a particular act. This matter is known not only as a tradition of faith, but also through clear philosophical proofs.

Rabbi Moshe ben Maimon
(Maimonides, Rambam)
1135–1204

Halachist, philosopher, author, and physician. Maimonides was born in Cordoba, Spain. After the conquest of Cordoba by the Almohads, he fled Spain and eventually settled in Cairo, Egypt. There, he became the leader of the Jewish community and served as court physician to the vizier of Egypt. He is most noted for authoring the *Mishneh Torah*, an encyclopedic arrangement of Jewish law, and for his philosophical work, *Guide for the Perplexed*. His rulings on Jewish law are integral to the formation of halachic consensus.

QUESTION FOR DISCUSSION

Why did Maimonides not provide the answer offered by Rabbi Shmuel de Uceda?

KEY POINTS

- God's knowledge does not influence our choices; our choices influence His knowledge. He knows our choices ahead of time because He sees the future in the present.

- Our free choice must always remain a given. How God could foreknow may remain a theological mystery.

4. Why does the Torah permit slavery?

Lesser of Two Evils

Text 10a

Rabbi Samson Raphael Hirsch, Exodus 12:44 ▐

The consideration of certain circumstances is necessary to correctly understand the fact that the Torah presupposes and allows the possession and purchase of slaves from abroad to a nation itself just released from slavery. No Jew could make any other human being into a slave. He could only acquire by purchase people who, by then universally accepted international law, were already slaves. But this transference into the property of a Jew was the one and only salvation for anybody who, according to the prevailing laws of the nations, was stamped as a slave.

Rabbi Samson Raphael Hirsch
1808–1888

Born in Hamburg, Germany; rabbi and educator; intellectual founder of the *Torah Im Derech Eretz* school of Orthodox Judaism, which advocates combining Torah with secular education. Beginning in 1830, Hirsch served as chief rabbi in several prominent German cities. During this period he wrote his *Nineteen Letters on Judaism*, under the pseudonym of Ben Uziel. His work helped preserve traditional Judaism during the era of the German Enlightenment. He is buried in Frankfurt am Main.

Why Does Jewish Law obcess over Details:
e.g. גלאט כשר's, why have separate Dishes,
why go to mikveh. Why do we need it for
see page 164

Text 10b

Rabbi Ben Zion Uziel, *Machmanei Uziel*, p. 263

יֵשׁ שֶׁמְּלַגְלְגִים עַל תּוֹרַת יִשְׂרָאֵל שֶׁהִתִּירָה קִנְיָן עֶבֶד כְּנַעֲנִי בְּגוּפוֹ. אֲבָל
לוּ חָכְמוּ מְלַגְלְגִים אֵלּוּ הָיוּ מְבִינִים שֶׁקִּנְיָן זֶה לֹא הֻתַּר אֶלָּא לְאֵלֶּה
שֶׁהָיוּ נִמְכָּרִין לַאֲחֵיהֶם בְּאוֹתָם הַתְּנָאִים . . . לְהַצִּילוּ מִיַּד אֶחָיו הַכְּנַעֲנִים
שֶׁלֹּא יִשְׁתַּעְבְּדוּ בּוֹ בְּאַכְזָרִיּוּת וְיִשְׁתַּלְּטוּ בְּגוּפוֹ עַד כְּדֵי מִיתָה.

בָּזֶה מִתְבָּאֶרֶת הַהֲלָכָה (תַּלְמוּד, גִּיטִין מג,ב–מד,א) שֶׁאִם מָכְרוֹ רַבּוֹ
יִשְׂרָאֵל לָעַכּוּ"ם, יָצָא בֶּן חוֹרִין וְכוֹפִין אֶת רַבּוֹ לַחֲזוֹר וְלִקְנוֹתוֹ מִן
הָעַכּוּ"ם עַד עֲשָׂרָה בְּדָמָיו, וְכוֹתֵב לוֹ גֵּט שִׁחְרוּר וְיוֹצֵא . . .

בְּתוֹרַת יִשְׂרָאֵל לֹא הֻתִּירָה אֲפִילוּ עַבְדוּת שֶׁל עֶבֶד כְּנַעֲנִי, אֶלָּא הִגְבִּילָה אוֹתוֹ
בְּהַגְבָּלוֹת מְרֻבּוֹת וְקַפְּדָנִיּוֹת, לְטוֹבָתוֹ שֶׁל יְצוּר זֶה שֶׁהָיָה נָתוּן לִהְיוֹת עֶבֶד
עוֹלָם בְּגוּפוֹ, וְנָפְלוּ בִּידֵי אֶחָיו הַכְּנַעֲנִים, וְהִצִּילָה אוֹתוֹ מֵעַבְדוּת שֶׁל בִּזָּיוֹן שִׁלְטוֹן
בְּגוּפוֹ וְנַפְשׁוֹ, וּמָסְרָה אוֹתוֹ לִידֵי יִשְׂרָאֵל שֶׁיִּתְנַהֲגוּ בּוֹ בְּמִדַּת חֶסֶד וְרַחֲמִים.

Rabbi Ben Zion Meir Chai Uziel
1880–1953

Scion of a prestigious family of Torah scholars, he served as Sephardic chief rabbi of Israel from 1939 to 1954. Rabbi Uziel founded many educational and charitable institutions and served in many rabbinical and communal posts, often at great personal sacrifice. He actively participated in establishing the Religious-Zionist Mizrachi movement and promoted its activities. He authored numerous halachic works and is best known for his responsa, *Mishpetei Uziel*.

There are those who scoff at the Torah of Israel for its permitting the purchase of the Canaanite slave. But had these scoffers been wise, they would have understood that this purchase was only permitted regarding those who were sold to their brothers as slaves. . . . The purpose was to save them from their Canaanite brothers, who would work them cruelly and subjugate their bodies to the point of death.

With this, we can understand the Talmudic law (Gitin 43b–44a) that if a Jewish master sold the slave to an idolater, the master would be forced to buy him back at up to ten times his market worth, write him a writ of manumission, and let him go.

The Torah of Israel did not permit even the servitude of a Canaanite without setting many strict limitations for the benefit of he who had been sold into life-long bodily servitude, having fallen into the hands of his Canaanite brothers. This saved him from abusive domination of his body and soul and transferred him to the hands of Israel, who would treat him kindly and compassionately.

Text 11

Rabbi Zadoc Kahn, *Ha'avdut Al Pi HaTorah VehaTalmud*, p. 78 📖

אֵין קִבּוּץ חֲבָרְתִי בַּתֵּבֵל אֲשֶׁר הָעֲבָדִים מָצְאוּ בּוֹ חֲנִינָה וְאַהֲבַת־אָדָם יוֹתֵר מֵאֲשֶׁר אֵצֶל הַיְהוּדִים. מִלְּבַד הַהוֹכָחָה הַנִּצַּחַת הַכְּלוּלָה בְּהַחֻקִּים בְּעַצְמָם, וּמִלְּבַד מַעֲשֵׂה הַחֶסֶד וְהָרַחֲמִים הַלוֹקְחִים לֵב אֲשֶׁר יְסֻפַּר לָנוּ הַתַּלְמוּד, יֵשׁ דָּבָר אֶחָד הַמּוֹכִיחַ עַל אֲמִיתַת מִשְׁפָּטֵנוּ בְּאוֹפֶן הַיּוֹתֵר טוֹב, וְהוּא כִּי בְּכָל קוֹרוֹת עַם יִשְׂרָאֵל לֹא מָצָא אַף הָרוֹשֶׁם הַיּוֹתֵר קַל מִתְלוּנָה כְּלָלִית מִצַּד הָעֲבָדִים, וְאַף הַנִּסָּיוֹן הַיּוֹתֵר קָטָן לְהִתְקוֹמֵם וּלְהִתְפָּרֵץ מִפְּנֵי אֲדוֹנֵיהֶם, בְּעוֹד אֲשֶׁר מְרִידוֹת כָּאֵלֶּה עָשׂוּ שַׁמּוֹת בְּאֲרָצוֹת אֲחֵרוֹת.

There is no society in the world in which slaves found such kindness and love of humanity as in that of the Jews. Aside from the decisive proof implicit in the laws themselves, and aside from the heart-capturing deeds of kindness and compassion described in the Talmud, there is one thing that verifies the true nature of our claim in the best way. That is seen in the fact that in all of recorded Jewish history, one does not find even the faintest trace of complaint from slaves, not even the smallest attempt at an uprising against their masters, when at the same time, there were revolts that caused devastation in other lands.

Rabbi Zadoc Kahn
1839–1905

Chief rabbi of France. The son of a peddler, Rabbi Kahn was born in Mommenheim, Alsace. He was educated in a *yeshivah* at Strasbourg and then at the Ecole Rabbinique in Metz. In 1889, Kahn was appointed chief rabbi of France. He was the editor of a French Bible translation and wrote his dissertation about slavery in Talmudic law.

Text 12a

Rabbi Nachum Eliezer Rabinowitz, *Darkah Shel Torah*, p. 11 📖

מַעֲרֶכֶת הַתּוֹרָה וְהַמִּצְוָוה הִיא כְּפוּלָה. מִצַּד אֶחָד, הַקְנָיַית דֵּעוֹת וְהַשְׁרָשַׁת
עֲרָכִים נִצְחִיִּים, הַנְחָיָה לְעֲבוֹדַת ה' בַּדְּרָגָּה הַגְּבוֹהָה בְּיוֹתֵר, וְעִיצוּב חֶבְרָה הָרְאוּיָה
לִהְיוֹת מֶרְכָּבָה לַשְּׁכִינָה. וּמֵאִידָךְ, חֲקִיקָה וְצִיוּוּיִים לְהִתְמוֹדֵד עִם כּוֹחוֹת הָרַע
וְהַהֶרֶס הַמִּתְפָּרְצִים בְּנַפְשׁוֹ שֶׁל הַיָּחִיד וּבְרוּחוֹ שֶׁל הָעָם . . . לְפִי הַנְּסִיבּוֹת
הַחֶבְרָתִיּוֹת הַכַּלְכָּלִיּוֹת וְהַתַּרְבּוּתִיּוֹת הַשּׁוֹרְרוֹת בְּאוֹתוֹ זְמַן וּבְאוֹתוֹ מָקוֹם.

לְהַשָּׂגַת הַמַּטָּרָה הָרִאשׁוֹנָה מַעֲמִידָה הַתּוֹרָה לְפָנֵינוּ יְעָדִים עִילָאִיִּים הַמְּשַׁמְּשִׁים
אֶתְגָּר וְתַמְרִיץ לְדוֹרוֹת רַבִּים, וַאֲפִילוּ בְּנֵי עֲלִיָּיה לֹא יַשִׂיגוּם בִּשְׁלֵמוּת. בַּד בְּבַד
הִיא קוֹבַעַת לַמַּטָּרָה הַשְּׁנִיָּיה אַמּוֹת מִידָה לְהִתְנַהֲגוּת לְפִי כּוֹחָן שֶׁל הַבְּרִיּוֹת
לְקַבֵּל - קְנֵי מִידָה שֶׁאֵין לִפְחוֹת מֵהֶן מִבְּלִי לְסַכֵּן אֶת עֶצֶם קִיּוּמָם שֶׁל הַיָּחִיד
וְהַחֶבְרָה שֶׁבָּה הוּא נָתוּן וּבְלֹא לְבַטֵּל אֶת הַסִּיכּוּיִים לְהִתְעַלּוּת רוּחָנִית . . .

Rabbi Nachum Eliezer Rabinowitz

1928–

Israeli rabbi and Maimonidean scholar. Born in Montreal, Canada, Rabbi Rabinowitz received rabbinic ordination at Ner Israel, Baltimore, and a PhD in Philosophy of Science at the University of Toronto. An authority on Maimonides, he has published scientific, theological, and halachic works examining Maimonides' writings. He heads Yeshivat Birkat Moshe in Ma'ale Adumim, Israel.

The system of Torah and commandments is two-fold. On the one hand, it conveys concepts, instills eternal values, and directs people to the service of God at the highest levels and to the formation of a society worthy to be the bearer of God's presence. On the other hand, it encompasses legislation and commands to combat the forces of evil and destruction that erupt within the individual's soul and the nation's spirit . . . given each generation's situation and the social, economic, and cultural circumstances prevalent at any given time and place.

For the first objective, the Torah places before us lofty goals that challenge and motivate us, for even the noblest of people cannot attain them in full. At the same time, it establishes, for the second objective, minimum standards for conduct that people can, as a practical matter, accept, and that are needed to avoid endangering the survival of the individual and society and to enable the possibility of spiritual uplift.

Text 12b

Rabbi Nachum Eliezer Rabinowitz, ibid., pp. 13–14 📖

"לְפִיכָךְ נִבְרָא אָדָם יְחִידִי בָּעוֹלָם . . . מִפְּנֵי שְׁלוֹם הַבְּרִיּוֹת, שֶׁלֹּא יֹאמַר אָדָם לַחֲבֵרוֹ, אַבָּא גָּדוֹל מֵאָבִיךָ" . . . (מִשְׁנָה, סַנְהֶדְרִין ד,ה)

כָּךְ, מִבְּרֵאשִׁית, לִימְּדָתְנוּ הַתּוֹרָה **שֶׁמַּעֲמָדָן שֶׁל כָּל בְּנֵי הָאָדָם שָׁוֶוה בֶּאֱמֶת** . . . וְאַף עַל פִּי כֵן, הֲלֹא **הַתּוֹרָה מַכִּירָה בְּמוֹסָד הָעַבְדוּת**! מִצַּד אֶחָד אֵין לְךָ הַצְהָרָה בְּרוּרָה וּבְהִירָה מִזּוֹ שֶׁ"נִּבְרָא אָדָם רִאשׁוֹן יְחִידִי" וְחוֹתָמוֹ שֶׁל ה' מוּטְבָּע עַל עֶבֶד כְּעַל אֲדוֹנָיו, עַל אָמָה כְּעַל גְּבִרְתָּהּ. וּמֵאִידָךְ "מֵהֶם תִּקְנוּ עֶבֶד וְאָמָה . . . וְהָיוּ לָכֶם לַאֲחֻזָּה" (וַיִּקְרָא כה,מד–מה)!

אֶלָּא הוּא הָעִיקָּרוֹן אֲשֶׁר הִסְבִּיר רַבֵּנוּ (מוֹרֵה נְבוּכִים ג,לב) "מַחֲמַת חֲשָׁשׁ מַה שֶׁאֵין יְכוֹלֶת לַנֶּפֶשׁ לְקַבְּלוֹ כְּפִי הַטֶּבַע . . . הֵסֵב ה' אוֹתָם מִן הַדֶּרֶךְ הַיְשָׁרָה שֶׁהָיְתָה הַמַּטָּרָה הָרִאשׁוֹנָה". מִפְּנֵי כּוֹרַח הַמְּצִיאוּת וִיתְּרָה הַתּוֹרָה עַל יִישׂוּמוֹ הַמָּלֵא שֶׁל הָעִיקָּרוֹן מִיָּד, **וְהֶעֱדִיפָה לְקַדֵּם אֶת הַחֶבְרָה צַעַד אַחַר צַעַד עַד שֶׁתּוּשַּׂג הַמַּטָּרָה בִּמְלוֹאָהּ.**

הַדְּבָרִים מְבוֹאָרִים בַּאֵר הֵיטֵב בְּסִפְרָא (לְוַיִּקְרָא כה,מד) . . . "שֶׁמָּא תֹּאמְרוּ . . . בַּמֶּה נִשְׁתַּמֵּשׁ? תַּלְמוּד לוֹמַר: 'וְעַבְדְּךָ וַאֲמָתְךָ אֲשֶׁר יִהְיוּ לָךְ - מֵאֵת הַגּוֹיִם'". בָּעוֹלָם הָעַתִּיק כִּמְעַט שֶׁלֹּא הָיְתָה אֶפְשָׁרוּת לְקַיֵּם מֶשֶׁק תָּקִין בְּלִי כּוֹחַ אָדָם רַב, וּבְדֶרֶךְ כְּלָל אוֹתוֹ כּוֹחַ גּוּיֵּיס לָרוֹב מִן הָעֲבָדִים. גַּם הוֹגֵי דֵעוֹת דְּגוּלִים בֵּין הָעַמִּים לֹא הֶעֱלוּ עַל דַּעְתָּם שֶׁתִּיתָכֵן חֶבְרָה מַצְלִיחָה בְּלִי עֲבוֹדָה רַבָּה. מִבְּחִינָה כַּלְכָּלִית בִּלְתִּי אֶפְשָׁרִי הָיָה הַדָּבָר. "בַּמֶּה נִשְׁתַּמֵּשׁ?" הָיְתָה טַעֲנָה רְצִינִית שֶׁאֵין לְהִתְעַלֵּם מִמֶּנָּה.

בְּרַם, הַתּוֹרָה עָשְׂתָה מַהְפֵּכָה בְּמוֹסָד הָעַבְדוּת. עַל כַּמָּה עֶקְרוֹנוֹת יְסוֹד אִי אֶפְשָׁר הָיָה לְוַותֵּר, וְהֵם כְּאִילוּ יָצְרוּ רִיצְפָּה אֲשֶׁר תִּמְנַע הִידַּרְדְּרוּת לִתְהוֹם הַתַּרְבּוּת הָרָעָה שֶׁל הָאֻמּוֹת. כָּךְ לְמָשָׁל, בְּנִיגּוּד לְכָל חוּקֵּי הָעוֹלָם הָעַתִּיק, נִשְׁמָתוֹ שֶׁל הָעֶבֶד אֵינָהּ רְכוּשׁ שֶׁל הָאָדָם, כִּי אִם שֶׁל אֲדוֹן כֹּל. "וְכִי יַכֶּה

אִישׁ אֶת עַבְדּוֹ אוֹ אֶת אֲמָתוֹ בַּשֵּׁבֶט וּמֵת תַּחַת יָדוֹ - נָקֹם יִנָּקֵם" (שְׁמוֹת
כא,כ). כְּמוֹ כֵן, אָמְנָם נִמְסַר הָעֶבֶד לַעֲבוֹדָתוֹ שֶׁל בְּעָלָיו, אֲבָל גַּם לְנַפְשׁוֹ שֶׁל
הָעֶבֶד דָּאֲגָה תּוֹרָה. יוֹם הַשַּׁבָּת הוּא מְקוּדָּשׁ גַּם לָאָדוֹן וְגַם לָעֶבֶד ...

אֶלָּא שֶׁעִם כָּל זֹאת נִשְׁאֶרֶת עַבְדּוּת, כִּי בַּתְּנָאִים הַשּׁוֹרְרִים
אָז לֹא נִיתַּן הָיָה לְבַטְּלָהּ בְּאוֹפֶן מוּחְלָט.

> **T**he original person was created a single individual in order to promote peace among people, so no person could say to another, 'my progenitor is greater than your progenitor'" (Mishnah, Sanhedrin 4:5). . . . From Creation itself the Torah teaches us that all people are truly equal. . . . Yet the Torah recognizes the institution of slavery! On the one hand, there is no clearer declaration than the creation of but one man [which underscores our equality], and the declaration that all people, slaves and masters alike, are created in the divine image. On the other hand, the Torah states (Leviticus 25:44–45), "From them you shall purchase slaves and maidservants . . . and they shall be your possession"!

This is an instance where Maimonides' principle is relevant: "Out of concern over what people, by their nature, could not accept . . . God did not mandate the ideal path, which was the primary goal (*Guide to the Perplexed* 3:32)" Given the circumstances, the Torah did not require that the principle be applied in full from the outset. Rather, it taught society to advance gradually, until the goal could be fully achieved.

The point is clearly made in *Sifra* (to Leviticus 25:44): "Lest you say . . . 'Whom shall we employ?' Scripture therefore states, 'Slaves and maidservants that may be yours from among the nations.'" In the ancient world, it was almost impossible to sustain a proper economy without vast amounts of human labor, and that human labor was usually recruited from slaves. The leading thinkers among the nations could not conceive of a successful society without bonded servants; as a matter of economics, it was simply impossible. "Whom shall we employ?" was a serious question that could not be avoided.

The Torah revolutionized the institution of slavery. It set out certain fundamental principles that could not be violated, and that set a floor that prevented descent to the vile conduct of the surrounding nations. For example, in contrast to the laws of other nations, the slave's life did not become the master's property but remained in the possession of the Master of all, as it says (Exodus 21:20), "If a man strikes his slave or his maidservant with a rod, causing death, the death shall be avenged." Similarly, although the slave must labor for the master, the Torah remains concerned about the slave's soul. The Shabbat is sacred not only for the master but also for the slave. . . .

Despite these limitations, the institution of slavery remained, for the prevailing conditions precluded its abolition.

QUESTION FOR DISCUSSION

How does Rabbi Rabinowitz's explanation differ from that of Rabbis Hirsch and Uziel?

KEY POINTS

- According to Rabbis Hirsch and Uziel, the Torah allowed the acquisition of existing slaves to save them from their Canaanite owners who would work them cruelly, as opposed to Jews, who were known to treat slaves with kindness and compassion.

- The Torah sets forth grand ideals for us to strive toward, but it also acknowledges reality. Rabbi Rabinowitz asserts that because the Jewish people were not yet ready to live without slaves, the Torah permitted slavery with the aim that they would eventually be weaned from this practice.

5. Why does Jewish law obsess over details?

Describe an area of life where details matter very much to you.	
Describe an area of life where details matter very little to you.	
What is the difference?	
Might this provide insight as to why "God cares about the details"?	

More Than a Mere Dot

Text 13

Rabbi Aron Moss, "Why Is Jewish Law So Petty Minded?" www.chabad.org 📖

Rabbi Aron Moss

Rabbi and author. Rabbi Moss is a teacher of Kabbalah, Talmud, and practical Judaism in Sydney, Australia. He serves as rabbi of the Nefesh Synagogue and authors a popular weekly syndicated article on modern Jewish thought.

Question:

Why does the Jewish religion seem to obsess over insignificant details? How much matza do we have to eat, which spoon did I use for milk and which for meat, what is the right way to tie my shoelaces? It seems to me that this misses the bigger picture by focusing on minutiae. Is this nitpicking what Jews call spirituality?

(I actually already sent you this question over a week ago and didn't receive a reply. Could it be that you have finally been asked a question that you can't answer?!)

Answer:

I never claimed to have all the answers. There are many questions that are beyond me. But it happens to be that I did answer your question, and you did get the answer. I sent a reply immediately. The fact that you didn't receive it is itself the answer to your question.

You see, I sent you a reply, but I wrote your email address leaving out the "dot" before the "com." I figured that you should still receive the email, because after all, it is only one little dot missing. I mean come on, it's not as if I wrote the wrong name or something drastic like that! Would anyone be so nitpicky as to differentiate between "yahoocom" and "yahoo.com"? Isn't it a bit ridiculous that you didn't get my email just because of a little dot?

No, it's not ridiculous. Because the dot is not just a dot. It represents something. That dot has meaning far beyond the pixels on the screen that form it. To me it may seem insignificant, but that is simply due to my ignorance of the ways of the internet. All I know is that with the dot, the message gets to the right destination; without it, the message is lost to oblivion.

Jewish practices have infinite depth. Each nuance and detail contains a world of symbolism. And every dot counts.

God Desires the Heart

Text 14a

Song of Songs 2:4 🔊

וְדִגְלוֹ עָלַי אַהֲבָה.   →   *(handwritten Hebrew) וְנֵצֵל וֹ ... skipping over luring*

His luring me was an act of love.

(handwritten) Details are important because G-D wants it question is not a question in a relation it only enhances it.

Text 14b

Midrash, *Shir Hashirim Rabah 2* 📖

Shir Hashirim Rabah

A midrashic text and exegetical commentary on the book of Song of Songs. This Midrash explicates this biblical book based on the principle that its verses convey an allegory of the relationship between God and the people of Israel. It was compiled and edited in the Land of Israel during the 6th century.

אָמַר רַב אַחָא: עַם הָאָרֶץ שֶׁקּוֹרֵא לְ"אַהֲבָה" "אֵיבָה", כְּגוֹן "וְאָהַבְתָּ" "וְאָיַבְתָּ" - אָמַר הַקָּדוֹשׁ בָּרוּךְ הוּא, "וְדִילוּגוֹ עָלַי אַהֲבָה".

Said Rav Acha, "When an uneducated person says 'eivah' (hatred) instead of 'ahavah' (love)—so for example, [when reading *Shema*], instead of 've'ahavta' ('you shall love'), he recites 've'ayavta' ('you shall hate')—God says about this person, 'His error is beloved unto me.'"

KEY POINTS

- God chose to desire a relationship with us through particular avenues. This is why the details of *mitzvot* are important and why they enable us to connect with God in a meaningful way.

- The details of *mitzvot* matter very much because each mitzvah is meant to accomplish something, and each nuance and detail plays a part in ensuring the desired outcome.

6. Why is it permitted to have sexual relations on Shabbat?

Procreating is a biological instinct.

The Tabernacle

Text 15

Exodus 20:8–10

זָכוֹר אֶת יוֹם הַשַּׁבָּת לְקַדְּשׁוֹ.

שֵׁשֶׁת יָמִים תַּעֲבֹד וְעָשִׂיתָ כָּל מְלַאכְתֶּךָ. וְיוֹם הַשְּׁבִיעִי
שַׁבָּת לַה' אֱלֹקֶיךָ לֹא תַעֲשֶׂה כָל מְלָאכָה.

Remember to sanctify the day of Shabbat.

Six days you shall labor and perform all your work.
But the seventh day is Shabbat for God. You shall perform no work.

Any work it was done in the _ מלאכה → creative labor
Mishkan
vs
עבודה → labor

Anything that changes the nature of:-
↳ from it's life source
e.g. removing a plant from the ground

Creative Labor

Text 16a

Rabbi Ya'akov Tsvi Mecklenburg, *Haketav Vehakabbalah*, Exodus 35:1

דַּע כִּי יֵשׁ הֶבְדֵּל בֵּין מִלַּת עֲבוֹדָה וּבֵין מִלַּת מְלָאכָה:

עֲבוֹדָה כּוֹלֵל כָּל הַמַּעֲשִׂים שֶׁאָדָם עוֹשֶׂה, וַאֲפִילוּ אֵין בְּמַעֲשֵׂהוּ עִנְיָן הַמִּצְטָרֵךְ לִידִיעָה וְחָכְמָה. גַּם אֵינוֹ מְשַׁנֶּה דָבָר בְּמַעֲשֵׂהוּ וְלֹא מְתַקֵּן דָּבָר. כְּמוֹ לָשֵׂאת מַשָּׂאוֹת אֲבָנִים, לָרוּץ מִמָּקוֹם לְמָקוֹם, לְהוֹלִיךְ כֵּלִים אַחַר רַבּוֹ לְבֵית הַמֶּרְחָץ, לְהַלְבִּישׁוֹ, וְכַיּוֹצֵא מִמַּעֲשִׂים הַלָּלוּ שֶׁהֵם מַעֲשֵׂה עֶבֶד. וְזֶהוּ עִנְיָן הַמִּלָּה עֶבֶד, וְהַשֵּׁם עֲבוֹדָה . . .

וְאֵין שֵׁם מְלָאכָה נוֹפֵל אֶלָּא עַל הַמְחַדֵּשׁ דָּבָר בְּעִנְיָנִים הַטִּבְעִיִּים וּמְשַׁנֶּה אוֹתָם בְּמַעֲשֵׂהוּ מִמַּה שֶׁהָיוּ, וְעַל יְדֵי הַחִדּוּשׁ הַזֶּה יִהְיֶה תִּקּוּן הַדָּבָר, הֵן שֶׁיִּבְנֶה הֵן שֶׁיַּהֲרוֹס, תָּמִיד יְשַׁנֶּה, וּכְשֶׁיֵּשׁ בְּמַעֲשֵׂהוּ תִּקּוּן לְיִשּׁוּב הָעוֹלָם הֲרֵי זֶה מְלָאכָה. וְלָכֵן מוֹחֵק עַל מְנַת לִכְתּוֹב, הוֹרֵס עַל מְנַת לִבְנוֹת, כּוּלָם מְלָאכוֹת הֵן.

וְכָל מְלָאכָה יֵשׁ לִמּוּד וִידִיעָה בְּאֵיזֶה זְמַן וּבְאֵיזֶה כְּלִי יַעֲשֶׂה . . .

Rabbi Ya'akov Tsvi Mecklenburg
1785–1865

German rabbi and biblical exegete. Rabbi Ya'akov served as rabbi in Königsberg, East Prussia. In 1839, he published *Haketav Vehakabbalah*, an important commentary that often demonstrates the indivisibility of the Written Torah and the Oral Torah.

Know that there is a difference between the word *avodah* and the word *melachah*.

Avodah refers to actions that do not require knowledge or wisdom and where nothing is being changed or fixed by the action. Examples include carrying loads of stones, running from place to place, carrying the clothing of one's master to the bathhouse, dressing him, or any similar work of a slave. These tasks are associated with the word *avodah* and *eved*.

The term *melachah* applies when someone creates something new from raw materials, changing it from its previous state and improving it. Whether building or destroying [in order to rebuild], there must always be a change. When a person's work makes the world more habitable, it is called *melachah*. Therefore, *melachah* includes erasing with the intention to rewrite or demolishing with the intention to rebuild.

Every *melachah* requires learning and knowledge to know when it should be performed and with what implement....

Text 16b

Rabbi Ya'akov Tsvi Mecklenburg, ibid. 📖

וְיוֹצֵא מִזֶּה עַל דֶּרֶךְ כְּלָל, כִּי כָל מַעֲשֵׂה אֱלֹקִים שֶׁעָשָׂה בְּשֵׁשֶׁת הַיָּמִים נִקְרָאִים מְלָאכוֹת לֹא עֲבוֹדוֹת. עַל כֵּן כְּתִיב "מִכָּל מְלַאכְתּוֹ" (בְּרֵאשִׁית ב,ב), "כִּי בוֹ שָׁבַת מִכָּל מְלַאכְתּוֹ" (שָׁם, ג). וְלָכֵן אֵלֶּה הַמְּלָאכוֹת כּוּלָּם אֲסוּרִים לָנוּ לַעֲשׂוֹת בְּיוֹם הַשַּׁבָּת, כִּי הִזְהִיר "לֹא תַעֲשֶׂה כָל מְלָאכָה". וְלֹא אָסַר עָלֵינוּ הָעֲבוֹדוֹת, כִּי לֹא מָצִינוּ "לֹא תַעֲבוֹד בְּיוֹם הַשַּׁבָּת", אוֹ "לֹא תַעֲשֶׂה בּוֹ עֲבוֹדָה", לְפִי שֶׁלֹּא הִזְהִירָנוּ עֲלֵיהֶן. וְיֵצֵא לָנוּ מִזֶּה שֶׁמּוּתָּר לְטַלְטֵל בְּשַׁבָּת שׁוּלְחָנוֹת וְכִסְאוֹת אוֹכְלִים וּמַשְׁקִים ... כְּשֶׁהֵם לְצוֹרֶךְ עוֹנֶג שַׁבָּת. וְכֵן מוּתָּר לָרוּץ כָּל הַיּוֹם מִבַּיִת לְבַיִת וְכַיּוֹצֵא, אַף עַל פִּי שֶׁהֵן עָמֵל וְטוֹרַח, לְפִי שֶׁאֵינָן אֶלָּא עֲבוֹדוֹת, וְהַשֵּׁם יִתְבָּרֵךְ לֹא אָסַר עֲשִׂיַּת הָעֲבוֹדָה זוּלַת הַמְּלָאכָה. וְלָכֵן הַחוֹרֵשׁ כָּל שֶׁהוּא, וְהַזּוֹרֵעַ כָּל שֶׁהוּא, וְהַכּוֹתֵב שְׁתֵּי אוֹתִיּוֹת בַּשַּׁבָּת, וְאַף עַל פִּי שֶׁאֵין בְּכָל זֶה עָמָל וְטוֹרַח, כְּבָר חִלֵּל אֶת הַשַּׁבָּת, לְפִי שֶׁעָשָׂה מְלָאכָה ...

We now understand why all the work God did during the six days of Creation is called *melachah*, not *avodah*, as we see in the second chapter of Genesis. Therefore, we are forbidden to do *melachah* on Shabbat, as it says, "You shall perform no *melachah*." But we do not find a prohibition that says, "You shall perform no *avodah* on Shabbat."

Consequently, it is permitted to carry tables and chairs, food and drink . . . when they are needed for the joy of Shabbat. Similarly, it is permitted to run from house to house all day, and so forth. Despite the fact that there is toil and trouble, it is *avodah*—and God did not forbid *avodah*, only *melachah*.

On the other hand, although there is no toil and trouble when one plows just a bit, plants just a bit, or writes just two letters, these acts desecrate Shabbat because they constitute *melachah*. . . .

Text 16c

Rabbi Ya'akov Tsvi Mecklenburg, ibid. 📖

וְהִנֵּה כָּל הַמַּעֲשִׂים שֶׁהֵכִין הַשֵּׁם יִתְבָּרֵךְ בְּמַעֲשֵׂה בְּרֵאשִׁית לְצוֹרֶךְ הָאָדָם רַבּוֹת מְאֹד, קְצָתָן תְּלוּיִים בָּאֲדָמָה בַּזְּרָעִים וּבַצְּמָחִים שֶׁהֵן לְצוֹרֶךְ מַאֲכָלוֹ, וּקְצָתָם תְּלוּיִים בִּמְלָאכוֹת שֶׁהֵן לְצוֹרֶךְ כֵּלָיו וּבְגָדָיו, כְּמוֹ מְלֶאכֶת חֹרֵשׁ וְחוֹשֵׁב תּוֹפֵר וְצוֹבֵעַ וְכַיּוֹצֵא, וּקְצָתָן לְצוֹרֶךְ דִּירָתוֹ כְּמוֹ מְלֶאכֶת הַבִּנְיָן וְכַיּוֹצֵא. וְאֵלּוּ הֵן ל"ט אֲבוֹת מְלָאכוֹת שֶׁקִּבְּלוּ רַזַ"ל הַשְּׁנוּיִים בְּפֶרֶק כְּלָל גָּדוֹל, וְהוּא קַבָּלָתָם עַל דֶּרֶךְ הֲלָכָה לְמשֶׁה מִסִּינַי, שֶׁבְּחָכְמַת אֱלֹקִים כְּלוּלִים בְּמִסְפָּר זֶה כָּל הַמְּלָאכוֹת הָרַבּוֹת שֶׁהֵן בַּמְּצִיאָת. כִּי אוֹתָן שֶׁלֹּא נִזְכְּרוּ, הֵן תּוֹלָדוֹת וּכְלוּלוֹת בְּאָבוֹת הַלָּלוּ.

Now, there are many types of *melachot*. Some relate to extracting food from the ground, like plowing. Some relate to the production of garments, like weaving, sewing, and dyeing. Others relate to building homes for shelter. All these are included in the thirty-nine categories of labor that our sages taught in Tractate Shabbat, going all the way back to Moses at Sinai. With divine wisdom, this number includes all potential *melachot*. For anything not included in the thirty-nine would be a corollary of one of the thirty-nine.

QUESTION FOR DISCUSSION

How might Rabbi Ya'akov Tsvi respond to our question—"Why is it permitted to have sexual relations on Shabbat?"

KEY POINTS

- The definition of *melachah* is limited to acts that were associated with building the *mishkan* and their corollaries. Procreation was not one of them.

- A *melachah* requires learning and knowledge. This does not apply to marital relations.

7. Why does the Bible refer to sexual relations as "knowing"?

Text 17a

Genesis 4:1

וְהָאָדָם יָדַע אֶת חַוָּה אִשְׁתּוֹ וַתַּהַר וַתֵּלֶד אֶת קַיִן.

Adam knew Chavah his wife; and she conceived and gave birth to Cain.

Knowledge connects:- emotionally & physically

Text 17b

Rabbi Naftali Tsvi Yehudah Berlin, *Ha'amek Davar*, ad loc.

Rabbi Naftali Tsvi Yehudah Berlin
(Netziv)
1817–1893

Rosh yeshivah of the famed Volozhin *yeshivah* in Lithuania. The Netziv's works include his commentary on the *She'iltos* of Rabbi Achai, his biblical commentary, and *Meishiv Davar*, a collection of his responsa. His two sons were Rabbi Chaim Berlin and Rabbi Meir Bar-Ilan.

שֶׁבְּכָל מָקוֹם דִּכְתִיב בְּלָשׁוֹן יְדִיעָה גַּבֵּי תַּשְׁמִישׁ הַמִּטָּה, מַשְׁמָעוֹ שֶׁהִכִּירָה, וְיָדַע אֶת מִי שֶׁהוּא מְשַׁמֵּשׁ, וּבִשְׁבִיל שֶׁהִיא הִיא הָאִשָּׁה וְלֹא אַחֶרֶת. וְהַיְנוּ בְּתוֹרַת קְדוּשִׁין. וְזֶהוּ דִּיּוּק הַלָּשׁוֹן "יָדַע אֶת חַוָּה אִשְׁתּוֹ", בִּשְׁבִיל שֶׁהִיא אִשְׁתּוֹ וְלֹא בִּשְׁבִיל שֶׁהִיא נְקֵבָה מִמִּין אָדָם, כְּמוֹ שֶׁהַשּׁוֹר בּוֹעֵל אֶת הַפָּרָה בִּשְׁבִיל שֶׁהִיא מִינוֹ, אֶלָּא אֵדַע אֶת זוֹ הַנְּקֵבָה דַּוְקָא בִּשְׁבִיל זֶה שֶׁהִיא מְיֻחֶדֶת לוֹ לְבַדּוֹ.

When the Torah uses the word "knew" to refer to sexual intercourse, it means that the man knew the woman, namely, that she was his wife, not just any person. Indeed, the verse says, "Adam knew Chavah *his wife*"—he had intercourse with her because he knew her as his wife, not merely because she was a human female. This is unlike an ox that mates with a cow merely because it is of the opposite gender of the same species. Adam "knew" this specific woman because she was designated to him alone.

KEY POINTS

- The word "knowing" in reference to sexual relations means that we recognize the other as our spouse, sanctified to us through marriage. When we approach sexual relations as an expression of "knowing" our spouse, we affirm its sanctity and enable a deep, all-encompassing attachment.

8. Why aren't vegan foods and restaurants kosher by default?

A Trace of Nonkosher

Text 18

http://vegan.org/vegan-certifications/

We do allow companies to use shared machinery (machinery that ran products containing eggs or dairy) in the production of their products, but most of those products carry a label that says so. Companies must provide documentation of the steps that are taken to thoroughly clean the machinery. Even though the machines are guaranteed to be cleaned thoroughly between non-vegan and vegan batches, shared machinery may contain trace amounts of eggs or dairy. For this reason, a Vegan Certified Product may not be acceptable to individuals with food allergies.

Many vegan companies lease non-vegan kitchens and equipment from other companies to produce their products and many companies make vegan and non-vegan items on the same machines. It is extremely expensive for these small companies to purchase dedicated vegan machinery of their own. In fact, many vegan companies may not exist if they had to purchase their own equipment.

When we were starting the Vegan Certification Campaign we had to establish what was going to be considered vegan. Most products with vegan ingredients would not be considered vegan under the strictest standards because of some form of processing contamination. We decided that we would not exclude products that may possibly contain trace amounts of contamination. We consulted with other prominent vegan organizations and we all agree that vegan purity is more harmful than helpful.

Text 19

Numbers 31:21–23 📖

וַיֹּאמֶר אֶלְעָזָר הַכֹּהֵן אֶל אַנְשֵׁי הַצָּבָא הַבָּאִים לַמִּלְחָמָה,
זֹאת חֻקַּת הַתּוֹרָה אֲשֶׁר צִוָּה ה' אֶת מֹשֶׁה.

אַךְ אֶת הַזָּהָב, וְאֶת הַכָּסֶף, אֶת הַנְּחֹשֶׁת, אֶת הַבַּרְזֶל, אֶת הַבְּדִיל, וְאֶת הָעֹפָרֶת.

כָּל דָּבָר אֲשֶׁר יָבֹא בָאֵשׁ תַּעֲבִירוּ בָאֵשׁ וְטָהֵר. אַךְ בְּמֵי נִדָּה
יִתְחַטָּא. וְכֹל אֲשֶׁר לֹא יָבֹא בָּאֵשׁ תַּעֲבִירוּ בַמָּיִם.

Elazar the Priest said to the men of war who went to battle: "This is the law that God commanded Moses.

"Only the gold, the silver, the brass, the iron, the tin, and the lead—anything that is used in fire shall pass through fire, and it shall be clean. It must, however, [also] be cleansed with sprinkling water.

"Whatever is not used in fire you shall pass through water."

Text 20

Rabbi Yosef Caro, *Shulchan Aruch, Yoreh De'ah* 121:1–2 🕮

הַלּוֹקֵחַ כֵּלִים יְשָׁנִים מִן הָעוֹבְדֵי כּוֹכָבִים, כְּדֶרֶךְ שֶׁנִּשְׁתַּמֵּשׁ
בָּהֶן הָעוֹבֵד כּוֹכָבִים כָּךְ הוּא הֶכְשֵׁרָן.

לְפִיכָךְ הַלּוֹקֵחַ כְּלֵי תַשְׁמִישׁ יְשָׁנִים שֶׁנִּשְׁתַּמֵּשׁ בָּהֶם בְּצוֹנֵן, כְּגוֹן
כּוֹסוֹת וְצַלּוֹחִיּוֹת וְכַיּוֹצֵא בָּהֶן, מְדִיחָן, וְצָרִיךְ לְשַׁפְשְׁפָן הֵיטֵב בְּמַיִם
בִּשְׁעַת הֲדָחָה כְּדֵי לְהָסִיר וּלְמָרֵק הָאִיסּוּר שֶׁעַל גַּבֵּיהֶן. . .

לָקַח מֵהֶן כֵּלִים שֶׁנִּשְׁתַּמֵּשׁ בָּהֶם בְּחַמִּין, בֵּין שֶׁהֵם
שֶׁל מַתֶּכֶת אוֹ שֶׁל עֵץ אוֹ אֶבֶן, מַגְעִילָן.

Rabbi Yosef Caro
(Maran, *Beit Yosef*)
1488– 1575

Halachic authority and author. Rabbi Caro was born in Spain, but was forced to flee during the expulsion in 1492 and eventually settled in Safed, Israel. He authored many works including the *Beit Yosef*, *Kesef Mishneh*, and a mystical work, *Magid Meisharim*. Rabbi Caro's magnum opus, the *Shulchan Aruch (Code of Jewish Law)*, has been universally accepted as the basis for modern Jewish law.

If someone purchases used utensils from a non-Jew [that were used for nonkosher food], the manner of making them kosher depends on how they were used.

If the utensils, like certain cups and plates, were used for cold food or drink, they only need to be washed to be rendered kosher. They need to be cleansed thoroughly to ensure that the [residue of the] prohibited food is erased. . . .

If one purchases utensils that were used for hot food, whether they are made of metal, wood, or stone, they need to be washed with boiling water.

Insects and Larvae

Text 21a

Leviticus 11:43 📖

אַל תְּשַׁקְּצוּ אֶת נַפְשֹׁתֵיכֶם בְּכָל הַשֶּׁרֶץ הַשֹּׁרֵץ.

Do not defile yourselves by any of these creeping creatures.

Text 21b

Rabbi Shlomo ben Aderet, *Responsa* 1:113 📖

דַּע שֶׁזּוּ הֲלָכָה רוֹוַחַת בְּיִשְׂרָאֵל. וּמְפוֹרָשׁ בִּגְמָרָא חוּלִּין (נח,ב), שֶׁכָּל דָּבָר שֶׁהַתַּרְחַשׁ מָצוּי בּוֹ, אָסוּר לְאָכְלוֹ וּלִשְׁתּוֹתוֹ עַד שֶׁיִּבָּדֵק.

Know that this is a widespread law among the Jewish community. It is clearly stated in the Talmud (Chulin 58b) that food or drink in which insect infestation is common requires examination prior to its consumption.

Rabbi Shlomo ben Aderet (Rashba)
1235–1310

Medieval Halachist, Talmudist, and philosopher. Rashba was born in Barcelona, Spain, and was a student of Nachmanides and Rabbi Yonah of Gerona. He was known as *El Rab d'España* ("the Rabbi of Spain") because of his fame as a rabbinical authority. More than 3,000 of his responsa are extant, dealing with varied questions on Halachah and religious philosophy, addressed to him from Spain, Portugal, Italy, France, Germany, and even from Asia Minor. Among his numerous students were the Ritva, Rabbeinu Bechaye, and the Re'ah.

FIGURE 4.1

FDA Defect Levels Handbook

Product	Defect	Action Level
Broccoli, Frozen	Insects and mites	Average of 60 or more aphids and/or thrips and/or mites per 100 grams
Asparagus, Canned or Frozen	Insect filth	10% by count of spears or pieces are infested with 6 or more attached asparagus beetle eggs and/or sacs
	Insects	Asparagus contains an average of 40 or more thrips per 100 grams OR Insects (whole or equivalent) of 3mm or longer have an average aggregate length of 7mm or longer per 100 grams of asparagus
Brussels Sprouts, Frozen	Insects	Average of 30 or more aphids and/or thrips per 100 grams

Product	Defect	Action Level
Corn: Sweet Corn, Canned	Insect larvae	Insect larvae (corn ear worms, corn borers) 2 or more 3mm or longer larvae, cast skins, larval or cast skin fragments of corn ear worms or corn borer and the aggregate length of such larvae, cast skins, larval or cast skin fragments exceeds 12 mm in 24 pounds (24 No. 303 cans or equivalent)
Berries: Lingon, Canned (European cranberry)	Insect larvae	Average of 3 or more larvae per pound in a minimum of 12 subsamples
Citrus Fruit Juices, Canned	Insects and insect eggs	5 or more Drosophila and other fly eggs per 250 ml or 1 or more maggots per 250 ml

Source: US Food and Drug Administration, *Defect Levels Handbook* http://tinyurl.com/JCOW4c

9. Why do we say *lechayim* as a drinking salutation?

Text 22

Talmud, Shabbat 67b ▯

מַעֲשֶׂה בְּרַבִּי עֲקִיבָא שֶׁעָשָׂה מִשְׁתֶּה לִבְנוֹ, וְעַל כָּל כּוֹס וְכוֹס שֶׁהֵבִיא אָמַר:
חַמְרָא וְחַיֵּי לְפוּם רַבָּנָן, חַיֵּי וְחַמְרָא לְפוּם רַבָּנָן וּלְפוּם תַּלְמִידֵיהוֹן.

Rabbi Akiva made a feast for his son. For every cup that he poured, he said, "Wine and life to the mouths of the sages; life and wine to the mouths of the sages and their students!"

Text 23

Rabbi David Abudraham, *Siddur, Ma'ariv Shel Shabbos* ▯

עוֹד שָׁמַעְתִּי טַעַם אַחֵר, וְאַתְיָא כְּמַאן דְּאָמַר (בְּרָכוֹת מ,א) "עֵץ שֶׁאָכַל
מִמֶּנּוּ אָדָם הָרִאשׁוֹן גֶּפֶן הָיָה", וּלְפִיכָךְ נִקְנְסָה עָלָיו מִיתָה. וְלָכֵן הוּא אוֹמֵר
"סַבְרִי מָרָנָן?" הֲיֵשׁ בְּדַעְתְּכֶם שֶׁזֶּה הַכּוֹס הוּא לְחַיִּים, וְלֹא לַמָּוֶת כְּאוֹתוֹ
שֶׁל אָדָם הָרִאשׁוֹן? וְהֵם עוֹנִים לְחַיֵּי, לְחַיִּים יִהְיֶה וְלֹא יִהְיֶה לַמָּוֶת.

I heard another explanation. It follows the Talmudic view (Berachot 40a) that the forbidden fruit that Adam ate was a grape, and as a result, death was decreed upon humankind. The reciter of *Kidush* therefore says, "*Savri*

Rabbi David ben Yoseph Abudraham
14th century

Resided in Seville, Spain, and is famous for his work on Jewish prayers and blessings. The work—completed around the year 1340—is a commentary on the daily, Shabbat, and festival prayers and collects many customs and laws relating to them. He is believed to have been a disciple of Rabbi Ya'akov ben Asher, author of *Arba'ah Turim*.

maranan? Do you agree that this cup should be for life, and that it should not be for death as were the grapes that Adam consumed?" And they all answer "*Lechayei!* Let it be for life and not for death!"

Continue your learning experience ONLINE

Visit www.myJLI.com/why4

for insightful and inspiring videos, articles, and readings on this topic.

KEY POINTS

- Alcohol has the dual power to be utterly destructive or spiritually uplifting. Toasting *lechayim* is a reminder and blessing that we should make the choice to drink mindfully and purposefully.

ADDITIONAL READINGS

MAIMONIDES ON FREE WILL

TRANSLATED BY RABBI ELIYAHU TOUGER

Chapter Five
Halacha 1

Free will is granted to all men. If one desires to turn himself to the path of good and be righteous, the choice is his. Should he desire to turn to the path of evil and be wicked, the choice is his.[1]

This is [the intent of] the Torah's statement (Genesis 3:22): "Behold, man has become unique as ourselves, knowing good and evil," i.e., the human species became singular in the world with no other species resembling it in the following quality: that man can, on his own initiative, with his knowledge and thought, know good and evil, and do what he desires. There is no one who can prevent him from doing good or bad. Accordingly, [there was a need to drive him from the Garden of Eden,] "lest he stretch out his hand [and take from the tree of life]."

Halacha 2

A person should not entertain the thesis held by the fools among the gentiles and the majority of the undeveloped among Israel that, at the time of a man's creation, The Holy One, blessed be He, decrees whether he will be righteous or wicked.

This is untrue. Each person is fit to be righteous like Moses, our teacher, or wicked, like Jeroboam. [Similarly,] he may be wise or foolish, merciful or cruel, miserly or generous, or [acquire] any other character

---

Rabbi Moshe ben Maimon. (Maimonides, Rambam, 1135–1204) Halachist, philosopher, author, and physician. Maimonides was born in Cordoba, Spain. After the conquest of Cordoba by the Almohads, he fled Spain and eventually settled in Cairo, Egypt. There, he became the leader of the Jewish community and served as court physician to the vizier of Egypt. He is most noted for authoring the *Mishneh Torah*, an encyclopedic arrangement of Jewish law, and for his philosophical work, *Guide for the Perplexed*. His rulings on Jewish law are integral to the formation of halachic consensus.

---

traits. There is no one who compels him, sentences him, or leads him towards either of these two paths. Rather, he, on his own initiative and decision, tends to the path he chooses.

This was [implied by the prophet,] Jeremiah who stated [Eichah 3:38: "From the mouth of the Most High, neither evil or good come forth." Accordingly, it is the sinner, himself, who causes his own loss.

Therefore, it is proper for a person to cry and mourn for his sins and for what he has done to his soul, the evil consequences, he brought upon it. This is implied by the following verse [*ibid.*:39]: "Of what should a living man be aggrieved? [A man of his sins.]" [The prophet] continues explaining, since free choice is in our hands and our own decision [is what prompts us to] commit all these wrongs, it is proper for us to repent and abandon our wickedness, for this choice is presently in our hand. This is implied by the following verse [*ibid.*:40]: "Let us search and examine our ways and return [to God]."

Halacha 3

This principle is a fundamental concept and a pillar [on which rests the totality] of the Torah and mitzvot as [Deuteronomy 30:15] states: "Behold, I have set before you today life [and good, death and evil]." Similarly, [Deuteronomy 11:26] states, "Behold, I have set before you today [the blessing and the curse]," implying that the choice is in your hands.

Any one of the deeds of men which a person desires to do, he may, whether good or evil. Therefore, [Deuteronomy 5:26] states:

"If only their hearts would always remain this way." From this, we can infer that the Creator does not compel or decree that people should do either good or bad. Rather, everything is left to their [own choice].

Halacha 4

Were God to decree that an individual would be righteous or wicked or that there would be a quality which draws a person by his essential nature to any particular path [of behavior], way of thinking, attributes, or deeds, as imagined by many of the fools [who believe] in astrology—how could He command us through [the words of] the prophets: "Do this," "Do not do this," "Improve your behavior," or "Do not follow after your wickedness?"[According to their mistaken conception,] from the beginning of man's creation, it would be decreed upon him, or his nature would draw him, to a particular quality and he could not depart from it.

What place would there be for the entire Torah? According to which judgement or sense of justice would retribution be administered to the wicked or reward to the righteous? Shall the whole world's Judge not act justly!

A person should not wonder: How is it possible for one to do whatever he wants and be responsible for his own deeds?—Is it possible for anything to happen in this world without the permission and desire of its Creator as [Psalms 135:6] states: "Whatever God wishes, He has done in the heavens and in the earth?"One must know that everything is done in accord with His will and, nevertheless, we are responsible for our deeds.

How is this [apparent contradiction] resolved? Just as the Creator desired that [the elements of] fire and wind rise upward and [those of] water and earth descend downward, that the heavenly spheres revolve in a circular orbit, and all the other creations of the world follow the nature which He desired for them, so too, He desired that man have free choice and be responsible for his deeds, without being pulled or forced. Rather, he, on his own initiative, with the knowledge which God has granted him, will do anything that man is able to do.

Therefore, he is judged according to his deeds. If he does good, he is treated with beneficence. If he does bad, he is treated harshly. This is implied by the prophets' statements: "This has been the doing of your hands" [Malachi 1:9]; "They also have chosen their own paths" [Isaiah 66:3].

This concept was also implied by Solomon in his statement [Ecclesiastes 11:9]: "Young man, rejoice in your youth . . . but, know that for all these things God will bring you to judgment," i.e., know that you have the potential to do, but in the future, you will have to account for your deeds.

Halacha 5

One might ask: Since The Holy One, blessed be He, knows everything that will occur before it comes to pass, does He or does He not know whether a person will be righteous or wicked?

If He knows that he will be righteous, [it appears] impossible for him not to be righteous. However, if one would say that despite His knowledge that he would be righteous, it is possible for him to be wicked, then His knowledge would be incomplete.

Know that the resolution to this question [can be described as]: "Its measure is longer than the earth and broader than the sea." Many great and fundamental principles and lofty concepts are dependent upon it. However, the statements that I will make must be known and understood [as a basis for the comprehension of this matter].

As explained in the second chapter of *Hilchot Yesodei HaTorah,* The Holy One, blessed be He, does not know with a knowledge that is external from Him as do men, whose knowledge and selves are two [different entities]. Rather, He, may His name be praised, and His knowledge are one.

Human knowledge cannot comprehend this concept in its entirety for just as it is beyond the potential of man to comprehend and conceive the essential nature of the Creator, as [Exodus 33:20] states: "No man will perceive, Me and live," so, too, it is beyond man's potential to comprehend and conceive the Creator's knowledge. This was the intent of the prophet's [Isaiah 55:8] statements: "For My thoughts are not your thoughts, nor your ways, My ways."Accordingly, we do not have the potential to conceive how The Holy One, blessed be He, knows all the creations and their deeds. However, this is known without any doubt: That man's actions are in his [own] hands and The Holy One, blessed be He, does not lead him [in a particular direction] or decree that he do anything.

This matter is known, not only as a tradition of faith, but also, through clear proofs from the words of wisdom. Consequently, the prophets taught that a person is judged for his deeds, according to his deeds - whether good or bad. This is a fundamental principle on which is dependent all the words of prophecy.

Chapter 6
Halacha 1
There are many verses in the Torah and the words of the prophets which appear to contradict this fundamental principle. [Thus,] the majorities of the people err because of them and think that the Holy One, blessed be He, does decree that a person commit evil or good and that a person's heart is not given over to him to direct it towards any path he desires.

Behold, I will explain a great and fundamental principle [of faith] on the basis of which the interpretation of those verses can be understood. [As a preface,] when an individual or the people of a country sin, the sinner consciously and willfully committing that sin, it is proper to exact retribution from him as explained. The Holy One, blessed be He, knows how to exact punishment: There are certain sins for which justice determines that retribution be exacted in this world; on the sinner's person, on his possessions, or on his small children.

[Retribution is exacted upon a person's] small children who do not possess intellectual maturity and have not reached the age where they are obligated to perform mitzvot [because these children] are considered as his property. [This concept is alluded to] by the verse [Deuteronomy 24:16]: "A man will die because of his own sins." [We may infer: This rule only applies] after one has become "a man."There are other sins for which justice determines that retribution be exacted in the world to come with no damages coming to the transgressor in this world. There are [other] sins for which retribution is taken in this world and in the world to come.

Halacha 2
When does the above apply? When [the transgressor] does not repent. However, if he repents, his Teshuvah is a shield against retribution. Just as a person may sin consciously and willfully, he may repent consciously and willfully.

Halacha 3
A person may commit a great sin or many sins causing the judgment rendered before the True Judge to be that the retribution [administered to] this transgressor for these sins which he willfully and consciously committed is that his Teshuvah will be held back. He will not be allowed the chance to repent from his wickedness so that he will die and be wiped out because of the sin he committed.

This is implied by the Holy One, blessed be He's statement [related] by Isaiah[6:10]: "Make the heart of this people fat [and make their ears heavy. Smear over their eyes, lest they see with their eyes . . . understand with their hearts, repent and be healed]."

Similarly, [II Chronicles 36:16] states "They mocked the messengers of God, scorned His words, scoffed at His prophets until the anger of God mounted up against His people until there was no remedy."

Implied [by these verses] is that they willingly sinned, multiplying their iniquity until it was obliged to hold back their Teshuvah, [which is referred to as] the "remedy."

For these reasons, it is written in the Torah [Exodus 14:4], "I will harden Pharaoh's heart." Since, he began to sin on his own initiative and caused hardships to the Israelites who dwelled in his land as [Exodus 1:10] states: "Come, let us deal wisely with them," judgment obligated that he be prevented from repenting so that he would suffer retribution. Therefore, The Holy One, blessed be He, hardened his heart.

Why did [God] send Moses to [Pharaoh], telling him: "Send [forth the people], repent"? The Holy One, blessed be He, had already told that he would not release [the people], as [Exodus 9:30] states: "I realize that you and your subjects [still do not fear God]."

[The reason is stated in Exodus 9:16:] "For this alone, I have preserved you . . . so that My name will be spoken about throughout the earth]," i.e., to make known to all the inhabitants of the world that when the Holy One, blessed be He, withholds repentance from a sinner, he cannot repent, but he will die in the wickedness that he initially committed willfully.

Similarly, Sichon was held liable for repentance to be withheld from him, because of the sins he committed, as [Deuteronomy 2:30] states: "God, your Lord, hardened his spirit and strengthened his heart."

Also, the Canaanites held back from repenting, because of their abominable acts, so that they would wage war against Israel as [Joshua 11:20] states: "This was inspired by God, to harden their hearts so that they should come against Israel in battle in order to utterly destroy them."

Similarly, the Israelites during the era of Elijah committed many iniquities. Repentance was held back from those who committed these many sins, as [I Kings 18:37] states: "You have turned their heart backwards," i.e., held repentance back from them.

In conclusion, the Almighty did not decree that Pharaoh should harm the Israelites that Sichon should sin in his land, that the Canaanites should perform abominable acts, or that the Israelites should worship idols. They all sinned on their own initiative and they were obligated to have Teshuvah held back from them.

Halacha 4
This is what is implied in the requests of the righteous and the prophets in their prayers, [asking] God to help them on the path of truth, as David pleaded [Psalms 86:11]: "God, show me Your way that I may walk in Your truth;" i.e., do not let my sins prevent me from [reaching] the path of truth which will lead me to appreciate Your way and the oneness of Your name.

A similar intent [is conveyed] by the request [Psalms 51:14]: "Support me with a spirit of magnanimity;" i.e., let my spirit [be willing] to do Your will and do not cause my sins to prevent me from repenting. Rather, let the choice remain in my hand until I repent and comprehend and appreciate the path of truth. In a similar way, [one must interpret] all the [verses] which resemble these.

Halacha 5
What was implied by David's statement [Psalms 25:8-9]: "God is good and upright, therefore, he instructs sinners in the path. He guides the humble [in the path of justice and] teaches the humble His way]"? That He sends them prophets to inform them of the path of God and to encourage them to repent.

Furthermore, it implies that He granted them the power to learn and to understand. This attribute is present in all men: As long as a person follows the ways of wisdom and righteousness, he will desire them and pursue them. This [may be inferred from] the statement of our Sages of blessed memory: "One who comes to purify [himself] is helped;" i.e., he finds himself assisted in this matter.

[A question may still arise, for] behold, it is written in the Torah [Genesis 15:13]: "They shall enslave them and oppress them," [seemingly implying that] He decreed that the Egyptians would commit evil.

Similarly, it is written [Deuteronomy 31:16]: "And this nation will arise and stray after the alien gods of the land," [seemingly implying that] He decreed that Israel would serve idols. If so, why did He punish them?

Because He did not decree that a particular person would be the one who strayed. Rather, each and every one of those who strayed to idol-worship [could have chosen] not to serve idols if he did not desire to serve them. The Creator merely informed [Moses] of the pattern of the world.

To what can this be compared? To someone who says, there will be righteous and wicked people in this nation. [Thus,] a wicked person cannot say that because God told Moses that there will be wicked people in Israel, it is decreed that he will be wicked. A similar concept applies regarding the statement [Deuteronomy 15:11]: "The poor will never cease to exist in the land."

Similarly, in regard to the Egyptians, each and every one of the Egyptians who caused hardship and difficulty for Israel had the choice to refrain from harming them, if he so desired, for there was no decree on a particular person. Rather, [God merely] informed [Abraham] that, in the future, his descendants would be enslaved in a land which did not belong to them.

We have already explained that it is beyond the potential of man to know how God knows what will be in the future.

Chapter 7
Halacha 1

Since free choice is granted to all men as explained, a person should always strive to do Teshuvah and to confess verbally for his sins, striving to cleanse his hands from sin in order that he may die as a Baal-Teshuvah and merit the life of the world to come.

Halacha 2

A person should always view himself as leaning towards death, with the possibility that he might die at any time. Thus, he may be found as a sinner.

Therefore, one should always repent from his sins immediately and should not say: "When I grow older, I will repent," for perhaps he will die before he grows older. This was implied by the wise counsel given by Solomon [Ecclesiastes 9:8]: "At all times, your clothes should be white."

Halacha 3

A person should not think that repentance is only necessary for those sins that involve deed such as promiscuity, robbery, or theft. Rather, just as a person is obligated to repent from these, similarly, he must search after the evil character traits he has. He must repent from anger, hatred, envy, frivolity, the pursuit of money and honor, the pursuit of gluttony, and the like. He must repent for all [of the above].

These sins are more difficult than those that involve deed. If a person is attached to these, it is more difficult for him to separate himself. In this context, [Isaiah 55:7] exhorts: "May the wicked abandon his path and the crooked man, his designs."

Halacha 4

A Baal Teshuvah should not consider himself distant from the level of the righteous because of the sins and transgressions that he committed. This is not true. He is beloved and desirable before the Creator as if he never sinned.

Furthermore, he has a great reward for he has tasted sin and yet, separated himself from it, conquering his [evil] inclination. Our Sages declared: "In the place where Baalei Teshuvah stand, even the completely righteous are not able to stand." The level of Baalei Teshuvah transcends the level of those who never sinned at all, for they overcome their [evil] inclination more.

Halacha 5

All the prophets commanded [the people] to repent. Israel will only be redeemed through Teshuvah.

The Torah has already promised that, ultimately, Israel will repent towards the end of her exile and, immediately, she will be redeemed as [Deuteronomy 30:1-3] states: "There shall come a time when [you will experience] all these things . . . and you will return to God, your Lord. . . . God, your Lord, will bring back your [captivity]."

Halacha 6

Teshuvah is great for it draws a man close to the *Shechinah* as [Hoshea 14:2] states: "Return, O Israel, to God, your Lord;" [Amos 4:6] states: "'You have not returned to Me,' declares God;" and [Jeremiah 4:1] states: "'If, you will return, 0 Israel,' declares God, 'You will return to Me.'" Implied is that if you will return in Teshuvah, you will cling to Me.

Teshuvah brings near those who were far removed. Previously, this person was hated by God, disgusting, far removed, and abominable. Now, he is beloved and desirable, close, and dear.

Similarly, we find God employs the same expression with which He separates [Himself] from the sinners to draw close those who repent. [Hoshea 2:1] states: "Instead of saying to you: 'You are not My nation,' He will tell you: 'You are the children of the living God.'"[Also, Jeremiah] speaks of Yecheniah while he was wicked [with the expression (22:30)]: "Write down this man as childless, a man who shall never prosper in his days," and [22:24]: "Would Cheniah, the son of Yehoyakim, king of Judah, be the signet ring on My right hand, I would tear him off." However, after he repented when in exile, [Chaggai 2:23] said concerning Zerubavel, his son: "'On that day,' declares the God of Hosts, 'I will take you, Zerubavel, the son of Shaltiel, My servant,' declares God, 'and I will place you as a signet ring.'"

Halacha 7

How exalted is the level of Teshuvah! Previously, the [transgressor] was separate from God, the Lord of Israel, as [Isaiah 59:2] states: "Your sins separate between you and your God." He would call out [to God] without being answered as [Isaiah 1:15] states: "Even if you pray many times, I will not hear."

He would fulfill mitzvot, only to have them crushed before him as [Isaiah 1:12] states: "Who asked this from you, to trample in My courts," and [Malachi 1:10] states: "'O were there one among you who would shut the doors that you might not kindle fire on My altar for no reason! I have no pleasure in you,' says the God of Hosts, 'nor will I accept an offering from your hand.'"Now, he is clinging to the *Shechi-nah* as [Deuteronomy 4:4] states: "And you who cling to God, your Lord." He calls out [to God] and is answered immediately as [Isaiah 65:24] states: "Before, you will call out, I will answer." He fulfills mitzvot and they are accepted with pleasure and joy as [Ecclesiastes 9:7] states, "God has already accepted your works," and [Malachi 3:4] states: "Then, shall the offering of Judah and Jerusalem be pleasing to God as in days of old and as in the former years."

Halacha 8

The manner of Baalei Teshuvah is to be very humble and modest.

If fools shame them because of their previous deeds, saying to them: "Yesterday, you would commit such and such [sins]. Yesterday, you would commit these and these [transgressions]," they will pay no attention to them. On the contrary, they will hear [this abuse] and rejoice, knowing that it is a merit for them.

Whenever they are embarrassed for the deeds they committed and shamed because of them, their merit increases and their level is raised.

It is an utter sin to tell a Baal Teshuvah, "Remember your previous deeds," or to recall them in his presence to embarrass him or to mention the surrounding circumstances or other similar matters so that he will recall what he did. This is all forbidden. We are warned against it within the general category of verbal abuse which Torah has warned us against as [Leviticus 25:17] states: "A man should not mistreat his colleague."

Excerpted from *Mishneh Torah: Sefer Madda* [New York and Jerusalem: Moznaim Publishers, 2010].
Reprinted with permission of the publisher.

SPIRITUAL MOLECULES

BY DR. VELVL GREENE

Even before we met Rabbi Moshe Feller in 1962 we would have been considered active and even committed Jews. Most of our friends were Jewish, our families were Jewish, our interests included Jewish "things," and our outlook was certainly Jewish. We read books published by the JPS, we listened to Jewish records, we treasured the Chagall prints in our home, and were dues-paying members of a Conservative synagogue. Gail was a leading soprano in the synagogue choir and I was one of the very few members who attended on most Friday nights, regardless of whose bar mitzvah was being celebrated that weekend. We were probably Zionists, too. We regularly contributed to the UJA, attended our city's Farband picnics, and were officers on the board of Herzl Camp.[2]

Before we met Rabbi Feller, however, I don't remember doing anything deliberately, or for that matter, abstaining from anything deliberately, because and only because it was a Torah Commandment. Such thoughts never really entered my mind. One went to synagogue and lit candles and ate gefilte fish and wore a *tallit* (prayer shawl) because it was a traditional thing to do, and a pleasant tradition at that. Not to do so would be making a statement of denial, or of disinterest, or of apathy. I didn't care to deny or to be disinterested. It wasn't part of my self-image. On the other hand, we didn't keep kosher or refrain from driving on Shabbat, or any of those other things. They were simply not relevant. They played no role in my value system. Note that we were not consciously protesting or transgressing, as one hears about the early Jewish socialists or freethinkers having done. Those would be statements that we didn't care to make. We were, quite simply, "good American Jews" who didn't want to make waves. Of course, we knew that some Jews avoided non-kosher food and didn't drive

on Shabbat. (There were remarkably few of them in our town, then.) And those were *their* traditions and *their* choices. We didn't think they were wrong—only slightly behind on the social evolution scale.

Looking back at those simpler days, I think that our lives reflected the characteristic paradox of the modern secular Jew: interested in Jewish things but basically ignorant; active in Jewish circles but limited in choice; committed to community, family, profession and the "Jewish People" but quite unaware of the foundation that informs this commitment. And above all, quite devoid of the learning and experience which permit discrimination between significance and triviality, reality and fraud. There must have been thousands like me. There still are. You see them arriving in Israel by the busload in "young leadership groups" or "fact-finding missions" or "synagogue tours." They are too busy raising funds to spend much time thinking; they are too involved with the present to research the past; they are too committed to the global picture to worry about the Jewish survival of their own children, or even themselves.

Actually, if we hadn't been in this kind of pattern ourselves, we probably wouldn't have met Rabbi Feller. He sought me out because I was a potentially rising star of the Jewish community. He was trying to organize his first banquet and wanted my name as well as others like me on his sponsors' committee.

The story of our first meeting has been told often enough (it was even mentioned in *Time* magazine) to obviate the need for retelling. On the surface it looked like a comedy. A strange, bearded, black-hatted young man remembers, just before sunset, that he has not yet said his afternoon prayers. Disregarding the fact that he is in my office, that he had asked for the appointment, that he is requesting a favor—he stands up, walks to the wall, ties a black cord around his waist and proceeds to mumble and shake. I will never forget my bewilderment and embarrassment. I didn't know what he was doing or why. I didn't know

Velvl Greene. Earned a PhD in bacteriology and biochemistry at the University of Minnesota, where he was professor of public health and microbiology for many years. In 1986, he and his family settled in Israel, where he directed the Sir Immanuel Jakobovits Center for Jewish Medical Ethics.

Jews prayed outside a synagogue. I didn't know they prayed in the afternoon. I didn't know they prayed on weekdays. And I didn't know how anyone could pray without someone announcing the page!

There were a lot of things I didn't know, then. But I did develop a definite interest and a special affection for this young man who was so pleasant and so different. He had a completely different set of rules to guide him—at once so radical and so archaic. He not only marched to the beat of a different drum—he seemed to enjoy the music more than we did ours. Above all, he was committed and consistent. I related to that. It is a beautiful trait in a world of laissez-faire religion and situation ethics.

In a short time we became friends—his family and ours. We discussed, we debated, we visited, we socialized. Gail and I were impressed with their sincerity and genuine warmth, but we still thought of them as anachronisms—as remnants of a past, as out of tune with the realities and needs of the modern American world. We didn't change our lifestyle because of them. Instead we kept waiting for them to change theirs. After all, nearly everyone else who had started out with a beard and hat ultimately did.

If he tried to influence us, during those early months, it must have been a very subtle effort. There was certainly no overt pressure or demand. Of course, they wouldn't eat at our house. But that wasn't a signal that something was wrong. They were so far out that their dietary idiosyncrasies were the least things one noticed. We started studying together, but our progress was infinitesimal. I asked too many questions, challenged too many axioms. I was definitely not a compliant student.

It could have gone on like this for a long time, if it weren't for our trip to Warsaw.

In the summer of 1963 I was invited to participate as a member of the American delegation in an international conference on space research in Poland. My balloon-borne samplers had discovered viable microorganisms in the stratosphere at a time when the field of exobiology was too full of speculation and embarrassingly lacking in real biological data. Whatever the real reasons for the invitation, it was an opportunity to be grabbed. In 1963, visits to Warsaw and Eastern Europe were very rare. Few of my professional colleagues had been to Warsaw since the war. None of my Jewish friends, certainly.

Gail and I left the three children with my parents in Canada and we flew to Warsaw. It was a dismal visit. In those years the city had not yet recovered from the destruction of World War Two. Physical destruction was evident in the piles of rubble that covered huge sections of the city. The emotional destruction was worse. The indigenous Polish anti-Semitism which had been fueled generously by the German occupation was now being nurtured by the Jew-hatred of the new Russian masters. We were told that there were a few thousand lonely Jews left in Warsaw: a handful of Jewish Communists, some of whom we met in the office of the Yiddish newspaper; less than a handful of old men who attended services in the only synagogue left standing; several in the performing arts; and the rest who had returned from the camps after the war and didn't want to leave their dead and/or their memories. They had survived the war and now they were surviving the peace.

One evening we attended a performance in the Jewish Theater. It was an edited version of *Tevyeh the Milkman* in Yiddish. The only part of the script written by Sholem Aleichem that remained described the misery and pogroms of the Tzarist times. The rest of the play dealt with the promise of the coming Soviet revolution. The hero of the play was not even Tevyeh. As one can imagine, it was Tevyeh's son-in-law Feferl, the revolutionary who was exiled to Siberia. It made no difference. We were the only ones in the theater who listened to the performance. The rest of the audience was a tour group from Sweden who were listening to a simultaneous translation with earphones.

Even twenty years later, I still remember the chill (it was the middle of June) as we walked through the area where the ghetto had once stood. The walls and all the buildings had been leveled. Piles of stone and burned timbers still lay there. But one could see where the streetcar tracks had ended because a wall had once been built across them. And it was possible, with the aid of maps we had copied from Holocaust literature, to recognize the original street lines, and even their identities. We could find our way to the Umschlagge Platz, to Mila Street and to the old Jewish cemetery.

I remember crying at the tomb of I.L. Peretz, the great Jewish writer after whom the day school I attended in Winnipeg was named. I remember crying at the large mounds of earth that covered unmarked mass graves. I remember walking a lot and crying a lot. This, after all, was the Jewish heritage that I knew. There, but for the luck of somebody emigrating in time, was my home or my grave. This was the end of the Yiddishist, Socialist, Zionist, European Judaism I knew. I was affected more by Warsaw than I would be ten years later by the Yad Vashem Holocaust Memorial in Jerusalem. The latter is a more beautiful monument, tastefully done. It is a museum, a history lesson, a shrine, an antiseptic display. Warsaw was death and cultural annihilation.

Through it all, I wondered how Gail was being affected. After all, I was a product of the "Old Country" culture of Winnipeg. She came from the sterile culture of Southern California's Reform temples. Peretz and Sholem Asch and Warsaw were part of my upbringing. How was all of this moving her?

I found out on Saturday afternoon. We had visitors—a Polish Jew and his two children whom we had met at the cemetery and whom we invited for tea. We had heard that there was a Jewish school and wanted to hear more about it. He, it developed, was looking for a handout. The seven-year-old child knew nothing. The eleven-year-old proudly recited the sum total of his Jewish knowledge: the four questions from the Passover Haggadah. We drank tea. I gave them a gift and my business card, and they left. Then we both cried. The end of Warsaw's centuries of Jewish creativity was a little boy who could barely stammer out *"Mah Nishtanah."*

Then Gail reacted. She sat up on her bed where she had been crying and spoke the most firm words I had heard in our seven years of marriage:

"I don't know what you think and I don't really care, but I've made up my mind. As soon as we get back I'm going to ask Moishe to make our house kosher. We're the only ones left. There's no one else. If we lose it, if we don't do it, if our children don't know about it, there won't be any Jews anymore. You can do what you want. But our house is going to be Jewish."

It was a defiant proclamation and she meant it. The pictures, the books and the music were not enough. She intended to transform the house organically, its very essence. Moreover, she was as good as her word. When we arrived in Minneapolis, the first person she called was Rabbi Feller, and he was only too willing to comply.

I don't remember all of the details. But I do remember the shocked look on his face when he first looked into our refrigerator. To this sweet young man, fresh out of the *yeshiva,* non-kosher meant a scar on the pleura of the animal who supplied the meat; or one drop of milk in fifty drops of chicken soup. The sight of real pork and shellfish must have been shattering. But bit by bit he "put our house in order." He introduced us to a kosher butcher; he taught us to look for the *kashrut* emblem on packaged food; he spent hours boiling silverware and metal utensils; he supervised the blowtorching of our oven; Mrs. Feller helped Gail buy new dishes.

One item gave him trouble: an expensive set of English bone china which we had received as a wedding gift from my sisters in Canada. It was a beautiful set and without doubt, one of our more precious possessions. Gail was quite eager to "kasher" the dishes by soaking and heating. She wanted to use them for Shabbat. I'm sure the whole project would have ended if she had been told then that the only way to kasher china, even English bone china, is to break it. He didn't have the heart to destroy our china. Or maybe he was a better psychologist than we took him for. When he discovered these dishes and what foods they had been used to serve, he suggested that we put them away. "Don't use them until I ask about such things in New York. Someone in New York must have more experience with things like this than I do."

They were put away. Every time he returned from a New York trip, Gail would ask what he had learned. And each time he had "forgotten." But he would be sure to remember next time. In the meantime, "Make sure they are put away in a safe place. You haven't used them, have you?"

This went on for months; then for years. The china was on display but it was never used. We kept waiting for expert advice that never came. Somehow, life went on without Minton Twilight in Grey.

We became closer to the Fellers during those years. Slowly the transformation which started in the kitchen moved into other areas of our life. Rabbi Feller introduced us to the Lubavitcher Rebbe, and we started growing in observance. Gail stopped singing in the synagogue choir; I started to put on *tefillin* sporadically at first, a little more regularly later on. I stopped driving on Shabbat. A few months later, so did Gail. We stopped eating at McDonalds. One Shabbat, we didn't switch on the television altogether. We bought a pair of *tzitzit* for the little boy. We switched membership to a synagogue with a *mechitzah* separating the men from the women. Gail started going to immerse in the *mikvah* (ritual bath). A few steps forward; a little backsliding; more steps forward. Years.

But the English bone china remained in the cabinet. Until one day, I came home from the university, and it was gone . . .

It was after a series of traumatic and melancholy miscarriages. Before observing *taharat ha'mishpacha* (the laws of family purity), it seems we had no difficulty having healthy and normal children. But when the *mikvah* became a feature of our family life, we started having trouble—three miscarriages in four years. Gail was sad; I was sad. Our friends comforted us. The Rebbe wrote letters of encouragement to Gail—private letters which I still have not read. But when I came home that singular day, she was smiling again:

"I took the china next door and sold it to Dorothy (our Gentile neighbor). Then I took the money and bought this *shaitel* (wig). What do you think of it?"

All this happened about 15 years ago. In 15 years you buy and discard a lot of *shaitlach*. Our two older daughters grew up and got married. They live with their husbands and their own children in Jerusalem. The little boy recently completed his rabbinic studies in the Lubavitch yeshiva in Montreal. We had two more children since then—the delights of our middle age. We have grown, both of us, both personally and professionally.

And we have another set of English bone china, from which we eat every Shabbat.

B'Or Ha'Torah Journal: Science, Art and Modern Life in the Light of Torah, 6 (1987): 167-171.
Available at www.borhatorah.org, info@borhatorah.org.
Reprinted with permission of the publisher.

THE SLOW END OF SLAVERY

BY RABBI JONATHAN SACKS

In Parshat Mishpatim we witness one of the great stylistic features of the Torah, its transition from narrative to law. Until now the Book of Exodus has been primarily narrative: the story of the enslavement of the Israelites and their journey to freedom. Now comes detailed legislation, the "constitution of liberty."

This is not accidental but essential. In Judaism, law grows out of the historical experience of the people. Egypt was the Jewish people's school of the soul; memory was its ongoing seminar in the art and craft of freedom. It taught them what it felt like to be on the wrong side of power. "You know what it feels like to be a stranger," says a resonant phrase in this week's parsha (23: 9). Jews were the people commanded never to forget the bitter taste of slavery so that they would never take freedom for granted. Those who do so, eventually lose it.

Nowhere is this clearer than in the opening of today's parsha. We have been reading about the Israelites' historic experience of slavery. So the social legislation of Mishpatim begins with slavery. What is fascinating is not only what it says but what it doesn't say.

It doesn't say: abolish slavery. Surely it should have done. Is that not the whole point of the story thus far? Joseph's brothers sell him into slavery. He, as the Egyptian viceroy *Tzofenat Paneach*, threatens them with slavery. Generations later, when a Pharaoh arises who "knew not Joseph," the entire Israelite people become Egypt's slaves. Slavery, like vengeance, is a vicious circle that has no natural end. Why not, then, give it a supernatural end? Why did God not say: There shall be no more slavery?

Rabbi Jonathan Sacks, PhD. (1948–) Former chief rabbi of the United Kingdom. Rabbi Sacks attended Cambridge University and received his doctorate from King's College, London. A prolific and influential author, his books include *Will We Have Jewish Grandchildren?* and *The Dignity of Difference*. He received the Jerusalem Prize in 1995 for his contributions to enhancing Jewish life in the Diaspora, was knighted and made a life peer in 2005, and became Baron Sacks of Aldridge in 2009.

The Torah has already given us an implicit answer. Change is possible in human nature but it takes time: time on a vast scale, centuries, even millennia. There is little doubt that in terms of the Torah's value system the exercise of power by one person over another, without their consent, is a fundamental assault against human dignity. This is not just true of the relationship between master and slave. It is even true, according to many classic Jewish commentators, of the relationship between king and subjects, rulers and ruled. According to the sages, it is even true of the relationship between God and human beings. The Talmud says that if God really did coerce the Jewish people to accept the Torah by "suspending the mountain over their heads," (Shabbat 88a) that would constitute an objection to the very terms of the covenant itself. We are God's *avadim*, servants, only because our ancestors freely chose to be (see Joshua 24, where Joshua offers the people freedom, if they so chose, to walk away from the covenant then and there).

So slavery is to be abolished, but it is a fundamental principle of God's relationship with us that he does not force us to change faster than we are able to do so of our own free will. So Mishpatim does not abolish slavery but it sets in motion a series of fundamental laws that will lead people, albeit at their own pace, to abolish it of their own accord. Here are the laws:

> "If you buy a Hebrew servant, he is to serve you for six years. But in the seventh year, he shall go free, without paying anything . . . But if the servant declares, 'I love my master and my wife and children and do not want to go free,' then his master must take him before the judges. He shall take him to the door or the doorpost and pierce his ear with an awl. Then he will be his servant for life." (Ex. 21: 2-6)

What is being done in these laws? First, a fundamental change is taking place in the nature of slavery. No longer is it a permanent status; it is a temporary condition. A Hebrew slave goes free after seven years. He or she knows this. Liberty awaits the slave not at the whim of the master but by divine command. When you know that within a fixed time you are going to be free, you may be a slave in body but in your own mind you are a free human being who has temporarily lost his or her liberty. That in itself is revolutionary.

This alone, though, was not enough. Six years are a long time. Hence the institution of Shabbat, ordained so that one day in seven a slave could breathe free air: no one could command him to work:

> "Six days you shall labor and do all your work, but the seventh day is a Sabbath to the Lord your God. On it you shall not do any work, neither you . . . nor your male or female servant . . . so that your male and female servants may rest, as you do. Remember that you were slaves in Egypt and that the Lord your God brought you out of there with a mighty hand and an outstretched arm. That is why the Lord your God has commanded you to observe the Sabbath day." (Deut. 5: 12-14)

But the Torah is acutely aware that not every slave wants liberty. This too emerges out of Israelite history. More than once in the wilderness the Israelites wanted to go back to Egypt. They say: "We remember the fish we ate in Egypt at no cost—also the cucumbers, melons, leeks, onions and garlic" (Num. 11: 5). As Rashi points out, the phrase "at no cost" [chinam] cannot be understood literally. They paid for it with their labour and their lives. "At no cost" means "free of mitzvot," of commands, obligations, duties. Freedom carries a high price, namely, moral responsibility. Many people have shown what Erich Fromm called "fear of freedom." Rousseau spoke of "forcing people to be free"—a view that led in time to the reign of terror following the French Revolution.

The Torah does not force people to be free but it does insist on a ritual of stigmatization. If a slave refuses to go free, his master "shall take him to the door or the doorpost and pierce his ear with an awl." Rashi explains:

> "Why was the ear chosen to be pierced rather than all the other limbs of the body? Said Rabbi Yochanan ben Zakkai: . . . The ear that heard on Mount Sinai: "For to Me are the children of Israel servants" and he, nevertheless, went ahead and acquired a master for himself, should [have his ear] pierced! Rabbi Shimon expounded this verse in a beautiful manner: Why are the door and the doorpost different from other objects of the house? G-d, in effect, said: "The door and doorpost were witnesses in Egypt when I passed over the lintel and the two doorposts, and I said: 'For to me are the children of Israel servants' "—they are My servants, not servants of servants, and this person went ahead and acquired a master for himself, he shall [have his ear] pierced in their presence."

A slave may stay a slave but not without being reminded that this is not what God wants for His people. The result of these laws was to create a dynamic that would in the end lead to an abolition of slavery, at a time of free human choosing.

And so it happened. The Quakers, Methodists and Evangelicals, most famous among them William Wilberforce, who led the campaign in Britain to abolish the slave trade were driven by religious conviction, inspired not least by the biblical narrative of the Exodus, and by the challenge of Isaiah "to proclaim freedom for captives and for prisoners, release from darkness" (Is. 61: 1).

Slavery was abolished in the United States only after a civil war, and there were those who cited the Bible in defence of slavery. As Abraham Lincoln put it in his Second Inaugural: "Both read the same Bible and pray to the same God, and each invokes His aid against the other. It may seem strange that any men should dare to ask a just God's assistance in wringing their bread from the sweat of other men's faces, but let us judge not, that we be not judged."

Yet slavery was abolished in the United States, not least because of the affirmation in the Declaration of Independence that "all men are created equal," and are endowed by their Creator with inalienable rights, among them "life, liberty and the pursuit of happiness." Jefferson, who wrote those words, was himself a slave-owner. Yet such is the latent power of ideals that eventually people see that by insisting on their right to freedom and dignity while denying it to others, they are living a contradiction. That is when change takes place, and it takes time.

If history tells us anything it is that God has patience, though it is often sorely tried. He wanted slavery abolished but he wanted it to be done by free human beings coming to see of their own accord the evil it is and the evil it does. The God of history, who taught us to study history, had faith that eventually we would learn the lesson of history: that freedom is indivisible. We must grant freedom to others if we truly seek it for ourselves.

"The Slow End of Slavery," https://www.ou.org/torah/parsha/rabbi-sacks-on-parsha/the_slow_end_of_slavery/ December, 2015. Reprinted with permission of ou.org.

LESSON FIVE

1. Why are the Jewish holidays always "late" or "early"?

2. Why do we say *Mazal Tov*?

3. Why do Jews eat *gefilte* fish on Shabbat?

4. Why do Jews eat *cholent* on Shabbat?

5. Why is a God-fearing person praiseworthy? Isn't fear a negative emotion? Why isn't love enough?

6. Why does Jewish law recognize matrilineal descent as the deciding factor for Jewish identity?

7. Why do some Jews wear old-fashioned clothes?

8. Why would the Torah state, "Do not cook a kid in its mother's milk" if the intention—according to the Talmud—is a broader prohibition?

9. Why are eggs *pareve*, though the birds that lay the eggs are *fleishig*?

JLI

JEWISH LEARNING INSTITUTE

1. Why are the Jewish holidays always "late" or "early"?

An Integrated System

Text 1

Maimonides, *Mishneh Torah*, Laws of Sanctifying the New Month 1:1 📖

Rabbi Moshe ben Maimon
(Maimonides, Rambam)
1135–1204

Halachist, philosopher, author, and physician. Maimonides was born in Cordoba, Spain. After the conquest of Cordoba by the Almohads, he fled Spain and eventually settled in Cairo, Egypt. There, he became the leader of the Jewish community and served as court physician to the vizier of Egypt. He is most noted for authoring the *Mishneh Torah*, an encyclopedic arrangement of Jewish law, and for his philosophical work, *Guide for the Perplexed*. His rulings on Jewish law are integral to the formation of halachic consensus.

חָדְשֵׁי הַשָּׁנָה הֵם חָדְשֵׁי הַלְּבָנָה, שֶׁנֶּאֱמַר "עוֹלַת חֹדֶשׁ בְּחָדְשׁוֹ" (בַּמִּדְבָּר כח,יד). וְנֶאֱמַר "הַחֹדֶשׁ הַזֶּה לָכֶם רֹאשׁ חָדָשִׁים" (שְׁמוֹת יב,ב). כָּךְ אָמְרוּ חֲכָמִים (רֹאשׁ הַשָּׁנָה כ,א): הֶרְאָה לוֹ הַקָּדוֹשׁ בָּרוּךְ הוּא לְמֹשֶׁה בְּמַרְאֵה הַנְּבוּאָה דְּמוּת לְבָנָה וְאָמַר לוֹ, כָּזֶה רְאֵה וְקַדֵּשׁ.

The months of the year are lunar months, as it says (Numbers 28:14), "The burnt offering of the month when it is renewed." [Monthly renewal is relevant to the lunar cycle.] It also says (Exodus 12:2), "This month shall be for you the first of months," about which our sages commented that God showed Moses in a vision of prophecy an image of the moon and told him, "When you see the moon like this, declare it [a new month]" (Talmud, Rosh Hashanah 20a).

Lunar — 12 mos. = 354   Just under 30 Days

Solar — 4 Seasons 365 Days

= 11 Days Difference

every 19

1 month is Added every Few Years

Text 2

Midrash, *Shemot Rabah* 15:26 📖

Shemot Rabah

An early rabbinic commentary on the Book of Exodus. Midrash is the designation of a particular genre of rabbinic literature usually forming a running commentary on specific books of the Bible. *Shemot Rabah*, written mostly in Hebrew, provides textual exegeses, expounds upon the biblical narrative, and develops and illustrates moral principles. It was first published in Constantinople in 1512 together with four other midrashic works on the other four books of the Pentateuch.

הַלְבָנָה בָּרִאשׁוֹן שֶׁל נִיסָן מַתְחֶלֶת לְהָאִיר. וְכָל שֶׁהִיא הוֹלֶכֶת מֵאִירָה, עַד ט"ו יָמִים וְדִסְקוֹס שֶׁלָּה מִתְמַלֵּא. וּמִט"ו עַד שְׁלֹשִׁים אוֹר שֶׁלָּה חָסֵר. בְּל' אֵינָה נִרְאֵית. כָּךְ יִשְׂרָאֵל . . .

The moon begins to shine on the first of Nisan. As the month proceeds, the moon's light increases until its disk becomes full on the fifteenth. From the fifteenth, its light diminishes. On the thirtieth, its light cannot be seen.

The Jews share a similar fate. . . .

As of the moon We have our ups & downs Just like the moon. We start over
as (מזל) = לֹז

Text 3

Deuteronomy 16:1 📖

שָׁמוֹר אֶת חֹדֶשׁ הָאָבִיב וְעָשִׂיתָ פֶּסַח לַה' אֱלֹקֶיךָ כִּי בְּחֹדֶשׁ הָאָבִיב הוֹצִיאֲךָ ה' אֱלֹקֶיךָ מִמִּצְרַיִם לָיְלָה.

Keep the month of spring, and make the Passover offering to God; for in the month of spring, God brought you out of Egypt at night.

LEARNING EXERCISE 1

Describe in what way the lunar message of change and the solar message of constancy would be beneficial in the following areas of life. ↳ NO Flexibility

	Moon	Sun
Relationships	Adapts is Flexible	
Education		
Judaism	Living with our principles but being flexible like The moon	
Career		

- Because the Jews are linked with the moon, ours is a lunar calendar. And because Passover needs to be in spring, the calendar features a built-in device, a leap year, to integrate the solar and lunar cycles.

- The Jewish calendar teaches us that we can reconcile our "lunar" and "solar" natures: we must be steadfast and unchanging in our principles, yet also be able to grow and adapt with respect to their applications.

2. Why do we say *Mazal Tov?*

Talmudic Astrology

Text 4

Babylonian Talmud

A literary work of monumental proportions that draws upon the legal, spiritual, intellectual, ethical, and historical traditions of Judaism. The 37 tractates of the Babylonian Talmud contain the teachings of the Jewish sages from the period after the destruction of the 2nd Temple through the 5th century CE. It has served as the primary vehicle for the transmission of the Oral Law and the education of Jews over the centuries; it is the entry point for all subsequent legal, ethical, and theological Jewish scholarship.

Talmud, Shabbat 156a 📖

הַאי מַאן דִּבְחַמָּה, יְהֵי גְּבַר זִיוְתָן, יְהֵי אָכִיל מִדִּילֵיה וְשָׁתֵי מִדִּילֵיה, וְרָזוֹהִי גַּלְיָין, אִם גָּנֵיב לֹא מַצְלַח. הַאי מַאן דִּבְכוֹכַב נוֹגַהּ, יְהֵי גְּבַר עַתִּיר, וְזַנַּאי יְהֵי . . . הַאי מַאן דִּבְכוֹכָב, יְהֵי גְּבַר נְהִיר וְחַכִּים . . . הַאי מַאן דִּבְלְבָנָה, יְהֵי גְּבַר סָבִיל מַרְעִין, בָּנַאי וְסָתִיר, סָתִיר וּבָנַאי, אָכִיל דְּלָא דִילֵיה וְשָׁתֵי דְּלָא דִילֵיה, וְרָזוֹהִי כַּסְיָין, אִם גָּנֵב מַצְלַח. הַאי מַאן דִּבְשַׁבְתַּאי, יְהֵי גְּבַר מַחֲשַׁבְתֵּיה בְּטֵלִין, וְאִית דְּאָמְרֵי כָּל דְּמְחַשְּׁבִין עֲלֵיה בְּטֵלִין. הַאי מַאן דִּבְצֶדֶק, יְהֵי גְּבַר צַדְקָן . . . הַאי מַאן דִּבְמַאדִּים, יְהֵי גְּבַר אָשִׁיד דְּמָא. אָמַר רַב אַשִׁי: אִי אוּמָּנָא אִי גַּנָּבָא אִי טַבָּחָא אִי מוֹהֲלָא . . .

אָמַר אַבְרָהָם לִפְנֵי הקב״ה . . . נִסְתַּכַּלְתִּי בָּאִיצְטַגְנִינוּת שֶׁלִי וְאֵינִי רָאוּי לְהוֹלִיד בֵּן. אָמַר לֵיה: צֵא מֵאִיצְטַגְנִינוּת שֶׁלְּךָ . . . מַאי דַעְתֵּיךְ דְקָאֵי צֶדֶק בְּמַעֲרָב, מַהֲדַרְנָא וּמוֹקְמִינָא לֵיה בְּמִזְרָח.

He who is born under the constellation of the sun will be a distinguished man, will eat and drink of his own, and his secrets will lie uncovered; if a thief, he will have no success.

He who is born under Venus will be wealthy and unchaste. . . .

He who is born under Mercury will be of a retentive memory and wise. . . .

He who is born under the Moon will be a man to suffer evil; he will build and demolish, demolish and build. He will eat and drink that which is not his, and his secrets will remain hidden. If a thief, he will be successful.

He who is born under Saturn will be a man whose plans will be frustrated. Others say that all [nefarious] designs against him will be frustrated.

He who is born under Jupiter will be a right-doing man....

He who is born under Mars will be a shedder of blood. Rav Ashi observed: He will be a surgeon, or thief, or slaughterer, or circumciser....

Abraham said before God, "I have looked at my constellation and found that I am not fated to beget a child."

God replied, "Cease your planet gazing.... What is your calculation? That Jupiter [the constellation you were born under] stands in the west? I will turn it back and place it in the east.

A Voice of Dissent (Optional)

Text 5

Maimonides, *Igerot Uteshuvot*, Letter to Community of Marseilles, p. 27

שֶׁכָּל דִּבְרֵי הַחוֹזִים בַּכּוֹכָבִים שֶׁקֶר הֵם אֵצֶל כָּל בַּעֲלֵי מַדָּע.

All predictions of the stargazers are lies in the opinion of all who are knowledgeable in science.

The Wish

Text 6

Rabbi Yehudah Hachasid, *Sefer Chasidim* 487 📖

Rabbi Yehudah ben Shmuel Hachasid
1140–1217

Mystic and ethicist. Born in Speyer, Germany, he was a rabbi, mystic, and one of the initiators of Chasidei Ashkenaz, a Jewish German moralist movement that stressed piety and asceticism. Rabbi Yehudah settled in Regensburg in 1195. He is best known for his work *Sefer Chasidim*, on the ethics of day-to-day concerns.

אִשָּׁה שֶׁיּוֹשֶׁבֶת עַל הַמַּשְׁבֵּר, אִם הִיא בְּחֶדֶר וּבְנֵי אָדָם בַּבַּיִת, יְבַקְשׁוּ עָלֶיהָ רַחֲמִים וְעַל הַיֶּלֶד שֶׁיִּוָּלַד בְּמַזָּל טוֹב.

When a woman is in labor and others are outside the room in the same house, they ought to pray for mercy upon her and that the child should be born under a good *mazal*.

KEY POINTS

- While the Talmud embraces some form of astrology—which explains the origins of *mazal tov*—it also asserts that God is always in control, that He can change any given outcome, and that human beings maintain their free choice.

- On a mystical level, *mazal* refers to God as He is beyond all limits and definitions. *Mazal tov* is a wish that one should receive blessings of goodness (*tov*) from this infinite level of God, which surpasses all calculations of merit.

---

3. Why do Jews eat *gefilte fish* on Shabbat?

Fish Pleasure

Text 7

Talmud, Shabbat 118b 📖

בַּמֶּה מְעַנְּגוֹ?

רַב יְהוּדָה בְּרֵיהּ דְּרַב שְׁמוּאֵל בַּר שִׁילַת מִשְּׁמֵיהּ דְּרַב אָמַר:
בְּתַבְשִׁיל שֶׁל תְּרָדִין, וְדָגִים גְּדוֹלִים, וְרָאשֵׁי שׁוּמִין.

רַב חִיָּיא בַּר אַשִׁי אָמַר רַב: אֲפִילּוּ דָּבָר מוּעָט וְלִכְבוֹד שַׁבָּת עֲשָׂאוֹ, הֲרֵי זֶה עוֹנֶג.

מַאי הִיא? אָמַר רַב פָּפָּא: כָּסָא דְּהַרְסָנָא.

How should one have pleasure on Shabbat?

Rav Yehudah son of Rav Shmuel bar Shilat said in Rav's name, "With a dish of beets, large fish, and heads of garlic."

Rav Chiya bar Ashi said in Rav's name, "Even something small, if it is prepared in honor of Shabbat, it satisfies the obligation to take delight."

What is [something small]?

Rav Papa said, "A pie of fish-hash."

One should have pleasure on Shabbat how so

Text 8

Rabbi Tsadok Hakohen of Lublin, *Peri Tsadik*, *Parashat Emor* 6 📖

שֶׁעִיקָר עוֹנֶג שַׁבָּת בְּדָגִים, מִשּׁוּם שֶׁאֵין בָּהֶם שׁוּם אִיסּוּר חֵלֶב,
וְגִיד הַנָּשֶׁה. וּבְעוֹפוֹת יֵשׁ עַל כָּל פָּנִים אִיסּוּר דָּם וּנְבֵילָה. מַה
שֶּׁאֵין כֵּן בְּדָגִים. מִכְּלָל דִּבְדָגִים אֵין בָּהֶם עִרְבּוּב טוֹב וָרַע.

The primary way to take pleasure on Shabbat is by consuming fish. Unlike animals, there are no prohibited fats in fish nor is there the prohibited sciatic nerve. Although poultry does not have these prohibited elements, the prohibition of blood still pertains to poultry and it must be slaughtered in a proper manner. None of these laws pertains to fish. With regard to fish, there is no mixture of the holy and unholy.

[Handwritten annotations:]
Fish represents holly
Fish Are always aware of its source (water) cannot live without it so should a Jew should Always be connected to its source

Stuffed Fish

Text 9

Eric G. Freudenstein, "Sabbath Fish," *Judaism: A Quarterly Journal of Jewish Life and Thought* 29:4 (1980), pp. 430–431

In the last two hundred years or so, the custom has [become] to eat the Sabbath fish as gefilte fish. That phrase is, of course, the Yiddish for stuffed fish. In the original version of this delicacy, the fish was chopped, mixed with flour and condiments, and this filling was used to stuff the skin of the fish. The whole was then cooked, cut into slices and served. . . .

Rabbi Tsadok Hakohen Rabinowitz of Lublin
1823–1900

Chasidic master and thinker. Rabbi Tsadok was born into a Lithuanian rabbinic family and later joined the Chasidic movement. He was a follower of the Chasidic leaders Rabbi Mordechai Yosef Leiner of Izbica and Rabbi Leibel Eiger. He succeeded Rabbi Eiger after his passing and became a rebbe in Lublin, Poland. He authored many works on Jewish law, Chasidism, Kabbalah, and ethics, as well as scholarly essays on astronomy, geometry, and algebra.

Eric Freudenstein
d. 2008

Nutritional scientist and Hebrew scholar. Freudenstein was chief chemist of the Jewish food giant Rokeach for 50 years and also an ardent Talmudist. His papers have been published in a volume entitled *Yad Gavriel*, that being Eric's Hebrew name.

An important reason why fish, rather than meat, became the preferred Sabbath fish dish was economics. Impoverished Jewish communities could hardly have afforded meat on every ordinary Sabbath, but some kind of fish was usually available at prices that were within reach. The utilization of every morsel was important for a poor community, and in the making of gefilte fish, the housewife could use every ounce. . . .

The Sabbath laws specify the preferred manner in which the edible part of the food shall be separated from the inedible portion, and even the manner in which the residue of the meal, such as the peelings and pits of fruit or the bones and skin of fish, can be removed from the table is laid down in the rules. To do so according to the strictures of *halakhah* requires learning, which not everyone possessed, and which could not be expected from the indigent guests who were often invited to the Sabbath table. All of these problems were eliminated by serving the fish in boneless and skinless portions.

"Come and let us give credit to Israel, the holy people," writes a halakhic authority in the name of the Brisker Rav, "for establishing the custom of eating fish on the Sabbath in the form of stuffed fish, thereby eliminating all manner of religious scruples and doubts."

KEY POINTS

- It is customary to eat fish on Shabbat as a way of having pleasure on this sacred day. In addition, fish is symbolic of a state in which spiritual failure is impossible due to the intimate connection to God that we have on Shabbat.

- The tradition of *gefilte* (stuffed) fish came about because of its economic benefit and the fact that it circumvents *halachic* concerns of separating on Shabbat.

4. Why do Jews eat *cholent* on Shabbat?

Princess Sabbath

Text 10

Heinrich Heine, "Princess Sabbath," in *The Standard Book of Jewish Verse* [New York: Dodd, Mead, 1917], p. 256

She denies her lover nothing
Save the smoking of tobacco;
"Dearest, smoking is forbidden,
For to-day it is the Sabbath.

"But at noon, as compensation,
There shall steam for thee a dish
That in very truth divine is—
Thou shalt eat to-day of schalet!

"Schalet, ray of light immortal!
Schalet, daughter of Elysium!"
So had Schiller's song resounded,
Had he ever tasted schalet,

For this schalet is the very
Food of heaven, which, on Sinai,
God Himself instructed Moses
In the secret of preparing . . .

Heinrich Heine
1797–1856

German poet. Heine was born Jewish and attended the universities of Bonn, Göttingen, and Berlin. In 1825, in order to open up the possibility of a civil service career, which was closed to Jews at that time, he converted to Protestantism with little enthusiasm and some resentment. Heine's international literary reputation and influence were established by the *Buch der Lieder* (*The Book of Songs*), frequently set to music, though the more somber poems of his last years are also highly regarded.

You Shall Not Cause to Burn

Text 11

Exodus 35:3 📖

לֹא תְבַעֲרוּ אֵשׁ בְּכֹל מֹשְׁבֹתֵיכֶם בְּיוֹם הַשַּׁבָּת.

Y ou shall not cause fire to burn in any of your dwelling places on the day of Shabbat.

KEY POINTS

- We are commanded to have pleasure on Shabbat, and meat, served hot, is generally a source of pleasure. In addition, eating hot food on Shabbat day demonstrates our belief in the authenticity of the oral tradition—that the Torah allows a fire lit before Shabbat to stay kindled throughout Shabbat.

5. Why is a God-fearing person praiseworthy? Isn't fear a negative emotion? Why isn't love enough?

Text 12

Deuteronomy 10:12

וְעַתָּה יִשְׂרָאֵל מָה ה' אֱלֹקֶיךָ שֹׁאֵל מֵעִמָּךְ כִּי אִם לְיִרְאָה אֶת ה אֱלֹקֶיךָ לָלֶכֶת בְּכָל דְּרָכָיו וּלְאַהֲבָה אֹתוֹ וְלַעֲבֹד אֶת ה' אֱלֹקֶיךָ בְּכָל לְבָבְךָ וּבְכָל נַפְשֶׁךָ.

And now, Israel, what does God require of you, but to fear God, to walk in all His ways, to love Him, and to serve God with all your heart and with all your soul.

Why do you want to "Fear" – Reward & Punishment? see text 14.

Positive vs. Negative (Optional)

QUESTION FOR DISCUSSION

When is fear positive and when is it negative?

Fear of Consequences (Optional)

Text 13

Rabbi Shalom Dovber Schneersohn
(Rashab)
1860–1920

Chasidic rebbe. Rabbi Shalom Dovber became the 5th leader of the Chabad movement upon the passing of his father, Rabbi Shmuel of Lubavitch. He established the Lubavitch network of *yeshivot* called Tomchei Temimim. He authored many volumes of Chasidic discourses and is renowned for his lucid and thorough explanations of Kabbalistic concepts.

Rabbi Shalom Dov Ber Schneersohn, *Sefer Hama'amarim* 5659, p. 19

הֲגַם דְּכָלְלוּת עִנְיָן יִרְאַת הָעוֹנֶשׁ הוּא לְגַרְמֵיהּ . . . מִכָּל
מָקוֹם, לְגַרְמֵיהּ זוּ דְיִרְאַת הָעוֹנֶשׁ אֵינָהּ רַע גָּמוּר.

Although fear of punishment is a selfish concern . . . nevertheless, it is not completely bad.

Immature Love (Optional)

QUESTION FOR DISCUSSION

Is love enough to sustain a relationship?

In Awe

Text 14

Maimonides, *Mishneh Torah*, Laws of the Foundations of the Torah 2:1–2

וְהֵיאַךְ הִיא הַדֶּרֶךְ לְאַהֲבָתוֹ וְיִרְאָתוֹ? בְּשָׁעָה שֶׁיִּתְבּוֹנֵן הָאָדָם בְּמַעֲשָׂיו וּבְרוּאָיו
הַנִּפְלָאִים הַגְּדוֹלִים, וְיִרְאֶה מֵהֶן חָכְמָתוֹ שֶׁאֵין לָהּ עֵרֶךְ וְלֹא קֵץ, מִיָּד הוּא אוֹהֵב
וּמְשַׁבֵּחַ וּמְפָאֵר וּמִתְאַוֶּה תַּאֲוָה גְדוֹלָה לֵידַע הַשֵּׁם הַגָּדוֹל, כְּמוֹ שֶׁאָמַר דָּוִד

"צָמְאָה נַפְשִׁי לֵאלֹקִים לְאֵל חָי" (תְּהִלִים מב,ג). וּכְשֶׁמְחַשֵּׁב בִּדְבָרִים הָאֵלּו עַצְמָן, מִיַּד הוּא נִרְתָּע לַאֲחוֹרָיו וְיִפְחַד, וְיוֹדֵעַ שֶׁהוּא בְּרִיָּה קְטַנָּה שְׁפֵלָה אֲפֵלָה, עוֹמֶדֶת בְּדַעַת קַלָּה מְעוּטָה לִפְנֵי תְּמִים דֵּעוֹת, כְּמוֹ שֶׁאָמַר דָּוִד (תְּהִלִים ח,ד–ה) "כִּי אֶרְאֶה שָׁמֶיךָ מַעֲשֵׂה אֶצְבְּעוֹתֶיךָ", "מָה אֱנוֹשׁ כִּי תִזְכְּרֶנּוּ".

What is the path to loving Him and fearing Him?

When we contemplate God's great and wondrous creations, and perceive thereby His infinite wisdom that surpasses all comparison, we will immediately love, praise, and acclaim God, and we will yearn with tremendous desire to know Him. As King David stated, "My soul thirsts for the living God" (Psalms 42:3).

When we continue to reflect on these matters, we will immediately recoil in awe. We will appreciate that we are tiny, humble, and obfuscated creatures, standing with flimsy and limited wisdom before He Who is of perfect knowledge. As David stated, "When I see Your heavens, the work of Your fingers . . . [I wonder] what is man that You should recall him?" (Psalms 8:4–5)

Translate Fear as → Awe – יראה
Fear – פחד

Taking it Personally

Text 15

Rabbi Shne'ur Zalman of Liadi, *Tanya*, ch. 41 📖

לְהִתְבּוֹנֵן בְּמַחֲשַׁבְתּוֹ עַל כָּל פְּנִים גְּדוּלַת אֵין סוֹף בָּרוּךְ הוּא,
וּמַלְכוּתוֹ אֲשֶׁר הִיא מַלְכוּת כָּל עוֹלָמִים עֶלְיוֹנִים וְתַחְתּוֹנִים,
וְאִיהוּ מְמַלֵּא כָּל עָלְמִין, וְסוֹבֵב כָּל עָלְמִין . . .

וּמַנִּיחַ הָעֶלְיוֹנִים וְתַחְתּוֹנִים וּמְיַחֵד מַלְכוּתוֹ . . . וְעָלָיו בִּפְרָט, כִּי "חַיָּב
אָדָם לוֹמַר בִּשְׁבִילִי נִבְרָא הָעוֹלָם" (מִשְׁנָה, סַנְהֶדְרִין ד,ה).

וְהוּא גַם הוּא מְקַבֵּל עָלָיו מַלְכוּתוֹ לִהְיוֹת מֶלֶךְ עָלָיו וּלְעָבְדוֹ וְלַעֲשׂוֹת רְצוֹנוֹ בְּכָל מִינֵי עֲבוֹדַת עֶבֶד.

וְהִנֵּה ה' נִצָּב עָלָיו . . . וּמַבִּיט עָלָיו וּבוֹחֵן כְּלָיוֹת וָלֵב אִם עוֹבְדוֹ כָּרָאוּי.

Rabbi Shne'ur Zalman of Liadi
(Alter Rebbe)
1745–1812

Chasidic rebbe, halachic authority, and founder of the Chabad movement. The Alter Rebbe was born in Liozna, Belarus, and was among the principal students of the Magid of Mezeritch. His numerous works include the *Tanya*, an early classic containing the fundamentals of Chabad Chasidism, and *Shulchan Aruch HaRav*, an expanded and reworked code of Jewish law.

Contemplate the greatness of the Infinite one, that His Kingship extends to all worlds, both higher and lower, and that He fills all worlds and encompasses them all.

Consider further that God leaves everything aside and uniquely bestows His Kingship upon . . . you in particular. Indeed, a person must say, "The world was created for my sake" (Mishnah, Sanhedrin 4:5).

Consider further that you ought to accept His Kingship upon yourself, that He be King over you, so that you serve Him and do His Will.

Consider further that God stands over you . . . and He looks at you and your innermost thoughts and emotions to determine if you are serving Him as is fitting.

KEY POINTS

- Love is crucial to our relationship with God, but for the relationship to be genuine, we must also acknowledge His awe-inspiring transcendence. Our relationship with God flourishes on love, but it must be borne out of reverence and awe.

- Our awe is intensified when we contemplate that this infinite, unfathomable God desires a relationship with us and awaits our fulfillment of our life's purpose.

6. Why does Jewish law recognize matrilineal descent as the deciding factor for Jewish identity?

A Given Identity

Text 16

Deuteronomy 29:13–14 📜

וְלֹא אִתְּכֶם לְבַדְּכֶם אָנֹכִי כֹּרֵת אֶת הַבְּרִית הַזֹּאת וְאֶת הָאָלָה הַזֹּאת. כִּי אֶת אֲשֶׁר יֶשְׁנוֹ פֹּה עִמָּנוּ עֹמֵד הַיּוֹם לִפְנֵי ה' אֱלֹקֵינוּ וְאֵת אֲשֶׁר אֵינֶנּוּ פֹּה עִמָּנוּ הַיּוֹם.

Not only with you am I making this covenant and this oath. [I am making this covenant] with those standing here with us today before God, and with those who are not here with us today.

A Yiddishe Mame

Text 17

Rabbi Yechiel Ya'akov Weinberg, *Responsa Seridei Eish* 4, p. 383 📖

לְפִי דִּינֵי הַתּוֹרָה, הוֹלֵךְ הַוָּלָד אַחֲרֵי הָאֵם.

אֵין אָנוּ יוֹדְעִים טַעֲמֵי הַתּוֹרָה.

יֵשׁ אוֹמְרִים שֶׁהוּא טַעַם בִּיוֹלוֹגִי בִּיצִירַת הַוָּלָד וּתְכוּנָתוֹ הַגּוּפָנִית וְהַנַּפְשִׁית.

וְיֵשׁ אוֹמְרִים שֶׁיֵּשׁ בָּזֶה טַעַם מוּסָרִי, שֶׁכֵּן הָאֵם וְהַשְׁפָּעָתָהּ
הַתְּמִידִית מַכְרִיעָה בְּחִינּוּךְ הַבָּנִים . . .

וַאֲחֵרִים רוֹאִים אֶת הַטַּעַם בְּוַודָּאוּת הַבִּלְתִּי מְפוּקְפֶּקֶת
בְּהִשְׁתַּיְּכוּת הַיֶּלֶד הַנּוֹלָד לְאִמּוֹ.

אֲבָל יִהְיוּ הַטְּעָמִים אֵיךְ שֶׁיִּהְיוּ, מַכְרִיעַ לֹא הַיְסוֹד הָרַאצִיוֹנָלִי שֶׁל
הַחֲקִירָה הַמַּדָּעִית, אֶלָּא הַיְסוֹד הַדָּתִי, שֶׁהוּא הָיָה הַגּוֹרֵם הַמַּכְרִיעַ
בְּעִיצוּב דְּמוּת הָאוּמָה וּבְעִיצוּב הַמִּשְׁפָּחָה הָעִבְרִית.

Rabbi Yechiel Ya'akov Weinberg
1885–1966

Talmudist and authority on Jewish law; known for his collection of responsa literature, *Seridei Eish*. Rabbi Weinberg studied in the famed Lithuanian *yeshivot* of Slabodka and Mir. In the 1930s, he served as rector at the Berlin Rabbinical Seminary, resulting in his shifting from traditional scholarship in the style of the Lithuanian yeshivah movement, to a more modern scientific approach. Following World War II, Rabbi Weinberg settled in Switzerland.

According to Torah law, a child's Jewishness depends on his or her mother.

We do not know the reasons for the Torah's laws.

Some offer a biological-based rationale—[that the mother is more involved] in the creation of a child and the formation of its body and soul.

Some offer a nurture-based rationale—that a mother's consistent influence is more decisive in shaping her children. . . .

Others suggest a practical rationale—that we know, indisputably, the identity of one's mother.

Ultimately, what matters is not the rationale for this law but the foundational law itself, which is the bedrock of the Jewish family and has shaped the Jewish people.

Text 18

Genesis 3:20 📖

וַיִּקְרָא הָאָדָם שֵׁם אִשְׁתּוֹ חַוָּה כִּי הוא הָיְתָה אֵם כָּל חָי.

Adam called his wife Chavah, because she was the mother of all life.

Text 19

Rabbi Joseph B. Soloveitchik, "A Tribute to the Rebbetzin of Talne," *Tradition* 17:2, Spring 1978, pp. 76–77 📖

What kind of a Torah does the mother pass on? I admit that I am not able to define precisely the masoretic [traditional] role of the Jewish mother. Only by circumscription I hope to be able to explain it.

Permit me to draw upon my own experiences. I used to have long conversations with my mother. . . . I used to watch her arranging the house in honor of a holiday. I used to see her recite prayers; I used to watch her recite the *sidra* [Torah portion] every Friday night and I still remember the nostalgic tune. I learned from her very much.

Rabbi Joseph B. Soloveitchik
1903–1993

Talmudist and philosopher. A scion of a famous Lithuanian rabbinical family, Rabbi Soloveitchik was one of the most influential Jewish personalities, leaders, and thinkers of the 20th century. In 1941, he became professor of Talmud at RIETS—Yeshiva University; in this capacity, he ordained more rabbis than anyone else in Jewish history. Among his published works are *Halakhic Man* and *Lonely Man of Faith*.

Most of all I learned that Judaism expresses itself not only in formal compliance with the law but also in a living experience. She taught me that there is a flavor, a scent and warmth to *mitzvot*. I learned from her the most important thing in life—to feel the presence of the Almighty and the gentle pressure of His hand resting upon my frail shoulders. Without her teachings, which quite often were transmitted to me in silence, I would have grown up a soulless being, dry and insensitive.

The laws of Shabbat, for instance, were passed on to me by my father. . . . The Shabbat as a living entity, as a queen, was revealed to me by my mother. . . . The fathers knew much about the Shabbat; the mothers lived the Shabbat, experienced her presence, and perceived her beauty and splendor.

KEY POINTS

→ • Possible reasons that God chose the mother to be the conveyer of her child's spiritual identity: (a) the mother is more involved in the creation of the child; (b) she has more influence on the child's emotional and spiritual development; (c) matrilineal lineage is definite.

7. Why do some Jews wear old-fashioned clothes?

Enclothed Cognition

Text 20

Rabbi Yehoshua Rokeach, cited in *Ta'amei Haminhagim*, p. 553 📖

דְּעֵשָׂו אָמַר לְיַעֲקֹב שֶׁתַּהֲלוּכֵי הַבְּגָדִים יִהְיֶה בְּשָׁוֶה . . . וּבִשְׁאָר הָעִנְיָנִים
תּוּכַל לֵילֵךְ בְּדֶרֶךְ אַחֵר מִמֶּנּוּ. וְהֵשִׁיב לוֹ: "הַיְלָדִים רַכִּים" (בְּרֵאשִׁית
לג,יג). אִם כִּי אֲנִי לֹא אֶפְחַד עוֹד לְהִתְקַלְקֵל עַל יְדֵי הַבְּגָדִים, אֲבָל
הַיְלָדִים יִתְקַלְקְלוּ עַל יְדֵי זֶה וְיִתְעָרְבוּ בַּגּוֹיִם וְיִלְמְדוּ מִמַּעֲשֵׂיהֶם.

Esau wanted Jacob to wear the same clothes as him. . . . In all other matters, he agreed that Jacob could choose to be different.

Jacob responded pointing to the fact that "the children are tender" (Genesis 33:13). Jacob was saying that although he would not be influenced by sharing Esau's way of dress, his children would be influenced and it would lead to assimilation.

Rabbi Yehoshua Rokeach
1825–1894

The second rebbe of the Belz Chasidic dynasty. Rabbi Rokeach's father was the first rebbe of Belz, Rabbi Shalom Rokeach, who passed away in 1855. Under the leadership of Rabbi Yehoshua Rokeach, Belz flourished and became one of the larger Chasidic sects. He was instrumental in founding the *Machzikei Hadas* organization, which sought to promote traditional orthodox values.

Text 21

"What Your Clothes Say About You," www.forbes.com, April 3, 2012

A study this year from Northwestern University examined a concept called "enclothed cognition." Researchers define it in their report as "the systematic influence that clothes have on the wearer's psychological processes," meaning what your clothes are saying to you, not about you. And how they make you feel.

The researchers distributed standard white lab coats to participants, telling some that it was a doctor's coat and some that it was a painter's smock. All participants performed the same task, but those wearing the "doctor's coat" were more careful and attentive. Their actions were influenced by their clothing. . . .

Enclothed cognition gives scientific proof to the idea that you should dress not how you feel, but how you want to feel. . . . The clothes you choose are sending a message to those around you, but also to you, yourself.

The Secret to Staying Power (Optional)

Text 22

Talmud, Shabbat 130a

כָּל מִצְוָה שֶׁמָּסְרוּ יִשְׂרָאֵל עַצְמָן עָלֶיהָ לְמִיתָה בִּשְׁעַת גְּזֵרַת הַמַּלְכוּת,

כְּגוֹן עֲבוֹדַת כּוֹכָבִים וּמִילָה - עֲדַיִן הִיא מוּחְזֶקֶת בְּיָדָם.

וְכָל מִצְוָה שֶׁלֹּא מָסְרוּ יִשְׂרָאֵל עַצְמָן עָלֶיהָ לְמִיתָה בִּשְׁעַת

גְּזֵרַת הַמַּלְכוּת, כְּגוֹן תְּפִילִין - עֲדַיִן הִיא מְרוּפָה בְּיָדָם.

Any commandment for which our ancestors accepted martyrdom in face of oppressive regimes—that mitzvah is firmly adhered to generations later. Examples include refusing idolatry and performing circumcision.

Any commandment for which our ancestors did not accept martyrdom in face of oppressive regimes—that mitzvah is feebly adhered to generations later. An example is the mitzvah of *tefilin*.

KEY POINTS

- The way we dress influences our thoughts and behaviors. Many Jews wear traditional clothes to foster and preserve a strong Jewish identity in themselves and their families.

---

8. Why would the Torah state, "Do not cook a kid in its mother's milk" if the intention—according to the Talmud—is a broader prohibition?

Text 23

Maimonides, *Mishneh Torah*, Laws of the Rebellious 2:9 🕮

הֲרֵי כָּתוּב בַּתּוֹרָה "לֹא תְבַשֵּׁל גְּדִי בַּחֲלֵב אִמּוֹ" (שְׁמוֹת כג,יט). מִפִּי הַשְׁמוּעָה לָמְדוּ שֶׁזֶּה הַכָּתוּב אָסַר לְבַשֵּׁל וְלֶאֱכוֹל בָּשָׂר בְּחָלָב.

The Torah states (Exodus 23:19), "You shall not cook a kid in its mother's milk." The received tradition teaches us that this verse forbids both the cooking and eating of milk with meat.

LEARNING EXERCISE 2

Considering the Talmudic laws pertaining to milk and meat, what would have been a clearer way for the Torah to state the verse? Write it in the box below.

Exodus 23:19 should have said:

3 Meaning of Bishul = ① Ripening, ② cooking ③ roasting.

Compatibility

LEARNING EXERCISE 3

The following chart contains a list of Talmudic laws pertaining to the prohibited mixture of meat and milk. Determine from which word of the verse ("You shall not cook a kid in its mother's milk") we can derive each law.

Word in verse	Law
[handwritten]	It is forbidden to eat milk and meat together, but this biblical prohibition only pertains if they were cooked together.
[handwritten]	The prohibition does not apply to meat from non-kosher species.
	The prohibition does not apply to meat from wild kosher species (such as deer).
	The prohibition does not apply to fowl.
	The prohibition applies to the animal's fat, not just its meat.
	The prohibition pertains to a kosher animal that died without proper slaughtering.
	The prohibition does not apply to milk from a non-kosher species.
	The prohibition does not apply to male lactation (male goats are known to lactate on occasion).
	The prohibition does not apply to milk extracted after the animal died.

Text 24

Rabbi Ya'akov Tsvi Mecklenburg, *Haketav Vehakabbalah,* Exodus 23:19

וְאִם יִקְשֶׁה בְּעֵינֶיךָ לָמָּה לֹא אָמְרָה הַתּוֹרָה לָשׁוֹן
הַיּוֹתֵר בָּרוּר "לֹא תְבַשֵּׁל בָּשָׂר בְּחָלָב"?

דַּע כִּי מִתְּנָאֵי אִסּוּר בָּשָׂר בְּחָלָב מִן הַתּוֹרָה, שֶׁיִּהְיֶה הַבָּשָׂר מִמִּין הַבְּהֵמָה הַטְּהוֹרָה,
לְהוֹצִיא בָּשָׂר מִן בְּהֵמוֹת הַטְּמֵאוֹת, וְגַם הֶחָלָב שֶׁנֶּאֱסַר בְּבִשּׁוּל הַבָּשָׂר יֵשׁ לָהּ תְּנַאי
זֶה, שֶׁאֵינֶנּוּ אָסוּר אֶלָּא הֶחָלָב מִן הַבְּהֵמָה, לְהוֹצִיא חֲלָב חַיָּה, וְגַם לֹא מִכָּל מִין אֶלָּא
דַּוְקָא הֶחָלָב מִמִּין בְּהֵמָה הַטְּהוֹרָה. וְהִנֵּה לִכְלוֹל כָּל הַתְּנָאִים הָאֵלֶּה בְּלָשׁוֹן כִּמְעַט
לֹא אֶפְשָׁר . . . לְזֶה בָּחֲרָה הַתּוֹרָה לָשׁוֹן קְצָרָה, לִכְלוֹל בּוֹ כָּל פְּרָטִים הַנִּזְכָּרִים.

Rabbi Ya'akov Tsvi Mecklenburg
1785–1865

German rabbi and biblical exegete.
Rabbi Ya'akov served as rabbi in
Königsberg, East Prussia. In 1839, he
published *Haketav Vehakabbalah*, an
important commentary that often
demonstrates the indivisibility of the
Written Torah and the Oral Torah.

You may ask, why did the Torah not write clearly, "Don't cook meat and milk"?

Know that there are many conditions that must be met before the combination of meat and milk amounts to a biblical prohibition—among them, that the meat and milk be of a kosher domesticated species. To include all this in a [succinct] written statement is virtually impossible. . . . The Torah therefore chose a brief statement that would include all of the details.

KEY POINTS

- The Torah states, "Do not cook a kid in its mother's milk" to enable us to derive the numerous laws regarding this prohibition contained in this verse.

9. Why are eggs *pareve*, though the birds that lay the eggs are *fleishig?*

Text 25

Maimonides, *Mishneh Torah*, Laws of the Rebellious 2:9 📖

גְּזֵרָה שֶׁלֹּא יָבֹא מִן הַדָּבָר חוֹבָה, וְיֹאמְרוּ הָעוֹף מוּתָּר מִפְּנֵי שֶׁלֹּא נִתְפָּרֵשׁ,
כַּךְ . . . בָּשָׂר בְּהֵמָה מוּתֶּרֶת חוּץ מִן הָעֵז. וְיָבֹא אַחֵר לוֹמַר אַף בְּשַׂר
הָעֵז . . . בְּחַלֵּב הָעֵז שֶׁאֵינָהּ אִמּוֹ מוּתָּר, שֶׁלֹּא נָאֱמַר אֶלָּא "אִמּוֹ".

t is a decree, lest the matter lead to harm. People might
say, "Fowl [with milk] is permitted, because the verse
only forbids a 'kid in its mother's milk.' Similarly, then
. . . the meat of all animals is permitted with the exception
of a goat." Another will add, "Even the meat of a goat . . . is
permitted with goat's milk as long as the milk is not from
its mother, for the verse only says, 'Its mother.'"

KEY POINTS

- The sages who issued the enactment forbidding the consumption of fowl with milk did not extend this to eggs, because it would yield no reasonable protective benefit.

Continue your learning experience ONLINE

Visit www.myJLI.com/why5

for insightful and inspiring videos, articles, and readings on this topic.

ADDITIONAL READINGS

"YET MY SOUL DREW BACK"
FEAR OF GOD AS EXPERIENCE AND COMMANDMENT IN AN AGE OF ANXIETY

BY RABBI SHALOM CARMY

I

They say that science has made it harder for people to fear God. Once upon a time, they say, illness was something over which people felt powerless, and so the sense of absolute dependence on God filled our spiritual horizon. Nowadays, we place ourselves under medical care first, and think of God second, if at all. Once we prayed for an adequate harvest. Today, when nature withholds her bounty, we either pay higher prices for tomatoes or eat something else instead. Far from the fleshpots of Modern Orthodoxy, R. Yehezkel Lowenstein, addressing the Ponivezh Yeshiva in Bnei Berak only fifteen years after the Holocaust, seems to agree that his hearers are prone to false security:

> Uprooting evil, is long and hard work, and it is possible only after recognizing the physical suffering that is liable to befall one because of his vices and sins. The reason one doesn't think of this is that human beings have presumptions, so to speak, about this world. One feels secure in his world and thinks it inconceivable that he will be harmed and will lose this world. Therefore he does not contemplate and fear physical punishment. One only lacks confidence in the world to come, and therefore we are more affected by promises about the world to come. For since we are not confident about the world to come, and we ask God to grant us the world to come, there-

fore we are agitated and worried that we will not merit the world to come."[1]

Has modern science indeed made us so secure? Leaving aside the unpredictable features of diagnosis and treatment even today, I want to ask, do scientifically controllable facts truly constitute the central reality for most of us? Are we really so assured that we have little room for God? Perhaps the opposite is true. Leave aside, again, the exceptional events that obsess some—terrorist acts, natural disasters and so forth—which, though most are sure they will never affect us, nonetheless happen. Can we honestly claim that our lives are free of uncertainty in the areas that count? You work for a company, let's say you even have job security and enjoy success. A new boss is appointed by people who know you not, nor have your interests at heart, a new set of priorities, and, from out of the blue, your situation is radically different from your reasonable expectations. At home, in an era of family instability and a culture of divorce, you wonder whether you are exempt from the failures that plague some of your friends. Because sheer physical survival is not your primary problem in life, these anxieties and tribulations are more important to you than they would have been in another era. No, science doesn't bestow upon you an easy mastery over your life.

Moreover, the "once upon a time," before modern life eliminated the fear of God, is earlier than you might think. Those moderns who chose to do so dismissed the fear of God without appealing to the marvels of

---

Rabbi Shalom Carmy. (1949–) Professor of Jewish philosophy and Bible. Rabbi Carmy is an expert on biblical theology and interpretation, modern Jewish thought, religious Zionism, and liberal arts and religion. He is the editor of *Tradition*, the theological journal of the Rabbinical Council of America. He is an affiliated scholar at Cardozo Law School and a member of the Erasmus and Dulles Forums.

---

[1] Yehezkel Lowenstein, *Or Yehezkel,* Vol. 6, 12 (Benei Berak, 1996).

omnipotent technology. Three centuries ago, Voltaire thought he had refuted Pascal's evocation of the terror aroused in him by the vast empty spaces that the astronomy of his day had discovered by pointing to the bustle of burgeoning urban centers. "As for me," he writes, "when I look at Paris or London I see no reason whatever for falling into this despair that M. Pascal is talking about; I see a town that in no way resembles a desert island, but is peopled, opulent, civilized, a place where men are as happy as human nature allows."[2] Happy city dwellers as we are, yet we know, as Voltaire did not know (or pretended not to know), that terrible loneliness and abandonment are often experienced in the midst of all that is opulent and civilized. *Plus ça change*—the desire to evade fear and terror are perennial; the rationalizations change, the underlying reality remains the same.

Someone suggests that the age of science may even enhance our sense of divine presence and human dependence on Him. She cites the famous aphorism ascribed to the *Hafets Hayyim*, according to which all the inventions of modern science strengthen faith: the telephone, for example, demonstrates that what is spoken here can be heard elsewhere, thus reinforcing our sense of divine omnipresence. Others react that this may have been the way the *Hafets Hayyim* perceived the world, but is not typical of the average modern man in the street. I have a different problem: to me the thought that my private world can be listened in on, via up-to-date technology, suggests not only an analogy to the divine omniscience I am committed to, but also the very real threat of being spied on. Rather than enhance my fear of God, it brings to the fore my fear of the secret police.

Why doesn't the *Hafets Hayyim* seem to share my worry? Because he takes it for granted that his audience accepts nominal belief in the governance of God. God's involvement in human affairs, however, is not always clearly manifested. As R. Israel Salanter put it in *Iggeret haMusar*—human beings are bound by their intellect but free in their imagination.[3] Comprehending the world through the imagination, the tangible present seems more real than invisible eternity. This principle explains many cases of weakness of will, what Aristotle called *akrasia*: the doctor, for example, who warns his patients but continues smoking. Just as one overindulges in food and drink, because the pleasures of the table are imminent while the morning after is remote, so the prospect of divine attention is not as vivid to us as it ought to be. If R. Yohanan ben Zakkai (*Berakhot* 28b) wished that his disciples fear God as much as they fear man, it is presumably because he knew that human surveillance is harder to ignore than the eye of God. For the *Hafets Hayyim*, the danger to faith is the feeling that "God does not see; God has abandoned the earth" (to quote Ezekiel 8:12); the telescope and the telephone reinforce our faith in the presence of things unseen and thus fortify our belief in God. The fear of God central to this conception is perfectly encapsulated in Vayikra's repeated phrase, "and you shall fear your God, I am the Lord," appended to prohibitions like offering misleading advice, taking advantage of others, taking usury, oppressing the slave, or the injunction to honor the elderly, as interpreted by Rashi, since in these cases one can easily disguise one's motives, we are reminded that one cannot do so unobserved. Regarding these verses it may be worth adding R. David Zvi Hoffmann's suggestion that these sins involve the abuse of people who cannot defend themselves and thus depend on divine protection.[4]

I have no wish to undervalue this traditional Musar insight. My concern, however, in this essay is with fear of God, not exclusively with belief in divine omniscience and omnipresence. For many whose piety is superior to mine, the very awareness of divine presence is tantamount to the fear of God: "the lion has roared, who does not fear?" (Amos 3:8). There are great, unforgettable moments, when Amos's pro-

---

[2] Voltaire, "On the Pensees of M. Pascal," Philosophical Letters, trans. E. Dilworth (New York, 1961), p. 124. Cf. R. Kook, Olat Reiyah, ii (Jerusalem, 1962), p. 122: "Yirat het (fear of sin) should be integrated with life. There are people who have yirat het but it is not strong in them; therefore, when they distance themselves from the clamor (hamon) of life and its tumult they fear sin, but when they connect themselves to life, in activities and business, yirat het withdraws from them." For R. Kook, it is the distractions of life, not its pleasures, which bring oblivion.

[3] *Iggeret haMusar*, ed. M. Pachter, *Kitvei R. Yisrael Salanter* (Jerusalem, 1972) 114ff.

[4] Leviticus 19:14, 31; 25: 17, 36, 43. Rashi derives his interpretations from *Safra* and *Kiddushin* 32b; at 25:36 he explains that usury requires the reminder because the avarice involved is hard to control. For additional sources, see *Encyclopedia Talmudit*, s.v. *yirat haShem*, Volume 25:89–91.

phetic words correspond to our own experience. And then the Musar formula is correct: our awareness of God, like that of Amos, engenders an overpowering motive to obey Him: "God spoke, who will not prophesy?"

Yet our hearts do not always resonate in this manner. One reason is the one we mentioned, the one that troubled the *ba'alei Musar* : the failure of our imagination, or rather its failure to testify to what we know intellectually. I believe that there are other factors, and that we will neither understand ourselves, nor understand what fear of God is for us, and should be for us, unless we analyze these factors in all their complexity. If the *Hafets Hayyim* worried about the imaginative failure to fear, we should worry whether our fear is the wrong kind of fear.

Given our sense that piety has declined in the modern and post-modern age, and the general spiritual shallowness of a community that is both vulnerable to the dominant secular atmosphere and disinclined to serious self-criticism, one is tempted to regard our confusion about the fear of God as a purely negative phenomenon, the best cure for which is a heavy dose of emotionally loaded Musar preaching. Nevertheless, I believe that we would do well to subject our ideas about fear of God to careful analysis in the hope that understanding will fortify our religious sensitivity.

There are at least three factors that complicate our conception of what it means to fear God properly: First, as we have noted, fear of God is in "competition," so to speak, with other kinds of fear, fear of human beings, natural disasters, fear of our own potentialities. Sometimes these fears motivate us to act rightly, as when we refrain from sin or do our duty for the sake of the social or natural consequences; sometimes our fears prevent us from obeying God, because we are swayed by concern about the unpleasant consequences of acting rightly or abstaining from evil. Sometimes our concern for social or natural effects helps to constitute our positive relationship to God.

Second, the fear of God, in Jewish sources, refers to a range of normative experiences and motives. Jewish ethical and halakhic literature distinguishes between fear of punishment (*yirat ha-onesh*), on the one hand, and the reverence or fear, associated with divine sublimity or the numinous (*yirat ha-romemut*), on the other hand. Theological liberals and moral latitudinarians obsessively denigrate the former as a means to presuming the latter. However, as we shall see, both Halakha and common decency require a combination of both strands of experience. Third, there is a creative tension between the fear of God, in all its varieties, and other normative feelings that seem to contravene fear. The most notable of these is the love of God; others are the commandment to imitate Him and to cleave unto Him (*devekut*). In the list of 613 biblical commandments, the *mitzvah* to fear God is not derived from the verses in Vayikra that link fear of God to specific prohibitions and injunctions, but from the passages in Devarim where fear of God is joined to these other experiential imperatives.[5]

Viewed comprehensively, the theme of *yirat haShem* (fear of God) and its kindred experiences and commandments comes close to being co-extensive with the Jewish moral orientation and with the Jewish experience of God. This terminological ambiguity threatens to make the investigation unmanageable because often the phrase *yirat shamayim* (fear of heaven) and its cognates are used so broadly that it becomes a synonym or synecdoche for Jewish piety, and this imprecision tends to blunt the acuity of any attempted analysis. Our goal is not to exhaust the literature. We intend rather to highlight some of the obvious elements of the mitzvah, including some that are regularly overlooked, some impediments to its fulfillment, and some ways it can be enhanced. Let us turn to the phenomenology and the practical implications of the fear of God and its relation to love.

II
Types of Fear

Fear is inherently distressing. We dislike fear. The most natural response to fear, virtually by definition, is the desire to avoid it, either by disabling the cause of the fear or by fleeing the occasion of fear. In the face of this fundamental, universal, perennial fact, it

---

[5] See Deuteronomy 6:2, 13, 24; 8:6; 28:58. Rambam *Hil. Yesodei haTorah* 2:1 and *Sefer haMizvot, Aseh* 4.

seems superfluous to invoke technological progress or the rise of the modern metropolis to explain why many people avoid thoughts that encourage or mandate fear of anyone, including fear of God. Given the natural inclination to avoid fear, the first question that comes to mind, it seems, is not why people no longer fear God much, but why they would want to fear God at all. Why should anyone regard the experience of fear as valuable in itself? The modernist seems to have reason on his side in feeling that a deity who commands fear is not promulgating the kind of religion that he would care to patronize. To cultivate the experience of fear deliberately, to accept the commandment of fear as part of a divinely bestowed regimen, carries a flavor of paradox.

At least three significant strategies promise to dispel the air of paradox. The first understands fear of God as a healthy means to an end—namely, moral obedience. Precisely because fear impels us to avoid the source of fear, it exercises a potent influence on behavior. A child is taught to fear fire to deter him from playing with matches or putting her hand on the gas burner. So too the fear of divine disapproval or retribution, as already noted, serves to motivate flagging commitment, to turn away from sin and to sustain the effort necessary to do one's duty. Thus *Sefer haHinnukh*, to take a representative medieval work, states that the reason we are commanded to fear God, which is clear to anyone with eyes to see, is that fear of punishment deters sin. From this perspective, God wants us to fear Him for our own good.

This approach is satisfactory up to a point. It provides a justification that agrees with everyday utilitarian ways of thinking about the instrumental value of fear. Just as adults accustomed to fire are not oppressed by their fear of it, so this kind of fear of God, once we internalize the norm, mellows into a sober caution of sin that no longer terrifies. There is even pleasure in recollecting the education in fear that makes us better able to conduct our lives. R. Nissim of Gerona applies the verse "Rejoice in trembling" (Psalms 2:10) to the sense of spiritual wholesomeness that accompanies the acquisition of this habit of mind.[6]

---

[6] *Derashot haRan* 10.

Yet because this approach to the fear of God focuses on the human inclination to sin, it is also problematic. If fear of God is merely a prophylactic, what place should it occupy in the ideal spiritual constitution? Augustine, forced to make room for the fear of God in the world to come, on the basis of Psalm 19 ("The fear of God is pure and everlasting") explains that this fear cannot be the fear that frightens away from evil, but rather the fear that helps one to persist in a good. Fully conscious of the oxymoron, he proposes the term "serene fear" for the eschatological form of punishment fear, by which he presumably meant an intellectual knowledge that God's wrath deserves to be feared without the occurrence of fear as an emotion.[7] Others, however, who oppose embracing fear of sin in any guise as a permanent ingredient in their spiritual outlook, would dismiss it as suitable only to those whose inherent motivation to act rightly is weak or undeveloped. The tendency to get beyond fear of sin is accentuated in our culture, which does not treat sin or moral failure with sufficient gravity. Hence, we don't imagine ourselves in need of sharp and constant reminders of our moral and religious fallibility, and concern about such matters is judged obsessive and damaging to the self-esteem we are set to cultivate with an earnestness that borders on the ferocious.

Consequently the first strategy soon requires assistance from the second. One distinguishes between the lower fear of God, which is merely the fear of punishment, and the higher fear, *yirat ha-romemut*, characterized by a sense of awe or reverence or sublimity; truly it resembles love of God more than the inferior kind of fear. Awe is patently different from ordinary fear: the intellectual underpinning of fear is the belief that one is threatened; awe entails the contemplation or encounter with what is overwhelming, majestic, and grand. Of course the distinction between higher and lower types of fear, well attested in the classic

---

[7] Augustine, *City of God* 14:9. If this explanation is unacceptable, he goes to suggest that the verse is not referring to the experience of fear at all, but instead to the everlasting character traits acquired through fear of God; (cf. R. S.R. Hirsch's commentary, ad loc). For a more extended sermonic commentary by Augustine, see James O'Donnell, *Augustine: A New Biography* (New York, 2005), pp. 157–59. It is worth noting that Radak interprets the verse as anti-Christian: the Torah's commandments are eternally binding.

medieval literature, is indispensable for the phenomenology of God-fearing. Anyone skeptical about the pedigree of the distinction can find it in the aftermath of the encounter at Sinai (Exodus 20:17). Moses tells the people not to fear, for God's will is that "His fear be upon your faces, that you sin not." If the word *yir'a* has the same meaning throughout the verse, there is a straightforward contradiction: the people should not fear, because they should fear! Obviously there must be a distinction between the fear born of terror at the theophany and a more reflective fear that is the intended result of the experience.[8]

According to the verse just quoted, the goal of refined fear of God is to transform the raw experience of terror into an inner apprehension that precludes sinning.[9] Indeed, we should beware the temptation to use the distinction between levels of fear to downplay fear of sin and punishment. Because fear of punishment is unpleasant and because we are so desperate to think well of ourselves, we are often tempted to ignore the fear of divine punishment. We rush ahead, organizing an accelerated graduation from the unsophisticated category of retribution-fear into the ranks of the elite whose experience of God is identical with a profound reverence. Apart from the likelihood of self-deception about our own spiritual state, there is also a danger that such easily achieved claims to reverence may remain little more than an aesthetic affair, like that experienced at the theater, attaching itself to religious images instead of Hamlet or Lear, where we reminisce or fantasize about reverence for God instead of fearing Him in the here and now.

For individuals who claim to have taken the fast track to *yirat ha-romemut*, the Halakha's stubborn adherence to *yirat ha-onesh* (fear of punishment) as a necessary component of the *mitzvah* becomes a problem. Rambam provides an experiential and intellectual description of the encounter with God that engenders His love and His fear: love is the thirst to know Him, rooted in our consciousness of His infinite wisdom; while fear is finite man's movement of recoil before the Infinite. This account says nothing about guilt, sin or fear of divine judgment. In *Hil. Berakhot* 1:4 he teaches that the recitation of blessings of pleasure and *mitzvot* and thanksgiving serves to "remember the Creator always and to fear Him."[10] Again, no guilt of fear of punishment. Moreover, in *Hil. Teshuva* 10, he disparages fear based on punishment as appropriate only to the spiritually immature.[11] At the same time, the definition of fear in *Sefer ha-Mitzvot* picks out fear of punishment as the primary characteristic of *Yir'a*.[12] It is as if the Halakha insisted on catering to a lowest common standard instead of recognizing that standard's irrelevance to spiritually mature people.

It is terribly easy to satirize the self-serving ingredients in this outlook that disparages fear of punishment. The normative perspective of Halakha and simple self-knowledge confirm that we do not outgrow *yirat ha-onesh*. But the obstacle here is not only the element of self-deception. There is something misleading, on phenomenological grounds, with the way we oppose the higher fear to the lower fear. Again, the distinction itself is well founded. But the problem with distinctions is that too often, in exhibiting the differences among different categories, we lose sight of what they have in common. The primary sources—most notably *Tanakh*—present in the raw, and without alluding explicitly to philosophical distinctions, an undifferentiated experience of fear; the medieval classification, for all its validity, comes later and, to that extent is secondary.

The oracle of doom in Isaiah 2, for example, contains a dramatic portrayal of fear and terror in the face of the divine. It is possible to read this chapter as a story of sin and punishment. The prophecy begins with chastisement for sins of idolatry, avarice and, in the

---

[8] See Malbim *ad loc.*

[9] R. Kook (*Olat Reiyah*, ii, p. 122) distinguishes fear of sin from fear of Heaven: "Fear of sin is sorrow and shame and incompleteness, when one gazes upon the majesty of supreme wisdom with downcast face, and sees that he cannot attach himself to it because he is defective, and he is mournful, so the defect of soul is sin, and the fear to beware of it is fear of sin. Fear because of the distance of the divine light from him, and the shamefacedness and sorrow, is fear of Heaven."

[10] See also R. Soloveitchik, *Shiurim l'Zekher Avi Mori*, Vol. 2 (Jerusalem, 1983), 179ff on God's "aweful" Name (*nora*). His illuminating comments on the *Hil. Berakhot* 1:4 passage are not yet published.

[11] See also R. Hutner, *Pahad Yitzhak* on Yom Kippur (Brooklyn, 1978), chap. 18.

[12] *Hil. Yesodei haTorah* 2:2 and *Sefer haMizvot, Aseh* 4.

most comprehensive sense, pride and arrogance. The "day" of the Lord is manifested in a frantic desire to flee from God, to hide from His crushing presence; human pretences are humbled. The retributive reading would view this frightening scene as no more and no less than the punishment inflicted upon the sin of pride. Yet the prophet is saying more than that—humility, the desire to flee and to hide is not only the punishment exacted by an angry deity for sinful arrogance. They are presented as the appropriate response to the overwhelming experience of divine Infinity and Mastery. The sense of awe and terror engendered by the consciousness of sin reflects the same reality that Rambam describes as a response to the magnificence of divine wisdom.

When R. Soloveitchik wishes to evoke the numinous, the sense of reverence and awe that is an integral part of religious experience, he cites Isaiah 2 among other biblical passages:

> To come close to God . . . is tantamount to self-effacement. Contact with Him undermines the very existence of man. The great fire engulfs the little candle. Infinity is not only the womb from which finitude emerges but also the bottomless abyss into which it plunges in its quest for the unattainable: "Enter into the rock and hide there in the dust for fear of the Lord and for the glory of His majesty."[13]

This blurring of the lines between fear of punishment and the encounter with divine infinity, is not accidental. To consider God's grandeur and our own smallness necessarily imbues us with an overpowering awareness of the magnitude of our debt to Him and profound dismay at the thought that we have failed Him and offended against Him. Conversely, confronting our sinfulness deepens the awareness of our unworthiness to stand before Him. Thus ontological finitude and moral guilt reinforce each other. In George Herbert's "Love," the soul draws back, laden with both "dust" and "sin," alluding to Job's final confession of insignificance and unworthiness (Job

42:6) which emerges, as we recall, not from remorse for his sins, but as response to the divine *mysterium tremendum*.

The catastrophic mood of Isaiah 2 is rarely part of our mediocre everyday religious experience. Even the minority for whom it is not too intense may be unable to make anything of the puzzling notion of flight and hiding from God. We will return to this text later. For the moment it is important to recognize that such imagery, and the powerful emotional response it precipitates, cannot be cleanly dissected into a fear of punishment, on the one hand, and the exalted fear of God's magnificence, on the other hand. Experientially, the two motives for fear are complementary, not contradictory. As we shall see, one of the strengths of R. Soloveitchik's teaching about fear and love of God is his insistence on the complex relationship between "lower" and "higher" types of fear and love. If, as I have suggested, we invoke too eagerly the distinction between different motives for fear of God in explaining our everyday religious existence, appealing to a distinction not readily accessible to introspection, perhaps we correspondingly neglect the more evident distinction between immediate, imminent, even instinctive fear of God and reflective fear. In its unadulterated incarnation, the former does not depend on the beliefs of the individual who experiences fear, flinching from a quick serpentine motion, for instance, without first verifying whether the apparition is a snake or merely a piece of rope. Sometimes (as with a harmless snake or other phobias) fear declares itself even when we know there is nothing to fear: The amygdala, scientists hypothesize, reacts fearfully faster than the response mediated through the cortex that overrides the fear as groundless.[14] Philosophers who view emotions like fear as essentially cognitive (and my own inclinations run in that direction) may feel compelled to deny such reactions the status of emotions. From this perspective, fear requires a propositional attitude towards the object that is causing the fear; a cat, on this account, cannot fear dogs, because it has no belief that the dog will attack, and

---

13 R. Joseph Soloveitchik, *Worship of the Heart*, ed. S. Carmy (Hoboken, 2003), p. 71. Of course, Rudolf Otto's *The Idea of the Holy* is part of the background of the Rav's discussion and my comments on it.

14 See, for example, Joseph LeDoux, *The Emotional Brain* (New York, 1996)

can best be described as being in a "state of fear," a physiological condition free of reflection.[15]

Traditional commentators may have captured something like this semantic distinction when they tried to explain the difference between the biblical words *yir'a* and *pahad*. Rashi (Deuteronomy 11:25, following *Sifre*) defines *pahad* (when parallel to *yir'a*) as affecting those who are nearby, while *mora* describes the reaction of those far away; he then states that *pahad* is sudden, while *mora* is a long-standing worry. *Pahad* thus is caused by immediate perception, imminent rather than distant, sudden rather than given to reflection.[16]

Many intelligent religious people would view this kind of instinctive fear as inferior to fear of punishment. Fear of retribution, at least, is a rational response to a potential threat. There is nothing irrational about an individual who chooses to reinforce his, or her, fear of God, either by meditating on the harm caused by sin, or by arousing sensitivity to the sacred and to the greatness of God along the lines urged by the Rambam and others. As R. Soloveitchik puts it: "*Pahad* and love are contradictory, *yira* and love are not contradictory."[17] The experience associated with *pahad*, however, does not seem dependent on reflection. If suddenness plays a constitutive role, it bears a disquieting resemblance to being startled involuntarily by a loud noise or a snake. Aristotle taught that being startled is not the same as being afraid: being alarmed in such cases does not impeach a man's reputation for bravery.[18] Whatever the case with courage, no Musar regimen I know advocates shouting boo at individuals as a dignified, reasonable part of their "working on" *yirat haShem*. Yet, if the goal is to shock the individual with a reminder of his psychic fragility and dependence on God, a sudden fright does the job as effectively, in the short run, as

more sublime methods. Netziv says that God came to Miriam and Aaron "suddenly" (Numbers 12:3) in order to frighten them. Ibn Ezra cites a view according to which Jacob's entreaty for divine help (Genesis 49:18) was his frightened reaction to the image of a snake representing his son Dan. In this connection, it is worth remembering that the prophecy in Isaiah 2 speaks constantly of the *pahad* aroused by God's overwhelming majesty.[19]

So far we have discussed the value of fear as a motive to obedience and as an opportunity for spiritual exaltation. Despite the initial expectation that fear of punishment serves only to spur obedience and that sublime fear addresses man's higher religious aspirations, we have seen that the phenomenological and psychological reality is more complicated. The overpowering fear of God that reduces the human being to confession of finitude and insufficiency cannot be separated from the knowledge of having fallen short in His service, and awareness of inadequacy before the moral claim of the Infinite leads directly to *yir'at ha-romemut*.

To these practical and emotional motives one may add a third, intellectual rationale for fear of God. Emotions like fear are more than events in the human nervous system. As we know through our reasoning capacity, we also grasp reality through properly functioning emotional capacities. Those who truly crave the most important kind of knowledge, that is the knowledge of God, and who believe that knowledge is not merely, or even primarily, a matter of knowing the truth of all the right propositions, would desire to experience the fear of God in all its varieties, both *yirat ha-onesh* and *yir'at ha-romemut*. The inherently distressing features of the experience would not deter

---

[15] See, for example, Robert Gordon, "Fear," *Philosophical Review*, 89, pp. 560–78.

[16] See Malbim to Isaiah 51:13, Micah 7:17 and Psalm 27:1 *inter alia*, stressing the imminent quality of *pahad*. Gra (Proverbs 3:25) argues for the element of suddenness, a view criticized (without mentioning his name) by Netziv to Deuteronomy.

[17] *U-Vikkashtem miSham*, in *Ish haHalakha, Galuy ve-Nistar* (Jerusalem, 1979), p. 174. See p. 173, n. 13 on the negative and positive connotations of *pahad*

[18] See, *inter alia*, Aristotle, *De Anima* 3:9.

[19] Netziv to Exodus 4:3 (and see further his comments in Numbers and *Emek haNetziv* to the verse in Numbers) maintains that Moses' flight from the rod that had turned into a snake was purely instinctive. He further argues that this reaction was improper, despite the fact that it was not under his control, and that the fear God inflicted upon him in Numbers 12 is a kind of punishment for that flight. Although Netziv does not link his approach here to his rejection of suddenness as an ingredient in *pahad*, I believe that he may have stressed the difference between fear, which is potentially a valuable religious experience, and being startled, which is not. Verses like Proverbs 3:25 or Job 22:10, which refer to sudden fear, therefore are not describing a good experience. See also Netziv to Genesis 22:1.

such individuals. Love of truth is sometimes strong enough to cast out the fear of fear.[20]

Although I do not wish to ignore this philosophical thread in the quest for authentic fear of God, most of us, a large part of the time, prefer the easy life to the examined life. Therefore, it is unwise to assign dominant status to the pure desire for theological truth. As we shall see momentarily, when we discuss R. Soloveitchik's doctrine on love and fear of God, giving appropriate weight to the "lower," primitive, biological sources of religious phenomena has its pragmatic advantages as well.

III
Love vs. Fear?

The commandment to fear God is routinely paired off with the commandment to love Him. Our present purpose is not to survey the extensive literature on the love of God, but better to elucidate the role of fear. As with the varieties of fear, we must guard against the theorist's inclination to overdraw the contrast between the two. As with the different levels of fear, we must also beware the impulse to praise love as a way of denigrating fear.

Offhand, the tendency to dispense with fear of God once one begins to speak of His love is demonstrably false and misleading. In the most basic sense, love is either an attraction to that which is loved, or the desire to promote what is loved. Fear, as the emotion corresponding to love, is either the desire to distance oneself from what is feared, or to resist and destroy it. When Rambam speaks of the love and fear of God, love is delineated as attraction and fear as recoil. In theory, and in practice as well, one might be strongly committed to what one loves, and express that love by promoting it—caring for the welfare of a human being, furthering the success of an idea—without feeling any desire for closeness with it. And one may

act against a person or idea and yet enjoy his company and feel attracted to the idea. In Rambam's account, the individual committed to God always loves God, if what is meant is the fulfillment of His will; yet there are moments where the worshipper experiences a powerful desire for His presence (love) and moments characterized by withdrawal (fear). Both are necessary.

At the outset we cited R. Hutner's dictum: "Fear without love—surely there is here a deficiency of love; love without fear—there is nothing here at all." Reflection on the classical ethical literature confirms his judgment. R. Bahye ibn Pakkuda's *Hovot ha-Levavot* is one of the most perfectionist of these treatises. He is impatient with spiritual aspirations willing to compromise the ideal. Yet, in the climactic section of the book (10:6), devoted to the love of God, when the subject is the marks identifying the lover of God, he lauds (following Exodus 20:17) "the signs of God's fear and dread upon his face." Interestingly, in this chapter the primary reason to prefer *yirat ha-romemut* to fear of punishment is that fear independent of considerations of reward and punishment is unconditional and therefore abiding. Ramban, commenting on the commandment of love in the first section of *Shma*, offers two reasons that fear-based chastisements in Deuteronomy persist, although one might think that love makes fear superfluous. One is that fear is still needed as a motivating factor; the other is that the truly pious person combines fear and love. Ramban betrays no sense that these two explanations are in conflict, because they are not.[21] Fear and love are intertwined.

Similarly, R. Kook asserts the Kabbalistic doctrine that the higher fear is above love alone, because only with the higher fear, whose source is *Bina*, does man understand the absolute nature of commitment to God, and only then is total love possible. In an early sermon from 1892, he suggests that we do not recite Hallel on Rosh haShana because the ultimate judgment reflects a superior consciousness to the gesture of thanksgiving (= love) represented by Hallel.

---

[20] A similar theme is sounded in Terry Eagleton's recent *Sweet Violence: the Idea of the Tragic* (London, 2003). To Aristotle's ancient question, why tragedy, dealing with misfortune and horror, provides pleasure, Eagleton responds, if I may simplify his lengthy analysis, that people appreciate and enjoy tragedy owing to a fundamental desire for truth, willing to confront the worst in order to comprehend the world as it is. Reviewers have observed that this orientation shares more with Eagleton's erstwhile Catholicism than with his present neo-Marxist affiliation.

[21] Commentary to Deuteronomy 6:5; cf. his remarks on 6:13 and 11:1 where Ramban says that the commandment of love ought to be, and is, commonly followed by the commandment to fear.

Along these lines he interprets the dispute about the permissibility of fasting on Rosh haShana: the ideal consciousness, integrating love and fear, has no place for fasting; for those who are not capable of comprehending this, fasting may be an appropriate way of marking the awesome day.[22]

The psychological and spiritual realism that is a hallmark of R. Soloveitchik's thinking is fully in evidence in his presentation of love and fear in *U-Vikkashtem miSham*. In the earlier sections of the work, where he focuses on the juxtaposition of "natural consciousness" (*havaya tiv'it*) and "revelational consciousness" (*havaya gilluyit*), he emphasizes that the natural love of God is rooted in ordinary human biology and psychology: we are attracted to God because we expect Him to satisfy various needs. For the Rav, this is no reason to disparage the "lower" love; we are biological creatures and do not leave our creaturely needs behind us any more than we outgrow the fear of harm if we offend against Him. The Halakha instructs us to fear God, and it also tells us to bless Him at moments of enjoyment, in the appreciation of food and special natural phenomena.[23] The centrality of petition in halakhic prayer, which the Rav did so much to explicate, testifies that these aspects of the human condition are dignified and respectable elements in our dialogue with the Creator.[24]

This natural self-interested outlook, however, cannot transcend its finite horizons. This occurs only when God breaks into our finite world with His commanding presence at Sinai. We are enjoined to remember the fear and trembling that accompanied that event and that continues until this very day as the divine commanding voice reverberates perpetually through our lives. Yet this God-man nexus, which exhausts itself in obedience to God, does not allow for a personal relationship. That is possible only when the human being identifies with the divine commandment (*devekut*). At this stage, both fear and love are transmuted from self-centered performances into gestures of genuine identification with the divine.[25] For our purposes, the crucial lesson is that love of God is not an alternative to fear, nor is it a stage of religious consciousness inherently superior to fear.

Despite all the halakhic, existential and Musar evidence for the honorable status of the fear of God as a Jewish virtue and its compatibility with love, fear is often set against love. What is the basis of this negative judgment? We shall examine three types of factors: one kind of objection to fear is that fear is inherently inferior to love and should be so recognized. Or one may hold that fear is a valuable component of religious life but is marred by baleful side effects. Lastly, we must return to our opening question: do certain elements in modern life impede the cultivation of *yirat haShem*?

IV
Love Better Than Fear?

It is customary to laud the love of God as *lishmah*, something pursued for its own sake, free of instrumental calculations. This is what Hazal mean when they oppose the idea of Abraham or Job serving God from love with the alternative of serving Him from fear.[26]

Rambam, in *Hilkhot Teshuva* 10, offers his magnificent vision of love of God as a kind of madness. Fear lacks a corresponding image of reckless commitment, and therefore suffers by comparison. It is disparaged as not being *lishmah*.

We tend to think of fear as driven by ulterior motives because we tend to identify fear with punishment-fear and love with unconditional love. As we have seen, however, fear is not always reducible to the calculus of self-interest. The highest praise for Abraham, the prototype of serving God out of love, is that he "feared God" (Genesis 22:14). Love, for its part, admits a variety of forms, some of which are as much

---

[22] R. Abraham Yitzhak Kook, *Meorot haReiyah, Yerah ha-Etanim* (Jerusalem, 1995), p. 89.

[23] *U-Vikkashtem miSham*, 135ff.

[24] See *Worship of the Heart* and S. Carmy, "Destiny, Freedom and the Logic of Petition," *Tradition*, 24:2, (Winter 1990), pp. 17–37 and "Without Intelligence, Whence Prayer?" ed. A. Mintz and L. Schiffman, *Jewish Spirituality and Divine Law* (New York, 2005), pp. 455–88.

[25] See *U-Vikkashtem miSham, passim*. According to the Rav, even *imitatio Dei* is a fundamentally submissive gesture (180f). See further my "Cleaving as Identification: R. Soloveitchik's Account of "*Devekut, U-Vikkashtem Mi-Sham*" (forthcoming in *Tradition*, Memorial issue for Rabbi Walter Wurzburger, guest editor Reuven Bulka).

[26] See Mishna *Sota* chapter 5, Bavli 31a, and E.E. Urbach, *The Sages*, chapter 14.

she-lo lishmah as the inferior model of fear. Just as fear may be nothing but the desire to escape punishment, there is a love that is no more than the desire for benefit. The *Hovot ha-Levavot*, listing several levels of worship, classifies serving God for the sake of reward in this world and the next slightly below service motivated by fear of punishment in this world and the next.[27] While unconditional commitment is superior to self-interested motivation, and that distinction is often associated with the contrast between love and fear, it is important to recognize the interaction between love and fear in their various forms.[28]

A more weighty theological formulation of the superior standing of love derives from Ramban's dictum that love corresponds to the positive *mitzvot* (*mitzvot aseh*) and that fear corresponds to the negative commandments (*mitzvot lo ta'aseh*). The halakhic principle that, in certain circumstances, positive obligations override negative ones indicates that, in the halakhic and theological arena, the works of love predominate over the imperatives of fear.[29] Explicating this principle R. Hutner develops the insight that positive obligations, rooted in love, differ from negative precepts, rooted in fear. The latter is simply a matter of obedience to God's will; the former additionally constitutes the idea of the *mitzvah*.

R. Hutner's language here is opaque. At the risk of psychologizing the metaphysical, we may take him to mean that the life of the *mitzvah* creates a positive identity, while adherence to prohibitions does not.[30] If the goal of religious practice is to form a positive identity, then educating towards positive actions is more important than concentrating on the necessity of avoiding sin. In concrete terms: lighting Sabbath candles, from this perspective, is more positive than refraining from violation of the Sabbath prohibitions; being a philanthropist is a more positive expression than abstaining from the abuse of people exposed to one's power.

Sound familiar? R. Hutner goes on to observe: "the discerning person recognizes that among the people of our generation it is much easier to get them to make an effort to do something good than to get them to refrain from an improper act, and this demonstrates that even the general element of good in them, hovers in the air, because in the healthy process turning away from evil is the basis of doing good." Why modern people are that way is a question for later. The immediate moral is that any attempt to demote fear of God in the name of love founders because good intentions without self-discipline and the ability to turn away from evil lack substance.[31] Elsewhere, R. Hutner champions the integration of love and fear as expressions of different psychological powers. Love is expansive in both the practical and intellectual spheres—it reflects man's desire to do and

---

27 *Hovot haLevavot* 3:4, categories 7 and 8. R. Bahye does not appear to see much difference between the two. He writes that the person who hopes for reward (level 7) lacks any conception of God's exalted nature. Perhaps the one who fears punishment is more advanced in this respect; more likely R. Bahye applies the same criticisms in both cases and simply chose not to repeat the detailed diagnosis.

28 I wonder whether we are consciously or unconsciously influenced by the temporal asymmetry between love and fear. Ancient philosophers like the Stoics contrasted love, not with fear, but with hate. Love and hate are both oriented to the present; hope and fear are attitudes towards the future. Thus the structure of hope and fear, as these terms are commonly used, entails calculation about the future, while love and hate are more easily understood as ends in themselves. The use of these terms in Jewish thought and Halakha is not rigidly committed to this convention. While Rambam treats love and fear of God as immediate responses to contemplation and experience in *Hil. Avodat Kokhavim* 3:10 he makes the conventional temporal differentiation: worshipping idols out of love means enjoying them aesthetically and the like; worshipping out of fear means fear of reprisal by idolaters for failure to worship.

29 Ramban to Exodus 20:8. For further discussion see *Hatam Sofer* to *Bava Kama* 9b (Jerusalem, 5743) and notes *ad loc.* and R. Yosef Engel, *Tsiyyunim laTorah* section 24. See also R. Aharon Lichtenstein, "The Woman's Obligation in Levirate Marriage," in E. Daum *et al*, *Maamar Yevamim* (Alon Shevut, 2004), pp. 11–25, and particularly 19ff on a possible distinction between agent-based and act-based clashes between positive and negative *mitzvot*.

30 R. Yitzchak Hutner, *Iggerot u-Ketavim*, 346ff. One could extend this insight about the distinctive nature of positive commandments by pointing to the principle according to which involvement in one *mitzvah* (*osek be-mitzvah*) exempts one from other *mitzvot*, and the philosophical idea that the ideal observance of one commandment with pure intent can bestow upon the soul eternal life; see Rambam's Commentary to Mishna *Makkot*, end of chapter 3, and R. Yosef Albo, *Sefer haIkkarim* 3:29 (note that Albo located this chapter within his discussion of Torah rather than in Part 4, where he addresses questions of reward and punishment).

31 Compare the argument in my "Use It or Lose It: On the Moral Imagination of Free Will," in Y. Berger and D. Shatz, eds. *Judaism, Science, and Moral Responsibility* (Lanham, 2006), pp. 104–54, especially 126–33. There I contrasted R. Dessler's idea of freedom, based on triumphant inner struggle, with R. Kook's doctrine, for which freedom is deepest self-expression. Like a good modern, I let R. Kook get the better of the discussion. One important principle of R. Dessler's account survived all critical scrutiny: freedom is possible only when the individual has had the experience of successful self-control, and self-control is normally manifest, not in creativity, but in the capacity for renunciation.

to know. Fear contracts the scope of human initiative—refraining from action and accepting the limits of human intellectual aspiration.[32]

In view of R. Hutner's famous affinity for Maharal of Prague, his failure to engage Maharal here is telling. Maharal maintains that the virtue of fearing God does not come under the category of *imitatio Dei*, since God does not fear Himself. For that reason fear of God is lower than humility. Humility creates a community between God and man—God dwells with the humble; this cannot be said about fear.[33] R. Hutner, by contrast, holds emphatically that every component of human virtue, fear of God included, must be rooted in God's ways. With respect to fear of God, the model is His will to contract His creativity by completing His work on the seventh day and affirming a finite world.[34]

V
Is Fear of God Debilitating?

The Talmud (*Megilla* 25b) discusses whether the curses and blessings and warnings in Leviticus 26 should be translated during public reading. Why not? Because dwelling on these matters could dishearten the people with thoughts of inevitable doom or motivate them to act out of fear of punishment or love of reward.[35] The fact that curtailing exposure to the word of God is even raised as a possibility implies that the concerns expressed are, in principle, legitimate. Although fear of God is a vital component of Jewish piety, allowing an intense emphasis on fear to flood the religious awareness is dangerous. Speaking of fear in general, R. Soloveitchik suggests that a modicum of fear is good, and too much is bad.[36]

Does fear of God have side effects that would deter us from its uncritical encouragement? Modern academic ideologists would say yes. Here are two American social historians. Commenting on the changes wrought by nineteenth to twentieth century capitalism they write, "A fearful individual was no longer appropriately pious but rather risked being incapable of taking the kinds of initiatives, of displaying the kinds of confidence, desirable in the new world shaped by republican optimism and business dynamism. Fear was dangerous, and the individual who deliberately sowed it was abusing authority."[37]

The complaint about lack of initiative is echoed by R. Avigdor Nebenzal, who tells of a student whose childhood dream was to be a pilot, but who was eventually dropped from pilot training course, along with the other religious fellows. One of the officers explains that the religious were educated from childhood to obey, while the pilot requires the ability to improvise as well. Is the imputation true? R. Nebenzal, while rejecting the view that religion is inherently tied to lack of initiative, acknowledges the problem with respect to contemporary education.[38]

The social historians go further than R. Nebenzal: they indict the traditional religious mentality of deficient confidence and optimism. No doubt defenders of traditional religion can point with pride to examples of entrepreneurial resourcefulness and realism in taking the measure of human beings and situations. And in the intellectual realm I hear a familiar voice retort: "Rabbenu Tam did not improvise? Rambam did not create? R. Hayyim of Brisk displayed no initiative?"

Whether confidence in modern society and optimism are unqualified virtues is also open to question. No doubt some traditionally religious people are timid investors and unduly pessimistic in evaluating people and situations. One wonders, however, whether, at least to some extent, the objections mask

---

[32] See *Pahad Yitzhak* on Pesah (Brooklyn, 1970), chapters 50 (pilgrimage to the Temple as a joyous occasion that requires gestures of withdrawal and reverence) and 54 (the delight of Sabbath is rooted in the injunction to abstain from creative work, and the positive imitation of God requires acceptance of His "dark," unknowable and hence not given to imitation, side).

[33] See Maharal, *Netivot Olam, Netiv ha-Anava*, chapter 1. See also *Gur Aryeh* to Deuteronomy 10:12 and n. 34 in the Hartman edition (Jerusalem, 5754), about the compatibility of closeness to God with fear of God.

[34] *Pahad Yitzhak* on Pesah, chapter 54.

[35] See Rashi and Maharsha *ad loc* and *Hovot ha-Levavot* 10:6. For the sake of conciseness I have conflated different versions of the Talmudic text.

[36] *U-Vikkashtem miSham*, p. 173.

[37] Peter Stearns and Timothy Haggerty, "The Role of Fear: Transitions in American Emotional Standards for Children, 1850–1950," *American Historical Review*, 96, pp. 63–94.

[38] R. Avigdor Nebentzal, *Sihot leRosh haShana* (Jerusalem, 5748), p. 67.

a discomfort less with the fear of God than with the fear of sin. It is likely that God-fearing people, tempted by the chance to exploit new social, economic, political or technological orders, hesitate more than others due to moral qualms or concern about unforeseen consequences. If sin is as grievous an affair as religion makes it out to be, then, when in doubt, caution is advisable. It is thus possible that conscience, from the modern point of view, makes cowards of religious people, and that this side effect, if it exists, must either be tolerated or circumvented.

Though there are times when we are indebted to practical boldness, the political record of recent generations indicates that caution is often justified. In any event, our firm commitment to a life of *yirat shamayim* and *yirat het* should not blind us to the need to examine how these commitments affect us.

The great role model for such self-examination is R. Kook. He was profoundly concerned about the harm caused by fear to the Jewish life of his time. Mostly, he believed that "evil, wild fear" resulted from "continued exile and persecution by base and evil enemies." The diminution of joy undermines individual elevation; even more so does it cripple the nation. "The first condition [of redemption] is removal of surplus fear from the collective soul, and particularly from the souls of the exceptional individuals. . . ."[39] He knows that "the fear of punishment that enters the bones, to the point of pervasive cringing, prevents the spread of the holy light of love and reverence toward the sublime, and this causes spiritual and physical sicknesses, to the community and the individual," and he believes that contemporary vulgar heresy (*kefira gassa*), which wrecks faith in divine providence, may serve as an antidote to excessive punishment-fear.[40] Passages like this abound in R. Kook's writings. But so does the assertion that even under ideal circumstances, fear can have deleterious effects. Discussing repentance, he argues that Yom Kippur must be followed by the joy of Sukkot because the hard work of repentance is psychological-

ly exhausting, like a necessary but difficult surgery, and requires joyful, pleasure-filled recuperation to restore a healthy psychic balance.[41]

VI
Cheap Grace, Hellfire, Shul Presidents—Obstacles to Fear of God

So far we have considered only critiques and qualifications regarding *yirat shamayim* with a place in traditional Jewish thought. Before seeking distinctively modern aids to fear of God, let us deepen our understanding by thinking about some of the obstacles.

The most substantial of these is our spiritual slackness. Most of the time, reminders of our finitude and moral inadequacy are unwelcome. In our communities, equanimity about our spiritual attainments is strengthened by the low level of halakhic observance among our fellow Jews and by the moral failings of society as a whole. Since we don't hold our fellow Jews responsible for their deviance, and they are therefore beyond divine chastisement, we naturally assume that we, who are superior to them, as we see it, are likewise above trembling before God's mysterious wrath. It is all too easy to congratulate ourselves for not being as other human beings, if I may coin a phrase. It makes no sense that God would demand of us more than we have given, or that we, of all people, ought to feel uncomfortable, let alone overwhelmed, by His presence.

Liberalized Protestantism, which, in a secularized form, passes for common therapeutic wisdom, smiles on what the German theologian and martyr Dietrich Bonhoeffer called "cheap grace," "the grace we bestow on ourselves," the notion that human beings are saved by divine grace and therefore no unpleasant effort to change is required.[42] The believer has nothing to fear. Over two centuries ago, when Dr. Johnson contemplated the mournful possibility that he might be damned, and a nice clergyman wondered what he meant, he slapped him down by saying, passionately and loudly,: "Sent to Hell, Sir, and punished

[39] "On Fear," *HaPahad*, in *Eder ha-Yekar* (Jerusalem, 1967), pp.119–21; likewise, "On Literature" in *Maamrei haReiyah* (Jerusalem, 1984), 502ff.
[40] See *Orot haKodesh*, iv, 32–33, pp. 421–22.
[41] *Olat Reiyah*, ii, pp. 367–68, and *Orot haTeshuva* 9:10.
[42] See Bonhoeffer, "Costly Grace," *The Cost of Discipleship* (New York, 1963), pp. 35–47.

everlastingly." Even then, Boswell felt compelled to apologize: Johnson's temperament was melancholy, and on his deathbed, when it counted, he was more confident in his salvation; Christianity and tranquility must go together.[43] What would have been made of him today, or of R. Yohanan ben Zakkai (*Berakhot* 28b), who expressed deathbed uncertainty about his final destination, one can only imagine.

Hell, of course, is not in fashion, by which I mean not only the idea of eternal damnation, but the colorful panoply of future torments portrayed in works like the *Reshit Hokhma* or Dante's "*Inferno*." Not knowing what to say about hell presents a second obstacle to *yira*. Consider this recently reprinted anecdote: The Gra once remarked that it is wrong to view the descriptions of hell in the *Reshit Hokhma* as hyperbole. Whereupon one of his disciples fell into a prolonged illness, from which he almost died. When he recovered and took his master to task for precipitating the ordeal, the Gra repeated that the book should be taken literally, but softened the impact of these words by adding that if a human being knew how much suffering in this world could alleviate the pangs of hell, he would not hesitate to suffer like Job all his days.[44]

Why would this type of discourse fall flat in many places? We may gain constructive insight by identifying factors not evident in our previous discussion:

1. The media saturate us with numbing images of violence, both real and fictional. Increasingly lurid descriptions of pain and torment are necessary to sustain interest and arouse horror. Eventually these too pall. At the same time, because of medical and political advances, we are unaccustomed to, and therefore extraordinarily sensitive to graphic descriptions of pain. Earlier generations may have responded affirmatively or tuned out repetitive accounts of hellfire; they were unlikely to treat them as exercises in camp, or, alternatively, to be scandalized by their verisimilitude.

2. Counseling against hellfire sermons, the prominent nineteenth-century rabbi R. Yaakov Ettlinger writes: "Mentioning the punishment of hell and other things (and he is angry and rebukes and offends the audience), these things provoke hatred. But when he reproves them with the words of the Torah itself, saying: "Listen brothers, this is what God spoke," nobody can hate him, for everyone will recognize the truth . . . and this arouses love."[45] One could interpret this statement as counseling soft words and a mild tone. Hell is inadvisable because nineteenth-century German Jews don't care for it. R. Ettlinger's precise language suggests another reading: when the preacher speaks about hell, he is not citing mainstream biblical or halakhic sources, but relatively marginal and overwrought invective; as he fulminates away, the discourse has the idiosyncratic flavor of the preacher's wrath where he would do better to call upon the word of God. And the lesson to contemporary speakers is to avoid subjectivity when broaching unpleasant subjects like rebuke or fear of God.

3. Most significantly for a constructive analysis of the fear of God today is the change that has occurred in our conception of what it means to experience the wrath of God. In the old preaching, sin was understood primarily as transgressions to be punished, the imagery was similar to that of conventional corporal punishment or torture.[46] Fear of God's rod was fear that He would visit upon us our iniquities. For many people today, the primary fear is that of meaninglessness. To fear God is to fear abandonment by God. The desolate soul is less frequently overwhelmed by God's numinous presence than by His thundering absence. In a word, the dominant emotion of spiritual apprehension is anxiety rather than fear.

The causes and scope of this change will not further occupy us here. One could view the development with dismay, as it testifies to an etiolated sense of responsibility: the individual for whom "turning

---

43 James Boswell, *Life of Johnson*, June 12, 1784. For background, see Stephen Miller, *Three Deaths and Enlightenment Thought: Hume, Johnson, Marat* (Lewisburg, 2001).

44 Zeev Grinvald, *Moreshet Avot, Bereshit* (Jerusalem, 1992), p. 24.

45 *Minhat Ani* (Jerusalem, 1966) to *Vayelekh* (129b). Thanks to my student Ephraim Meth, who thought this sermon would interest me.

46 For rabbinic hell imagery, see Saul Lieberman, "Of Sins and Their Punishment," *Texts and Studies* (Hoboken, 1974), pp. 29–51.

away from evil" and fear of evil's consequences is not a pre-condition of doing good, is deficient in the old-fashioned conception of guilt. One may be justified in going against the grain of the modern temperament, attempting to reverse it by strenuously reaffirming the punishment model. Or one may recognize that, for better or for worse, new analogies, new ways of thinking about fear of God, are needed. The new can supplement the old, or at least, for those whose yearning for love is lacking in fear, help to build a bridge from spiritual numbness to sensitivity.

In an age of anxiety, our fear of others is also transformed. Here is a third challenge to the God-fearing life. We are less obsessed with whether we have done right than we are anxious about where we stand with others and how we measure up to their standards. At the outset we noted that fear of other people and subjugation to their judgment can be a barrier to the fear of God. By the same token, fear and reverence towards those whom we are commanded to respect, and who merit our reverence, is an important ingredient in attaining the fear of God.

R. Soloveitchik reports that a psychiatrist once told him that he would like to eliminate the "Impress Your fear" (*U-ve-khen ten pahdekha*) from the Rosh haShana and Yom Kippur prayers because fear is the primary cause of neurosis. The Rav responded that most people are plagued by many fears: anxiety about one's career, status, wealth, popularity or fame; fear of illness, old age and vulnerability; great fears and little fears. Only the fear of God can transcend and cast out the multitude of petty fears.[47] The fear of God liberates. If rabbis prayed properly, the Rav said on another occasion, they would not be intimidated by shul presidents. Conversely, one may suggest, shaking off the yoke of petty fear frees us to fear the One worthy of our fear and awe.

The practical realization of this ideal is difficult. One strand in Jewish ethical literature seems to negate absolutely any notion of legitimate fear of unworthy objects. The *Hovot haLevavot*, for instance, praises the saint who sleeps in the open air, unprotected against wild animals, and who explains that he would be ashamed to show fear of anyone but his Creator.[48] R. Bahye b. Asher states flatly that it is wrong to fear any human being except for those whose fear is commanded—parents, teachers and lawful political authority.[49] Nonetheless the Halakha recognizes fear of a belligerent litigant as an acceptable reason for a judge to excuse himself from hearing a case.[50] Samuel, aware of the likely threat from Saul, hesitates to anoint a king in his stead, and does not initially rely upon divine intervention to safeguard him.[51]

R. Yeruham of Mir, one of the most eminent pre-Holocaust Musar instructors, teaches that great personalities, like Jacob preparing to meet Esau, relate their experience of fear to their situation before God, even while recognizing that, when threatened by another person or by a wild animal, the object of fear itself is the ordinary fear of the adversary.

> Obviously Jacob's fear of Esau was not what we understand regarding the weak person's fear of the violent; surely Scripture does not speak about this and such fear would not be laudable in the holy Patriarchs. Jacob's fear was that he had become defiled by sin (Rashi to Genesis 32:11). Yet in the end, the expression of this fear was his fear of Esau and his four hundred retainers, a natural fear characteristic of every human being to fear a robber or a wild animal . . . and that fear of Esau, that is part of every human being's nature, was for Jacob a fear of Heaven.[52]

Most readers of these words do not align themselves with the radical school of *bittahon* (trust in God),

---

[47] R. Soloveitchik, *Al ha-Teshuva* (Jerusalem, 1975). pp. 140–41.

[48] *Hovot ha-Levavot* 10:6. One could moderate the import by suggesting that the saint does not deliberately act recklessly but that, finding himself exposed, his trust in God enables him to sleep serenely. However, the simple sense of the story is that the saint is totally indifferent to worldly danger.

[49] *Kad haKemah* s.v *yir'a*, in *Kitvei Rabbenu Bahye* (Jerusalem, 1970), pp. 192–96 and Commentary to Deuteronomy 20:1.

[50] *Sanhedrin* 6b. The commandment "Do not fear any man" (Deuteronomy 1:17), addressed to the judge, applies once the judge discerns which party is in the right or hears the case. For that reason R. Bahye b. Asher does not appeal to this verse, as the Halakha would undermine his case. Instead he uses the prohibition of fear in war, despite the obvious rebuttal that fearlessness is forbidden in battle for tactical psychological considerations, not for ethical or theological reasons.

[51] I Samuel 16:2. See *Pesahim* 8b.

[52] R. Yeruham Leibovitz, *Daat Hokhma u-Musar* (New York, 1967), p. 23.

which denies and frowns upon the efficacy of human effort and scorns all forms of worldly fear. The unreality we rightly or wrongly impute to this pious approach may lead us to abandon any orientation to *bittahon*. When the fear of God does not tower above all other fears, we exaggerate the potency of those threats and misinterpret the harm that adversity and hostility can visit upon us. We grant the Shul president from hell, of whom we would be less afraid, according to the Rav, if we prayed properly, an almost metaphysical supremacy over us. In truth, much of the time, he and his ilk may not have the power over us that he, or we, ascribe to him, and even if he does, we can, with God's help, overcome. Because [we as] members of an anxious community are especially prone to measure [our] happiness by the weather inside our heads, progress in *yirat shamayim* depends on our success, as individuals and as a community, in ridding ourselves of the bully's shadow, the snob's vulgar sneer, and the desire to be liked by the charming social manipulator. And that success, in turn, is measured by the degree to which we are able to place God and His service at the center of our existence: "The haughtiness of man will be prostrate, and the loftiness of man abased; and God alone will be exalted on that day. And the idols will pass away completely." (Isaiah 2:17–18).

VII
Your Heart Will Fear and Expand

At the inauguration of the Hebrew University in 1925, R. Kook quoted Isaiah 60:5: "Then you shall see and brighten, and your heart will fear (*pahad*) and expand." Why fear at the moment of eschatological glory? Because novelty is not always an unmixed blessing. The same events may rightly cause shock and a contraction of the heart for some, even when a sense of expansion and satisfaction are also appropriate. The most realistic response to many new developments is not uncritical optimism but a fear that is nevertheless ready to ripen into joy.[53] Fear, the subject of this essay, is an inherently disturbing experience. Much of our discussion has compounded the unease by elaborating upon the difficulty attendant upon the acquisition of fear of God as a virtue, the danger of the wrong kind of fear, the perennial and contemporary obstacles to fear of God. Yet the very difficulties

we have confronted may also yield distinctively modern ways of fulfilling the commandment to fear God. In the spirit of the heart contracting and expanding, let us examine new practical, experiential and intellectual directions arising from our analysis.

Hazal, of course, recommended a number of practices as conducive to *yirat shamayim*: Torah study, respect for elders, and worship in Jerusalem during the Temple period.[54] R. Hutner, in particular, called our attention to the difficulty contemporary people, those who have a yearning to do good, experience in turning away from evil. In the light of his insight it would appear that by concentrating on those *mitzvot* that integrate love and fear, psychological expansion with psychological contraction, we could take advantage of the positive impulses and overcome the crippling defects. These include the observance of Shabbat (the paradigmatic *zakhor veshamor*), prayer and the culture of the synagogue. Educators indeed devote attention to these areas and successfully nurtured students show the results.

All the same, the most trying challenges of renunciation often take place in private. One reason that turning away from evil is so difficult is that our community is so fixated on moral reinforcement through public display that we are untrained in private struggle. None of our institutions confers honors on people who make the best of an intolerable job or make a blessing of an unmanageable family situation. There is no *Keter Perishut* award for homosexuals who remain celibate or for the insulted and injured who bury their anger and grief. These are quintessential scenes of *yirat haShem*.

What motivates us to succeed in these tasks? Fear alone? Sometimes. But fear is not sufficient, especially not for our generation. Maharal taught that *imitatio Dei* cannot apply to fear of God, and that fear therefore may not facilitate closeness to God. But *gevura*, in the sense of restraint and self-control, *is* a divine attribute.[55] The individual who renounces his or her imperious desires and embraces the yoke of obe-

---

[53] *Maamrei haReiyah* 306–308.

[54] See *Encyclopedia Talmudit*, Vol. 25, pp.85–86.

[55] For the ethical meaning of *gevura*, see R. Soloveitchik's "Catharsis," *Tradition*, 17, 2.

dience and self-negation can imitate his Creator in that way. Whenever the lonely individual fulfills the commandment of fearing God through the gesture of heroic renunciation, he or she forges a bond of love with God as well. Maharal's *Netivot Olam* does not contain a treatise on *gevura*; the twenty-first century version must provide one.

Some of you may have felt that I devoted too much attention to biblical descriptions of human beings overwhelmed and virtually annihilated by the numinous presence of God. Many members in good standing of religious institutions know nothing of such experiences. For the rest of us such experiences are mostly associated more with a religious awareness of sin and guilt rather than with the religious per se (though in the light of our analysis this distinction may be factitious). In any event, such moments are rarely as intense as those portrayed in the Bible, and they are not frequent or prolonged. Whatever their value for phenomenology of religion, it is unclear how they translate into the world of our everyday life.

What can we learn from Isaiah 2, for example, beyond the excoriation of pride and other vices? The depiction of lowly man vainly attempting to flee from God, seeking out cracks and caves in which to hide, while mountains crash around him probably reflects the great earthquake during the reign of Uzziah.[56] Yet running away from God, in the literal sense, is impossible. Appealing to such language easily becomes a cliché.[57] How can imagining the attempt enrich our grasp of what it means to fear God?

Appropriating the message of this prophecy identifies several elements that speak to all of us, and not only to those whose religious imagery is especially vivid. First, the desire to flee from God's presence, however absurd, is part of our experience. This is obviously true where we feel guilt and moral shame, as is the case in Isaiah 2. It is no less true when we are overwhelmed by an encounter that is too much for us, even in the aesthetic realm. And as we have seen, the experience of God's grandeur intrinsically communicates a sense of our unworthiness and finitude. Second, the realization that flight is impossible. The inability to escape God is an essential component of the experience of fear, whether it arises primarily from moral or ontological inadequacy. The awareness that God is with us, no matter how far we fly, is often a source of overwhelming comfort, as magnificently expressed in Psalm 139. Sometimes it gives comfort even at times when God's presence and solicitude is the occasion of reproach, as in Jonah 2. In Isaiah 2, however, the impossibility of not being in His presence is depicted exclusively as the cause of terror.

Lastly, and most important from the point of view of spiritual education, there is the one verse that moves from the descriptive to the prescriptive. It happens to be the verse from this chapter quoted by R. Soloveitchik in *Worship of the Heart*: "Enter into the rock and hide there in the dust for fear of the Lord and for the glory of His majesty" (2:10).[58] On one way of interpreting the verse, the speakers are panicky sinners futilely seeking to elude divine detection (see Ibn Ezra, Radak, and Metzuddot). I believe the imperative form here is not accidental: the speaker is the prophet; he is saying that the proper response in the face of the *mysterium tremendum* is humility. The proud human being is to lower himself, and the physical expression of this is hiding in the cleft of the rock, making oneself less prominent, taking up less space.[59] "The reward of humility is the fear of God" (Proverbs 22:3). "Humility leads to fear of God" (*Avoda Zara* 20b). Shame (in the sense of modesty, though not necessarily sexual) is likewise the mark of the person who is afraid of sin: so the Talmud (*Nedarim* 20a) identifies the "fear of God on your faces" (Exodus 20:17) that follows the revelation at Sinai.

One reason that humility is a virtue especially appropriate to our generation is that it is manifested not only

---

[56] See Jacob Milgrom, "Did Isaiah Prophesy During the Reign of Uzziah?" *Vetus Testamentum*, 14, 164–82, 178–82.

[57] Francis Thompson's melodramatic confession "The Hound of Heaven," with God pursuing the desperate sinner through the lurid, labyrinthine demimonde streets of late nineteenth century London, is one instance where the figure of speech comes to life.

[58] In *U-Vikkashtem miSham*, 158, R. Soloveitchik quotes more extensively from this prophecy.

[59] Francine Prose's recent novel *A Changed Man* describes the moral rehabilitation of a half-hearted neo-Nazi who drifts away from that way of life without a clear project of repentance and regeneration but ends up growing into a responsible person. Readers of the book may notice how often the hero and other sympathetic characters arrange their bodies so as to take up less room.

in how we walk before God, but also in our relations with other human beings. All of us succeed in deceiving ourselves, much of the time, about our standing before God, in particular regarding the intrinsically private aspects. Many are tone deaf when it comes to the kind of religious life that has occupied so much of this essay. The arrogant and vulgar can, of course, succeed in remaining oblivious to their impact on other human beings; when they are powerful or charming enough, the victims often connive to cover up the truth. Yet even the swaggering individual who has no shame before God may nonetheless be appalled by moments of insight when he or she realize how they are perceived by others and how their behavior and attitudes debase their human environment. Democratic, anti-hierarchic trends in our society make it harder for us to cultivate honor, respect, and awe towards our superiors, but provide better opportunities to detect arrogance in our treatment of those dependent on our good will. As religious individuals and as members of observant communities, we ought to make the most of the advantages our age offers, as we seek to minimize the obstacles it places before us.[60]

We began our discussion by puzzling over the difficulties that many modern people think they have achieving fear of God. We have discovered that the problems may be different than is commonly assumed. We have explored the variety of experiences subsumed under the fear and love of God, and the ways they are, and should be, inextricably intertwined. That our soul draws back from God's invitation is fear, born of dust and sin, finitude and guilt; yet it is a fear inseparable from love.

Let us return to our earlier insight that fear, in our culture, primarily takes the form of anxiety. We first made this observation when we listed some of the reasons that the apprehension of hell is no longer a powerful spur to religious obedience and awe, even among those who practice traditional religion. "We are afraid of pain but more afraid of silence," wrote W.H. Auden over sixty years ago.[61] Fear, in its traditional import, is identical with the desire to avoid or annihilate a threat. Anxiety, at one level, is an antipathetic experience. Yet to be anxious is to desire. Thus a fear informed by anxiety is a fear informed by love. It is a fear that even people who find it easier to summon up the effort to do something good than to refrain from an improper act (to recall R. Hutner's diagnosis) can aspire to.

John Donne, after reviewing the speculations of his time about literal interpretations of hell—fire, brimstone, the undying worm, and so forth, concludes: "when all is done, the hell of hells, the torment of torments is the everlasting absence of God, and the everlasting impossibility of returning to his presence. . . . Yet there was a case, in which David found an ease, to fall into the hands of God, to escape the hands of men . . . ; but to fall out of the hands of the living God, is a horror beyond our expression, beyond our imagination."[62] David's wish (ii Samuel 24) to be chastised directly by God, rather than fall into the hands of men, is familiar to us as the opening verse of the daily *tahanun*. Perhaps, for the reasons just adduced, Donne's evocation of the incident speaks to us today even more directly than it did four centuries ago. Our hell is the hell of silence and anxiety, not that of high tech tortures and gnashing of teeth. The greatest terror is not that God watches over us, counting our sins, and ordering our penalties, but that, responding to our estrangement from Him, He will leave us to our ultimately meaningless devices.[63]

After the death of his wife C.S. Lewis was surprised to realize that grief feels like fear. Fear, in the shape that most beleaguers and challenges us today, very much resembles grief.

Yirat Shamayim: The Awe, Reverence, and Fear of God [New York: Yeshiva University Press, 2008], pp. 265–299.
Reprinted with the permission of the author.

---

60 See Corey Robin, *Fear: the Political History of an Idea* (Oxford, 2004). Robin cites studies to the effect that our late capitalist culture is rife with behavior that systematically humiliates employees. The most dramatic examples involve strictly regulated bathroom breaks in low paying factory jobs and ridiculous techniques used in training middle management executives. I am more familiar, and more concerned about, less drastic and less creative practices.

61 W.H. Auden, "For the Time Being," lines 124–25.

62 George Potter and Evelyn Simpson, eds., *The Sermons of John Donne* (U. of California Press, 1962) Vol. v, p.266. I have modernized the spelling.

63 C.S. Lewis, *The Great Divorce*, is a fine dramatization of this point.

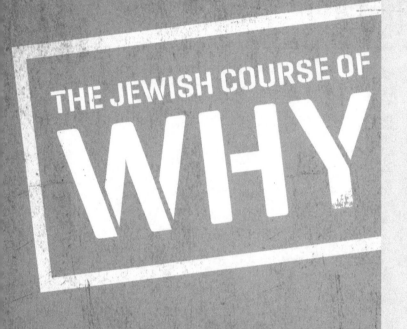

THE JEWISH COURSE OF
WHY

LESSON SIX

1. Why have the Jews been singled out for persecution and hate throughout history?

2. Why does Jewish adulthood begin at age twelve for girls and thirteen for boys?

3. Why do we pour a cup of wine for Elijah at the Passover *seder*?

4. Why is it not forbidden to submit petitions of prayer to a righteous person? Isn't it true that Judaism forbids using intermediaries to access God?

5. Why do Chasidim think it is necessary to have a rebbe? Isn't it true that Jews do not require intermediaries to access God?

6. Why is Moses' name absent from the *Haggadah*?

7. Why does Judaism associate so many of its celebrations with food?

JLI

JEWISH LEARNING INSTITUTE

1. Why have the Jews been singled out for persecution and hate throughout history?

Causes

LEARNING EXERCISE 1

List some of the primary causes of antisemitism.

1.	
2.	
3.	
4.	
5.	
6.	

Text 1a

Rabbi Jonathan Sacks, "Future Tense—The New Antisemitism. What Is It and How Do We Deal with It?" *The Jewish Chronicle*, November 1, 2007

Antisemitism is not an ideology, a coherent set of beliefs. It is, in fact, an endless stream of contradictions. The best way of understanding it is to see it as a virus. Viruses attack the human body, but the body itself has an immensely sophisticated defence, the human immune system. How then do viruses survive and flourish? By mutating. Antisemitism mutates, and in so doing, defeats the immune systems set up by cultures to protect themselves against hatred.

Rabbi Jonathan Sacks, PhD
1948–

Former chief rabbi of the United Kingdom. Rabbi Sacks attended Cambridge University and received his doctorate from King's College, London. A prolific and influential author, his books include *Will We Have Jewish Grandchildren?* and *The Dignity of Difference.* He received the Jerusalem Prize in 1995 for his contributions to enhancing Jewish life in the Diaspora, was knighted and made a life peer in 2005, and became Baron Sacks of Aldridge in 2009.

Text 1b

Rabbi Jonathan Sacks, ibid.

Antisemitism has always had to find legitimation in the most prestigious source of authority at any given time.

In the first centuries of the Common Era, and again in the Middle Ages, this was religion. That is why Judeo-phobia took the form of religious doctrine. In the nineteenth century, religion had lost prestige, and the supreme authority was now science. Racial antisemitism was duly based on two pseudo-sciences, social Darwinism (the idea that in society, as in nature, the strong survive by eliminating the weak) and the so-called scientific study of race.

By the late twentieth century, science had lost its prestige, having given us the power to destroy life on Earth. Today the supreme source of legitimacy is human rights. That is why Jews (or the Jewish state) are accused of the five primal sins against human rights: racism, apartheid, ethnic cleansing, attempted genocide and crimes against humanity.

A Mystical Perspective

Text 2

Talmud, Megilah 14a

מָשָׁל דַּאֲחַשְׁוֵרוֹשׁ וְהָמָן לְמָה הַדָּבָר דּוֹמֶה? לִשְׁנֵי בְּנֵי אָדָם, לְאֶחָד הָיָה לוֹ
תֵּל בְּתוֹךְ שָׂדֵהוּ, וּלְאֶחָד הָיָה לוֹ חָרִיץ בְּתוֹךְ שָׂדֵהוּ. בַּעַל חָרִיץ אָמַר: מִי
יִתֵּן לִי תֵּל זֶה בְּדָמִים. בַּעַל הַתֵּל אָמַר: מִי יִתֵּן לִי חָרִיץ זֶה בְּדָמִים.

לְיָמִים נִזְדַּוְּגוּ זֶה אֵצֶל זֶה. אָמַר לוֹ בַּעַל חָרִיץ לְבַעַל הַתֵּל:
מְכוֹר לִי תִּלָּךְ. אָמַר לוֹ: טוֹל אוֹתָהּ בְּחִנָּם. וְהַלְוַאי.

Babylonian Talmud

A literary work of monumental proportions that draws upon the legal, spiritual, intellectual, ethical, and historical traditions of Judaism. The 37 tractates of the Babylonian Talmud contain the teachings of the Jewish sages from the period after the destruction of the 2nd Temple through the 5th century CE. It has served as the primary vehicle for the transmission of the Oral Law and the education of Jews over the centuries; it is the entry point for all subsequent legal, ethical, and theological Jewish scholarship.

Ahasuerus and Haman can be compared to two people—one who had a mound in his field [Ahasuerus], and the other who had a deep ditch in his field [Haman]. The owner of the ditch mused to himself, "I wish I could buy that mound to fill up my ditch." And the owner of the mound mused to himself, "I wish I could purchase [the right to dump my mound into] his empty ditch."

Not long afterward, the two met. The owner of the ditch said, "Sell me your mound." The owner of the mound said, "Take it for free!"

[Handwritten notes:] Mound — Irritated by the Jewish people's very existence. The King was a fool Did not value his people. Haman had an understanding — his ditch feels empty as his life. The Jews had a meaningful life.

KEY POINTS

- Antisemitism survives by mutating to misappropriate the most sacred-held values of any given generation.

- An underlying cause of antisemitism might be—consciously or unconsciously—a resentment of the Jew for making the antisemite aware of his emptiness and insecurity.

- An answer to antisemitism is to stay true to our beliefs and lead by example, showing others how to infuse their lives with holiness and purpose.

2. Why does Jewish adulthood begin at age twelve for girls and thirteen for boys?

A Question of National Identity

Text 3

The Lubavitcher Rebbe, Rabbi Menachem Mendel Schneerson, *Reshimot* 19 📖

Rabbi Menachem Mendel Schneerson
1902–1994

The towering Jewish leader of the 20th century, known as "the Lubavitcher Rebbe," or simply as "the Rebbe." Born in southern Ukraine, the Rebbe escaped Nazi-occupied Europe, arriving in the U.S. in June 1941. The Rebbe inspired and guided the revival of traditional Judaism after the European devastation, impacting virtually every Jewish community the world over. The Rebbe often emphasized that the performance of just one additional good deed could usher in the era of Mashiach. The Rebbe's scholarly talks and writings have been printed in more than 200 volumes.

אֵצֶל בְּנֵי יִשְׂרָאֵל, גָּדוֹל לִי"ג שָׁנָה, מִלְּבַד פְּרָטִים שֶׁצָּרִיךְ יח', כ', וְגַם מ' . . .
מַה שֶּׁאֵין כֵּן בִּשְׁאָר אוּמּוֹת הָעוֹלָם גָּדוֹל לְכ' שָׁנָה, כא' שָׁנָה, וְכַיּוֹצֵא בָּזֶה.

הַטַּעַם: אוּמּוֹת הָעוֹלָם נַעֲשׂוּ לְעַם עַל יְדֵי שֶׁמִּתְּחִלָּה מִתְיַישְׁבִים
עַל אַדְמָתָם אַחֲרֵי הֱיוֹתָם נוֹדְדִים וְרוֹעֵי צֹאן, בּוֹחֲרִים לָהֶם
מֶלֶךְ וְכוּ' וְאַחַר כָּךְ מְיַיסְּדִים לָהֶם תּוֹרָה וְחוּקִים.

בְּנֵי יִשְׂרָאֵל הָיוּ בְּהֵיפֶךְ. תֵּיכֶף כְּשֶׁיָּצְאוּ מֵעַבְדוּת מִצְרַיִם, בִּהְיוֹתָם בָּאָרֶץ לֹא
זְרוּעָה, הִתְחִילוּ בַּתּוֹרָה וּמִצְוֹת . . . וְזֶה הָיָה יְסוֹד וְהַתְחָלַת הֱיוֹתָם לְעָם.

וְלָכֵן לֹא בֶּן כ' לְכֹחַ בְּמִלְחֶמֶת הַקִּיּוּם נַעֲשֶׂה גָּדוֹל, אֶלָּא בֶּן יג', כְּשֶׁהוּא בַּר דֵּעָה
לְהָבִין גּוֹדֶל הַזְּכוּת וְגוֹדֶל הָאַחֲרָיוּת שֶׁיֵּשׁ עָלָיו עַל יְדֵי הֱיוֹתוֹ אֶחָד מִבְּנֵי יִשְׂרָאֵל.

The age of majority for Jewish males is thirteen, although to obtain certain rights and privileges one must be eighteen, twenty, or even forty. . . . This stands in contrast to the laws of the nations, which stipulate that one reaches the age of majority around the age of twenty.

Most nations were formed when tribes abandoned their nomadic existence as herdsmen to settle on a land, banded together to choose a leader, and organized militarily to defend their territory. Only afterward did they establish a legal system.

Regarding the Jewish nation, however, the opposite is true. Immediately upon being liberated from bondage in Egypt, while still in the desert, an uninhabitable land, they united under the Torah and *mitzvot*. . . . This was the foundation and beginning of Jewish nationhood.

Therefore, according to Jewish law, one need not be twenty—the age when a citizen is strong enough to contribute to his country's existence by defending it—to reach the age of majority. Rather, the Jewish nation confers adult status when youngsters are mature enough to understand the great privilege and responsibility of being a part of the Jewish people.

Text 4

Jean-Baptiste de La Curne de Sainte-Palaye,
Memoirs of Ancient Chivalry [London, 1784], pp. 42–43

It was not only to the sons of princes, or on some peculiar occasions, that knighthood was established before the age of twenty-one, prescribed by the ancient laws; a peculiar degree of merit and genius in attaining the necessary qualifications, often gained this prize in early life. . . . The regular age was, however, twenty-one; for though the minority of the nobles ended at seventeen, because they were judged strong enough, and sufficiently qualified, for the culture of their lands, the mechanic arts, and commerce,

Jean-Baptiste de La Curne de Sainte-Palaye
1697–1781

French medievalist and lexicographer. La Curne, son of a gentleman of the household of the duke d'Orléans, was elected in 1724 to the Académie des Inscriptions and devoted himself to historical studies. In 1758, he was elected to the Académie Française after publishing a brochure outlining his ambitious plan for a glossary of Old French. In 1759, he published the first edition of his *Memoirs of Ancient Chivalry*.

in which they were all employed; yet the profession of the arms demanded an ability and strength, not to be acquired till the age of twenty-one; and this extended to those nobles whose only profession was a military life: their majority was fixed at that age.

Soul Maturity (Optional)

Text 5

Rabbi Shne'ur Zalman of Liadi
(Alter Rebbe)
1745–1812

Chasidic rebbe, halachic authority, and founder of the Chabad movement. The Alter Rebbe was born in Liozna, Belarus, and was among the principal students of the Magid of Mezeritch. His numerous works include the *Tanya*, an early classic containing the fundamentals of Chabad Chasidism, and *Shulchan Aruch HaRav*, an expanded and reworked code of Jewish law.

Rabbi Shne'ur Zalman of Liadi, *Shulchan Aruch HaRav*, *Orach Chayim* 4:2 (*Mahadura Tinyana*)

שֶׁגִּמַר וְעִיקָּר כְּנִיסַת נֶפֶשׁ הַקְּדוֹשָׁה בָּאָדָם הוּא בִּי"ג שָׁנִים וְיוֹם א' לְזָכָר, וּבִי"ב לַנְּקֵבָה. שֶׁלָּכֵן נִתְחַיְּיבוּ אָז בְּמִצְוֹת מִן הַתּוֹרָה.

The sacred soul integrates fully with a boy at age thirteen and with a girl at age twelve. This is why, when they reach those ages, they become obligated to fulfill the Torah's commandments.

Earlier Maturity (Optional)

Text 6

Genesis 2:22

וַיִּבֶן ה' אֱלֹקִים אֶת הַצֵּלָע אֲשֶׁר לָקַח מִן הָאָדָם לְאִשָּׁה.

God built the side that He had taken from man into a woman.

Built up — comes from Binah (וַיִּבֶן)

Text 7

Talmud, Nidah 45b

דִּכְתִיב "וַיִּבֶן ה' [אֱלֹקִים] אֶת הַצֵּלָע" - מְלַמֵּד שֶׁנָּתַן הַקָּדוֹשׁ
בָּרוּךְ הוּא בִּינָה יְתֵירָה בָּאִשָּׁה יוֹתֵר מִבָּאִישׁ.

"**G**od built the side." This teaches us that <u>God</u> bestowed <u>earlier</u> <u>maturity</u> upon <u>the woman</u> than He did upon the man.

KEY POINTS

- Because Jewish nationhood is founded upon and defined by Torah, the Jewish age of majority is therefore at the age when one can perform and appreciate the Torah's teachings.

- Only when the Godly soul is completely integrated with the human body do we become fully responsible for going beyond our natural selfishness to serve our existential purpose. This integration corresponds to the Jewish age of majority.

---

3. Why do we pour a cup of wine for Elijah at the Passover *seder*?

Herald, Solve, and Testify

Text 8a

Malachi 3:23 ▥

הִנֵּה אָנֹכִי שֹׁלֵחַ לָכֶם, אֵת אֵלִיָּה הַנָּבִיא לִפְנֵי בּוֹא יוֹם ה'.

I am sending to you Elijah the Prophet before the day of God comes.

[handwritten: every item in the Seder represents something Elijah fought many Idol worshipers to defeut our faith. Rebuking the prophets & kings.]

Text 8b

Rashi, Leviticus 26:42 ▥

Rabbi Shlomo Yitschaki (Rashi)
1040–1105

Most noted biblical and Talmudic commentator. Born in Troyes, France, Rashi studied in the famed *yeshivot* of Mainz and Worms. His commentaries on the Pentateuch and the Talmud, which focus on the straightforward meaning of the text, appear in virtually every edition of the Talmud and Bible.

"וְזָכַרְתִּי אֶת בְּרִיתִי יַעֲקוֹב" (וַיִּקְרָא כו,מב): בַּחֲמִשָּׁה מְקוֹמוֹת נִכְתַּב מָלֵא, וְאֵלִיָּהוּ חָסֵר בַּחֲמִשָּׁה מְקוֹמוֹת, יַעֲקֹב נָטַל אוֹת מִשְּׁמוֹ שֶׁל אֵלִיָּהוּ עֵרָבוֹן שֶׁיָּבוֹא וִיבַשֵּׂר גְּאוּלַת בָּנָיו.

❝ I will remember My covenant [with] Ya'akov (Jacob)" (Leviticus 16:42).

The name Ya'akov is written in full, [i.e., with a "*vav*,"] in five places in scripture, and the name Elijah is written defectively [without a "*vav*,"] in five places in scripture. Jacob took a letter ["*vav*"] from the name of Elijah as security, so that he would come and herald the redemption of his [Jacob's] children.

Text 9

Rabbi Yeshayah Halevi Horowitz, *Torah Shebe'al Peh*, *Kelal Leshonot Sugyot* 📜

תֵּיקוּ. בְּכָל דּוּכְתָּא בַּתַּלְמוּד שֶׁהַתְּשׁוּבָה אֵינָהּ נוֹדַעַת לִפְשֹׁט מִמֶּנָּה הָאִבַּעְיָא, אוֹמֵר "תֵּיקוּ". וּלְשׁוֹן "תֵּיקוּ" הוּא מִלְּשׁוֹן "תִּיק". כִּי כְּמוֹ שֶׁהַתִּיק שֶׁבּוֹ הַסֵּפֶר אֵינוּ נוֹדַע מַה שֶּׁבְּתוֹכוֹ, כָּךְ פְּשִׁיטוּת הָאִבַּעְיָא אֵינוּ נוֹדַע. וְכֵן פֵּרֵשׁ הֶעָרוּךְ.

וְיֵשׁ אוֹמְרִים "תֵּיקוּ" רָאשֵׁי תֵּבוֹת "תִּשְׁבִּי יְתָרֵץ קֻשְׁיוֹת וְאִבַּעְיוֹת".

eiku: Whenever the Talmud does not know the answer to a question, it says *"teiku."* This is a cognate of *"tik,"* satchel. Just as when a book is in its satchel, we do not know what is inside, so too, we do not know the answer to the question. This explanation is given by Rabbi Nathan of Rome in his *Aruch.*

Some say *teiku* is an acronym for "Elijah will resolve questions and problems."

Rabbi Yeshayah Halevi Horowitz (*Shelah*) 1565–1630

Kabbalist and author. Rabbi Horowitz was born in Prague and served as rabbi in several prominent Jewish communities, including Frankfurt am Main and his native Prague. After the passing of his wife in 1620, he moved to Israel. In Tiberias, he completed his *Shenei Luchot Haberit*, an encyclopedic compilation of Kabbalistic ideas. He is buried in Tiberias, next to Maimonides.

Text 10

Zohar 1:93a

Zohar

The seminal work of Kabbalah, Jewish mysticism. The Zohar is a mystical commentary on the Torah, written in Aramaic and Hebrew. According to Arizal, the Zohar contains the teachings of Rabbi Shimon bar Yocha'i who lived in the Land of Israel during the 2nd century. The Zohar has become one of the indispensable texts of traditional Judaism, alongside and nearly equal in stature to the Mishnah and Talmud.

"קַנֹּא קַנֵּאתִי לַה' (אֱלֹקֵי צְבָאוֹת), כִּי עָזְבוּ בְרִיתְךָ בְּנֵי יִשְׂרָאֵל וְגוֹ'" (מְלָכִים א, יט,י).

אָמַר לֵיה: חַיֶּיךָ בְּכָל אֲתַר דְּהַאי רְשִׁימָא קַדִּישָׁא יִרְשְׁמוּן לֵיה בְּנֵי בְּבִשְׂרֵהוֹן, אַנְתְּ תִּזְדַּמֵּן תַּמָּן, וּפוּמָא דְּאַסְהֵיד דְּיִשְׂרָאֵל עָזְבוּ הוּא יַסְהֵיד דְּיִשְׂרָאֵל מְקַיְּימִין הַאי קַיְּימָא.

> have been very zealous for God. The Israelites have rejected your covenant" (I Kings 19:10).
>
> God responded, "Whenever they place the sign of the covenant on their flesh, you will be there. The mouth that said that they abandoned the covenant will testify that they have kept it."

Elijah and Passover

Text 11a

Talmud, Rosh Hashanah 11b

בְּנִיסָן נִגְאֲלוּ, בְּנִיסָן עֲתִידִין לִיגָּאֵל.

מְנָלָן? אָמַר קְרָא (שְׁמוֹת יב,מב) "לֵיל שִׁמֻּרִים" - לֵיל הַמְשׁוּמָּר וּבָא מִשֵּׁשֶׁת יְמֵי בְּרֵאשִׁית.

> n Nisan we were redeemed [from Egypt], and in Nisan we will be redeemed again.
>
> How do we know? For the verse says (Exodus 12:42) [regarding Passover eve], "It is a night of anticipation for God," which means a night that has been anticipated [as the date of the final redemption] since the six days of Creation.

Text 11b

Rabbi Ya'akov Reischer, *Chok Ya'akov* 480 📖

מִנְהָג בְּכַמָּה מְקוֹמוֹת, שֶׁאֵין נוֹעֲלִין הַחֲדָרִים שֶׁיְּשֵׁנִים שָׁם בְּלֵיל

פֶּסַח, כִּי "בְּנִיסָן נִגְאֲלוּ וּבְנִיסָן עֲתִידִים לִיגָּאֵל". דִּכְתִיב "לֵיל שִׁמֻּרִים"

– "לַיְלָה הַמְשׁוּמָּר מִשֵּׁשֶׁת יְמֵי בְּרֵאשִׁית". וְאִם יָבוֹא אֵלִיָּהוּ יִמְצָא

פֶּתַח פָּתוּחַ וְנֵצֵא לִקְרָאתוֹ מְהֵרָה. וְאָנוּ מַאֲמִינִים בְּזֶה . . .

וְנוֹהֲגִין בְּאֵלּוּ מְדִינוֹת לִמְזוֹג כּוֹס א' יוֹתֵר מֵהַמְסוּבִּין

וְקוֹרִין אוֹתוֹ כּוֹס שֶׁל אֵלִיָּה הַנָּבִיא.

I n numerous places, it is customary to leave the doors unlocked on Passover eve. For "in Nisan we were redeemed [from Egypt], and in Nisan we will be redeemed again." As it says, "It is a night of anticipation for God," which means "a night that has been anticipated [as the date of the final redemption] since the six days of Creation." If Elijah indeed arrives, he will find an open door, and we will be able to go out to greet him quickly. Indeed, we believe that he will arrive. . . .

It is customary in our regions to pour one additional cup. We call it "Elijah's cup."

Rabbi Ya'akov ben Yosef Reischer
ca. 1670–1733

Renowned rabbi, halachic authority, and author. He served on rabbinical courts in Prague, Ansbach, Worms, and Metz. He was accepted by contemporary rabbis as the ultimate authority on halachic issues, and problems were addressed to him from all over the Diaspora and Israel. His most famous works are *Chok Ya'akov*, an exposition on the section of the *Shulchan Aruch* pertaining to the laws of Passover, and his *Responsa Shevut Ya'akov*.

Text 12

Rabbi Eliyahu of Vilna, cited in *Ta'amei Haminhagim, Inyanei Pesach* 551 📖

טַעַם לַמִּנְהָג שֶׁמוֹזְגִין כּוֹס חֲמִישִׁי, וְקוֹרְאִין אוֹתוֹ כּוֹס שֶׁל אֵלִיָּהוּ הַנָּבִיא,
מִשּׁוּם דְּאִיכָּא פְּלוּגְתָּא בַּגְּמָרָא אִם צְרִיכִין כּוֹס חֲמִישִׁי, וְלֹא אִפְסְקָא הִלְכְתָא.
וּכְשֶׁיָּבוֹא אֵלִיָּהוּ יִתְבָּרֵר הַסָּפֵק. וְעַל כֵּן מוֹזְגִין הַכּוֹס מִסָּפֵק וְאֵין שׁוֹתִין אוֹתוֹ,
וְקוֹרְאִין אוֹתוֹ כּוֹס שֶׁל אֵלִיָּהוּ, כִּי בְּבוֹאוֹ יִתְבָּרְרוּ כָּל הַסְּפֵקוֹת וְגַם סָפֵק זֶה.

Rabbi Eliyahu of Vilna
(Vilna Gaon, Gra)
1720–1797

Talmudist, halachist, and Kabbalist. The Vilna Gaon was one of the greatest scholars of his day. In addition to Talmud, he excelled in all aspects of Torah study, including Kabbalah, and was proficient in secular subjects as well. He left a tremendous legacy, both from his vast writings on the Tanach, Talmud, and *Shulchan Aruch*, and from the many students that he inspired to Torah and scholarship.

The following is why it is customary to pour a fifth cup, which we call Elijah's cup. There is a Talmudic dispute whether we ought to drink a fifth cup at the *seder*. The final ruling was never issued, so Elijah will resolve this question when he arrives. Because there is a doubt about this matter, we pour the fifth cup but do not drink it. We call it Elijah's cup to indicate that when he comes, this doubt, among all others, will be resolved.

Rabbi Moshe Chagiz, in *Birkat Eliyahu*, p. 55 📖

וַדַּאי שָׁמַעְתָּ עַד כֹּה טַעַם הֲכָנַת הַכִּסֵּא לְאֵלִיָּהוּ בִּשְׁעַת הַמִּילָה, וְכִנּוּי
הַשֵּׁם שֶׁהוּא אֵלִיָּהוּ מַלְאַךְ הַבְּרִית . . . וְהַפֶּה שֶׁהֵאסִיר לְדַבֵּר עַל יִשְׂרָאֵל
שֶׁהֵפֵרוּ אֶת הַבְּרִית, הוּא הַפֶּה שֶׁמְּאַשֵּׁר וּמֵעִיד עַל יִשְׂרָאֵל, וְנַעֲשָׂה
עַצְמוֹ סַנֵּיגוֹר בִּהְיוֹת עֵד הָרוֹאֶה שֶׁיִּשְׂרָאֵל מְקַיְּמִין אֶת הַבְּרִית.

אִם כֵּן, הָכָא זָכִינוּ לְקַיֵּם מִנְהָגָן שֶׁל יִשְׂרָאֵל בְּלֵיל פֶּסַח לְהָכִין לוֹ כִּסֵּא דִּמְהֵמְנוּתָא,
וּמִטָּה, וְשׁוּלְחָן עָרוּךְ, שֶׁבּוֹ יִשְׂרָאֵל מְקַיְּמִים אֶת הַפֶּסַח, שֶׁאֶחָד מֵחֻקּוֹתָיו וּמִשְׁפָּטָיו
הַיְשָׁרִים הוּא ית׳ אֲשֶׁר צִוָּה עָלָיו "וְכָל עָרֵל לֹא יֹאכַל בּוֹ" (שְׁמוֹת יב,מח) . . .

אֵין כָּאן סָפֵק כִּי בָּא יָבֹא בִּרְכַּת אֵלִיָּהוּ ז"ל בְּכָל בָּתֵּי יִשְׂרָאֵל, לִרְאוֹת קִיּוּם הַמִּצְוָה
אַחַת שֶׁהוּא שְׁתַּיִם פֶּסַח וּמִילָה שֶׁהֵם מְקַיְּמִים. וְיַעֲלֶה לָנוּ הַשָּׁמַיְמָה לְהָלִיץ בַּעַד
כְּלַל וּפְרַט יִשְׂרָאֵל לְמַהֵר וּלְהָחִישׁ גְּאוּלָתָם וּפִדְיוֹן נַפְשָׁם בִּגְאוּלָה אַחֲרוֹנָה.

You have certainly heard the reason for preparing Elijah's chair at a circumcision, and the reason we refer to him as the "angel of the covenant." . . . The mouth that indicted Israel by stating that they forsook the covenant is the very mouth that gives testimony in support of Israel when he sees them keeping the covenant.

On the night of Passover, we observe the custom to prepare a cup of wine for Elijah along with a seat at the table at which we fulfill the Passover mitzvah. One of the laws regarding the consumption of the Paschal lamb [during Temple times] was that "no uncircumcised male may eat it" (Exodus 12:48), [which indicates that there is a link between circumcision and the Passover meal]. . . .

There is no doubt, then, that the blessing of Elijah's presence comes to every Jewish house to observe that they have fulfilled the mitzvah of Passover, which is linked to circumcision. He will then go before God to pray on

Rabbi Moshe Chagiz
ca. 1671–1750

Talmudic scholar, kabbalist, and author. Rabbi Chagiz was born in Jerusalem and traveled to Europe to raise funds for the impoverished Jewish community of the Holy Land. While in Amsterdam and Altona, he became embroiled in communal disputes, alleging that various Jews were secret Sabbateans. He authored polemical works about these disputes and some halachic works as well.

behalf of all of us, collectively and individually, and that God hasten the final redemption.

KEY POINTS

- According to tradition, Elijah the Prophet will herald the final redemption. On this night, whose theme is redemption, we pour an additional cup of wine in Elijah's name as a symbol of our faith in this redemption.

- We are taught that Elijah will resolve unanswered questions, such as the question of whether we drink a fifth cup at the *seder*. We therefore name the fifth cup for Elijah.

- Elijah is present at every circumcision and *seder* to testify that the Jews are keepers of the covenant.

---

4. Why is it not forbidden to submit petitions of prayer to a righteous person? Isn't it true that Judaism forbids using intermediaries to access God?

A Time-Honored Tradition

Text 14

Rabbi Moshe of Trani, *Beit Elokim, Sha'ar Hatefilah* 12 📖

שֶׁאָנוּ רוֹאִים בַּתּוֹרָה וּבַנְּבִיאִים שֶׁכְּשֶׁהָיוּ יִשְׂרָאֵל נִמְצָאִים בְּצָרָה, הָיוּ בָּאִים אֶל הַנָּבִיא שֶׁיִּתְפַּלֵּל בַּעֲדָם אֶל ה' שֶׁיַּצִּילֵם מִצָּרָתָם.

כְּמוֹ שֶׁנֶּאֱמַר בְּמִתְאוֹנְנִים שֶׁבָּעַר בָּם אֵשׁ ה' (בְּמִדְבָּר יא,ב), "וַיִּצְעַק הָעָם אֶל מֹשֶׁה וַיִּתְפַּלֵּל מֹשֶׁה אֶל ה' וַתִּשְׁקַע הָאֵשׁ", כִּי נִרְאָה שֶׁצַּעֲקָתָם הָיְתָה לְמֹשֶׁה שֶׁיִּתְפַּלֵּל בַּעֲדָם, וְהוּא הִתְפַּלֵּל וְשָׁמַע הָאֵ-ל תְּפִלָּתוֹ.

וְכֵן בִּשְׁמוּאֵל (א, יב,יט): "וַיֹּאמְרוּ כָל הָעָם אֶל שְׁמוּאֵל, הִתְפַּלֵּל בְּעַד עֲבָדֶיךָ אֶל ה' אֱלֹקֶיךָ וְאַל נָמוּת, כִּי יָסַפְנוּ עַל כָּל חַטֹּאתֵינוּ רָעָה לִשְׁאוֹל לָנוּ מֶלֶךְ".

וְכֵן יִרְמְיָהוּ שָׁלַח לוֹ הַמֶּלֶךְ צִדְקִיָּהוּ, "הִתְפַּלֵּל נָא בַעֲדֵנוּ אֶל ה' אֱלֹקֵינוּ" (יִרְמְיָהוּ לז,ג). וְכֵן שָׂרֵי הַחַיָּילִים אָמְרוּ אֶל יִרְמְיָהוּ (יִרְמְיָהוּ מב,ב), "תִּפָּל נָא תְחִנָּתֵנוּ לְפָנֶיךָ וְהִתְפַּלֵּל בַּעֲדֵנוּ אֶל ה' אֱלֹקֶיךָ".

וְכֵן מָצִינוּ (בְּרָכוֹת לד,ב) בְּרַבָּן גַּמְלִיאֵל שֶׁשָּׁלַח זוּגָא דְרַבָּנָן לר' חֲנִינָא בֶּן דּוֹסָא שֶׁיִּתְפַּלֵּל עַל חוֹלִי בְּנוֹ, וְכֵן רַבָּן יוֹחָנָן בֶּן זַכַּאי, אָמַר לֵיהּ: חֲנִינָא בְּנִי בַּקֵּשׁ עָלָיו רַחֲמִים וְיִחְיֶה . . .

וְכֵן כַּיּוֹצֵא בָזֶה בִּשְׁאָר הַדּוֹרוֹת.

Throughout the Torah and Prophets, we find that Jews petitioned their prophets to pray for them in times of trouble.

When the complainers were plagued by fire, "The people cried out to Moses; Moses prayed to God and the fire died down" (Numbers 11:2). It seems that their cry to Moses was that he should pray for them, which he did, and God heard his prayer.

So it was with Samuel: "And the entire nation said to Samuel, 'Pray on behalf of your servants to God that we might not die, for we have added to our wickedness by petitioning for a king'" (I Samuel 12:19).

Similarly, King Zedekiah petitioned Jeremiah, "Please pray to God for us" (Jeremiah 37:3); also the military officers beseeched Jeremiah, "May our supplications come before you so that you might pray to God for us" (Jeremiah 42:2).

Similarly, we find in the Talmud (Berachot 34b) that Rabban Gamliel sent emissaries to petition Rabbi Chanina ben Dosa to pray on behalf of his ill son. Rabban Yochanan ben Zakai also petitioned Rabbi Chanina, saying, "Chanina my son, beg for mercy so that he might live." . . .

And so it was in all other generations.

In the Presence of God

Text 15

Rabbi Yisrael Bruna, *Responsa* 275 📖

מַה שֶּׁאָנוּ אוֹמְרִים "נָא מִדָּה נְכוֹנָה", וְכֵן "מִדַּת רַחֲמִים", וּמַכְנִיסֵי רַחֲמִים",
"מַלְאֲכֵי רַחֲמִים", אֵינוּ אֶלָּא דֶּרֶךְ שִׁפְלוּת וְעַבְדוּת, שֶׁמְּדַבֵּר בִּפְנֵי הַמֶּלֶךְ לְיוֹעֲצָיו
לְדַבֵּר לַמֶּלֶךְ וְהוּא בּוֹשׁ בְּדָבָר לְקָרֵב אֶל הַמֶּלֶךְ. וְאֵין זֶה דֶּרֶךְ אֶמְצָעִי כְּלָל.

When we appeal to angels in various prayers
. . . it is only out of a sense of humbleness and
servitude. It is similar to when we speak before
the king and ask his advisers to beseech him, because
we are too awestruck to approach the king. This is in no
way intermediation.

Rabbi Yisrael Bruna
(Mahari Bruna)
d. 1480

Halachic authority. Rabbi Yisrael
was a student of Rabbi Yisrael
Iserlein, author of *Terumat
Hadeshen*. Shortly after 1440, he
moved to Regensburg, where he
opened a *yeshivah*, and was later
appointed rabbi of the city. After
the death of his teachers, he was
considered the foremost Torah
scholar in Germany. In his old age,
he was the victim of a blood libel
and was imprisoned. His halachic
work consists of 284 responsa,
first published in Salonika in 1798.

LEARNING EXERCISE 2

With a partner, answer the following three questions.

Questions	Answers
1. "It is only out of a sense of humbleness." What is Rabbi Yisrael of Bruna negating?	
2. "We *speak before the king and* ask his advisers. . . ." Why are the italicized words necessary for his thesis? Would removing these words compromise his message?	
3. "This is in no way intermediation." What is the meaning of these words?	

Brain Petition

Text 16

Rabbi Moshe Sofer, *Responsa Chatam Sofer, Orach Chayim* 1:166 📖

אַךְ כָּל יִשְׂרָאֵל שׁוּתָּפִים, וְגוּף אֶחָד, וְנֶפֶשׁ א'. וּכְשֶׁאֶחָד מִצְטַעֵר, גַּם חֲבֵירוֹ
מַרְגִּישׁ וְעִמּוֹ מִצְטַעֵר . . . וְכֵיוָן שֶׁשְּׁנֵיהֶם בְּצַעַר, טוֹב יוֹתֵר שֶׁיִּכָּנֵס הָרֹאשׁ
מִשֶּׁיִּכָּנֵס הָרֶגֶל . . . כֵּיוָן שֶׁשְּׁנֵיהֶם בַּעֲלֵי דְבָרִים. וְלֹא כְּמֵלִיץ בְּעַד אַחֵר.

Together, the Jewish people form one body and one soul. When one person is in pain, another is able to sense this pain.... Because both people are suffering, and the matter relates to both of them, it is preferable that the "head"—rather than the "foot"—offers the prayer.... This is not a case of one person interceding before God on someone else's behalf.

The brain knows it best & know how to act in favor of the foot.
& Ask

> **Rabbi Moshe Sofer**
> (*Chatam Sofer*)
> 1762–1839
>
> A leading rabbinical authority of the 19th century. Born in Frankfurt am Main, *Chatam Sofer* ultimately accepted the rabbinate of Pressburg (now Bratislava), Slovakia. Serving as rabbi and head of the *yeshivah* that he established, Rabbi Sofer maintained a strong traditionalist perspective, opposing deviation from Jewish tradition. *Chatam Sofer* is the title of his collection of halachic responsa and his commentary to the Talmud.

KEY POINTS

- It is a long-established tradition to petition a righteous person to pray to God on one's behalf. It is clear that this tradition does not imply that we have no direct access to God.

- Some attribute this custom to the fact that we are so awe-struck by God's presence that we feel uncomfortable speaking for ourselves.

- Others explain that a righteous person is akin to the head, whose job it is to care for and seek remedy for the body's needs.

We should All be in synch when you feel each others pain.

5. Why do Chasidim think it is necessary to have a rebbe? Isn't it true that Jews do not require intermediaries to access God?

Positive Environment

Text 17

Maimonides, *Mishneh Torah*, Laws of Temperaments 6:1–2 📖

Rabbi Moshe ben Maimon
(Maimonides, Rambam)
1135–1204

Halachist, philosopher, author, and physician. Maimonides was born in Cordoba, Spain. After the conquest of Cordoba by the Almohads, he fled Spain and eventually settled in Cairo, Egypt. There, he became the leader of the Jewish community and served as court physician to the vizier of Egypt. He is most noted for authoring the *Mishneh Torah*, an encyclopedic arrangement of Jewish law, and for his philosophical work, *Guide for the Perplexed*. His rulings on Jewish law are integral to the formation of halachic consensus.

דֶּרֶךְ בְּרִיָּתוֹ שֶׁל אָדָם לִהְיוֹת נִמְשָׁךְ בְּדֵעוֹתָיו וּבְמַעֲשָׂיו אַחַר רֵעָיו וַחֲבֵרָיו, נוֹהֵג כְּמִנְהַג אַנְשֵׁי מְדִינָתוֹ. לְפִיכָךְ צָרִיךְ אָדָם לְהִתְחַבֵּר לַצַּדִּיקִים וְלֵישֵׁב אֵצֶל הַחֲכָמִים תָּמִיד כְּדֵי שֶׁיִּלְמֹוד מִמַּעֲשֵׂיהֶם . . .

מִצְוַת עֲשֵׂה לְהִדָּבֵק בַּחֲכָמִים וְתַלְמִידֵיהֶם כְּדֵי לִלְמוֹד מִמַּעֲשֵׂיהֶם, כָּעִנְיָן שֶׁנֶּאֱמַר (דְּבָרִים י,כ) "וּבוֹ תִדְבָּק". וְכִי אֶפְשָׁר לָאָדָם לְהִדָּבֵק בַּשְּׁכִינָה? אֶלָּא כָּךְ אָמְרוּ חֲכָמִים בְּפֵירוּשׁ מִצְוָה זוֹ (סִפְרֵי, עֵקֶב מט): הִדָּבֵק בַּחֲכָמִים וְתַלְמִידֵיהֶם . . . וְכֵן צִוּוּ חֲכָמִים וְאָמְרוּ (אָבוֹת ד,ד): "וֶהֱוֵי מִתְאַבֵּק בַּעֲפַר רַגְלֵיהֶם וְשׁוֹתֶה בַּצָּמָא אֶת דִּבְרֵיהֶם".

People's character and actions are influenced by their friends and associates, and they follow the local norms of behavior. Therefore, we should associate with righteous people and always be in the company of the wise to learn from their deeds. . . .

Indeed, it is a positive commandment to <u>cleave</u> unto the <u>wise</u> and <u>their</u> disciples to learn from their deeds, as it states (Deuteronomy 10:20), "You shall cleave to God."

Is it possible for a human being to cleave to God? The sages explained this commandment thus (*Sifrei, Ekev* 49): "Cleave to the wise and their disciples." . . . Similarly, our sages have directed (Ethics of the Fathers 4:4), "Sit in the dust of their feet and drink in their words thirstily."

Finding the Switch

Text 18

Interview with the Lubavitcher Rebbe [New York: Vaad Hanochos Hatemimim, 1996], pp. 8–11 📖

Question: *What was the role that the Baal Shem Tov played in the Chasidic movement?*

Rebbe: We can understand what the Baal Shem Tov did by the simile of the relationship of an electric powerhouse with a lamp that is connected to it by a wire. In order to light his lamp, one must find the right switch, or push the correct button. The soul of every Jew is a part of and is connected with G-d Almighty, but in order that one can enjoy the great benefits of it, the correct switch must be found or the proper button pushed. It was the Baal Shem Tov's mission to explain and proclaim that every Jew without exception is connected with "the powerhouse," and every one of them has a switch in his innermost, that will be found if searched for. . . .

Question: *What is the function of a Rebbe?* → Guidance, shows us who we are and connect us to higher Achiwments.
Rebbe: As was said earlier, to find the switch in every Jew and help him become connected with the powerhouse.

The righteous when they die they are not dead Since their lives was filled with spiritual Richness Therefore they are considered Alive.

Stem Souls

Text 19

Rabbi Shne'ur Zalman of Liadi, *Tanya*, ch. 2 🕮

וּבָזֶה יוּבָן מַאֲמַר רַבּוֹתֵינוּ זִכְרוֹנָם לִבְרָכָה עַל פָּסוּק "וּלְדָבְקָה בּוֹ",
שֶׁכָּל הַדָּבֵק בְּתַלְמִידֵי חֲכָמִים מַעֲלֶה עָלָיו הַכָּתוּב כְּאִלוּ נִדְבַּק
בַּשְּׁכִינָה מַמָּשׁ. כִּי עַל יְדֵי דְבֵיקָה בְּתַלְמִידֵי חֲכָמִים, קְשׁוּרוֹת נֶפֶשׁ
רוּחַ וּנְשָׁמָה שֶׁל עַמֵּי הָאָרֶץ וּמְיוּחָדוֹת בִּמְהוּתָן הָרִאשׁוֹן.

This explains the comment of our sages on the verse, "And to cleave unto Him"—"Those who cleave unto a scholar [of Torah] is deemed by the Torah as if they had become attached to God," which is quite literally true. For, through attachment to the scholars, the soul of each person is bound up and united with its original essence.

KEY POINTS

- We do not require intermediaries to access God, for we all have a "direct line" to God. The role of a rebbe is to help us find the switch—so that we can ignite our souls and reveal our connection to God.

- God places souls in each generation that maintain a conscious connection to God and that help us connect to the latent knowledge within us that we too are part of God.

---

6. Why is Moses' name absent from the *Haggadah*?

An Honorable Mention

Text 20

Passover *Haggadah*, from *Mechilta*, *Parashat Beshalach* 6 📜

רַבִּי יוֹסֵי הַגְּלִילִי אוֹמֵר: מִנַּיִן אַתָּה אוֹמֵר שֶׁלָּקוּ הַמִּצְרִים
בְּמִצְרַיִם עֶשֶׂר מַכּוֹת וְעַל הַיָּם לָקוּ חֲמִשִּׁים מַכּוֹת?

בְּמִצְרַיִם מַהוּ אוֹמֵר, "וַיֹּאמְרוּ הַחַרְטֻמִּים אֶל פַּרְעֹה
אֶצְבַּע אֱלֹקִים הִיא" (שְׁמוֹת ח,טו).

וְעַל הַיָּם מַהוּ אוֹמֵר, "וַיַּרְא יִשְׂרָאֵל אֶת הַיָּד הַגְּדוֹלָה אֲשֶׁר עָשָׂה ה' בְּמִצְרַיִם
וַיִּרְאוּ הָעָם אֶת ה' וַיַּאֲמִינוּ בַּה' וּבְמֹשֶׁה עַבְדּוֹ" (שְׁמוֹת יד,לא).

כַּמָּה לָקוּ בְּאֶצְבַּע, עֶשֶׂר מַכּוֹת. אֱמוֹר מֵעַתָּה, בְּמִצְרַיִם
לָקוּ עֶשֶׂר מַכּוֹת, וְעַל הַיָּם לָקוּ חֲמִשִּׁים מַכּוֹת.

Rabbi Yosei the Galilean said: How do we know that God struck the Egyptians in Egypt with ten plagues and at the sea with fifty plagues?

[With regard to the plague of lice that occurred] in Egypt, it says (Exodus 8:15), "The necromancers said to Pharaoh, 'It is the *finger* of God.'"

At the sea it says (Exodus 14:31), "Israel saw the great *hand* that God used upon the Egyptians, and the people feared God, and they believed in God and in Moses His servant."

Mechilta

A halachic Midrash to Exodus. Midrash is the designation of a particular genre of rabbinic literature usually forming a running commentary on specific books of the Bible. The name "*Mechilta*" means "rule" and was given to this Midrash because its comments and explanations are based on fixed rules of exegesis. This work is often attributed to Rabbi Yishmael ben Elisha, a contemporary of Rabbi Akiva, though there are some references to later sages in this work.

How many plagues were there [in Egypt, where it uses] the word finger? Ten. If in Egypt there were ten plagues, then at sea [where it says "hand"] there were five times the amount, namely fifty plagues.

God, Not Moses

Text 21

Rabbi Menachem Mendel of Shklov,
Seder Haggadah Shel Pesach [Horodna 5559], p. 91 📖

בְּכָל הַסִּיפּוּר יְצִיאַת מִצְרַיִם, אֵין לָנוּ זִכָּרוֹן לִזְכּוֹר, חַס וְשָׁלוֹם, אֶת מֹשֶׁה. כִּי אָסוּר לָנוּ לְשַׁתֵּף שׁוּם דָּבָר לִכְבוֹדוֹ וּלְעַצְמוֹ. וְאֵין הַשֶּׁבַח תָּלוּי בְּמֹשֶׁה, רַק בַּה' לְבַדּוֹ . . .

וְלָכֵן כְּתִיב "וַיַּאֲמִינוּ בַּה' וּבְמֹשֶׁה עַבְדּוֹ", כְּלוֹמַר לֹא לִגְדוּלַת מֹשֶׁה נֶאֱמַר זֶה. אַדְרַבָּה, לְהַאֲמָנַת יִשְׂרָאֵל וְעַנְוַת מֹשֶׁה שֶׁהֶאֱמִינוּ שֶׁה' עָשָׂה כָּל זֹאת וּמֹשֶׁה אֵינוֹ רַק עַבְדּוֹ כְּכָל הַבְּרוּאִים שֶׁבָּעוֹלָם שֶׁמְּחוּיָּבִין לַעֲשׂוֹת רְצוֹנוֹ.

Rabbi Menachem Mendel of Shklov
d. 1827

Kabbalist. Rabbi Menachem Mendel was a devout student of Rabbi Eliyahu of Vilna (Gra), and spent many hours with him during his last two years of life. After his passing, Rabbi Menachem Mendel took upon himself the task of bringing the Gra's teachings to print. In 1808, together with other students of the Gra, he settled in Israel, first in Tiberias, then Safed, and finally in Jerusalem. Most of his writings are on subjects of Kabbalah.

Throughout the entire story of the Exodus, we do not mention Moses, God forbid, because it is forbidden to attribute a partner to God. We do not praise Moses but God alone. . . .

It therefore says, "They believed in God and in Moses His servant." This is not said to speak of Moses' greatness. On the contrary, this conveys that the Jews believed that God did everything, and that Moses was nothing but His humble servant—that he was like all creatures in the world that are obligated to do God's will.

Moses' Wish

Text 22

Rabbi Shmuel Greineman, *Chafets Chayim Al HaTorah*,
Parashat Beha'alotecha, p. 199 📖

וּפַעַם בַּאֲמִירַת הַהַגָּדָה בְּלֵיל הִתְקַדֶּשׁ חַג הַפֶּסַח, הֵסֵב תְּשׂוּמַת לִבָּם שֶׁל הַמְּסֻבִּים
לְשׁוּלְחָנוּ, עַל הָעוּבְדָּא, כִּי בְּכָל הַהַגָּדָה לֹא נִזְכַּר אַף פַּעַם שְׁמוֹ שֶׁל מֹשֶׁה רַבֵּינוּ,
לַמְרוֹת שֶׁכָּל הַנֵּס שֶׁל יְצִיאַת מִצְרַיִם נַעֲשָׂה עַל יָדוֹ, לְלַמְּדֵנוּ, שֶׁ"רְצוֹן יְרֵאָיו יַעֲשֶׂה"
(תְּהִלִּים קמה,יט). וּמִכֵּיוָן שֶׁהָיָה עָנָיו מִכָּל הָאָדָם, לָכֵן לֹא נִזְכַּר שְׁמוֹ עַל הַנֵּס.

Once, when Rabbi Yisrael Meir, the *Chafets Chayim,* was reciting the *Haggadah* on the first night of Passover, he pointed out to those dining with him the fact that Moses' name is not mentioned in the *Haggadah* even once, despite the fact that the entire miracle of the Exodus transpired through him. It teaches us that "God fulfills the wishes of those who are in awe of Him" (Psalms 145:19), and because Moses was the most humble person to ever live, his name is not associated with the miracle.

Rabbi Yisrael Meir Hakohen Kagan
(*Chafets Chayim*)
1839–1933

Pre-WWII Polish Halachist and ethicist. Rabbi Kagan was the dean of the illustrious yeshivah in Radin, Poland. A prolific author on topics of Halachah and ethical behavior, he is often called *Chafets Chayim* after his first work, a comprehensive digest of laws pertaining to ethical speech. His magnum opus, on which he worked for 28 years, is *Mishnah Berurah*, a concise commentary on the first section of the *Shulchan Aruch*. He also authored *Bi'ur Halachah* on the *Shulchan Aruch* and numerous other works.

Rabbi Shmuel Greineman
1889–1957

Communal activist, educator, and scholar. Rabbi Greineman was a student of and an aide to Rabbis Yisrael Meir of Radin (*Chafets Chayim*) and Chaim Ozer Grodzinski. In 1935, he settled in Israel, but later moved to America where he authored *Chafets Chayim al HaTorah*, a collection of teachings that he heard from Rabbi Yisrael Meir, divided by the weekly Torah portion.

KEY POINTS

- One theory offered as to why Moses' name is not (prominently) mentioned in the *Haggadah* is that we do not wish to ascribe praise to anyone but God.

- Alternatively, Moses' name is not mentioned in the *Haggadah*, because he would have preferred this due to his humility.

7. Why does Judaism associate so many of its celebrations with food?

To Mind the Body

Text 23

The Lubavitcher Rebbe, Rabbi Menachem Mendel Schneerson, *Likutei Sichot* 23:29 🎙

דָאס וואָס תּוֹרָה זאָגְט אָן, אַז שַׁבָּת (אָדֶער יוֹם טוֹב) דאַרְף זַיין אַ זְמַן פֿון עוֹנֶג בַּיי אִידְן ("לָכֶם"), מֵיינְט עֶס נִיט, אַז (נאָר) דִי נְשָׁמָה זאָל הָאבְּן תַּעֲנוּג (רוּחָנִי) פֿון יוֹם הַשַּׁבָּת (וְיוֹם טוֹב), נאָר אַז (אוֹיךְ) דֶער **גוּף** זאָל פִֿילְן אַן עוֹנֶג דֶערְפֿון וואָס דאָס אִיז יוֹם הַשַּׁבָּת (יוֹם טוֹב). וְאַדְּרַבָּה: דֶער עִיקָר הַמְכֻוָּן פֿון דֶער מִצְוָה אִיז דַוְקָא דֶער (לְצַרֶךְ דֶעם) גוּף.

אוּן וויבַּאלְד אַז דֶער תַּעֲנוּג **טִבְעִי** פֿון גוּף אִיז פֿון אֲכִילָה וּשְׁתִיָה, דֶערִיבְּעֶר זאָגְט תּוֹרָה אַז חִיּוּב הָעוֹנֶג אִיז דוּרְךְ אֲכִילָה דַוְקָא; וויל דַוְקָא בְּאוֹפַן זֶה ווֶערְט אוֹיפְֿגֶעטאָן אַז דֶער עוֹנֶג שַׁבָּת אִיז מְצַרֶף, נֶעמְט דוּרְךְ דֶעם גוּף מַמָּשׁ.

מַה שֶׁאֵין כֵּן אַ תַּעֲנִית שֶׁל תְּשׁוּבָה (וְכַיּוֹצֵא בָּזֶה) אִיז דאָךְ דאָס נִיט קֵיין (הֲנָאָה) עוֹנֶג פֿאַרְן גוּף (נאָר אַ תַּעֲנוּג (רוּחָנִי) פֿאַר דֶער נְשָׁמָה); אוּן אֲפִֿילוּ ווֶען אַ אִיד הָאט גֶע'פּוֹעֶל'ט אוֹיף זִיךְ אַז זַיין גוּף זאָל נִיט פִֿילְן קֵיין צַעַר פֿון דֶעם תַּעֲנִית, אָדֶער נאָךְ מֶער: אוֹיךְ דֶער גוּף פִֿילְט אַ גֶעוויסְן עוֹנֶג דֶערְפֿון וואָס דִי נְשָׁמָה הָאט תַּעֲנוּג... אִיז דאָךְ דאָס אָבֶּער נִיט קֵיין עוֹנֶג הַגוּף **מִצַּד עַצְמוֹ**... נאָר מִצַּד דֶער **שְׁלִיטָה** (בְּטֶבַע אָדֶער דוּרְךְ עֲבוֹדָה) פֿון דֶער נְשָׁמָה אוֹיפְֿן גוּף **הֵיפֶּךְ** טֶבַע הַגוּף, אֲפִֿילוּ פֿון גוּף צָרוּף וְקָדוֹשׁ.

The Torah command that Shabbat (and holidays) be a time of pleasure for the Jewish people does not mean that only the soul should derive (spiritual) pleasure from Shabbat (or the holiday). The body must (also) derive pleasure from Shabbat (or the holiday). Moreover, the primary objective of the mitzvah [of pleasure] is specifically (to refine) the body.

Because the natural pleasure of the body is in eating and drinking, the Torah says that the obligation to take pleasure [on Shabbat] is through eating. It is only in this way that the pleasure of Shabbat can truly permeate and refine the body.

On the other hand, fasting in order to repent (and so forth) brings no pleasure to the body (although it brings spiritual pleasure to the soul). Even if someone has refined himself to the point that fasting does not cause his body pain, and even provides his body with some satisfaction because his soul is having pleasure ... still, this is not a natural pleasure for the body. ... Rather it is a result of the soul forcing the body to deny its basic nature, and this pertains even to a holy and refined body.

The body should have a pleasant experience just as the soul does on Shabbat.

Continue Learning:
www.myjLi.com/why

Text 24

Rabbi Chaim Vital, *Ets Chayim*, Sha'ar 26, 1:42

Rabbi Chaim Vital
ca. 1542–1620

Lurianic Kabbalist. Rabbi Vital was born in Israel, lived in Safed and Jerusalem, and later in Damascus. He was authorized by his teacher, Rabbi Yitschak Luria, the Arizal, to record his teachings. Acting on this mandate, Vital began arranging his master's teachings in written form, and his many works constitute the foundation of the Lurianic school of Jewish mysticism. His most famous work is *Ets Chaim*.

וְאָמְנָם יָדַעְתָּ גַּם כֵּן כִּי כָּל הַמִּצְוֹת אֵינָם אֶלָּא לְצָרֵף וּלְבָרֵר הַצֶּלֶם וְהַחוֹמֶר. אַךְ הַצּוּרָה אֵינָהּ צְרִיכָה תִּיקוּן כְּלָל. וְלֹא הוּצְרְכָה לְהִתְלַבֵּשׁ בְּצֶלֶם וְחוֹמֶר רַק לְהַמְשִׁיךְ בָּהֶם אוֹר לְתַקְּנָם. וְהָבֵן זֶה מְאֹד. כִּי זֶה טַעַם יְרִידַת הַנְּשָׁמָה בָּעוֹלָם הַזֶּה לְתַקֵּן וּלְבָרֵר.

Know as well that all of the *mitzvot* are only intended to purify the physical [body], but the spiritual [soul] does not need any rectification. The soul did not need to enclothe itself into the body for any other reason than to illuminate the body and to rectify it. Understand this well: The reason the soul descended to this world was to fix [not to be fixed].

Continue your learning experience ONLINE

Visit www.myJLI.com/why6

for insightful and inspiring videos, articles, and readings on this topic.

KEY POINTS

- The soul was placed into a physical body to refine the body. We eat for pleasure on Shabbat and Jewish holidays to allow the body to experience the holiness of the day in a language that it can understand.

- Pleasure for its own sake is an empty, transient experience. Pleasure for a higher purpose, with holy intention, refines and elevates the body and fulfills the purpose of the soul's descent into the body.

ADDITIONAL READINGS

A STRANGER AND A RESIDENT

BY RABBI J. B. SOLOVEITCHIK

The first patriarch, Abraham, introduced himself to the inhabitants of Canaan with the words, "I am a stranger and a resident among you" (Gen. 23:4). Are not these two term mutually exclusive? One is either a stranger, an alien, *or* one is a resident, a citizen. How could Abraham claim both identities for himself?

Abraham's definition of his dual status, we believe, describes with profound accuracy the historical position of the Jew who resides in a predominantly non-Jewish society. He was a resident, like other inhabitants of Canaan, sharing with them a concern for the welfare of society, digging wells, and contributing to the progress of the country in loyalty to its government and institutions. Here, Abraham was clearly a fellow citizen, a patriot among compatriots, joining others in advancing the common welfare. However, there was another aspect, the spiritual, in which Abraham regarded himself as a stranger. His identification and solidarity with his fellow citizens in the secular realm did not imply his readiness to relinquish any aspects of his religious uniqueness. His was a different faith and he was governed by truths, and observances which set him apart from the larger faith community. In this regard, Abraham and his descendants would always remain "strangers."

Like other people, the Jew has more than one identity. He is a part of the larger family of mankind, but he also has a Jewish identity which separates him from others. Each identity imposes upon him particular responsibilities. As a citizen of a pluralistic society, the Jew assumes the social and political obligation to contribute to the general welfare and to combat such common dangers as famine, corruption, disease, and foreign enemies. Where the freedom, dignity, and security of human life are at stake, all people—irrespective of ethnic diversity—are expected to join as brothers in shouldering their responsibilities. These are concerns which transcend all boundaries of difference.

Years ago, the prophet Jeremiah counseled the Jewish inhabitants of Babylonia to "seek the welfare of the city whither I have caused you to be carried away captive, and pray unto the Lord for it; for in its prosperity you shall prosper" (29:7). In Talmudic days, Samuel of Nehardea promulgated the enduring rule that, in civil matters, the law of the land is as binding upon Jews as are the religious commandments of their own faith (Git. 10b).[3] Even under the cruel oppression of Rome, Rabbi Hanina enjoined: "Pray for the peace of the realm, since but for the fear thereof, men would swallow each other alive" (Avot 3:2).

The Jew, however, has another identity which he does not share with the rest of mankind: the covenant with God which was established at Mt. Sinai over 3,000 years ago. All of Jewish history only makes sense in terms of the validity of this covenant, which entrusted the Jewish people of all generations with a particular national destiny and a distinctive religious heritage. This identity involves responsibilities and a way of life which are uniquely Jewish and which, inevitably set the Jew apart from non-Jews. It is particularistic, rather than universalistic. As fellow human beings, the Jew and the non-Jew are members of a broad-based fraternity. Jews, however, must often confront others and insist on their right to be different and not

---

Rabbi Joseph B. Soloveitchik. (1903–1993) Talmudist and philosopher. A scion of a famous Lithuanian rabbinical family, Rabbi Soloveitchik was one of the most influential Jewish personalities, leaders, and thinkers of the 20th century. In 1941, he became professor of Talmud at RIETS—Yeshiva University; in this capacity, he ordained more rabbis than anyone else in Jewish history. Among his published works are *Halakhic Man* and *Lonely Man of Faith*.

to be derogated. The political and social structure of society must not interfere with the religious, cultural, and social institutions which the Jew finds necessary to preserve his separate identity. Here, the emphasis is not on similarity but on difference, not on togetherness but on apartness.

There is an inevitable tension in trying to uphold the two identities. Many Jews maintain that the universal and the covenantal cannot be combined in our relation hip with other faiths. It is absurd, they argue, to claim unity in the secular realm, and the next instant to make an about-face by emphasizing our distinctiveness and separateness in the religious sphere. There is something contradictory and psychologically discordant in maintaining this dual role. They feel the need to choose between being human and being Jewish, and very frequently it is the secular reality which becomes their dominant concern. They become ardent supporters of humanistic and philanthropic causes and they passionately identify with efforts to enhance the moral and aesthetic quality of life, while neglecting the spiritual-religious element as far as they themselves and the Jewish people are concerned.

Among these one-identity proponents one can find many who persist in expressing an unabashed pride in their heritage. Their total immersion in secular affairs has not severed their Jewish connections. Yet they often tend to redefine their Judaism in universal terms, to dilute its aspects of distinctiveness, and to present it as not very dissimilar from the majority faith. Their reformulation of the theology, worship, and rituals of Judaism tends to de-emphasize the religious differences that are deemed to form barriers to full social and political integration.

Such misrepresentation of one's identity betrays cowardice and self-delusion. In fact, both identities are compatible and in most instances, they are inescapable. The secularized Jew who either denies or distorts his faith is purchasing acceptance and integration into the general society at the expense of his intellectual honesty. There is something fraudulent and disingenuous in the effort to one's roots and one's soul. It scars the psyche and, in fact, is rarely

successful. While this group loudly proclaims its exclusive human identity and its denial of all sectarian loyalties, the non-Jewish world adamantly regards all Jews, including the assimilated, as member of a separate and distinct community with its own specialized interests and concerns. The concept of a totally shared humanity is a utopian ideal which is rarely fully achieved.

Where Judaism Differs

From its very inception, Judaism has been strikingly different from other faiths. It has embodied ideas, a way of life, and aspirations for the future which set the Jewish people apart from other groups. Even a rather unfriendly observer, Balaam felt compelled to characterize the Jews as a "people that shall dwell alone, and shall not be reckoned among other nations" (Num. 23.9).

There are three primary areas of distinctiveness without which Judaism would lose its essential character.

Commandments. These are the *mitzvot,* behavioral imperatives, which are derived from the Divine Will. They find their precise formulation in the *Halakhah,* Jewish Law, and have been codified by Torah scholars over the centuries. These commandments are very personal to the observant Jew and they reflect the inner mystery of Israel's commitment to God. They have suggestive meanings and emotional overtones which are known only to the two partners of the covenant. To equate these *mitzvot* with the ritual observances of another faith is to belie the distinctiveness of both. To declare these *mitzvot* as no longer obligatory is to divest Judaism of its primary mark of singularity. Such acts of reductionism are basically fraudulent.

Doctrines. Judaism regards its dogmas and values as verities which are rooted in the Torah tradition and whose authority is ultimately Divine. Our theological and philosophical premises about God, man, and creation are uniquely Jewish and, through the course of centuries, have been preserved despite efforts at dissuasion, ridicule, and torture. We, in modern times, have not been authorized by our millennia-old history to revise these historical attitudes or to trade the fundamentals of our faith for the illusory pursuit of interfaith goodwill. Such would be a betrayal of our great tradition and would, furthermore, produce no practical benefits. A cringing readiness to barter away our identity will never evoke the respect of any who confront us. Only a staunch and unequivocal bearing, reflecting our firm commitment to God and a sense of pride and privilege in being what we are, will impress other faith communities.

Future Expectations. Judaism foresees and eagerly awaits the coming of the Messiah, the vindication of Jewish singularity and chosenness, the ingathering of the dispersed in the Holy Land, the reestablishment of the Temple, the universal acknowledgment of ethical monotheism, and the realization of world peace. These beliefs have sustained us for countless centuries in periods of trial. They are called eschatological expectations, since they represent our vision of the future which we anticipate with exultant certainty. Other faiths define their eschatological expectations in other terms.

Adopting the religious practices of others, the dilution of dogmatic certitudes, and the waiving of eschatological expectations would spell the end of the vibrant and great faith experience of our four-thousand-year-old history.

We have been critical of the one-identity proponents who choose the universal-human response at the expense of their Jewish identity. One can equally question the parochialism of those whose Jewish identity excludes any interest in the larger concerns of society and who seem to live insulated from all that is beyond their immediate group. In all fairness, however, we insist that this self-involvement is frequently due to the fact that, for centuries, the non-Jewish world has reduced its Jewish inhabitants to a subordinate level of bare toleration and has excluded them from equal citizenship and opportunities, regarding them, until modern times, as being bereft of noble instincts and creative abilities. Jews should not be held responsible for this cruelty and blindness, which precluded any possibility of their joining others in advancing the progress of society. When given equal status, they were always ready to fulfill the Divine challenge

to "fill the earth and to subdue it" (Gen. 1:28). As demonstrated in most modern Western societies, Jews, when given the opportunity, have contributed far more than their proportionate share to the welfare of humanity.

The Confrontation of Jacob and Esau

The confrontation of Jacob and Esau, after twenty years of separation, has been interpreted by our Sages and commentators as a paradigm, guiding future generations of Jews in their relation to other groups. Many years earlier, the two brothers had parted under threatening circumstances and now, hopefully mellowed by the passage of time, the two old adversaries were about to meet. The text is remarkably incisive: "And he [Jacob] commanded those at the front, saying, When Esau my brother meets you and asks you, saying: '*Whose* are you and where are you going? And whose [animals] are these ahead of you?' Then you shall answer that they are your servant Jacob's: 'It is a present sent to my lord, Esau, and behold he [Jacob] is right behind us' " (Gen. 32: 18-20).

Jacob anticipated that Esau would ask three questions of him and his family as they approached to take up residence in Canaan. "Whose are you?"—To whom do you pledge your ultimate loyalty? And where are you going?"—What objectives and goals do you seek for yourself in the future? Who is your God and what manner of life and discipline will He require of you and your descendants? These two inquiries relate to Jacob's soul and spiritual identity. Consequently, Jacob commanded his representatives to reply boldly, clearly, and precisely that their souls, their personalities, their metaphysical identities, their spiritual future and social commitment were the private concerns of Jacob. "They are your servant Jacob's," and no human power may interfere or attempt to sever this eternal bond with God which had been established in the covenant with Abraham.

Jacob anticipated, however, that Esau would also ask a third question: "And whose are these [cattle, gifts, etc.] ahead of you?"—Are you ready to contribute your talents. capabilities, and material resources toward the material and cultural welfare of the general society? Are you ready to give of your oxen, goats, camels, and bulls? Are you willing to pay taxes, to develop and industrialize the country? This third question is focused on secular aspects of life. To this question Jacob instructed his agents to answer in the affirmative: "It is a present to my lord, Esau." Yes, we are determined to participate in every civic, scientific, and political enterprise. We feel obligated to enrich society with our creative talents and to be constructive and useful citizens.

This testament handed down to us by Jacob is particularly relevant in our day when, after millennia of separation, various gestures of rapprochement are being made. The identical questions are implicitly being heard: "Whose are you? Where are you going? Whose are these before you?" A millennia-old history demands of us that we meet these challenges courageously and give the same answers which were entrusted to Jacob's messengers several thousand years ago.

Interreligious Discussion and Activity

It is self-evident that meetings between two faith communities are possible only if they are accompanied by a clear assurance that both parties will enjoy equal rights and full religious freedom. No relationship even remotely suggestive of subordination would be tolerable. A democratic confrontation certainly does not demand that we submit to an attitude of self-righteousness on the part of the majority faith community which, while debating whether or not to absolve the Jewish community of some mythical guilt, completely ignores its own historical responsibility for the suffering and martyrdom inflicted upon the few, the weak, and the persecuted.

Two basic ground rules must govern such group contacts. First, Judaism is not to be regarded as validating itself in history by virtue of its being the precursor of another faith. Any suggestion that the historical worth of our faith is to be gauged against the backdrop of another faith, and the mere hint that a revision of basic historical attitudes on our part is anticipated, are incongruous with the fundamentals of religious liberty and freedom of conscience and can only breed discord and suspicion. Such an approach is unacceptable to any self-respecting faith community that is proud of its past, vibrant and active in the present, and determined to live on in the future, and which intends to continue serving God in its own unique way. Only a full appreciation of the singular role, inherent worth, and basic prerogatives of each religious community will help promote the spirit of cooperation among faiths.

Secondly, the discussion should concern itself not with theological but with secular matters of mutual concern. In the private religious realm, each faith has its own "words" and forms which are uniquely intimate, reflecting its philosophical character, and are totally incomprehensible to people of other faiths. The claims of supernatural experiences on the part of each group differ, and an attempt to achieve dialogue on this level can cause more friction than amity, more confusion than clarity, and thereby prove harmful to the interrelationship. The areas of joint concern should be outer-directed, to combat the secularism, materialism, and atheistic negation of religion and religious values which threaten the moral underpinnings of our society. As far as religion is concerned, we should be guided by the words of Micah (4:5): "Let all people walk, each one in the name of its god, and we shall walk in the name of the Lord, our God, for ever and ever."Our approach to the outside world has always been of an ambivalent character. We cooperate with members of other faiths in all fields of human endeavor but, simultaneously, we seek to preserve our distinct integrity which inevitably involves aspects of separateness. This is a paradoxical situation. Yet, paraphrasing the words of our first ancestor, Abraham we are very much residents in general human society while, at the same time, strangers and outsiders in our persistent endeavor to preserve our historic religious identity.

Excerpted from *Reflections of the Rav* [Jewish Agency Publishing Department, Israel, 1979], pp. 169–177.

FUTURE TENSE—THE NEW ANTISEMITISM: WHAT IS IT & HOW DO WE DEAL WITH IT?

BY RABBI JONATHAN SACKS

On 27 January 2000, heads of state or senior representatives of 44 governments met in Stockholm to commit themselves to a continuing programme of Holocaust remembrance and the fight against antisemitism. Barely two years later, synagogues and Jewish schools in France and Belgium were being firebombed, and Jews were being attacked in the streets.

The distinguished Chief Rabbi of France, Rabbi Joseph Sitruk, advised Jews not to wear yarmulkas in the street. The French Jewish intellectual Alain Finkielkraut wrote, 'The hearts of the Jews are heavy. For the first time since the war, they are afraid.' Shmuel Trigano, professor of sociology at the University of Paris, openly questioned whether there was a future for Jews in France. Never again had become ever again.

On 28 February 2002 I gave my first speech on the new antisemitism. Never before had I spoken on the subject. I had grown up without a single experience of antisemitism. I believed, and still do, that the whole enterprise of basing Jewish identity on memories of persecution was a mistake. The distinguished Holocaust historian Lucy Dawidowicz reached the same conclusion at the end of her life. She warned of the danger of a whole generation of children growing up knowing about the Greeks and how they lived, the Romans and how they lived, the Jews and how they died. I wrote *Radical Then, Radical Now*, specifically to focus Jewish identity away from death to life, suffering to celebration, grief to joy.

Rabbi Jonathan Sacks, PhD. (1948–) Former chief rabbi of the United Kingdom. Rabbi Sacks attended Cambridge University and received his doctorate from King's College, London. A prolific and influential author, his books include *Will We Have Jewish Grandchildren?* and *The Dignity of Difference*. He received the Jerusalem Prize in 1995 for his contributions to enhancing Jewish life in the Diaspora, was knighted and made a life peer in 2005, and became Baron Sacks of Aldridge in 2009.

The return of antisemitism, after sixty years of Holocaust education, interfaith dialogue and antiracist legislation is a major event in the history of the world. Far-sighted historians like Bernard Lewis and Robert Wistrich had been sounding the warning since the 1980s. Already in the 1990s, Harvard literary scholar Ruth Wisse argued that antisemitism was the most successful ideology of the twentieth century. German fascism, she said, came and went. Soviet communism came and went. Antisemitism came and stayed.

It is wrong to exaggerate. We are not now where Jews were in the 1930s. Nor are Jews today what our ancestors were: defenceless, powerless and without a collective home. The State of Israel has transformed the situation for Jews everywhere. What is necessary now is simply to understand the situation and sound a warning. That is what Moses Hess did in 1862, Judah Leib Pinsker in 1882 and Theodor Herzl in 1896: 71, 51 and 37 years respectively before Hitler's rise to power. To understand is to begin to know how to respond, with open eyes and without fear.

Today's antisemitism is a new phenomenon, continuous with, yet significantly different from the past. To fathom the transformation, we must first define what antisemitism is. In the past Jews were hated because they were rich and because they were poor; because they were capitalists (Marx) and because they were communists (Hitler); because they kept to themselves and because they infiltrated everywhere; because they held tenaciously to a superstitious faith (Voltaire) and because they were rootless cosmopolitans who believed nothing (Stalin).

Antisemitism is not an ideology, a coherent set of beliefs. It is, in fact, an endless stream of contradictions. The best way of understanding it is to see it as a virus. Viruses attack the human body, but the body itself has an immensely sophisticated defence, the human immune system. How then do viruses survive and flourish? By mutating. Antisemitism mutates, and in so doing, defeats the immune systems set up by cultures to protect themselves against hatred. There have been three such mutations in the past two thousand years, and we are living through the fourth.

The first took place with the birth of Christianity. Before then there had been many Hellenistic writers who were hostile to Jews. But they were also dismissive of other non-Hellenistic peoples. The Greeks called them barbarians. There was nothing personal in their attacks on Jews. This was not antisemitism. It was xenophobia.

This changed with Christianity. As was later to happen with Islam, the founders of the new faith, largely based on Judaism itself, believed that Jews would join the new dispensation and were scandalized when they did not. Jews were held guilty of not recognizing—worst still, of being complicit in the death of—the messiah. A strand of Judeophobia entered Christianity in some of its earliest texts, and became a fully-fledged genre, the 'Adversos Judaeos' literature, in the days of the Church Fathers. From here on, Jews—not non-Christians in general—became the target of what Jules Isaac called the 'teaching of contempt'.

The second mutation began in 1096 when the Crusaders, on their way to conquer Jerusalem, stopped to massacre Jewish communities in Worms, Speyer and Mainz, the first major European pogrom. In 1144 in Norwich there was the first Blood Libel, a myth that still exists today in parts of the Middle East. Religious Judeophobia became demonic. Jews were no longer just the people who rejected Christianity. They began to be seen as a malevolent force, killing children, desecrating the host, poisoning wells and spreading the plague. There were forced conversions, inquisitions, burnings at the stake, staged public disputations, book burnings and expulsions. Europe had become a 'persecuting society'.

We can date the third mutation to 1879 when the German journalist Wilhelm Marr coined a new word: anti-Semitism. The fact that he needed to do so tells us that this was a new phenomenon. It emerged in an age of Enlightenment, the secular nation state, liberalism and emancipation. Religious prejudice was deemed to be a thing of the past. The new hatred had therefore to justify itself on quite different grounds, namely race. This was a fateful development, because you can change your religion. You cannot change your race. Christians could work for the conversion of the Jews. Racists could only work for the extermination of the Jews. So the Holocaust was born. Sixty years after the word came the deed.

Today we are living through the fourth mutation. Unlike its predecessors, the new antisemitism focuses not on Judaism as a religion, nor on Jews as a race, but on Jews as a nation. It consists of three propositions. First, alone of the 192 nations making up the United Nations, Jews are not entitled to a state of their own. As Amos Oz noted: in the 1930s, antisemites declared, 'Jews to Palestine'. Today they shout, 'Jews out of Palestine'. He said: they don't want us to be there; they don't want us to be here; they don't want us to be.

The second is that Jews or the State of Israel (the terms are often used interchangeably) are responsible for the evils of the world, from AIDS to global warming. All the old anti-Semitic myths have been recycled, from the Blood Libel to the Protocols of the Elders of Zion, still a best-seller in many parts of the world. The third is that all Jews are Zionists and therefore legitimate objects of attack. The bomb attacks on synagogues in Istanbul and Djerba, the arson attacks on Jewish schools in Europe, and the almost fatal stabbing of a young yeshiva student on a bus in North London in October 2000, were on Jewish targets, not Israeli ones. The new antisemitism is an attack on Jews as a nation seeking to exist as a nation like every other on the face of the earth, with rights of self-governance and self-defence.

How did it penetrate the most sophisticated immune system ever constructed—the entire panoply of international measures designed to ensure that nothing like the Holocaust would ever happen again, from the United Nations Universal Declaration of Human Rights (1948) to the Stockholm declaration of 2000? The answer lies in the mode of self-justification. Most people at most times feel a residual guilt at hating the innocent. Therefore antisemitism has always had to find legitimation in the most prestigious source of authority at any given time.

In the first centuries of the Common Era, and again in the Middle Ages, this was religion. That is why Judeophobia took the form of religious doctrine. In the nineteenth century, religion had lost prestige, and the supreme authority was now science. Racial antisemitism was duly based on two pseudo-sciences, social Darwinism (the idea that in society, as in nature, the strong survive by eliminating the weak) and the so-called scientific study of race. By the late twentieth century, science had lost its prestige, having given us the power to destroy life on earth. Today the supreme source of legitimacy is human rights. That is why Jews (or the Jewish state) are accused of the five primal sins against human rights: racism, apartheid, ethnic cleansing, attempted genocide and crimes against humanity.

That is where we are. How then shall we respond? There are three key messages, the first to Jews, the second to antisemites, and the third to our fellow human beings in this tense and troubled age. As Jews we must understand that we cannot fight antisemitism alone. The victim cannot cure the crime. The hated cannot cure the hate. Jews cannot defeat antisemitism. Only the cultures that give rise to it can do so.

European Jews in the nineteenth and early twentieth century made one of the most tragic mistakes in history. They said: Jews cause antisemitism, therefore they can cure it. They did everything possible. They said, 'People hate us because we are different. So we will stop being different.' They gave up item after item of Judaism. They integrated, they assimilated, they married out, they hid their identity. This failed to diminish antisemitism by one iota. All it did was to debilitate and demoralize Jews.

We need allies. Jews have enemies but we also have friends and we must cultivate more. I have helped lead the fight against Islamophobia; I ask Muslims to fight Judeophobia. I will fight for the right of Christians throughout the world to live their faith without fear; but we need Christians to fight for the right of Jews to live their faith without fear.

The most important thing Jews can do to fight antisemitism is never, ever to internalize it. That is what is wrong in making the history of persecution the basis of Jewish identity. For three thousand years Jews defined themselves as a people loved by God. Only in the nineteenth century did they begin to define themselves as the people hated by gentiles. There is no sane future along that road. The best psychological defence against antisemitism is the saying of Rav Nachman of Bratslav: 'The whole world is a very narrow bridge; the main thing is never to be afraid.'

To antisemites and their fellow travelers we must be candid. Hate destroys the hated, but it also destroys the hater. It is no accident that antisemitism is the weapon of choice of tyrants and totalitarian regimes. It deflects internal criticism away by projecting it onto an external scapegoat. It is deployed in country after country to direct attention away from real internal problems of poverty, unemployment and underachievement. Antisemitism is used to sustain regimes without human rights, the rule of law, an independent judiciary, a free press, liberty of association or accountable government. One truth resounds through the pages of history: To be free you have to let go of hate. Those driven by hate are enemies of freedom. There is no exception.

Finally to all of us together, we must say: Jews have been hated throughout history because they were different. To be sure, everyone is different; but Jews more than most fought for the right to be different. Under a succession of empires, and centuries of dispersion, Jews were the only people who for more than two thousand years refused to convert to the dominant religion or assimilate into the dominant culture. That is why antisemitism is a threat not just to Jews but to humanity.

For we are all different. After Babel there is no single culture. Instead there is a multiplicity of languages and identities, each one of which is precious. Judaism is the world's most sustained protest against empires, because imperialism is the attempt to impose a single truth, culture or faith on a plural world. God, said the rabbis, makes everyone in His image, yet He makes everyone different to teach us to respect difference. And since difference is constitutive of humanity, a world that has no space for difference has no space for humanity. That is why a resurgence of antisemitism has always been an early warning of an assault on freedom itself. It is so today.

We must find allies in the fight against hate. For though it begins with Jews, ultimately it threatens us all.

"Future Tense—The New Antisemitism: What Is It & How Do We Deal with It?" http://www.rabbisacks.org/future-tense-the-new-antisemitism-what-is-it-how-do-we-deal-with-it-published-in-the-jewish-chronicle/ December, 2015.
Reprinted with permission of the author.

ACKNOWLEDGMENTS

Our sages taught: If your son is capable, he should ask. . . . If not,
ask the question of yourself. Even two scholars who are proficient
in the laws of Passover should ask one another,
"Why is this night different from all other nights?"
—Talmud, *Pesachim* 116a

"Why?"

This most elementary of queries serves as an integral tool of Jewish education and fuels our lifelong pursuit of study. Education is not indoctrination, nor can genuine study flourish under blind compliance. "Why?" is a
hallmark of healthy curiosity, of wonder and reflection. As demonstrated
by the Talmud's countless queries, the timeless and cherished path to Jewish scholarship is not to silence minds or hearts, but to flex their muscles
in our service of G-d. The solutions we discover as a result of an unceasing
quest for knowledge are the bricks and mortar of the sophisticated structure of understanding and analysis that we build upon a bedrock of faith.

With this in mind, the Rohr Jewish Learning Institute (JLI) undertook the
ambitious task of creating *The Jewish Course of Why*, a learning experience that provokes discussion and offers perspectives on fifty of the most
popular and interesting "why" questions that Jews today ask about Jewish
theology, identity, history, law, and custom.

This course is unique inasmuch our students guided its development. We
selected the questions from those submitted by JLI students from around
the world, representing virtually every level of involvement in Jewish life.
We are grateful to all of these individuals who helped shape this course—a
partial list of whom follows these acknowledgments.

We extend our appreciation to **Rabbis Mordechai Dinerman** and **Naftali Silberberg**, who direct the JLI Curriculum Department and the Flagship editorial team; to **Rabbi Dr. Shmuel Klatzkin**, JLI's senior editor; and to **Rabbi Zalman Abraham**, charged with JLI strategic branding and marketing, who skillfully provides the vision for branding JLI course offerings.

We are grateful to **Rabbi Lazer Gurkow** for his extensive research and for composing many of the course's components; to **Chava Shapiro** for her precise and superb editorial review of the entire course; and to **Rabbis Avraham Bergstein, Yaakov Gerson, Eli Raksin,** and **Shmuel Super** of **JLI's Machon Shmuel: The Sami Rohr Research Institute** for their meticulous research that greatly aided the preparation of this course.

We are thankful to **Rivkah Slonim, Rabbi Ari Sollish,** and **Rabbi Avrohom Sternberg**, members of the JLI editorial board, for providing countless useful suggestions that enhanced the course and ensured its suitability for a wide range of students. We also extend our thanks to **Rabbis Menachem Feldman** and **Chaim Hanoka**, who, together with the editorial board, helped select the final fifty questions from the long list of submissions. We are grateful to **Rabbi Yossi Jacobson**, **Rabbi Manis Friedman,** and **Rivkah Slonim** for agreeing to be interviewed by the JLI editorial team in preparation for this course.

We thank **Zeldy Friedman** and **Rabbi Levi Kaplan** for managing the numerous components of course production. We are grateful to **Mendel Schtroks** for designing the textbooks with taste, expertise, and patience, and **Mendel Sirota** for directing book production. **Lynne Clamage**, **Rabbi Shmuel Super, Ya'akovah Weber,** and **Rachel Witty** enhanced the quality and professionalism of the course with their copyediting and proofreading.

Mushka Pruss and **Rivka Rapoport** designed the course's aesthetically pleasing PowerPoints. **Moshe** and **Getzy Raskin** headed the production team charged with producing the videos for this course. The video scripts were masterfully created by **Rabbi Yaakov Paley**.

We acknowledge the hard work and efforts of JLI's support staff and administration, whose contributions to this course were critical, but whose names are too many to enumerate here.

We are immensely grateful for the encouragement of JLI's visionary chairman and vice-chairman of Merkos L'Inyonei Chinuch—Lubavitch World Headquarters, **Rabbi Moshe Kotlarsky.** Rabbi Kotlarsky has been highly instrumental in building the infrastructure for the expansion of Chabad's international network, and is the architect of scores of initiatives and services to help Chabad representatives across the globe succeed in their mission. We are blessed to have the unwavering support of JLI's principal benefactor, **Mr. George Rohr,** who is fully invested in our work and continues to be instrumental in JLI's monumental expansion.

The commitment and sage direction of JLI's dedicated executive board—**Rabbis Chaim Block, Hesh Epstein, Ronnie Fine, Yosef Gansburg, Shmuel Kaplan, Yisrael Rice,** and **Avrohom Sternberg**—and the countless hours they devote to the development of JLI, are what drives the vision, growth, and flourishing of the organization.

Finally, JLI represents an incredible partnership of more than 1000 *shluchim* and *shluchot* in 960 locations across the globe, who give of their time and talent to further Jewish adult education. We thank them for generously sharing feedback and making suggestions that steer JLI's development and growth. They are our most valuable critics and our most cherished contributors.

Inspired by the call of the **Lubavitcher Rebbe,** of righteous memory, it is the mandate of the Rohr JLI to encourage all Jews throughout the world to experience and participate in their precious heritage of Torah learning. May this course succeed in fulfilling this sacred charge!

On behalf of the Rohr Jewish Learning Institute,

Rabbi Efraim Mintz, Executive Director
Rabbi Yisrael Rice, Chairman, Editorial Board
24 Teves, 5776

SPECIAL THANKS

We thank the thousands of JLI students from around the world who submitted questions for *The Jewish Course of Why*. The questions selected for inclusion in this course were submitted by the following individuals:

Chris Ahrens
Dallastown, PA

Alan Berkower
Great Neck, NY

Karen Bertilson
Flagstaff, AZ

Donna Lee Cohn,
Boynton Beach, FL

John de Haas
Richmond, BC Canada

Raymond Deneckere
Madison, WI

Mira Dessy
The Woodlands, TX

Rodolfo Eichberg
Tampa, FL

Alta Franco
Portland, OR

Sean Friesen
Victoria, BC Canada

Alex Ginsburg
Memphis, TN

Ram Goren
Wilmington, DE

Bruce Hoffen
Lake Mary, FL

Leo Hmelnitsky
Walnut Creek, CA

Gary Ickowicz
Teaneck, NJ

Randi Jablin
Scottsdale, AZ

Mariko Kawaguchi
Burlingame, CA

Karen King
Plantation, FL

Boruch Tuvye Kohn
Laurel, MD

Shaindee Kreit
Sherman Oaks, CA

Roni Leibovitch
West Bloomfield, MI

Heather Leibowitz
Cherry Hill, NJ

Frances Ludmer
Calgary, Canada

Max Minshull
Palos Verdes Estates, CA

Stephen Modell
Ann Arbor, MI USA

Michael Morris,
Rockville, MD

Lisbeth Ornstein
Pittsford, NY

Naomi Pless
Rochester, NY

Felicia Sampson
Truckee, CA

Melinda Snyder
Farmington Hills, MI

Myrna Solganick
Middleton, WI

Brenna Stein
Philadelphia, PA

Hal Switkay
Avondale, PA

Marianne Tettlebaum
Little Rock, AR

Julie Valinsky
Middleton, WI

Joel Verstaendig
Plainview, NY

Barbara Whatley
Owings Mills, MD

Lauren Weiss
Glenview, IL

Steve Weinstein
Milwaukee, WI

Edyce Winokur
Sprinfield, MA

Eugene Yelkin
Cherry Hill, NJ

Cheryl Zack
Calgary, AB Canada

JLI Teens
in partnership with
CTeeN: Chabad Teen Network

Rabbi Chaim Block
Chairman
San Antonio, TX

Rabbi Elya Silfen
Director

Rabbi Michoel Shapiro
Editor in Chief

Mrs. Nechi Gudelsky
Program Administrators

Advisory Board
Rabbi Mendy Cohen
Merion Station, PA

Rabbi Yitzi Hein
Pittsford, NY

Rabbi Zalman Marcus
Mission Viejo, CA

Land and Spririt
Israel Experience

Shmuly Karp
Director

Steering Committee
Rabbi Yechiel Baitelman
Rabbi Dovid Flinkenstein
Rabbi Chanoch Kaplan
Rabbi Levi Klein
Rabbi Mendy Mangel
Rabbi Sholom Raichik
Rabbi Avi Richler

Machon Shmuel
The Sami Rohr Research Institute

Rabbi Avrohom Bergstein
Dean

Rabbinic Advisory Board
Rabbi Chaim Rapoport
Rabbi Gedalya Oberlander
Rabbi Chaim Schapiro
Rabbi Levi Yitzchak Raskin
Rabbi Mordechai Farkash
Rabbi Moshe Miller
Rabbi Yossi Yaffe

Research Fellows
Rabbi Yehudah Altein
Rabbi Binyomin Bitton
Rabbi Moshe Chanunu
Rabbi Yaakov Gershon
Rabbi Nesanel Loeb
Rabbi Mendel Mellul
Rabbi Zushe Wilmowsky
Rabbi Eliezer Raksin

Mishnah Project
Rabbi Elya Silfen
Director

myShiur:
Advanced Learning Initiative

Rabbi Shmuel Kaplan
Chairman
Potomac, MD

Rabbi Levi Kaplan
Director

National Jewish Retreat
Rabbi Hesh Epstein
Chairman
Columbia, SC

Mrs. Shaina B. Mintz
Administrator

Bruce Backman
Coordinator

Rabbi Mendy Weg
Founding Director

Rochelle Katzman
Program Coordinator

Shmuly Karp
Shluchim Liaison

Rosh Chodesh Society
Rabbi Shmuel Kaplan
Chairman
Baltimore, MD

Mrs. Shaindy Jacobson
Director

Mrs. Chava Shapiro
Associate Director

Mrs. Fraydee Kessler
Administrator

Steering Committee
Mrs. Malka Bitton
Mrs. Shula Bryski
Mrs. Rochel Holzkenner
Mrs. Devorah Kornfeld
Mrs. Chana Lipskar
Mrs. Ahuva New
Mrs. Binie Tenenbaum

Sinai Scholars Society
in partnership with Chabad on Campus

Rabbi Menachem Schmidt
Chairman
Philadelphia, PA

Rabbi Dubi Rabinowitz
Director

Devorah Leah Notik
Associate Director

Mrs. Devorah Zlatopolsky
Administrator

Executive Committee
Rabbi Moshe Chaim Dubrowski
Rabbi Yossy Gordon
Rabbi Efraim Mintz
Rabbi Menachem Schmidt
Rabbi Nechemia Vogel
Rabbi Eitan Webb
Rabbi Avi Weinstein
Dr. Chana Silberstein

Curriculum Committee
Rabbi Zalman Bluming
Rabbi Shlomie Chein
Rabbi Shlomo Rothstien

Steering Committee
Rabbi Shlomie Chein
Rabbi Moshe Laib Gray
Rabbi Dovid Gurevitch
Rabbi Mendel Matusof
Rabbi Yisroel Wilhelm

TorahCafe.com
Online Learning

Rabbi Levi Kaplan
Director

Rabbi Yisroel Silman
Creative Director

Rabbi Simcha Backman
Dr. Michael Kigel
Consultants

Rabbi Mendy Elishevitz
Rabbi Elchonon Korenblit
Website Development

Moshe Levin
Mendel Serebryanski
Content Manager

Avrohom Shimon Ezagui
Rafi Roston
Filming Crew

Simcha Raskin
Yossi Rubin
Yossi Wagshul
Video Editing

Torah Studies
Rabbi Yosef Gansburg
Chairman
Toronto, ON

Rabbi Meir Hecht
Founding Director

Rabbi Zalman Margolin
Director

Rabbi Ahrele Loschak
Managing Editor

Steering Committee
Rabbi Levi Fogelman
Rabbi Yaacov Halperin
Rabbi Nechemia Schusterman
Rabbi Ari Sollish

JLI Central
Founding Department Heads

Rabbi Mendel Bell
Brooklyn, NY

Rabbi Zalman Charytan
Acworth, GA

Rabbi Mendel Druk
Cancun, Mexico

Rabbi Menachem Gansburg
Toronto, ON

Rabbi Yoni Katz
Brooklyn, NY

Rabbi Chaim Zalman Levy
New Rochelle, NY

Rabbi Benny Rapoport
Clarks Summit, PA

Dr. Chana Silberstein
Ithaca, NY

Rabbi Elchonon Tenenbaum
Napa Valley, CA

Rohr **JLI** Faculty

ALABAMA
BIRMINGHAM
Rabbi Yossi Friedman
205.970.0100

ARIZONA
CHANDLER
Rabbi Mendel Deitsch
480.855.4333

FLAGSTAFF
Rabbi Dovie Shapiro
928.255.5756

ORO VALLEY
Rabbi Ephraim Zimmerman
520.477.8672

PHOENIX
Rabbi Zalman Levertov
Rabbi Yossi Friedman
602.944.2753

SCOTTSDALE
Rabbi Yossi Levertov
480.998.1410

ARKANSAS
LITTLE ROCK
Rabbi Pinchus Ciment
501.217.0053

CALIFORNIA
AGOURA HILLS
Rabbi Moshe Bryski
Rabbi Shlomo Bistritsky
818.991.0991

BEL AIR
Rabbi Chaim Mentz
310.475.5311

BEVERLY HILLS
Rabbi Chaim I. Sperlin
310.734.9079

BURBANK
Rabbi Shmuly Kornfeld
818.954.0070

CARLSBAD
Rabbi Yeruchem Eilfort
Mrs. Nechama Eilfort
760.943.8891

CENTURY CITY
Rabbi Tzemach Cunin
310.860.1260

CHATSWORTH
Rabbi Yossi Spritzer
818.718.0777

CONTRA COSTA
Rabbi Dovber Berkowitz
925.937.4101

CORONADO
Rabbi Eli Fradkin
619.365.4728

ENCINO
Rabbi Joshua Gordon
Rabbi Aryeh Herzog
818.784.9986

FOLSOM
Rabbi Yossi Grossbaum
916.608.9811

GLENDALE
Rabbi Simcha Backman
818.240.2750

HUNTINGTON BEACH
Rabbi Aron Berkowitz
714.846.2285

IRVINE
Rabbi Alter Tenenbaum
Rabbi Elly Andrusier
949.786.5000

LA JOLLA
Rabbi Baruch Shalom Ezagui
858.455.5433

LAGUNA BEACH
Rabbi Elimelech Gurevitch
949.499.0770

LOMITA
Rabbi Eli Hecht
Rabbi Sholom Pinson
310.326.8234

LONG BEACH
Rabbi Abba Perelmuter
562.621.9828

LOS ANGELES
Rabbi Leibel Korf
323.660.5177

MARINA DEL REY
Rabbi Danny Yiftach-Hashem
Rabbi Dovid Yiftach
310.859.0770

NORTH HOLLYWOOD
Rabbi Nachman Abend
818.989.9539

NORTHRIDGE
Rabbi Eli Rivkin
818.368.3937

PACIFIC PALISADES
Rabbi Zushe Cunin
310.454.7783

PALO ALTO
Rabbi Yosef Levin
Rabbi Ber Rosenblatt
650.424.9800

PASADENA
Rabbi Chaim Hanoka
626.564.8820

RANCHO MIRAGE
Rabbi Shimon H. Posner
760.770.7785

RANCHO PALOS VERDES
Rabbi Yitzchok Magalnic
310.544.5544

RANCHO S. FE
Rabbi Levi Raskin
858.756.7571

REDONDO BEACH
Rabbi Yossi Mintz
Rabbi Zalman Gordon
310.214.4999

S. BARBARA
Rabbi Mendel Loschak
CHAPTER FOUNDED BY
RABBI YOSEF LOSCHAK, OBM
805.683.1544

S. CLEMENTE
Rabbi Menachem M. Slavin
949.489.0723

S. DIEGO
Rabbi Motte Fradkin
858.547.0076

S. FRANCISCO
Rabbi Peretz Mochkin
415.571.8770

S. LUIS OBISPO
Rabbi Chaim Leib Hilel
805.706.0256

S. MONICA
Rabbi Boruch Rabinowitz
310.394.5699

S. RAFAEL
Rabbi Yisrael Rice
415.492.1666

South Lake Tahoe
Rabbi Mordechai Richler
530.314.7677

Stockton
Rabbi Avremel Brod
209.952.2081

Studio City
Rabbi Yossi Baitelman
818.508.6633

Thousand Oaks
Rabbi Chaim Bryski
805.493.7776

Tustin
Rabbi Yehoshua Eliezrie
714.508.2150

Ventura
Rabbi Yakov Latowicz
Mrs. Sarah Latowicz
805.658.7441

West Los Angeles
Rabbi Mordechai Zaetz
424.652.8742

Yorba Linda
Rabbi Dovid Eliezrie
714.693.0770

COLORADO
Aspen
Rabbi Mendel Mintz
970.544.3770

Denver
Rabbi Mendel Popack
720.515.4337

Rabbi Yossi Serebryanski
303.744.9699

Fort Collins
Rabbi Yerachmiel Gorelik
970.407.1613

Highlands Ranch
Rabbi Avraham Mintz
303.694.9119

Longmont
Rabbi Yakov Dovid Borenstein
303.678.7595

Vail
Rabbi Dovid Mintz
970.476.7887

Westminster
Rabbi Benjy Brackman
303.429.5177

CONNECTICUT
Fairfield
Rabbi Shlame Landa
203.373.1118

Greenwich
Rabbi Yossi Deren
Rabbi Menachem Feldman
203.629.9059

Milford
Rabbi Schneur Wilhelm
203.878.4569

New London
Rabbi Avrohom Sternberg
860.437.8000

Stamford
Rabbi Yisrael Deren
Rabbi Levi Mendelow
203.3.CHABAD

West Hartford
Rabbi Yosef Gopin
Rabbi Shaya Gopin
860.659.2422

Westport
Rabbi Yehuda L. Kantor
Mrs. Dina Kantor
203.226.8584

DELAWARE
Wilmington
Rabbi Chuni Vogel
302.529.9900

FLORIDA
Bal Harbour
Rabbi Dov Schochet
305.868.1411

Boca Raton
Rabbi Zalman Bukiet
Rabbi Moishe Denburg
Rabbi Arele Gopin
561.417.7797

Boynton Beach
Rabbi Yosef Yitzchok Raichik
561.732.4633

Bradenton
Rabbi Menachem Bukiet
941.388.9656

Cape Coral
Rabbi Yossi Labkowski
239.541.1777

Coral Springs
Rabbi Yankie Denburg
954.471.8646

Delray Beach
Rabbi Sholom Ber Korf
561.496.6228

East Boca Raton
Rabbi Ruvi New
561.417.7797

Fleming Island
Rabbi Shmuly Feldman
904.290.1017

Fort Lauderdale
Rabbi Yitzchok Naparstek
954.568.1190

Fort Myers
Rabbi Yitzchok Minkowicz
Mrs. Nechama Minkowicz
239.433.7708

Hallandale Beach
Rabbi Mordy Feiner
954.458.1877

Hollywood
Rabbi Leizer Barash
954.965.9933

Rabbi Leibel Kudan
954.801.3367

Kendall
Rabbi Yossi Harlig
305.234.5654

Lakeland
Rabbi Moshe Lazaros
863.510.5968

Lake Mary
Rabbi Yanky Majesky
407.878.3011

Maitland
Rabbi Sholom Dubov
Rabbi Levik Dubov
470.644.2500

Ocala
Rabbi Yossi Hecht
352.291.2218

Orlando
Rabbi Yosef Konikov
407.354.3660

Ormond Beach
Rabbi Shmuel Konikov
386.672.9300

Palm Beach Gardens
Rabbi Dovid Vigler
561.624.2223

Palmetto Bay
Rabbi Zalman Gansburg
786.282.0413

Plantation
Rabbi Pinchas Taylor
954.644.9177

Ponte Vedra Beach
Rabbi Nochum Kurinsky
904.543.9301

Sarasota
Rabbi Chaim Shaul Steinmetz
941.925.0770

Satellite Beach
Rabbi Zvi Konikov
321.777.2770

South Palm Beach
Rabbi Leibel Stolik
561.889.3499

South Tampa
Rabbi Mendy Dubrowski
813.287.1795

Share the **Rohr JLI** experience with friends and relatives worldwide

SUNNY ISLES BEACH
Rabbi Alexander Kaller
305.803.5315

WESTON
Rabbi Yisroel Spalter
954.349.6565

WEST PALM BEACH
Rabbi Yoel Gancz
561.659.7770

VENICE
Rabbi Sholom Ber Schmerling
941.493.2770

GEORGIA
ALPHARETTA
Rabbi Hirshy Minkowicz
770.410.9000

ATLANTA
Rabbi Yossi New
Rabbi Isser New
404.843.2464

ATLANTA: INTOWN
Rabbi Eliyahu Schusterman
Rabbi Ari Sollish
404.898.0434

GWINNETT
Rabbi Yossi Lerman
678.595.0196

MARIETTA
Rabbi Ephraim Silverman
770.565.4412

IDAHO
BOISE
Rabbi Mendel Lifshitz
208.853.9200

ILLINOIS
CHAMPAIGN
Rabbi Dovid Tiechtel
217.355.8672

CHICAGO
Rabbi Meir Hecht
312.714.4655

Rabbi Dovid Kotlarsky
773.495.7127

Rabbi Yosef Moscowitz
773.772.3770

Rabbi Levi Notik
773.274.5123

CHICAGO-HYDE PARK
Rabbi Yossi Brackman
773.955.8672

ELGIN
Rabbi Mendel Shemtov
847.440.4486

GLENVIEW
Rabbi Yishaya Benjaminson
847.998.9896

HIGHLAND PARK
Mrs. Michla Schanowitz
847.266.0770

NAPERVILLE
Rabbi Mendy Goldstein
630.778.9770

NORTHBROOK
Rabbi Meir Moscowitz
847.564.8770

OAK PARK
Rabbi Yitzchok Bergstein
708.524.1530

PEORIA
Rabbi Eli Langsam
309.692.2250

ROCKFORD
Rabbi Yecheskel Rothman
815.596.0032

SKOKIE
Rabbi Yochanan Posner
847.677.1770

VERNON HILLS
Rabbi Shimmy Susskind
847.984.2919

WILMETTE
Rabbi Dovid Flinkenstein
847.251.7707

INDIANA
INDIANAPOLIS
Rabbi Mendel Schusterman
317.251.5573

KANSAS
OVERLAND PARK
Rabbi Mendy Wineberg
913.649.4852

KENTUCKY
LOUISVILLE
Rabbi Avrohom Litvin
502.459.1770

LOUISIANA
METAIRIE
Rabbi Yossie Nemes
Rabbi Mendel Ceitlin
504.454.2910

MARYLAND
BALTIMORE
Rabbi Elchonon Lisbon
410.358.4787

Rabbi Velvel Belinsky
CLASSES IN RUSSIAN
410.764.5000

BEL AIR
Rabbi Yekusiel Schusterman
443.353.9718

BETHESDA
Rabbi Bentzion Geisinsky
Rabbi Sender Geisinsky
301.913.9777

COLUMBIA
Rabbi Hillel Baron
Rabbi Yosef Chaim Sufrin
410.740.2424

FREDERICK
Rabbi Boruch Labkowski
301.996.3659

GAITHERSBURG
Rabbi Sholom Raichik
301.926.3632

OLNEY
Rabbi Bentzy Stolik
301.660.6770

OWINGS MILLS
Rabbi Nochum H. Katsenelenbogen
410.356.5156

POTOMAC
Rabbi Mendel Bluming
301.983.4200

Rabbi Mendel Kaplan
301.983.1485

ROCKVILLE
Rabbi Moishe Kavka
301.836.1242

MASSACHUSETTS
CAPE COD
Rabbi Yekusiel Alperowitz
508.775.2324

LONGMEADOW
Rabbi Yakov Wolff
413.567.8665

NEWTON
Rabbi Shalom Ber Prus
617.244.1200

MILFORD
Rabbi Mendy Kievman
508.473.1299

SUDBURY
Rabbi Yisroel Freeman
978.443.3691

SWAMPSCOTT
Mrs. Layah Lipsker
781.581.3833

MICHIGAN
ANN ARBOR
Rabbi Aharon Goldstein
734.995.3276

GRAND RAPIDS
Rabbi Mordechai Haller
616.957.0770

WEST BLOOMFIELD
Rabbi Elimelech Silberberg
248.855.6170

MINNESOTA
MINNETONKA
Rabbi Mordechai Grossbaum
952.929.9922

S. PAUL
Rabbi Shneur Zalman Bendet
651.998.9298

MISSOURI
CHESTERFIELD
Rabbi Avi Rubenfeld
314.258.3401

S. LOUIS
Rabbi Yosef Landa
314.725.0400

MONTANA
BOZEMAN
Rabbi Chaim Shaul Bruk
406.585.8770

NEVADA
SUMMERLIN
Rabbi Yisroel Schanowitz
Rabbi Tzvi Bronchtain
702.855.0770

NEW JERSEY
BASKING RIDGE
Rabbi Mendy Herson
908.604.8844

CHERRY HILL
Rabbi Mendy Mangel
856.874.1500

CLINTON
Rabbi Eli Kornfeld
908.623.7000

FAIR LAWN
Rabbi Avrohom Bergstein
718.839.5296

FANWOOD
Rabbi Avrohom Blesofsky
908.790.0008

FORT LEE
Rabbi Meir Konikov
201.886.1238

FRANKLIN LAKES
Rabbi Chanoch Kaplan
201.848.0449

HASKELL
Rabbi Mendy Gurkov
201.696.7609

HILLSBOROUGH
Rabbi Shmaya Krinsky
908.874.0444

HOLMDEL
Rabbi Shmaya Galperin
732.772.1998

MADISON
Rabbi Shalom Lubin
973.377.0707

MANALAPAN
Rabbi Boruch Chazanow
Rabbi Levi Wolosow
732.972.3687

MOUNTAIN LAKES
Rabbi Levi Dubinsky
973.551.1898

MULLICA HILL
Rabbi Avrohom Richler
856.733.0770

NORTH BRUNSWICK
Rabbi Levi Azimov
732.398.9492

OLD TAPPAN
Rabbi Mendy Lewis
201.767.4008

ROCKAWAY
Rabbi Asher Herson
Rabbi Mordechai Baumgarten
973.625.1525

TEANECK
Rabbi Ephraim Simon
201.907.0686

TENAFLY
Rabbi Mordechai Shain
Rabbi Yitzchak Gershovitz
201.871.1152

TOMS RIVER
Rabbi Moshe Gourarie
732.349.4199

WEST ORANGE
Rabbi Mendy Kasowitz
973.486.2362

WOODCLIFF LAKE
Rabbi Dov Drizin
201.476.0157

NEW YORK
BEDFORD
Rabbi Arik Wolf
914.666.6065

BINGHAMTON
Mrs. Rivkah Slonim
607.797.0015

BRIGHTON BEACH
Rabbi Zushe Winner
Rabbi Moshe Winner
718.946.9833

BROOKLYN HEIGHTS
Rabbi Mendy Hecht
Rabbi Ari Raskin
347.378.2641

BROOKVILLE
Rabbi Mendy Heber
516.626.0600

CEDARHURST
Rabbi Zalman Wolowik
516.295.2478

CHESTNUT RIDGE
Rabbi Chaim Tzvi Ehrenreich
845.356.6686

COMMACK
Rabbi Mendel Teldon
631.543.3343

DIX HILLS
Rabbi Yaakov Saacks
631.351.8672

EAST HAMPTON
Rabbi Leibel Baumgarten
Rabbi Mendy Goldberg
631.329.5800

FOREST HILLS
Rabbi Yossi Mendelson
917.861.9726

GREAT NECK
Rabbi Yoseph Geisinsky
516.487.4554

KINGSTON
Rabbi Yitzchok Hecht
845.334.9044

LARCHMONT
Rabbi Mendel Silberstein
914.834.4321

LONG BEACH
Rabbi Eli Goodman
516.897.2473

NYC KEHILATH JESHURUN
Rabbi Elie Weinstock
212.774.5636

NYC MIDTOWN
Mrs. Raizy Metzger
212.758.3770

OSSINING
Rabbi Dovid Labkowski
914.923.2522

PORT WASHINGTON
Rabbi Shalom Paltiel
516.767.8672

RIVERDALE
Rabbi Levi Shemtov
718.549.1100

ROCHESTER
Rabbi Nechemia Vogel
585.271.0330

ROSLYN
Rabbi Yaakov Reiter
516.484.8185

SEA GATE
Rabbi Chaim Brikman
718.266.1736

SOUTHAMPTON
Rabbi Chaim Pape
917.627.4865

STONY BROOK
Rabbi Shalom Ber Cohen
631.585.0521

SUFFERN
Rabbi Shmuel Gancz
845.368.1889

WESTBURY
Rabbi Mendy Brownstein
516.850.4486

NORTH CAROLINA
ASHEVILLE
Rabbi Shaya Susskind
828.505.0746

CARYY
Rabbi Yisroel Cotlar
919.651.9710

CHAPEL HILL
Rabbi Zalman Bluming
919.630.5129

CHARLOTTE
Rabbi Yossi Groner
Rabbi Shlomo Cohen
704.366.3984

GREENSBORO
Rabbi Yosef Plotkin
336.617.8120

RALEIGH
Rabbi Pinchas Herman
Rabbi Lev Cotlar
919.637.6950

WILMINGTON
Rabbi Moshe Lieblich
910.763.4770

NORTH DAKOTA
FARGO
Rabbi Yonah Grossman
701.212.4164

OHIO
BEACHWOOD
Rabbi Shmuli Friedman
Rabbi Moshe Gancz
216.370.2887

BLUE ASH
Rabbi Yisroel Mangel
513.793.5200

COLUMBUS
Rabbi Areyah Kaltmann
Rabbi Levi Andrusier
614.294.3296

OKLAHOMA
OKLAHOMA CITY
Rabbi Ovadia Goldman
405.524.4800

TULSA
Rabbi Yehuda Weg
918.492.4499

OREGON
PORTLAND
Rabbi Moshe Wilhelm
Rabbi Mordechai Wilhelm
503.977.9947

SALEM
Rabbi Avrohom Yitzchok Perlstein
503.383.9569

PENNSYLVANIA
AMBLER
Rabbi Shaya Deitsch
215.591.9310

BALA CYNWYD
Rabbi Shraga Sherman
610.660.9192

LAFAYETTE HILL
Rabbi Yisroel Kotlarsky
347.526.1430

LANCASTER
Rabbi Elazar Green
717.368.6565

NEWTOWN
Rabbi Aryeh Weinstein
215.497.9925

PHILADELPHIA: CENTER CITY
Rabbi Yochonon Goldman
215.238.2100

PITTSBURGH
Rabbi Yisroel Altein
412.422.7300 ext. 269

PITTSBURGH: SOUTH HILLS
Rabbi Mendy Rosenblum
412.278.3693

WYNNEWOOD
Rabbi Moishe Brennan
610.529.9011

RHODE ISLAND
WARWICK
Rabbi Yossi Laufer
401.884.7888

SOUTH CAROLINA
COLUMBIA
Rabbi Hesh Epstein
Rabbi Levi Marrus
803.782.1831

TENNESSEE
CHATTANOOGA
Rabbi Shaul Perlstein
423.490.1106

MEMPHIS
Rabbi Levi Klein
901.766.1800

TEXAS
ARLINGTON
Rabbi Levi Gurevitch
817.451.1171

BELLAIRE
Rabbi Yossi Zaklikofsky
713.839.8887

DALLAS
Rabbi Mendel Dubrawsky
Rabbi Moshe Naparstek
972.818.0770

HOUSTON
Rabbi Dovid Goldstein
713.774.0300

Rabbi Moishe Traxler
713.774.0300

HOUSTON: RICE UNIVERSITY AREA
Rabbi Eliezer Lazaroff
713.522.2004

LEAGUE CITY
Rabbi Yitzchok Schmukler
713.398.2460

MISSOURI CITY
Rabbi Mendel Feigenson
832.758.0685

PLANO
Rabbi Mendel Block
Rabbi Yehudah Horowitz
972.596.8270

S. ANTONIO
Rabbi Chaim Block
Rabbi Levi Teldon
210.492.1085

THE WOODLANDS
Rabbi Mendel Blecher
281.719.5213

UTAH
SALT LAKE CITY
Rabbi Benny Zippel
801.467.7777

VERMONT
BURLINGTON
Rabbi Yitzchok Raskin
802.658.5770

VIRGINIA
ALEXANDRIA/ARLINGTON
Rabbi Mordechai Newman
703.370.2774

Share the **Rohr JLI** experience with friends and relatives worldwide

FAIRFAX
Rabbi Leibel Fajnland
703.426.1980

NORFOLK
Rabbi Aaron Margolin
Rabbi Levi Brashevitzky
757.616.0770

RICHMOND
Rabbi Shlomo Pereira
804.740.2000

TYSONS CORNER
Rabbi Chezzy Deitsch
CHAPTER FOUNDED BY
RABBI LEVI DEITSCH, OBM
703.829.5770

WASHINGTON
LYNNWOOD
Rabbi Berel Paltiel
425.741.9633

MERCER ISLAND
Rabbi Elazar Bogomilsky
206.527.1411

OLYMPIA
Rabbi Cheski Edelman
360.584.4306

SPOKANE COUNTY
Rabbi Yisroel Hahn
509.443.0770

WISCONSIN
KENOSHA
Rabbi Tzali Wilschanski
262.359.0770

MADISON
Rabbi Avremel Matusof
608.231.3450

MEQUON
Rabbi Menachem Rapoport
262.242.2235

MILWAUKEE
Rabbi Mendel Shmotkin
414.961.6100

WAUKESHA
Rabbi Levi Brook
925.708.4203

PUERTO RICO
CAROLINA
Rabbi Mendel Zarchi
787.253.0894

ARGENTINA
CAPITAL FEDERAL
Rabbi Mendy Gurevitch
54.11.4545.7771

PALERMO NUEVO
Rabbi Mendy Grunblatt
54.11.4772.1024

AUSTRALIA
AUSTRALIAN CAPITAL TERRITORY
CANBERRA
Rabbi Shmuel Feldman
614.3167.7805

DOUBLE BAY
Rabbi Yanky Berger
Rabbi Yisroel Dolnikov
612.9327.1644

DOVER HEIGHTS
Rabbi Motti Feldman
612.9387.3822

NORTH SHORE
Rabbi Nochum Schapiro
Mrs. Fruma Schapiro
612.9488.9548

SOUTH HEAD
Rabbi Benzion Milecki
612.9337.6775

QUEENSLAND
BRISBANE
Rabbi Levi Jaffe
617.3843.6770

SOUTH AUSTRALIA
GLENSIDE
Rabbi Yossi Engel
618.8338.2922

VICTORIA
BENTLEIGH EAST
Rabbi Mendel Raskin
613.9570.6707

CAULFIELD NORTH
Rabbi Menachem Stern
614.4850.4301

CAULFIELD SOUTH
Rabbi Peretz Schapiro
613.9532.9180

ELSTERNWICK
Rabbi Chaim Cowen
614.3330.8584

Rabbi Motty Liberow
613.9533.0090

MALVERN
Rabbi Zev Slavin
614.0476.6759

Rabbi Shimshon Yurkowicz
613.9822.3600

MELBOURNE
Rabbi Sholem Gorelik
614.5244.8770

Rabbi Mendel Groner
613.9532.7299

Rabbi Dovid Gutnick
614.3038.4948

MOORABBIN
Rabbi Elisha Greenbaum
614.0349.0434

ST. KILDA EAST
Rabbi Moshe Kahn
613.9522.8217

Rabbi Dovid Leib Shmerling
613.9526.3874

WESTERN AUSTRALIA
PERTH
Rabbi Shalom White
618.9275.2106

BRAZIL
RIO DE JANEIRO
Rabbi Yehoshua Binyomin Goldman
Rabbi Avrohom Tsvi Beuthner
55.21.2294.3138

S. PAULO
Rabbi Avraham Steinmetz
55.11.3081.3081

CANADA
ALBERTA
CALGARY
Rabbi Mordechai Groner
403.238.4880

EDMONTON
Rabbi Ari Drelich
Rabbi Mendy Blachman
780.851.1515

BRITISH COLUMBIA
RICHMOND
Rabbi Yechiel Baitelman
604.277.6427

VANCOUVER
Rabbi Yitzchok Wineberg
604.266.1313

VICTORIA
Rabbi Meir Kaplan
250.595.7656

MANITOBA
WINNIPEG
Rabbi Shmuel Altein
204.339.8737

NOVA SCOTIA
HALIFAX
Rabbi Mendel Feldman
902.422.4222

LAWRENCE/EGLINTON
Rabbi Menachem Gansburg
416.546.8770

LONDON
Rabbi Eliezer Gurkow
519.434.3962

MISSISSAUGA
Rabbi Yitzchok Slavin
905.820.4432

NIAGARA FALLS
Rabbi Zalman Zaltzman
905.356.7200

OTTAWA
Rabbi Menachem M. Blum
613.823.0866

RICHMOND HILL
Rabbi Mendel Bernstein
905.770.7700

Rabbi Yossi Hecht
905.773.6477

TORONTO AREA BJL
Rabbi Leib Chaiken
416.916.7202

GREATER TORONTO
REGIONAL OFFICE & THORNHILL
Rabbi Yossi Gansburg
905.731.7000

YORK MILLS
Rabbi Levi Gansburg
647.345.3800

WATERLOO
Rabbi Moshe Goldman
226.338.7770

WHITBY
Rabbi Tzali Borenstein
905.493.9007

QUEBEC
COTE ST. LUC
Rabbi Levi Raskin
514.485.7221

MONTREAL
Rabbi Ronnie Fine
Pesach Nussbaum
514.342.3.JLI

Rabbi Levi Y New
514.739.0770

TOWN OF MOUNT ROYAL
Rabbi Moshe Krasnanski
Rabbi Shneur Zalman Rader
514.739.0770

VILLE S. LAURENT
Rabbi Schneur Zalmen Silberstein
514.808.1418

WESTMOUNT
Rabbi Yossi Shanowitz
Mrs. Devorah Leah Shanowitz
514.937.4772

SASKATCHEWAN
REGINA
Rabbi Avrohom Simmonds
306.585.1359

SASKATOON
Rabbi Raphael Kats
306.384.4370

CAYMAN ISLAND
GRAND CAYMAN
Rabbi Berel Pewzner
717.798.1040

COLOMBIA
BOGOTA
Rabbi Yehoshua B. Rosenfeld
Rabbi Chanoch Piekarski
571.635.8251

DENMARK
COPENHAGEN
Rabbi Yitzchok Loewenthal
45.3316.1850

ESTONIA
TALLINN
Rabbi Shmuel Kot
372.662.30.50

GEORGIA
TBILISI
Rabbi Meir Kozlovsky
995.593.23.91.15

GERMANY
BERLIN
Rabbi Yehuda Tiechtel
49.30.2128.0830

COLOGNE
Rabbi Mendel Schtroks
49.22.1240.3902

DUSSELDORF
Rabbi Chaim Barkahn
49.21.1420.9693

HAMBURG
Rabbi Shlomo Bistriztsky
49.40.4142.4190

HANNOVER
Rabbi Binyamin Wolff
49.511.811.2822

GREECE
ATHENS
Rabbi Mendel Hendel
30.210.520.2880

GUATEMALA
GUATEMALA CITY
Rabbi Shalom Pelman
502.2485.0770

ISRAEL
ASHKELON
Rabbi Shneor Lieberman
054.977.0512

BALFURYA
Rabbi Noam Bar-Tov
054.580.4770

CAESAREA
Rabbi Chaim Meir Lieberman
054.621.2586

EVEN YEHUDA
Rabbi Menachem Noyman
054.777.0707

GANEI TIKVA
Rabbi Gershon Shnur
054.524.2358

GIV'ATAYIM
Rabbi Pinchus Bitton
052.643.8770

HAIFA
Rabbi Yehuda Dunin
054.426.3763

KARMIEL
Rabbi Mendy Elishevitz
054.521.3073

KFAR SABBA
Rabbi Yossi Baitch
054.445.5020

KIRYAT BIALIK
Rabbi Pinny Marton
050.661.1768

KIRYAT MOTZKIN
Rabbi Shimon Eizenbach
050.902.0770

KOCHAV YAIR
Rabbi Dovi Greenberg
054.332.6244

MACCABIM RE'UT
Rabbi Yosef Yitzchak Noiman
054.977.0549

MODIIN
Rabbi Boruch Slonim
054.300.1770

NES ZIYONA
Rabbi Menachem Feldman
054.497.7092

NETANYA
Rabbi Schneur Brod
054.579.7572

RAMAT GAN-KRINITZI
Rabbi Yisroel Gurevitz
052.743.2814

RAMAT GAN-MAROM NAVE
Rabbi Binyamin Meir Kali
050.476.0770

RAMAT YISHAI
Rabbi Shneor Zalman Wolosow
052.324.5475

RISHON LEZION
Rabbi Uri Keshet
050.722.4593

ROSH PINA
Rabbi Sholom Ber Hertzel
052.458.7600

YEHUD
Rabbi Shmuel Wolf
053.536.1479

ITALY
FIRENZE
Rabbi Levi Wolvovsky
39.389.595.2034

Share the **Rohr JLI** experience with friends and relatives worldwide

KAZAKHSTAN
ALMATY
Rabbi Shevach Zlatopolsky
7.7272.77.59.77

LATVIA
RIGA
Rabbi Shneur Zalman Kot
371.6733.1520

NETHERLANDS
DEN HAAG
Rabbi Shmuel Katzman
31.70.347.0222

NOORD-HOLLAND
AMSTERDAM
Rabbi Yanki Jacobs
31.6.4498.8627

PANAMA
PANAMA CITY
Rabbi Ari Laine
Rabbi Gabriel Benayon
507.223.3383

RUSSIA
ASTRAKHAN
Rabbi Yisroel Melamed
7.851.239.28.24

BRYANSK
Rabbi Menachem Mendel Zaklas
7.483.264.55.15

CHELYABINSK
Rabbi Meir Kirsh
7.351.263.24.68

MOSCOW-MARINA ROSHA
Rabbi Mordechai Weisberg
7.495.645.50.00

NIZHNY NOVGOROD
Rabbi Shimon Bergman
7.920.253.47.70

OMSK
Rabbi Osher Krichevsky
7.381.231.33.07

PERM
Rabbi Zalman Deutch
7.342.212.47.32

SAMARA
Rabbi Shlomo Deutch
7.846.333.40.64

SARATOV
Rabbi Yaakov Kubitshek
7.8452.21.58.00

S. PETERSBURG
Rabbi Zvi Pinsky
7.812.713.62.09

ROSTOV
Rabbi Chaim Danzinger
7.8632.99.02.68

TOGLIATTI
Rabbi Meier Fischer
7.848.273.02.84

UFA
Rabbi Dan Krichevsky
7.347.244.55.33

VORONEZH
Rabbi Levi Stiefel
7.473.252.96.99

SINGAPORE
SINGAPORE
Rabbi Mordechai Abergel
656.337.2189

Rabbi Netanel Rivni
CLASSES IN HEBREW
656.336.2127

SOUTH AFRICA
JOHANNESBURG
Rabbi Dovid Hazdan
Rabbi Shmuel Simpson
27.11.728.8152

Rabbi Dovid Masinter
Rabbi Ari Kievman
27.11.440.6600

SWEDEN
STOCKHOLM
Rabbi Chaim Greisman
468.679.7067

SWITZERLAND
LUGANO
Rabbi Yaakov Tzvi Kantor
41.91.921.3720

LUZERN
Rabbi Chaim Drukman
41.41.361.1770

UKRAINE
DNEPROPETROVSK
Rabbi Dan Makagon
380.504.51.13.18

NIKOLAYEV
Rabbi Sholom Gotlieb
380.512.37.37.71

ZHITOMIR
Rabbi Shlomo Wilhelm
380.504.63.01.32

ODESSA
Rabbi Avraham Wolf
Rabbi Yaakov Neiman
38.048.728.0770 ext. 280

UNITED KINGDOM
CARDIFF
Rabbi Michoel Rose
44.292.221.0733

EDGEWARE
Rabbi Leivi Sudak
Rabbi Yaron Jacobs
44.208.905.4141

ILFORD
Rabbi Rafi Goodwin
44.208.554.1624

LEEDS
Rabbi Eli Pink
44.113.266.3311

LONDON
Rabbi Nissan D. Dubov
44.20.8944.1581

Rabbi Mendy Korer
44.794.632.5444

Rabbi Baruch Levin
44.208.451.0091

Rabbi Yisroel Lew
44.20.7060.9770

Rabbi Gershon Overlander
Rabbi Dovid Katz
44.208.202.1600

Rabbi Yossi Simon
44.20.8458.0416

MANCHESTER
Rabbi Akiva Cohen
Rabbi Levi Cohen
44.161.740.4243

Rabbi Shmuli Jaffe
44.161.766.1812

VENEZUELA
CARACAS
Rabbi Yehoshua Rosenblum
58.212.264.7011

Share the **Rohr JLI** experience with friends and relatives worldwide

NOTES

NOTES

NOTES

NOTES

JEWISH LEARNING INSTITUTE

THE JEWISH LEARNING MULTIPLEX

Brought to you by the Rohr Jewish Learning Institute

In fulfillment of the mandate of the Lubavitcher Rebbe, of blessed memory,
whose leadership guides every step of our work,
the mission of the Rohr Jewish Learning Institute is to transform
Jewish life and the greater community through the study of Torah,
connecting each Jew to our shared heritage of Jewish learning.

While our flagship program remains the cornerstone of our organization,
JLI is proud to feature additional divisions catering to specific populations,
in order to meet a wide array of educational needs.

THE ROHR JEWISH LEARNING INSTITUTE,
a subsidiary of *Merkos L'Inyonei Chinuch,*
is the adult education arm of the Chabad-Lubavitch Movement.